Givenness and God

Series Board

James Bernauer

Drucilla Cornell

Thomas R. Flynn

Kevin Hart

Richard Kearney

Jean-Luc Marion

Adriaan Peperzak

Thomas Sheehan

Hent de Vries

Merold Westphal

Edith Wyschogrod

Michael Zimmerman

John D. Caputo, *series editor*

Perspectives in
Continental
Philosophy

Givenness and God
Questions of Jean-Luc Marion

Edited by Ian Leask and Eoin Cassidy

FORDHAM UNIVERSITY PRESS
New York ▪ 2005

Copyright © 2005 Fordham University Press

All rights reserved. No part of this publication may be reproduced, stored in a retrieval system, or transmitted in any form or by any means—electronic, mechanical, photocopy, recording, or any other—except for brief quotations in printed reviews, without the prior permission of the publisher.

Perspectives in Continental Philosophy Series
ISSN 1089-3938

Library of Congress Cataloging-in-Publication Data

  Givenness and God : questions of Jean-Luc Marion / edited by Ian Leask and Eoin Cassidy. — 1st ed.
     p. cm. — (Perspectives in continental philosophy, ISSN 1089-3938 ; no. 43)
   Includes bibliographical references and index.
   ISBN 0-8232-2450-3 (hardcover) — ISBN 0-8232-2451-1 (pbk.)
   1. Marion, Jean-Luc, 1946– . I. Leask, Ian Graham. II. Cassidy, Eoin G. III. Series.
  B2430.M284G58   2005
  194—dc22   2005006441

Printed in the United States of America
07   5 4 3 2
First edition

Contents

Acknowledgments — ix

Abbreviations — xi

Foreword — xv
   Dermot A. Lane

Introduction — 1
   Ian Leask and Eoin Cassidy

PART ONE: MARION ON DESCARTES, HUSSERL, AND HEIDEGGER

1. The Conceptual Idolatry of Descartes's Gray Ontology: An Epistemology "Without Being" — 11
   Derek J. Morrow

2. I Am, I Exist — 37
   Lilian Alweiss

3. Hubris and Humility: Husserl's Reduction and Givenness — 47
   Timothy Mooney

4. Glory, Idolatry, Kairos: Revelation and the Ontological Difference in Marion — 69
   Felix Ó Murchadha

5. Reduced Phenomena and Unreserved Debts in Marion's Reading of Heidegger — 87
   Brian Elliott

PART TWO: MARION: GIFT AND RECEPTION

6 The Reason of the Gift — *101*
Jean-Luc Marion

7 The Gift: A Trojan Horse in the Citadel of Phenomenology? — *135*
Joseph S. O'Leary

8 Phenomenality in the Middle: Marion, Romano, and the Hermeneutics of the Event — *167*
Shane Mackinlay

9 The Dative Subject (and the "Principle of Principles") — *182*
Ian Leask

10 Marion's Ambition of Transcendence — *190*
Mark Dooley

PART THREE: MARION AND BEYOND

11 *Le phénomène érotique*: Augustinian Resonances in Marion's Phenomenology of Love — *201*
Eoin Cassidy

12 Hermeneutics of the Possible God — *220*
Richard Kearney

13 Giving More — *243*
Jean-Luc Marion and Richard Kearney in Dialogue

14 The Absent Threshold: An Eckhartian Afterword — *258*
John O'Donohue

Notes — *285*

Contributors — *341*

Index — *345*

Acknowledgments

This collection emerged from a symposium held at the Mater Dei Institute, Dublin City University, in January 2003. The editors wish to record their profound thanks to the staff and students of the Institute, especially its director, the Rev. Dr. Michael Drumm, and its president, the Rev. Dr. Dermot Lane, for their unstinting support and enthusiasm for that event and for the resultant publication project. We also thank Dr. Stijn Van den Bossche, of the Katholieke Universiteit Leuven; Dr. Joseph Dunne, of St. Patrick's College, Drumcondra, Dublin; and Prof. Dermot Moran, of University College Dublin. We owe a huge debt to Dr. Nicholas de Warren and the Rev. Shane Mackinlay for the thoroughness and rigor of their excellent translation work. And we offer sincere thanks to Prof. John Caputo and to the editorial team at Fordham University Press. Above all, however, we should like to record our gratitude to Prof. Jean-Luc Marion—for his profundity, his knowledge, and, especially, his generosity.

Abbreviations

AT *The Philosophical Writings of Descartes*, edited and translated from the original Latin and French by John Cottingham, Robert Stoothoff, and Dugald Murdoch, 2 vols. (Cambridge: Cambridge University Press, 1984). All the citations regarding the correspondence with Descartes rely on *The Philosophical Writings of Descartes*, vol. 3, edited and translated from the original Latin and French by John Cottingham, Robert Stoothoff, Dugald Murdoch, and Anthony Kenny (Cambridge: Cambridge University Press, 1991). The page numbers refer to the standard twelve-volume editions of Descartes's works edited by Charles Adam and Paul Tannery known as *AT* (*Oeuvres de Descartes*, rev. ed. (Paris: Crin/C.N.R.S., 1964–76).

BG *Being Given: Toward a Phenomenology of Givenness*, translated by Jeffrey L. Kosky (Stanford, Calif.: Stanford University Press, 2002).

CPR Immanuel Kant, *Critique of Pure Reason*, translated by Norman Kemp Smith (London: Macmillan, 1934). All references are to the standard first and second editions' pagination.

CQ *Cartesian Questions: Method and Metaphysics*, translated by Jeffrey L. Kosky, John Cottingham, and Stephen Voss,

	foreword by Daniel Garber (Chicago: University of Chicago Press, 1999).
DMP	*On Descartes' Metaphysical Prism: The Constitution and the Limits of Onto-theo-logy in Cartesian Thought*, translated by Jeffrey L. Kosky (Chicago: University of Chicago Press, 1999).
DS	*De surcroît: Études sur les phénomènes saturés* (Paris: Presses Universitaires de France, 2001).
DSE	*Dieu sans l'être: Hors-texte* (Paris: Arthème Fayard, 1982; 2nd ed., Paris: Presses Universitaires de France [Quadrige], 1991; 2nd ed., rev. and enl. [Quadrige], 2002).
ED	*Étant donné: Essai d'une phénoménologie de la donation* (Paris: Presses Universitaires de France, 1997).
GWB	*God Without Being: Hors-texte*, translated by Thomas A. Carlson, foreword by David Tracy (Chicago: University of Chicago Press, 1991).
IAD	*The Idol and Distance: Five Studies*, translated by Thomas A. Carlson (New York: Fordham University Press, 2001).
ID	*L'idole et la distance: Cinq études* (Paris: Grasset, 1977; 2nd ed., 1989; 3rd ed. [Poche/Biblio], 1991).
IE	*In Excess: Studies of Saturated Phenomena*, translated by Vincent Berraud and Robyn Horner (New York: Fordham University Press, 2002).
ITN	"In the Name: How to Avoid Speaking of 'Negative Theology,'" in *God, the Gift, and Postmodernism*, edited by J. D. Caputo and M. J. Scanlon (Bloomington and Indianapolis: Indiana University Press, 1999), pp. 20–41.
OFP	"The Other First Philosophy and the Question of Givenness," translated by Jeffrey Kosky, *Critical Inquiry* 25 (1999): 784–800.
OG	*Sur l'ontologie grise de Descartes: Science cartésienne et savoir aristotélicien dans les Regulae* (Paris: Vrin, 1975; 2nd ed., rev. and enl., 1981; 3rd ed., 1993; 4th ed., 2000).
OTG	"On the Gift: A Discussion Between Jacques Derrida and Jean-Luc Marion," moderated by Richard Kearney, in *Of God, the Gift, and Postmodernism*, edited by John D. Caputo and Michael Scanlon, O.S.A. (Bloomington: Indiana University Press, 1999), pp. 54–78.
PAC	*Prolégomènes à la charité* (Paris: Éditions de la Différence, 1986; 2nd ed., 1991).

PC	*Prolegomena to Charity*, translated by Stephen E. Lewis (New York: Fordham University Press, 2002).
PMD	*Sur le prisme métaphysique de Descartes: Constitution et limites de l'onto-théo-logie cartésienne* (Paris: Presses Universitaires de France, 1986).
PS	"Le phénomène saturé," in *Phénoménologie et théologie*, edited by Jean-François Courtine (Paris: Criterion, 1992), pp. 79–128.
PWD	*The Philosophical Writings of Descartes*, vol. 1, trans. John Cottingham, Robert Stoothoff, and Dugald Murdoch (Cambridge: Cambridge University Press, 1985).
QC	*Questions cartésiennes: Méthode et métaphysique* (Paris: Presses Universitaires de France, 1991).
RD	*Réduction et donation: Recherches sur Husserl, Heidegger et la phénoménologie* (Paris: Presses Universitaires de France, 1989).
RdD	"La raison du don," *Philosophie*, 78 (June 2003): 3–32.
RG	*Reduction and Givenness: Investigations of Husserl, Heidegger and Phenomenology*, translated by Thomas Carlson (Evanston, Ill: Northwestern University Press, 1998).
SP	"The Saturated Phenomenon," translated by Thomas Carlson, *Philosophy Today*, 40 (1996): 103–24.
SPCG	"Sketch of a Phenomenological Concept of Gift," translated by John Conley, S.J., and Danielle Poe, in *Postmodern Philosophy and Christian Thought*, edited by Merold Westphal (Bloomington: Indiana University Press, 1999), pp. 122–43.
TB	*Sur la théologie blanche de Descartes: Analogie, création des vérités éternelles et fondement* (Paris: Presses Universitaires de France, 1981; 2nd ed., corrected and completed [Quadrige], 1991).

Foreword

Dermot A. Lane

It is a pleasure for me as President of Mater Dei Institute to welcome the publication of this collection of essays celebrating the work of Jean-Luc Marion. Most of the papers were first delivered in the Mater Dei Institute, a college of Dublin City University, in January 2003, at a conference attended by Marion. It was Marion's first visit to Ireland, and it was most appropriate that a college specializing in religious education should host the occasion: after all, Marion has not only been central in the "turn toward the theological" in recent French phenomenology, but has also generated massive interest within theology itself.

What is outstanding about Marion's writings is the way he provokes his readers to go beyond ontology, beyond onto-theology, beyond ontological difference, so that they can begin to think in a way that is liberated from the confines of traditional metaphysics. In phenomenology, this liberation means thinking "after the traditional subject" and "after" Heideggerian ontology; beyond both of these, Marion suggests, we have the sheer givenness of phenomena without condition. In theology, this liberation means rethinking God: not as a conceptual "idol," and not through the heavy metaphysical language of "Being" or substance or essence, but, instead, in terms of phenomena such as love, gift, and excess.

Further, from a theological point of view, what is particularly significant about Marion's multifaceted project is the way it seeks to go beyond the dialectics of affirmation and negation, beyond the hyperessentialism of certain forms of analogy, to embrace "a third way" that he calls the way of mystical theology. This way of mystical theology culminates not in concepts or theories but in what Marion calls the pragmatics of prayer and praise. For Marion, all talk about God disrupts, destabilizes, and disestablishes philosophical and theological discourse.

How all this happens and what is the basis of this dazzling discourse, how he arrives at this new theological phenomenology, and in what way he connects this original phenomenology with the Catholic heritage—these are some of the questions addressed in this collection.

What is surely distinctive and enduring about the contribution of Marion is the way he has safeguarded the academy and the church and religion from the constant temptation toward idolatry. Equally outstanding is the way he always seeks to go beyond current categories, breaking new ground, disturbing philosophical systems, and challenging theological complacencies. For these provocations we are deeply indebted to his immense labor.

Toward the end of his landmark *God Without Being*, Marion writes: "We are infinitely free in theology: we find all already given, gained, available. It only remains to understand, to say, and to celebrate." It is hoped that the publication of these essays will promote a deeper philosophical and theological understanding of Marion's work, as well as a celebration of it.

Dublin
March 2005

Givenness and God

Introduction

Ian Leask and Eoin Cassidy

Jean-Luc Marion's body of work has already secured his place among the top rank of twentieth-century philosophers; it seems inconceivable that his reputation will not grow even further in the twenty-first century and beyond. Though equally renowned for his scholarly work on early modern philosophy and on Husserl and Heidegger, Marion is perhaps best known for his renewal of phenomenology, for his remarkable, ongoing inquiry into the question of God, and for work bridging all of these areas. The oeuvre resulting from this fertile constellation places Marion's writings at the center of the "theological turn" in recent French phenomenology; as such, his work is a central resource in any attempt to think after the "end of metaphysics" without subscribing or succumbing to an unfettered nihilism.

Indeed, the "postmetaphysical" confrontation with nihilism is probably the defining feature of Marion's intellectual and spiritual project. Born in 1946, and educated at the École Normale Supérieure and the Sorbonne, the young Marion enjoyed a quintessentially Parisian formation: the events of 1968, the teaching of Derrida and Althusser, the realization that "old" thought was exhausted and unable to withstand the combination of Nietzschean, Heideggerian, structuralist, and deconstructive critique. Far from undermining his Christian experience and commitment, however, this same formation propelled Marion into thinking about God (and so thinking about meaning and significance) while also thinking within the broadly postmodern critique of so much previous intellectual endeavor. The result has been a series of writings in which the heavy terminology of older metaphysics—"ground," "cause," "substance," and even "Being," for example—plays no positive role, and in which the "traditional subject" is refused primacy or ultimacy. Instead, the theological focus has been on God overflowing the subject's knowing grasp or intentional gaze, exceeding any conceptual "idol," and becoming manifest in terms of charity, love, and praise (rather than knowledge, proposition, or ratiocination). The philosophical focus, likewise, has been on a description of the phenomena that overwhelm autarchy, on phenomenality "beyond" phenomenology, on the primordial givenness (*donation*) of phenomena, and—perhaps above all—on the significance of a singular, unique, and "ultimate" phenomenon: love. This work, as a whole, has released an explosion of energy within both phenomenological and theological study.

The roots of this thinking lie in Marion's first great confrontation with the tradition: his postgraduate research (supervised by Ferdinand Alquié) on Descartes. The young Marion recognized in Descartes a crucial conflict between the respective "poles" of the ego and God. This, he suggested, took the form of a profound ambivalence—or, more particularly, an undecidability—regarding the question of "foundation": despite the conventional contemporary understanding of Descartes as instigating the metaphysics of (inflated) subjectivity, Marion proposed a Cartesianism in which there is constant oscillation between ego and God, between human conceptuality and the Infinite itself. This instability, in turn, throws into question any assumption of self-sufficiency or self-presence: Marion's Descartes is never wholly an onto-theo-logical system builder but, instead, always open to (and opened by) the unknown, the transcendent.

These two poles—the ego without self-sufficiency and the unthinkable Infinite—have remained the central features of Marion's subsequent endeavor. Most significantly, they have allowed Marion to work both "for" and "against" Heidegger: the *destruktion* of metaphysics, *Ereignis*, and the critique of onto-theo-logy are utterly basic for Marion's project; but Heideggerian thinking is itself subjected to a Lévinasian (and, perhaps, Neoplatonic) questioning of Being and its supposed primacy. For Marion, postmetaphysical thinking does not confront us with the ultimacy of the *Seinsfrage*; instead, it takes us *beyond* Being.

This "thinking otherwise than Being" manifested itself as early as 1977, when Marion's *The Idol and Distance* suggested that a divine *distance* surpasses even Heidegger's ontological difference; Marion already speaks here of God *giving*, outside of the horizon of ontology. But it is Marion's most famous theological work, *God Without Being*, that more fully establishes this insight, suggesting—famously—that Heideggerian Being becomes an idolatrous precondition that philosophy imposes upon God. Furthermore, it is not just that, for Marion, the Heideggerian thought of Being-as-ultimacy is a kind of idolatry. It is also that, as long as Being is privileged, so too is *Dasein*: the human being, qua "access" to or opening on *Sein*, is phenomenologically anterior; as such, *Dasein* is a crucial "condition" for unveiling and establishing the ultimacy of Being. The overall point, Marion suggests, is that Being and its conduit, *Dasein*, combine to edge out any possible priority or anteriority for God. The decision has already been taken, so to speak: God is not ultimate, but secondary. Thus, for Marion, Heidegger *enframes* God within Being; he sets up an idol, a "higher-or-greater-than-God." The critic of onto-theo-logy remains trapped by metaphysical assumptions.

Marion's now celebrated theological response to this idolatrous precedence is to suggest that we try to think a God *without* Being, a God who is free from any condition whatsoever. As far as Marion is concerned, the search for "the divine god" obliges us not just to go beyond onto-theo-logy but also to go beyond the Heideggerian ontological difference. How might we achieve this? By rethinking the whole problematic in terms of an *icon* that is not reducible to idolatry.

The idol, Marion stresses, is a human projection. It is about the subject's intentions, aspirations, expectations, or volition; it "comes from me." In turn, it reflects back "me"—*my* assumptions, presumptions, conceptions, and so on. Idolatrous ideas of God are thus "mirrors": they are reflections of our subjectivity. We remain the center of gravity, and our conceptions of the divine are precisely that: *our conceptions*. What Marion seeks, instead (again following Lévinas), is a "counterintentionality," brought about by "counterphenomena" that are imposed upon us and never reducible to our intentional grasp. In this respect, Marion suggests that, in addition to the gaze that comprehends and domesticates, there is also the possibility of an *icon* that ruptures visibility, representation, or even intentionality. The icon is "defined" by an infinite origin "without original": it overflows my gaze and my intentionality, my conceptual grasp. It "comes from elsewhere" and aims at us, regards us. Just as the Lévinasian face reverses intentionality, so does Marion's icon: this is no longer my mirror image (the idol) but, instead, the transgression of visibility. Accordingly, the icon is not so much seen as *venerated*: with the icon, the invisible can (if we might put it like this) "make its presence felt" without ever becoming an object for my gaze. To think iconically is thus to think in a way that renounces claims to comprehend the incomprehensible: this is a thinking that lets itself be measured by the excess it receives. It hardly needs stating, then, that the Cartesian idea of Infinity (mediated, of course, through its Lévinasian reception) remains a crucial point of reference for Marion's project.

To a huge extent, these same concerns—thinking "otherwise than Being," without any a priori conditions, without assuming the primacy of an active, constituting ego, and in reference to an overwhelming excess—are also central to Marion's strictly philosophical, nonconfessional work. Thus, as with the theological writings, the phenomenology stresses a subjectivity saturated by a surplus over and beyond constitution and the intentional gaze. In this philosophical register, though, God gives way (so to speak) to the ultimacy of the given: the historical survey in *Reduction and Givenness* and the systematic survey in *Being Given* combine to stress the sheer givenness of phenomena, over and above either the transcendental ego or the *Seinsfrage*. Marion's "third reduction" aims to take us to the inner truth of phenomenology: sheer phenomenality in its givenness.

Despite the radicality of these investigations, they are still—to a huge extent—about a consolidation and extension of the phenomenological tradition that Marion not only knows intimately but also inhabits fully. Specifically, Marion is working with what we might term the standard phenomenological understanding of how our "reality" always exceeds what we *see* directly, what we intend, what we constitute—and even what "is." Marion's phenomenology of givenness is, at base, a rigorous engagement with this *excess* of phenomenality, given but not necessarily constituted. He wants to think through what it is to allow phenomena their "full rights," without supposing any a priori horizon or condition.

The work of art provides an excellent example of how Marion treats the "excessive" nature of phenomenality. The effect or power of the painting, he tells us, is (or can be) far more than the conglomeration of paint and spatial organization on canvas: with the painting, Marion suggests, the invisible can "insert" itself into the visible; he describes this insertion in terms of the *unseen* (*l'invu*) suggested by, implied by, but more than, the seen. Thus the power of a painting is not reducible to its purely visible elements: in principle, the painting can reach a depth and a glory that exceed the "idolatrous" gaze. And here, Marion argues, seeing becomes *reception* (more than constitution, domination, domestication, etc.). The Rothko chapel, a late self-portrait by Rembrandt, a Balthus street scene: always, as well as what is seen, there is an excess, beyond vision. What we see is definitely not all that we get.

And, of course, painting is by no means unique in terms of its "excessiveness." Over a range of his writings, Marion has given us a plethora of examples of so-called saturated phenomena. The historical event, for one, is always more than any perspective we might have; it can never be exhausted by any number of accounts. Similarly, the Other, self-affection, the sublime, the idea of Infinity, inner time consciousness . . . the basic experience we have of phenomena, he stresses, is of their saturating whatever intention we bring to bear. (Nonsaturated phenomena are the exceptions rather than the rule, he suggests.) In general, Marion wants to say, we are given more than we can take (in) at any (given) moment. The "I" is in no sense sole authority; it is, ultimately, a *recipient*, interlocuted, *subject to*; I always receive more than I constitute. Once givenness is freed from any horizons—in other words, once phenomenology is true to the phenomena themselves—the subject can never be lord and master. The ultimate term is never the subject, nor the object, nor even Being, but givenness.

Marion's contribution to this volume, "The Reason of the Gift," is his most recent, and perhaps fullest, meditation on yet another example—perhaps the best possible, he suggests—of pure givenness: paternity. A subject that has engaged Marion theologically throughout his career (God as Father is a key concern in both *The Idol and Distance* and *God Without Being*), the theme of paternity has also received a specifically phenomenological treatment stretching back to Marion's 1996 homage to Lévinas,[1] and has been in continuous development since.

In the present volume, the phenomenological treatment of paternity becomes a crucial element in Marion's debate with Jacques Derrida over the possibility of there being "pure" givenness. As is now well known, Derrida argues that what we call the gift is always inserted into a certain economy, a "mode" that means, in turn, the *impossibility* of the gift. There is never a genuine gratuitousness, Derrida suggests: when I give anything, there always a risk (or perhaps inevitability) that this gift will become enmeshed in a relationship of exchange. Thus, I may give a gift to you, but I always expect to get another gift in return (even if it is "merely" gratitude); as such, there are no "real" or "pure" gifts. And if, as seems inevitable, my so-called gift puts the recipient under some compulsion, it is not a gift at all: it is an obligation (for example), or a demand, but not a gift. What seems a gift in fact contradicts the recipient's freedom. Conversely, if I receive a gift, *I* am put under compulsion—and so my freedom is compromised. Either way, the integrity of the gift is always undermined: the conditions of its possibility (giver and receiver) are, simultaneously, the conditions of its impossibility.

Furthermore, it is not just freedom that is an issue vis-à-vis the gift: there is also the question of the *presence* of the present. The less a gift is actually "here," the less of a gift it seems (or so Derrida claims); conversely, the more the gift is "here and now," the more it seems to be a proper gift—real, substantial, and so on. And, as far as Derrida is concerned, herein lies the problem. The more a gift is literally present, the more we can measure it, weigh it up, take account of it, value it (in monetary terms), or commodify it. Thus the more present it is, the less of a present it is. A pure gift would be something given freely, without condition, without obligation, and not subject to any "currency conversion" or commodified measurement. It seems, then, that the very requirements here—giver, gift, recipient—undo the possibility of there being a pure gift. Every gift can be reduced to "economic" terms; no gift can escape the circle of exchange. Which means there is not really any "gift" at all! Or, more accurately: we could never *know* any such gift; it will always be a noumenon beyond any phenomenological description.[2]

In response to all of this, Marion wants to argue that we can arrive at "pure givenness" by means of the phenomenological reduction. He insists that it is possible to bracket each of the factors involved here, and so to delineate a principle of sufficient givenness that is not subject to Derrida's critique. Thus, Marion argues that there can be givenness without any object or "thing" given (for Marion, the most important phenomena are not in any sense present); givenness without anyone giving; and givenness without anyone receiving. In short, we can have givenness beyond the economy of the gift given and received. And the significance of paternity is that, for Marion, it provides the supreme example of a phenomenon that "reduces" (in the phenomenological sense) to sheer givenness.

Fatherhood, Marion tells us, is about giving, but it always gives more than itself. It does not "produce" any strictly quantifiable or predictable commodity; what is given is pure possibility. Furthermore, what is given cannot possibly be repaid: the child can never repay the giver himself with the gift of life he or she has received. And what is given, as gift, is in no sense an *object*: life itself cannot be regarded as a "thing." Above all, though, fatherhood "achieves" all of this, or is "responsible" for it, while (unlike motherhood) it is essentially an *absence*: after procreation, the father is missing, literally and directly, from the life that develops in utero. Fatherhood can be established (juridically, say, or medically) only after it has given, without the full presence of what it has given, in constant renewal of itself—making itself present again and again—to what it has given. For these reasons, Marion suggests, paternity is the supreme example of givenness beyond the (Derridean) economy of the gift. Overall, the analysis here forms one of Marion's most startling—and provocative—theses.

No doubt the efficacy of Marion's explorations and analyses will provoke further explorations and analyses; the first such reactions—appropriately enough, in one case, from Joseph O'Leary, probably the first thinker in the English-speaking world to engage with Marion's work—are contained in this volume. We are delighted at the prospect of such an encounter contributing significantly to some of the most important ongoing debates in contemporary phenomenology and theology.

Elsewhere, *Givenness and God* offers a suitably wide-ranging engagement with the work of a thinker whose work is renowned for its breadth, depth, and scope. As such, it represents the first collection in English dedicated to Marion's oeuvre. Yet, despite acknowledging Marion's status and significance, the collection is a genuinely critical encounter: none of the contributors is reluctant to identify difficulties, aporiai, or possible blind spots in aspects of Marion's work. This engagement takes various forms: critical analyses of Marion's historical interpretations of, respectively, Descartes (Alweiss), Husserl (Mooney), and Heidegger (Elliott, Ó Murchadha); analyses of the structural efficacy of Marion's texts (Leask); comparative readings of Marion and a "pure" postmodernism (Dooley), of Marion and Romana (Mackinley), and of Marion and Augustine (Cassidy); critical analysis of the lacunae in the reception of Marion (Morrow); and also wider philosophical and theological explorations based upon (or launched from) Marion's own breakthrough thinking (Kearney, O'Donohue). The volume reflects its provenance—a hugely successful symposium held at the Mater Dei Institute, Dublin, in January 2003—by including not only fuller versions of papers delivered at that event but also the transcript of a unique open forum featuring Marion, Richard Kearney, and various interlocutors in dialogue. Together, all of these contributions provide a comprehensive engagement with Marion, as well as allowing Marion to continue his engagement, in English, with the wider philosophical and theological communities. Instead of needlessly summarizing such a rich assortment, we merely state here our sincere conviction that *Givenness and God* provides a landmark in the ongoing reception of a profound and profoundly significant thinker.

The translation of any important philosopher's work is always likely to become a fraught affair—and, needless to say, Marion's is no exception. The most obvious question concerns the translation of *donation*. Most of the contributors here opt for "givenness," in accord with both established practice and Marion's own preference[3]; the title of this volume reflects our own preference as editors. Nonetheless, we recognize that there are important questions over the English translation of *donation*, and even over Marion's use of *donation* as a French translation of the German *Gegebenheit*. For example, there may be a certain case for leaving *donation* untranslated (just as one would, say, *Dasein*); there may also be legitimate or quasi-legitimate claims from a newcomer like "givingness." Similar questions arise over other important terms in Marion's thought: "objectness" or "objectivity"?; "givee" or "recipient" (or *donataire*, untranslated)?; "gifted" or *adonné*? And so on. . . . At the risk of apparent inconsistency, we have decided not to impose a uniform policy or style throughout this volume: our concern was that any such editorial intervention might contribute to a premature closure or ossification of an important debate. Therefore, we have allowed individual contributors to follow their own preferences—notwithstanding our own. We hope that any questions raised as a result are wholly fruitful.

PART I

Marion on Descartes, Husserl, and Heidegger

1

The Conceptual Idolatry of Descartes's Gray Ontology
An Epistemology "Without Being"

Derek J. Morrow

As even a cursory glance at the current literature will confirm, the task of investigating the many philosophical and theological questions raised by Jean-Luc Marion's explorations into the phenomenology of the gift and of givenness (*donation*) has only begun. Not least of these questions, of course, is the purely formal one of methodology. For although Marion's phenomenology of *donation* has generated significant criticism from several quarters—both from scholars who regard it as insufficiently phenomenological and thus as a betrayal of phenomenology (Janicaud[1]), and from scholars who consider it to have unduly compromised the theological prerogatives of the Christian faith (Milbank[2])—all such criticism suffers nonetheless from one glaring methodological omission: it fails to situate Marion's phenomenological concerns within the larger context of his extensive scholarship on Descartes. And insofar as this scholarship antedates and, to a large degree, sets the stage for Marion's phenomenological project, that this project is seen to be too "theological" for some and too "metaphysical" for others amounts to something of a nonsequitur. That is, from a methodological point of view, all such assessments of Marion's thought betray a certain impertinence in assuming, quite gratuitously, that one can safely ignore a substantial portion of Marion's corpus and still arrive at an accurate understanding of his intention. How or even whether this intention is conditioned by the concerns evinced by his work as a whole has not been deemed worthy, it seems, of serious consideration.

In this chapter, I seek to redress this deficiency, at least in part, by expositing a key element in Marion's interpretation of Cartesian metaphysics: the "gray" ontology elaborated by the *Regulae ad directionem ingenii*. My aim in doing so will be to show how what Marion calls the "schizocosmic" ambivalence of this ontology is animated by a fundamentally idolatrous impulse that seeks to master the world by reconstructing its intelligibility according to the demands of the *mens humana* and its methodic gaze that longs for the certainty of a fully transparent evidence. Construing Descartes's gray ontology explicitly as a form of conceptual idolatry promises to furnish a viable thematic link between Marion's Cartesian studies and his more recent writings in phenomenology, the gift, and negative theology. Accordingly, if this link can be established, it might serve to illuminate and evaluate the ongoing debates in the literature over the nature and legitimacy of the "theological turn" in phenomenology. And although an investigation of this latter question goes beyond the scope of this chapter, it is my hope that the analysis presented here will facilitate such work in the future.

The Hidden Interlocutor: Aristotle

It is no secret that the "utopic"[3] anonymity of the *Regulae ad directionem ingenii* tempts even the skilled interpreter of Descartes to despair of unlocking its meaning. Yet for all its beguiling, this temptation betrays a certain paradox. The *Regulae* do indeed contain many anonymous features that (a) may urge exegetes to regard the work as impregnable and (b) may cause them to doubt whether it contributes anything of consequence to Cartesian thought generally. Paradoxically, however, these anonymous features, even while they shroud the *Regulae* in obscurity and suggest their irrelevance, are also the same features that convey their philosophic singularity and render them indispensable for ascertaining "the true 'birth' of the Cartesian genesis of Descartes" (*OG*, 16).[4]

According to Marion, three main proposals for resolving the hermeneutic problem of the *Regulae* have been put forward in the scholarly literature, each of which attempts "to overcome" its "utopic situation" (*OG*, 16) by situating it with respect to Descartes's published writings. Each of these proposals has serious deficiencies,[5] however, and for this reason, Marion himself recommends that we look "*outside* of the Cartesian corpus" (Marion's emphasis) to find "the point of reference, or at least of illumination" from which to interpret the *Regulae*'s obscurities. Adopting such a standpoint would make it possible to view the *Regulae* as a "bordering text" (*texte limitrophe*) that stands between the thought of Descartes that is properly Cartesian (as articulated in the published writings) and "the other currents of ideas" that comprise the conceptual mise-en-scène within which Descartes finds himself. In a word, Marion suggests that we regard the *Regulae* as a sustained — but *furtive* — Cartesian polemic against views then regnant in contemporary thought. Reading the *Regulae* in this way, as a "bordering text" intent on accomplishing a veiled polemic, could account for those features of the work — its "bordering concepts" (*concepts limitrophes*) — that either fail to appear in the published corpus or seem incompatible with the principles informing that corpus. The presence of such "bordering concepts" in the *Regulae* could then be explained and justified in terms of the methodological constraints imposed by the work's polemical aim "to confront, gather up, and reinterpret a conceptual material that is not Cartesian" — a provisional aim whose fulfillment the published works presuppose and for which they no longer have need (*OG*, 18–19).

If, however, the *Regulae* are to be understood as a deliberate but silent polemic, against what conceptuality do they polemicize, and how shall one identify their unnamed opponent? Marion contends that "[t]he singularity of the *Regulae*'s concepts comes to it from the critical relation these concepts bear to the topoi of Aristotelian themes" (*OG*, 180). Throughout the *Regulae*, Descartes conducts "a strangely constant and precise dialogue with Aristotle"[6] that the interpreter can detect only if he executes "an Aristotelian deciphering"[7] of the *Regulae*'s themes by comparing them systematically with their counterparts in Aristotle — the hidden interlocutor of the *Regulae*.

Rejection by Displacement: Cartesian "Metaphorization"

Several indications support this hypothesis. (a) The text of the *Regulae* betrays a de facto preoccupation with Aristotle insofar as it refers "incessantly" to theses of Aristotelian philosophy that are so recognizable and commonplace ("pour ainsi dire banales"; so to speak, banal) as to suggest that Descartes deploys "a precise knowledge" of Aristotle in the *Regulae* to effect "a consciously critical reprise of Aristotelian thought" (*OG*, 19). (b) Descartes undoubtedly read Aristotle's texts, probably in the original Greek, as a constitutive part of his scholastic formation in philosophy at La Flèche. In light of this Aristotelian training, one could reasonably conclude that "Aristotle remained for Descartes, culturally if not metaphysically, 'a contemporary.'"[8] (c) Descartes himself testifies to this contemporaneity, "at least programmatically," if one considers his repeated declarations in various letters regarding his intention to publish a comparison of his philosophy with that of the schools (*OG*, 20–21). Curiously, however, (d) he never undertook this comparison—perhaps intentionally. For such a task would have been superfluous if in fact the *Regulae* had already managed to accomplish it implicitly:

> Perhaps . . . Descartes never took up this project because he had *already* brought it to completion in some way—in the *Regulae*. For if in fact the real confrontation with Aristotle had already given rise to a complete debate [in the *Regulae*], a new comparison would have only been a fastidious, parallel enumeration of contrary theses: an apologetic work for its own sake, or a work of advertising intended for everyone. (*OG*, 21; emphasis in the original)

Do the *Regulae* themselves offer any evidence to support this (admittedly controversial[9]) assumption? More precisely, does Descartes give any specific indication in the text of the *Regulae* that would not only confirm the *existence* of such a comparison but also, and more importantly, one that would alert the reader as to *the way in which* the comparison is to be carried out? Does Descartes, in effect, provide his interpreter with a "smoking gun"?

On this point, Marion is perhaps at his most original: quite early on in the *Regulae*, in what appears to be an incidental digression from the main topic at hand, Descartes inserts a passage whose "decisive importance" is perhaps for that reason "not usually noted" (*OG*, 21).[10] In this passage, he expressly announces to his reader that he intends to use the traditional language of the schoolmen in a wholly untraditional way; that is, the *Regulae* will apply the "old" scholastic terminology in a "new" manner that *entirely transforms its sense*:

> In case anyone should be troubled by my *novel* use of the term "intuition" [*intuitus*] *and of other terms* [*aliarumque*] to which I shall be forced to give a different meaning from their ordinary one, I wish to point out here that I am paying no attention to the way these terms have lately been used in the [s]chools. For it would be very difficult for me to employ the same terminol-

ogy, when my own views are profoundly different. I shall take account only of the meanings in Latin of individual words and, when appropriate words are lacking, I shall use what seem the most suitable words, adapting them to my own meaning [*transferam ad meum sensum*] (emphasis added).[11]

What comparison, specifically, is in view here? That Descartes should single out the term *intuitus* to illustrate his general methodology ("and of other terms," *aliarumque*)[12] is instructive, since *intuitus* had long since been used by the scholastics to translate Aristotle's νοῦς (*OG*, 22).[13] Accordingly, here we see Descartes declaring that he plans to take up traditional Aristotelian vocabulary and invest it with a new meaning (*transferam ad meum sensum*), one that is suitable to his own purpose. The comparison in question, then,

> consists in correlating the Latin etymology [of a given word] . . . with the organically Cartesian *sensus* (or the Cartesian "value" of the word). On the part of the reader, [detecting] this direct correlation can depend on an indirect process: [viz.] measuring the gap (*transferre*, 369, 9) that Descartes institutes between the concept or concepts designated by such a word and the peculiar semantics that he substitutes for it. (*RUC*,[14] 126, "Annotations," n. 12)

The systematic transformation (better: reconfiguration) of sense revealed by this process of comparison Marion will designate "the principle of metaphorization" (*OG*, 22) because the "Cartesian innovation" it deploys "is to be sought less in the lexicon than in the transfers that metaphorize the conceptual semantics of this or that term" (*RUC*, 127, "Annotations," n. 12). In other words, one must realize that in the *Regulae*, Descartes "does not exactly limit himself to contradicting" Aristotelian doctrines:

> On the contrary, he translates their meaning into his new conceptual universe . . . [where] [e]ach concept thus undergoes a multiple displacement and rearrangement that is measured by its gap with the concept of Aristotelian origin. More than a critique, Descartes institutes a metaphor. (*OG*, 22)[15]

Indeed, in an unrelated fragment found outside the *Regulae*, "Descartes informs us that what is essential" on this point "resides less in the concepts [he employs], or their names, than in the new relation that the former bear to the latter." (*OG*, 22)[16]

If the *Regulae* elaborate an extended metaphor (or set of metaphors) by transferring (μετα–φέρειν)[17] Aristotelian terminology into a conceptual domain that is foreign to it, it becomes clear that the "principle of metaphorization" at work in the *Regulae* does not aim to *replace* Aristotle so much as it seeks to *displace* him. And this operation of displacement—in which Descartes "sets to one side" (*mise à l'écart*; *OG*, 181)[18] an Aristotelian metaphysics that he will refrain from challenging directly only so that he may freely institute an epistemological project of his own devising[19]—provides Marion with one of the governing principles informing his analysis of Descartes's gray ontology.

The Displaced (Gray) Ontology of the Object

In the preceding section, we set forth Marion's contention that the *Regulae* must be read as a systematic but covert disputation with Aristotle, the hidden interlocutor of the work who is never expressly acknowledged as such by Descartes. As we have seen, Marion holds that the *Regulae*'s tacit confrontation with Aristotle proceeds by way of a "metaphorization" in which Descartes assigns his own meanings to traditional vocabulary in order to achieve his desired effect. Nevertheless, precisely *why* Descartes should resort to such an elaborate ruse in the first place remains to be articulated. Indeed, to grant the existence of what one might call a "hermeneutics of displacement" in the *Regulae* is one thing; to determine its purpose, quite another. Put simply, what does Descartes hope to gain from his silent polemic against Aristotle?

One can begin to answer this question by recalling what is perhaps the most salient feature of Cartesian displacement, namely, its strictly *tactical* character. That is, Descartes does not insist upon, nor does he see the need for, a *refutation* of Aristotle so much as he assumes that Aristotle's doctrine can be safely *disregarded* as irrelevant. Thus, when Marion states that the *Regulae* execute "the deconstruction of the [Aristotelian] εἶδος and the construction of the [Cartesian] object" (*OG*, 113), he understands this deconstruction as purely formal, and one that "conceals itself under an epistemological discourse."[20] Accordingly, Descartes's "bracketing of the thing itself and of its εἶδος" (*la mise entre parenthèses de la chose même et de son eidos*, *OG*, 140)[21] does not deny their ontological validity as such; rather, this validity is merely placed to one side and "dismissed" methodologically so that Descartes can "constitute" another parallel, "gray" ontology[22] — gray, ironically,

> because it is an ontology that does not acknowledge itself as such, but goes beyond a simple theory of knowledge by over-investing this theory. Indeed, the great inaugural and incomplete text of the *Regulae* reverses term for term the enterprise of Aristotle to think being insofar as it is being in order to substitute for it the thought of being insofar as it is known, of being insofar as it is an object.... From this point forward, a *mathesis universalis* is imposed [that] constitutes its objects according to measure and especially according to order. At the same time, however, by defining every possible thing principally and universally as knowable — [and] thus as an object rather than as a being (indeed, without reference to any being whatsoever) — this science, de facto and by right, takes on the rank of the Aristotelian science of being qua being.[23]

Here we see — in a very compressed form — Marion's articulation of the complexity and the ambivalence of the *Regulae*'s metaphysical situation.[24] Paradoxically, Marion interprets Descartes as embracing a nonontological ontology that is nonetheless ontological, since it simultaneously denies and affirms a *logos* regarding the Being of beings. Cartesian ontology is nonontological because it "challenges every *logos* that would adequately announce it" (Descartes's gray ontology).[25] Yet this same ontology is not so nonontological that it lacks an ontology altogether — as though it were, so to speak, a "nonontology" in terms of its content.[26] Rather, the Cartesian nonontological ontology is also fully ontological because it constructs a *logos* of the object (whose status as "object" is derived from the indeterminate ontic status of the *ego cogito* and its certainty); functionally, at least, the *Regulae*'s ontology of the object [27] ascribes to epistemology the prerogatives of first philosophy. *Mathesis universalis*, which ostensibly is purely epistemological in character, in fact possesses — as *universalis* — unmistakable (however unacknowledged) metaphysical designs, for it seeks to replace in a surreptitious fashion Aristotle's first philosophy of *ens inquantum ens* with a gray ontology of *ens inquantum objectum* that treats *de omni re inquantum scibili*.[28]

Moreover, Descartes's gray ontology of the object supplants Aristotle's ontology of οὐσία only by displacing it and marginalizing it in the name of an epistemology that has neither refuted it nor replaced it with an alternative ontology—at least not with one that has been justified as such:

> The theory of science won by the first four *Rules* cannot be founded, however, or at least cannot be made intelligible, by itself. Indeed, the epistemic operations this science puts into practice, de facto . . . only advance on a terrain that is ready to collapse: the condition of their epistemic possibility requires the destruction of certain ontological concepts—a destruction that is neither justified, *nor, perhaps, effected*, but is merely sketched by a simple setting to one side. (*OG*, 71; emphasis added)

As this citation makes clear, Marion considers the "destruction" of Aristotelian ontology to be merely assumed by the *Regulae*'s gray ontology, never "justified" nor even "effected." Yet Descartes does not hesitate to act on this assumption and to draw from it what seem to him irrefragable epistemic conclusions—conclusions whose irrefragability is evidenced, plainly, from the methodological "utility" (*nec ulla utilior est in toto hoc Tractatu, AT*, X, 381.8–10) they promise. Thus the *Regulae*'s destruction (*destruction*) of Aristotle really amounts to a deconstruction (*déconstruction*) of Aristotle so that he may be selectively reassembled according to the demands of the method. That is, Descartes deconstructs Aristotelian οὐσία only to the extent necessary in order to construct the epistemically certain object as its surrogate.[29] In this way, the *Regulae* evince "a double movement of deconstruction as construction" in which "*déconstruction* is also *de construction*."[30] This paradoxical but characteristic feature of the *Regulae*, in which Aristotelian οὐσία is methodologically suppressed, reconfigured, and supplanted—in a word, "metaphorized"—by a dissimulated gray ontology of the knowable object, will lead Marion in a later work to assert that "[t]he initial and recurrent decision of the *Regulae*, thus also of all the thought that follows, will consist in *not* [my emphasis] taking into view things that are susceptible of being made into objects of *intuitus* in terms of the categorical figures of *ens*" (*DMP*, 74/*PMD*, 81), such that "the question of the ὄν ᾗ ὄν disappears, leaving as its beneficiary the arrangement according to the order of knowledge" (*DMP*, 71/*PMD*, 78). And from this result, as we have already seen, Marion provocatively concludes that "[f]ormally, Cartesian philosophy is deployed as an explicit and avowed nonontology" (*DMP*, 73/*PMD*, 80).

Mathesis Universalis: Epistemology "Without Being"

Just how do the *Regulae* construct this "nonontology," and what purpose does this construction serve? This and the following section will address the first of these questions, while the second question will be taken up in the final two sections. To begin, it is important to note more precisely the way in which Descartes's *mathesis universalis* passes beyond the abstraction from matter attained in Aristotle's common mathematics to a second, "more radical and therefore more universal," level of abstraction (*OG*, 61). This second level of abstraction Marion names "the principle of mathematicity," which vouchsafes "abstraction in general" (*OG*, 61) as applicable to all the genera of being, and not simply to the mathematicals. In postulating a *mathesis universalis*, Descartes at once displaces and revaluates Aristotle's doctrine (Cartesian metaphorization) by seeking

> no longer a universal mathematics, that is, one that furnishes the particular mathematical sciences with their principles, and one that is therefore limited to quantity alone . . . —but a "universal science" that does not govern quantity (from which it can abstract) so much as it does order and measure. A decisive substitution: whereas universal mathematicity (in Aristotle, as also for Proclus and Iamblichus) ratifies the break from the "physical" and from the mathematical by being defined through abstract quantity, *mathesis universalis* attains the nonmathematical mathematicity of mathematics only to erase immediately this break from abstraction. In effect, in passing to the second degree of abstraction (order and measure), *mathesis universalis* abolishes just as quickly the distinctions imposed by the first (quantity, being outside of "matter"). The universal mathematics [of which Aristotle speaks] is such only by remaining mathematical; *mathesis universalis* is universal only insofar as it is no longer purely mathematical. (*OG*, 63–64)[31]

Of cardinal importance here is the unrestricted scope of *mathesis universalis*, for it is this unqualified universality that signals the distinctively *metaphysical* pretensions of such a *mathesis* to stand alongside of, and on a par with, Aristotle's first philosophy of *ens inquantum ens*.[32] In order to attain this privileged status, however, *mathesis universalis* must first displace the primacy of οὐσία not only in the order of being but also—and more decisively—in the order of knowledge.

To achieve this end, the *Regulae* must at their very outset "accomplish a considerable task: [they must] invert the center of gravity regarding the relation of knowledge to that which it knows—the thing itself" (*OG*, 25). Such an inversion requires more than merely positing an isomorphism between the order of being and the order of knowing; it requires that "the center of gravity of the epistemic relation" between knower and known be "situated in the understanding" alone (*OG*, 151).[33] For although an Aristotelian ontology of οὐσία does indeed imply a corresponding order of knowledge in which "there is undoubtedly a correlation between the known and the knower," nonetheless it remains true that

> never for Aristotle (nor for Saint Thomas) does this correlation become reciprocal. This relation alone does not admit its inversion and imposes a center of gravity that is radically located in the thing to be known. (*OG*, 28; see also *DMP*, 134–36/*PMD*, 143–45)

For Descartes, on the other hand, by means of the "omnipotent relation" (*OG*, 82) that is *mathesis universalis*, the relation between knower and known depends on the knower in such a way that knower and known become reciprocal, or even convertible. With Descartes,

> therefore, the center of gravity for knowledge [*la science*] resides less in that which is known than in that which knows; less in the thing itself than in that which apprehends this thing; or again, more essential than the thing known appears, for each thing, the knowledge of the mind that constitutes it as an object. (*OG*, 29)

Despite—or, indeed, because of—this radical shift in the epistemic "center of gravity"[34] effected by the universal method of *mathesis universalis*, Marion insists that "in the *Regulae* the primacy of epistemology does not conceal the necessity for having a *metaphysica generalis*, because the science of the object plays for it the role of an ontology of the thing, tinted gray" (*OG*, 197). In other words,

> the gap between the *Regulae* and Aristotelian thought is due, therefore, not to a critique of metaphysical themes, but to the intensification and erasure of these themes by a construction of epistemological models. The absence of metaphysics [in the *Regulae*] becomes, more radically, the setting aside of the inquiry

into the nature of the thing, leaving as its beneficiary a preoccupation with pure intelligibility. (*OG*, 181)

Thus, "when ontology becomes gray (depends on methodical knowledge),"[35] "[u]niversality is ascribed to *mathesis universalis* on the basis of the unconditioned efficacy of the criterion of order. This order [as deployed by *mathesis universalis*] can lay claim to all objects since it does not depend on any of them, but only on the relation—by definition always possible—of the object to the knowing mind" (*DMP*, 60 [mod.]/*PMD*, 66). In its own fashion, then, the universality of *mathesis universalis* emulates the metaphysics of Aristotelian first philosophy, but paradoxically so, since with *mathesis universalis*

> the universal no longer characterizes the ὂν ᾗ ὂν that can be made visible by means of φιλοσοφία πρώτη; it characterizes . . . the universality produced by submitting things to the thought that contains them, inasmuch as it orders (itself and) them. (*DMP*, 61 [mod.]/*PMD*, 66–67)[36]

Accordingly, insofar as "the function of *mathesis universalis*" in the *Regulae* "will remain thus strictly epistemological" because its primacy "remains . . . purely epistemological" (*OG*, 69),[37] the metaphysics of gray ontology—a metaphysics of "*ens non in quantum ens, sed in quantum repraesentatum, ut objectum*" ([being, not insofar as it is being, but insofar as it is represented, as an object]; *DMP*, 78/*PMD*, 85)— reveals an ontology devoid of ontology (*un néant d'ontologie*),[38] because it boasts a universality and a primacy that are, *stricto sensu*, "without Being."

Construction of the Object: *Idea* (*Natura Simplex*) as Construct

The gray ontology of the *Regulae* is without Being, Marion argues, "since the demands of the epistemological order bracket all ontic foundation" (*DMP*, 66/*PMD*, 72). In stipulating that "when we consider things in the order that corresponds to our knowledge of them [*res singulas in ordine ad cognitionem nostram*], our view of them must be different [*aliter spectandas esse*] from what it would be if we were speaking of them in accordance with how they exist in reality [*prout revera existunt*]" (*PWD*, I, 44),[39] Descartes announces "a fundamental thesis of the method and of gray ontology" (*DMP*, 164 [mod.]/*PMD*, 175). This thesis holds that "the required order is constituted first *in ordine ad cognitionem nostram,*"⁴⁰ and not in terms of how each *res singula* is constituted *revera*, since this is disregarded in the name of a *mathesis universalis* that regards (*spectare*) them solely according to the strictures of the *ordo vel mensura* prescribed by the method.⁴¹ In this way, *mathesis universalis* introduces a "gap" (*écart*) between "the 'natural' order" (*l'ordre "naturel"*) of the world and "the methodic order" (*l'ordre méthodique*) of the mind in which the latter "by a fiction of thought" does not falsify the former so much as it ignores it (*OG*, 77).⁴² Yet, as we have seen, this gap is purely methodological and, as such, it "exposes a rift between [the] two orders, yet without one being able to reduce the other to a status of disorder" (*OG*, 78). In effect, then, "the radical and irreversible innovation" of gray ontology consists "in the very schizocosmenia [*la schizocosmie même*] that presides over the bifurcation of order [*le dédoublement de l'ordre*] rather than in the undecided supremacy of one order over the other" (*OG*, 78).

In virtue of this "schizocosmenia," Marion will claim in a more mature version of his argument that

> what is peculiar to Descartes, which establishes him as the metaphysician par excellence of modernity, is found in this: the question of the beginning and of the first term—in short, the question of the primacy at work in *prima philosophia*—passes from Being to thought. (*DMP*, 68 [mod.]/*PMD*, 74)⁴³

The above quotation should not be taken to imply that Marion aligns himself straightforwardly with those interpreters who castigate Descartes as an "idealist" who rejects the preceding tradition of philosophical "realism." The controversy over the supposed realism or idealism of Descartes conducted by an earlier generation of Cartesian scholars⁴⁴ Marion considers to obfuscate what is more fundamentally at issue, at least in the *Regulae*:

> Before debating the realism or idealism of Descartes, the entire question should consist in inquiring after the conditions by which the problem of a gap between the two orders can be posed here [in the *Regulae*]. If the *Regulae* do not resolve the difficulty of the duplication of orders, it is perhaps because their unique task is *to institute the gap* [my emphasis] in which alone the con-/de-formity of the orders would become possible. (*OG*, 78, n. 17)⁴⁵, ⁴⁶

For Marion, the debate over whether Descartes is more properly classified as a realist or as an idealist—as well as whether such classification can fruitfully serve to assess Cartesian thought as either a modern advance over premodern realism (Liard) or as a "degradation" of that same realism (Maritain)—misses the point because it fails to see that what is truly significant in Descartes's "epistemological revolution"[47] is precisely the installation of that schizocosmic *dédoublement de l'ordre*[48] which gives rise to the debate as such and constitutes its a priori condition of possibility:

> Instead of asking whether the order of thought . . . is reconciled finally, or not, with the order of the world, . . . should not a [different] question—the most pressing one—be asked first? [Namely:] How could this disjunction become possible? In a word, what stake is being wagered in this game of the order with its *alter ego*? (*OG*, 78)

In a similar vein, Marion has observed more recently that although "it is a commonplace to consider Descartes as the founder of modern 'idealism,'" one should beware of adopting the "questionable habit" indulged by many scholars "of hastily evaluating [*apprécier*] this so-called 'idealism' positively or (most of the time) negatively, without bothering to define it" (*CQ*, 43 [mod.]/*QC*, 75). For, in the case of Descartes at least, it is by no means clear that in the effort to detect a presence or absence of idealism in his thought, the logically prior "attempt to determine the Cartesian definition of the idea" (*CQ*, 43 [mod.]/*QC*, 75) has been realized satisfactorily, with its results secured, such that its theoretical implications can simply be taken for granted. Indeed, to interpret the text of Descartes on this question without first defining the terms by which that interpretation is formulated evinces a methodological impropriety that is betrayed by its very gratuity,

> for only if Descartes presents a unified, coherent, and operational concept of the idea will it eventually be possible to evaluate [*mesurer*] its originality and influence, and even—if one really insists—to speak of "idealism." (*CQ*, 43/*QC*, 76)

At first glance, this objection may strike the reader as somewhat facile, even dismissive. Does it not merely state the obvious? Despite appearances, however, the hermeneutic challenge posed by "the Cartesian definition of the idea" remains particularly acute and is far from admitting a straightforward solution—not least because, in the wake of the definitive work of Jean-Robert Armogathe,[49] we now know that the texts of Descartes employ two distinct (and not fully compatible) conceptualities for the words *idea/idée*, "one belonging for the most part to the *Regulae ad directionem ingenii* and another deriving especially from the *Meditationes*" (*CQ*, 43 [mod.]/*QC*, 76). Indeed, from the definition of the idea found in the *Regulae*, a definition that through Cartesian displacement and metaphorization "rejects *idea* in the sense of εἶδος (that is, the essence of a thing) while retaining in the new meaning of the term two traits borrowed from Aristotle" (*CQ*, 44/*QC*, 76), to that given in the *Meditationes*, in which "these two characteristics of the idea are reversed" (*CQ*, 45/*QC*, 78), we find that

> Descartes' doctrine [of the *idea*] has evolved to the point that it has now inverted itself: Either an idea processes things by means of figures [the presentation of the *Regulae*], or thought is informed by the idea [that of the *Meditationes*]. Ideas depend upon the imagination [in the *Regulae*] or are freed from it on the basis of the *cogitatio* [in the *Meditationes*]. (*CQ*, 46/*QC*, 80)

For if, in virtue of their schizocosmenia, the *Regulae* understand *idea* as (a) "the equivalent of a figure" and as (b) "belong[ing] both to the realm of the imagination and to that of the intellect," such that "*here* [Marion's emphasis] at least, Descartes is willing to maintain the hylomorphic determination of the εἶδος of 'physical' beings," the *Meditationes* reverse the polarity of these terms by presenting a doctrine in which (a') "the idea, as a figure, instead of remaining a form of the thing, forms [*met en forme*] thought itself,"[50] and (b') "against Aristotle, the idea is defined by thought only, independently of the imagination."[51]

Perhaps more important than the disparate "variations" (*CQ*, 46/*QC*, 80) of *idea* in the Cartesian texts is the rationale that accounts for their existence in the first place: the evolving status of *idea* in Descartes's thought reflects not "Descartes' own contribution to the definition of the idea, but rather echo[es] some of its consequences for the pre-Cartesian definitions that were prevalent at that time" (*CQ*, 46/*QC*, 80–81). In other words, the multiple and equivocal significations for the term *idea* in the *Regulae* and the *Meditationes* furnish yet another example of those "bordering concepts" (*concepts limitrophes*) employed by Descartes "to confront, gather up, and reinterpret a conceptual material that is not Cartesian" (*OG*, 13). On this assumption, one must reckon with the possibility that

> the [properly] Cartesian doctrine of the idea does not at first use the term *idea*. Instead, it uses a perfectly new and original substitute: namely, the simple nature. (*CQ*, 46 [mod.]/*QC*, 81)

Marion contends that in the second part of *Rule XII*, Descartes "abandons" the language of *idea* — a language bequeathed to him by the philosophical tradition based on Aristotle's *De Anima* — "and introduces an utterly new concept" as its surrogate, "that of the 'simple nature' (*natura simplicissima, res simplex*)" (*CQ*, 46–47/*QC*, 81). As such, the supplanting of *idea* by *natura simplex* (*simplicissima*)[52] yields a further installment in the *Regulae*'s systematic metaphorization of Aristotle, and in particular, here in *Rule XII*, a metaphorizing that reworks the Aristotelian faculties of the soul, especially those of sensibility and intellection.[53] Moreover, as with all instances of Cartesian displacement, the simple nature initiates "not only, or primarily, a terminological innovation"; it also (and more importantly) executes a profound transformation of Aristotle's doctrine — indeed, so profound in this particular case that Marion will go so far as to claim that the neologism *natura simplex* subjects all subsequent philosophical discourse to nothing less than "an epistemological revolution" (*CQ*, 47/*QC*, 81) — and this precisely because, as the definitive replacement for Aristotelian οὐσία,

> far from antecedently determining or regulating [*normer*] our knowledge, this nature is the result of our knowledge, its product. And insofar as the simple nature is a knowable object — that is, an object precisely because it is knowable — it substitutes itself for οὐσία, which it banishes once and for all from modern metaphysics.[54]

In that, "paradoxically," both in terms of its function and of its content, "it contradicts both nature and simplicity" (*CQ*, 47 [mod.]/*QC*, 81), Descartes's simple nature is neither if these terms are taken in their traditional sense. On the contrary, the "simplicity" of such "natures" (*res singulae*) is artificially constructed *in ordine ad cognitionem nostram* (*Rule XII, AT,* X, 418.2), and therefore "consist[s] entirely in the knowledge that the constitutive mind has of them" (*DMP*, 77/*PMD*, 83).[55] In a manner that reflects the *Regulae*'s gray ontology — or rather, as a constitutive element of this ontology,

> the simple nature remains the simplest term, but the simplicity is an epistemological, not an ontological one: It does not concern οὐσία.... The result is a concept of idea that is distinctly and originally Cartesian: *idea* defined as an object that is first insofar as it is known, and not according to οὐσία — first insofar as it is "easy" to know, and not according to some indivisible form or εἶδος. (*CQ*, 47–48 [mod.]/*QC*, 82–83)

Here we see that in speaking of the simple nature, Rule *XII* deploys "several conceptual divisions" (*OG*, 132), each of which embodies and illustrates the schizocosmenia at work implicitly throughout the *Regulae* but effectively put into play only by the *mathesis universalis* of Rule *IV* and the reciprocity of relations outlined in *Rule VI*.[56] First, "the concept of simplicity undergoes a division" in which either "it can be envisaged *a parte rei*," or "it can be understood, not with reference to the thing itself, but . . . with reference to the epistemic *ego*" that constructs the simplicity of its object—*ens inquantum objectum*—which is knowable exclusively *respectu intellectus nostri* and is regarded (*spectandas*) by the mind's conscious gaze (*intuitus mentis*) solely *in ordine ad cognitionem nostram* (*OG*, 131).

Next, "simple nature" denies "nature" by splitting the concept of nature into two acceptations: "*Natura* no longer designates exclusively the φύσις of each individual thing," but in addition, it also signifies

> the logical elements to which the thing is reduced through the application of a schema of correlation: simple *natura* makes possible a reconstitution [*la recomposition*]. [In *Rule XII*,] *Res* designates as much the element that the *ego* selects and constructs as its privileged object, as it does the irreducibly given thing; "nature" is as much the reconstituted object as it is the "thing" which is observed [*c'est autant que la "chose" constatée, l'objet reconstitué*]. (*OG*, 132)[57]

The crucial equivocation of *Rule XII*, where Descartes moves almost imperceptibly from an ontological construal of *natura*—that is, nature in the sense of φύσις—to its reconstitution as *objectum*, in the name of an epistemic *simplicitas*,[58] reveals that the constituent elements of the simple nature—namely, its simplicity and its nature—are mutually imbricated in the fabric of Descartes's *artis secretum*. That is, the simplicity of the simple nature enacts the schizocosmic bifurcation of order posited by the method and amounts to "a simplicity by simplification," since it "does not recognize, but produces the simple elements" constitutive of it. For such a "nature," "[*s*]*implex*, finally, takes on a radically new meaning: it is not the simplicity that the 'solitary nature' [of Aristotle] delimits . . . but the result of a process of simplification" and "reduction that only advances by simultaneously elaborating the terms of its [own] simplicity" (*OG*, 132).[59] Indeed, *Rule XII* construes *simplex* no longer as referring only to those natures "individuated as a τόδε τι" (*OG*, 133), but, more decisively, it simplifies the latter by reducing them methodologically to "the simplicity of those things which are to be known" (*OG*, 132), effecting thereby a "strict dissolution of the thing [that is] concretely given and in fact simple" in order to abstract "from it an object that is certain" and "distinct for the needs of intellection" (*OG*, 133).[60]

The ambiguous double reference of the simple nature enables Descartes to engage in the construction of the *ens inquantum objectum* without having to justify his refusal of the *ens inquantum ens* and its intrinsic validity: Cartesian schizocosmenia. For although within the province of the method, "[u]ndoubtedly it is still a matter of knowing things, and thus of organizing them insofar as they are knowable," nonetheless

> it is precisely the rupture [*la scission*] of an organizing knowledge with the κόσμος of beings which reveals that knowledge only becomes possible at the expense of such a schizocosmenia — hence a dual ontology where knowledge bifurcates the world so as to organize a docile image of it. (*OG*, 132)

When subjected to the epistemic constraints of the schizocosmic *artis secretum*, the *ens* is tacitly stripped of its rights[61] to be *inquantum ens*, only to be (re)constructed, domesticated, and made "docile" as *objectum*, with the result that the *ens* of Aristotle is acknowledged "only in the exact measure in which it is reduced to precisely what the elimination [of the *ens*, effected in the *Regulae*] aimed to extract — a pure, simple, empty, and uniform objectivity" (*DMP, 77/PMD*, 83). Clearly, the revolutionary doctrine of the simple nature owes its central importance in the *Regulae* to that which it makes possible: Cartesian schizocosmenia understood as the mind's active construction of a world of objects reduced to evidence for the intuitive gaze — that is, the construction of (mental) constructs that can be perfectly known, because perfectly (in both senses)[62] constructed.

The Conceptual Idolatry of Gray Ontology

The series of displacements produced by the *Regulae*'s methodological refusal to confront Aristotle directly — with first philosophy now a *mathesis universalis* prescinding from οὐσία; simple nature bereft of nature and of ontological simplicity; *ens* reduced to epistemic *objectum*; a gray ontology of *ordo vel mensura* whose distinguishing mark is its lack of ontology; a schizocosmic world whose bifurcation posits a methodic order that at once parallels and rivals the ontic order from which it is derived; an *idea* that informs thought itself rather than the hylomorphic thing (τόδε τι) of which it is the form (εἶδος); a deconstruction of *natura* that permits its (re)construction for the *intuitus mentis*—all of these displacements show clearly and unmistakably the astonishing degree to which Descartes is concerned to (mis)appropriate Aristotle without first having to refute him. What these displacements purport to accomplish, however, still remains unclear. What, precisely, does Descartes hope to gain by such a procedure? Or, to put the question in slightly different terms: What is the philosophic purpose undergirding the *Regulae*'s gray ontology?

At the beginning of this chapter, we noted the paradoxical character of the *Regulae*'s hermeneutical situation. There we observed embedded in the *Regulae* a critical encounter with Aristotle that is marked, notably, by its absence. Aristotle is at once present to the argument of the *Regulae* and absent from their text; it is as though Descartes wishes to found the Cartesian *ego*—or at least to prepare for its advent—by assimilating the residuum of its Aristotelian alter ego. Toward this end, Descartes develops an elaborate hermeneutics of displacement that confronts the reader with the following paradox: Aristotle is countered in the text of the *Regulae* only by not being encountered.

Yet insofar as they take up, by means of a gray ontology, the Aristotelian thematic of the Being of beings—with the latter now redefined as *ens inquantum repraesentatum, ut objectum*—the *Regulae* must equally be understood as a fundamental engagement with Aristotle, "thanks to the permanence of the Aristotelian site, as metaphysics."[63] For if Descartes's epistemological revolution marks a new beginning, a "novelty" in which the Being of beings is transformed by the universality of *mathesis universalis* into "an overdetermination of knowledge as ontology—to the second degree, and as though by proxy"—nonetheless "it is precisely insofar as being is known that, for the *Regulae*, being appears as such."[64] Cartesian displacement, then, is predicated upon the very metaphysics it rejects, in such a way that

> [i]t is the Aristotelian constitution of metaphysics that can and that must usher in the novelty according to which Descartes takes up the Aristotelian *topoi*, displaces them, and therefore (re)thinks them: against Aristotle, thereby encountering him [*à l'encontre d'Aristote, donc à sa rencontre*].[65]

In fact, it is exactly because "[t]he way of Being that leads beings back to their status as pure beings is put forth in what Descartes inaugurated—Being in the mode of *objectum*" (*DMP*, 91/*PMD*, 98–99), that Descartes's gray ontology of the object constitutes a simultaneous displacement, reduction, and "reconduction"⁶⁶ of Aristotle's doctrine on the Being of beings. For Marion, grasping the interrelation of these three features is crucial for understanding the overall aim of the Cartesian project:

> Here is the decisive point about which everything else revolves: the Cartesian reduction of the world to its reduced and conditional status as object does not totally abandon reconducting the world to the status of being; it repeats it, with a slight displacement. (*DMP*, 90/PMD, 98)

Contrary to appearances, then, and despite its thoroughly epistemological orientation—indeed, *because* of this very orientation—the thought of the *Regulae* remains inescapably metaphysical. While appearing to sidestep the question of the Being of beings through a re(-con)duction of being to its "conditional status as object," Descartes in fact takes up the question all the more resolutely.⁶⁷ Within the strictures of gray ontology, no longer does the world gain its intelligibility and its ontological foothold on the basis of οὐσία, because this latter has been displaced in favor of the self-produced intelligibility and being of the *mens humana* and its *universalis Sapientia* (Rule I, AT, X, 360.19–20) that willfully subjects the Aristotelian "subject" (*hypokeimenon*) to conditions of evidence set in advance and imposed by the Cartesian subject—the *mens humana* itself alone.

Willfully: a rigorously apt description, inasmuch as the philosophic significance of the *Regulae*'s gray ontology resides less in a theoretical insight than in an act of will, in a deliberate and sustained *decision* to disregard the inherent intelligibility of the world. To be sure, the *Regulae* do not deny the world or its intelligibility outright; rather, they merely bracket these—and this peremptorily—so that the method is free to assign its own intelligibility to a world of its own (wholly mind-immanent) construction. Next comes the moment of subjection: to erect this constructed world of intelligible objects presupposes that "the substrate of an irreducible (and perhaps irreducibly unknowable) thing" be rendered completely transparent to the gaze of the *mens humana*—and thus placed at its disposal; in the schizocosmic universe of the *Regulae*, "'subject,' originally from substrate, comes to designate a *subjection* of the substrate."⁶⁸ In a word, the requisite amount of intelligibility stipulated by the method demands the submission of the *ens* to the reduced status of "object" for the representative gaze of the human mind, as "subject." The human subject thus subjects the traditional subject (οὐσία) by subjugating, subduing, and transforming the being of this subject into that of an object—or rather, an idol—whose being is represented, produced, and exhausted by the gaze of the human subject. Conceptual idolatry, in which the Being of beings becomes colored by the grayness of the object, falls beneath, because it arises from, the gaze.

Regarding *Le Regard*: The Idolatrous Gaze of Gray Ontology

Being, conceived as an object produced by and for the gaze of the human mind that represents this object to itself: here we arrive at the heart of the matter in which Descartes is seen to have made "a mask, a representation, an idol" (*IAD*, 71/*ID*, 97) out of Being by subjecting it, "through the idolatrous filter of the concept or through the facelike conception of the idol" (*IAD*, 9/*ID*, 27), to the demands of *mathesis universalis*. In their original context, the citations of the preceding sentence refer to the idolatry of the Nietzschean Eternal Return in which the Christian "God of love" is judged and found wanting by the will to power that "delivers to each being that which for it is Being-value, reproducing thus the investigation and the difference of the ὄν ᾗ ὄν" (*IAD*, 73/*ID*, 99). Here I apply to Cartesian gray ontology Marion's analysis of the conceptual idol embraced by Nietzsche; the justification for doing so will become apparent shortly. As a preliminary remark, however, the reader should note from the foregoing citation the decisive role played by "the investigation and the difference of the ὄν ᾗ ὄν" in Marion's explication of conceptual idolatry—the very same investigation to which, by means of gray ontology, Descartes devotes himself in the *Regulae*.

Descartes's gray ontology of the object and its willful inversion of the center of gravity between knower and known bring us to the very threshold of Cartesian idolatry, since, as Marion notes elsewhere, "the idol places its center of gravity in a human gaze" (*GWB*, 24/*DSE*, 37).[69] Let us make no mistake: the "epistemology without being" of the *Regulae* is at once metaphysical and idolatrous, for

> when the world must run the gauntlet, or rather prostrate itself before the rostrum of the *objectum purae Matheseos*, which constitutes what is essential in the legacy passed on to the *Meditationes* from the *Regulae* (a point that cannot be emphasized too

much)—when this is so, the *ens in quantum ens* is, again and finally, at issue. (*DMP*, 90/*PMD*, 98)[70]

The *ens inquantum ens* is indeed again at issue in the *Regulae*, but in a profoundly different key, and one that strikes a consistently idolatrous note. For in contrast to Aristotle's ontology, in which the Being of beings is defined by οὐσία in such a way that the divine νοῦς remains its supreme instance, Descartes's gray ontology transfers the site of supreme intelligibility from the divine οὐσία to the (in the *Regulae*, as yet unacknowledged) οὐσία of the *mens humana*. This substitution of the human for the divine, while literally constituting an idolatry, nonetheless serves only to institute a more fundamental and far-reaching idolatrous intention: to master the world of οὐσίαι by representing its being as so many *objecta* to be brought under the human gaze, a gaze within which οὐσία "takes on the aspect of an object, *being entirely submitted* to the demands of human knowledge" (*OG*, 186; emphasis added). The Cartesian subject, it seems, does not want to *be* God so much as it wants to know what God knows. Yet it is just this desire that indicts Cartesian "subjectity"[71] of its most profound idolatry, since with it

> the very situation of the thinker becomes divine, since he gathers in himself the estimation of the world. It is not that he establishes himself as the supreme being. But the supreme sum of beings—where the world alone becomes the supreme being—is stated only in a *yes*, which the thinker alone can say. And which he must say divinely, like Dionysus. (*IAD*, 43–44/*ID*, 68; Marion's emphasis)

That this passage in its original context has directly in view the idolatry of the Nietzschean *Ja-Sagen*, which wills the Eternal Return of the same, and not the idolatry of Cartesian gray ontology, detracts not one iota from its pertinence. For, as we shall see, Marion considers both forms of idolatry to be rooted in the metaphysical function of the gaze (*le regard*) that furnishes their a priori condition of possibility. Thus, with respect to the former, Marion can say that

> [m]ore essential than all of its valuations, valuating accepts the condition that makes those valuations possible: to support with the gaze what the gaze has to put in perspective [*supporter du regard ce que le regard doit mettre en perspective*]. To support does not indicate only that one endures, but that one sustains and provides. (*IAD*, 42/*ID*, 67)

And with respect to the latter, Marion holds that

> Descartes, and through him modern thought, only approaches the thing by "regarding [in it] precisely the thing that is (an) object(ified) to him, *rem sibi objectam*" (*Rule XII*, *AT*, X, 423.2–3), the thing inasmuch as it is an object. The object is summed up in what the gaze of the mind admits within the field of its evidence. It thus recovers from the initial thing only that which the composite interplay of simple natures takes hold of and offers up to the gaze. (*OG*, 186)[72]

In Nietzsche's *Ja-Sagen*, as with Descartes's *mathesis universalis*, the metaphysical function of the gaze—and therefore its idolatry—lies in its pretended capacity to determine the Being of all beings; the human gaze plays the role of supreme arbiter in the dispute over the Being of beings precisely because it arbitrates a case whose verdict it has already decided, in advance, by a prejudicial hearing of only that evidence which alone will ensure the sole outcome admissible for the gaze of the *mens humana*:

> It falls to man to establish the value of every being without exception: this is no arbitrarily idealist subjectivism but the establishment of man as the place of the production of beings in their Being. In order to reach their Being, beings must pass through valuation itself, through man. (*IAD*, 41–42/*ID*, 66)

Lest this association of Cartesian gray ontology with Nietzschean will to power under the common cover of idolatry appear too hasty or overdrawn, it is important to see that for Marion, what unites them is "the domain of the gaze [*le domaine du regard*]" in which the idol "reigns undividedly" (*GWB*, 10/*DSE*, 18). And insofar as "[t]he idol presents itself to man's gaze in order that representation, and hence knowledge, can seize hold of it" (*GWB*, 9–10/*DSE*, 18), the representative gaze of the *intuitus mentis* is joined to the valuating gaze of the *Wille zur Macht* as two sides of the same idolatrous coin; for both, *ens* is represented—and representable—by "the gaze [which] alone characterizes the idol" (*GWB*, 10/*DSE*, 19) only so that it can be manipulated by the will of the one who gazes.

Thus when Descartes displays his contempt for the history of philosophy as just so many untrustworthy "stories" (*historias*; *Rule III*, *AT*, X, 367.23), his otherwise banal dismissal can be made intelligible as reflecting a certain idolatrous conception of truth that, when read in terms of the gaze with its desire to possess and to master, in fact anticipates Nietzsche. For Descartes, truth must be possessed in person, without an intermediary: all knowledge must be direct and immediate (*OG*, 44). According to the analysis presented here, this arbitrary (read: *arbitrium*) restriction of the domain of legitimate inquiry to that which is immediate and direct to *one's own* mind gives one reason to think of the later, and more obviously willful, form of idolatry that makes its appearance with Nietzsche:

> Not admitting any other forms of knowledge than that of possession, does the will to knowledge [in the *Regulae*] subject itself to the modest desire of investigating the real so much that it anticipates the will to truth—and perhaps, therefore, the will to power? (*OG*, 44)

If one is to view *le regard* as the source of Cartesian idolatry—as also with all forms of conceptual idolatry—then perhaps it is no coincidence that Descartes singles out *intuitus* (*le regard*)[73] as his term of choice to illustrate the principle informing his methodological "metaphorization" of Aristotle. For *intuitus* in Descartes's usage signals "the gaze [*le regard*] that keeps its object in view" and that "keeps within its sight the thing it places in evidence" for itself (*RUC*, "Annexe I," 302).[74] As such, it is perhaps not too much to say that the philosophic function of *intuitus* in the *Regulae* cannot be fully appreciated if one does not grasp the idolatry it announces; Descartes, it may be said, constructs an idol out of Being by effecting the "de-realization of the thing into an object"[75] only because he first decides to restrict Being to the "gazeable" (*le regardable*), to that which is capable of filling the mind's gaze. Due to this restriction, Cartesian *intuitus* can be understood as fulfilling the essential condition of idolatry since it defines itself in terms of "that which will fill [its] gaze":

> The *decisive* moment in the erection of an idol stems not from its fabrication, but from its investment as gazeable [*le regardable*], as that which will fill a gaze [*un regard*]. That which characterizes the idol stems from the gaze. It dazzles with visibility only inasmuch as the gaze looks on it with consideration. It draws the gaze only inasmuch as the gaze has drawn it whole into the gazeable and there exposes and exhausts it. The gaze alone makes the idol, as the ultimate function of the gazeable. (*GWB*, 10/*DSE*, 19; emphasis added)

To this precise extent, then, one can apply to Descartes what Marion says of the philosophers generally in his exegesis of St. Paul's discourse to the Athenians: "Everything happens as if the philosophers also came under the jurisdiction of idolatry—only having purified it, that is, having conceptualized it" (*IAD*, 24/*ID*, 43).

Yet to say that Descartes commits conceptual idolatry is not, as might be suspected, to conflate the domains of philosophy and theology—domains that Descartes takes great pains to keep sharply distinct, a fact that Marion does not fail to notice.[76] Rather, it is to point out that, for Marion at least, what is philosophically significant in Descartes's gray ontology is precisely the affinities it bears to the theological, but only insofar as the latter "permits one to disclose a phenomenological conflict—a conflict between two phenomenologies" (*GWB*, 7/*DSE*, 15). Indeed, the celebrated analysis of the idol and the icon in *God Without Being* makes clear that "[t]he critical portion of this essay was accomplished within the field of philosophy"[77] and not theology, even if we admit with Marion that this was done "not without a certain violence."[78] Thus, insofar as "[t]he icon and the idol determine two manners of being for beings, not two classes of beings" (*GWB*, 8/*DSE*, 16),[79] Descartes's gray ontology can be classified phenomenologically—that is, as "indicat[ing] a manner of being for beings" (*GWB*, 7/*DSE*, 15)—under the theological rubric of the idol, even though it does not have God or the divine directly in view. Accordingly, the idolatry of the *Regulae* may be said to be the*io*-logic, rather than theological in the strict or narrow sense.[80]

From these considerations, it would seem to follow that if one interprets the *Regulae*'s gray ontology in a phenomenological manner, Marion's various descriptions of the idolatry that is properly *theo*logical—in its conceptual guise at least—can be rightly applied to its Cartesian, the*io*-logic variant. For example, when *God Without Being* asserts that "[t]he idol offers to, or rather imposes on, the gaze, its first visible—whatever it may be, thing, man, woman, *idea*, or god,"[81] one could infer that the idolatrous "first visible" in Cartesian gray ontology is the *objectum* that is constituted as such by the gaze of the *intuitus mentis* that erects the idol of the *natura simplex* on the ruins of the Aristotelian *idea*. Similarly, when Marion states that "[t]he idolatry of the concept is equivalent to that of sight: imagining oneself to have attained God and to be capable of maintaining him under our gaze, like a thing of the world,"[82] one could understand such conceptual idolatry to include not only those concepts that seek to capture the essence of God in order to maintain Him "under our gaze, like a thing of the world," but also those concepts (*objectum, natura simplex*) that seek to capture the very things of the world themselves (*entia*), once these have been reduced by the abstractive method of *mathesis universalis*, making it possible for them to be held as much "under our gaze" and at our disposal as the crudest of idols, whether of wood or stone.

To so bring the world "under our gaze" as to place its being at our disposal requires that the things of the world be stripped of their own being by the idolatrous gaze itself. Under the gaze, every *ens* "is degraded into an object" of the human mind and becomes a "thing that is taken outside of" and "alienated from its οὐσία" by a "gray ontology in which the *ego* possesses the Being of objects that are the gray shadows of things, because it has confiscated from these things— [now] devalued into objects—their οὐσία" (*OG*, 189–90). Just as a man who no longer retains the vitality of his youth is regarded as a "shadow" of his former self, so are these objects regarded—by *le regard*—as the "gray shadows of things" (*OG*, 190), things that have been emptied of the vitality of their being by the idolatrous gaze that has (re)constructed them as so many conceptual idols.

From *ens* to idol/object: the construction of (mental) constructs that are perfectly known, because perfectly transparent to the gaze of the *intuitus mentis*, reveals that the *Regulae*'s "schizocosmenia" conceives knowledge fundamentally in terms of production. That is, the "object" of the mind is in the decisive respect a *product* of the mind's own making. Within the schizocosmic method of the *Regulae*, the mind that gazes (*regarder*) soon gives rise to the will that constructs (*fabriquer*) the idols that will satisfy this gaze, since in the construction of these idols, one finds

> the pure intersection of epistemological parameters that are perfectly intelligible, because totally abstracted from all that does not satisfy, precisely, the conditions of intelligibility itself. The object is not merely defined by relation to the *mens* (*res sibi objecta*, Descartes says);[83] it reflects the *mens* and essentially prolongs it, as its first product. It is because it reproduces the *mens* that the object is its product. (*PC*, 36/*PAC*, 49–50)

Like the ideology[84] and technology[85] for which it is the metaphysical source, Cartesian schizocosmenia posits a "production [that] in effect supposes the substitution of one universe (planned, calculated, and in principle radically intelligible) for another—the world, precisely" (*PC*, 37/*PAC*, 51). By reducing Aristotle's εἶδος to an idolatrous *objectum*, such world production and substitution equally reduce—purely for the sake of Cartesian *utilitas*—Aristotelian ὕλη to "the homogeneous malleability of a material that is equally suitable for a thousand and one goals" (*OG*, 189). Under the idolatrous transformation (read: a-formation)[86] of the gaze, form becomes object, and matter becomes (raw) material for producing the being of the world. Yet insofar as the gaze is an idolatrous one, the production of the schizocosmic universe made possible by this gaze is nothing other than the gaze itself: production as self-production, since, according to a phenomenological analysis of idolatry,

> the idol returns the gaze to itself, indicating to it how many beings, before the idol, it has transpierced, thus also at what level is situated that which for its aim stands as first visible above all. The idol thus acts as a mirror, not as a portrait: a mirror that reflects the gaze's image, or more exactly, the image of its aim and of the scope of that aim. The idol, as a function of the gaze, reflects the gaze's scope. ... The idol, as invisible mirror, gives the gaze its stopping point and measures out its scope [*sa portée*]. (*GWB*, 12/*DSE*, 21)

The schizocosmic scope of the *Regulae* permits Descartes to reduce Aristotle's *ens* to the status of *objectum*, but this reduction itself is idolatrous because its highly restricted "scope" (*sa portée*) does not take into view the alterity of the things thus seen.[87] When the *intuitus mentis* gazes upon its world, it sees only itself and its "defined representations: idols, then" (*IAD*, 67/*ID*, 92). The final displacement of gray ontology, it seems, concerns neither Aristotle's terminology nor his doctrine, but that to which these are oriented: the thing itself, displaced and finally supplanted, by the Cartesian idol (*OG*, 187). The *Regulae*'s "gray ontology, because it maintains the thing in the grayness of the object, bears witness therefore to the intoxication (to the *hybris*?) of the *ego* as 'the master and possessor' of the world reduced to evidence" (*OG*, 187). And yet, one may ask with Marion, "What must one become in order to state that our perspective orders, lays out, appraises, constructs, organizes a world—in short, sees it by bringing it under its gaze." (*IAD*, 39–40/*ID*, 64)[88] Or again: "What must the human mind become in order to *be* under the figure of the *ego*?" (*OG*, 187; Marion's emphasis). Answer: To thus *be*, the human mind—or at least the Cartesian *ego*—must become an idolater, if not a god.

I Am, I Exist

Lilian Alweiss

The aim to lay knowledge on a foundation that is free of doubt is historically associated with the philosophy of Descartes. Moreover, with his observation that only one proposition escapes doubt—namely, the famous *cogito, ergo sum:* "I am thinking, therefore I exist"—it is claimed that Descartes inaugurated a philosophy of consciousness (*Bewußtseinsphilosophie*). It is important to note that Descartes's original contribution to philosophy does not so much consist in advancing the proposition itself (it can already be found in the writings of Augustine), but in making the *metaphysical* claim that the ego holds rank of a *first principle* or *substance*. "I use the argument," writes Descartes, "to show that this I, that is thinking, is an *immaterial substance* with no bodily elements."[1] The claim that "I am thinking and therefore exist," and the metaphysical interpretation of this discovery as a first principle, are "two very different things."[2]

Although this metaphysical proposition has turned Descartes into the founding father of modern philosophy, it is curious to note that from the time of its inception the validity of this proposition has been questioned by his contemporaries and by Kant and post-Kantian philosophers. They all claim in one way or another that Descartes's inference was either false or nonexistent. Against this objection, Jaakko Hintikka and Jean-Luc Marion have tried to show that Descartes's proposition can be saved if it is understood as a performance and not an inference.[3] The aim of this chapter is to look at Hintikka's and Marion's defense of Descartes's proposition and to ask whether, in the light of this downgrading from inference to performance, Descartes's metaphysical claim that the *ego cogito* ranks as a first principle can be upheld.

It seems to me that we can isolate four fundamental objections to Descartes's first principle: (1) Gassendi and Hobbes believed that Descartes's metaphysical thesis, that the *ego cogito* ranks as a first principle or substance, remains unfounded because the proposition *ambulo, ergo sum* (I walk, therefore I am) is just as good an inference as *cogito, ergo sum*:[4] "You could have made the same inference from any one of your other actions, since it is known by the natural light that whatever acts, exists."[5] (2) Further, it has been argued that the proposition "I am thinking, therefore I exist" provides us with a false syllogism based on the enthymeme that "everything that thinks is, or exists" (*AT*, VII, 140). In view of this, Leibniz argues that "to say, *I think, therefore I am*, is not properly to prove existence by thought, since to think and to be thinking is the same thing; and to say, I am thinking, is already to say, I *am*."[6] The problem seems to be that Descartes does not logically (syllogistically) deduce *sum* from the *cogito*; the equation between thinking and existence is merely assumed. The participle *ergo* is misplaced since no inference is taking place.[7] (3) Kant goes even further by pointing out that Descartes's inference is simply *false*: the equation between thinking and existence (*sum*) cannot be substantiated since thought is essentially reflexive. Only the empirical ego exists to the extent that it can be turned into an object of reflection; however, the ego that is aware of the fact that it is thinking does not exist, since it can never be represented. Descartes, so Kant claims, fails to see that "it must be possible for the 'I think' to accompany all my representations; for otherwise something would be represented in me that could not be thought at all, and that is equivalent to saying that the representation would be impossible, or at least would be nothing to me" (*CPR*, B131–32). We need to split the ego and differentiate between the "transcendental self" that accompanies all my representations, even the representation of myself, and the "empirical self" that appears or can be represented in time and space. The *ego cogito* as a first principle, however, can never be represented or known. (4) Finally, Heidegger claims that Descartes presupposes an understanding of existence that he leaves unexplored:

> *Descartes* . . . is credited with providing the point of departure for modern philosophical inquiry by his discovery of the "*cogito*

sum." He investigates the *"cogitare"* of the *"ego,"* at least within certain limits. [Yet . . .] he leaves the *"sum"* completely undiscussed, even though it is regarded as no less primordial than the *cogito*.[8]

Against these objections Hintikka and Marion argue that the inference "I am thinking, therefore I exist" appears inconsistent only if we understand it logically (Hintikka) or theoretically (Marion), and not existentially (Hintikka) or ontologically (Marion). "The famous debate that surrounded the formulation 'in order to think, one has to exist,'" says Marion, "almost entirely privileged theoretical considerations about knowledge and neglected the formulation's ontological realm and metaphysical status" (*CQ*, 170, n. 25). Similarly, Hintikka maintains that we can uphold the *cogito* as a first principle once we realize that we should not understand the statement "cogito, ergo sum" as an inference (theoretically) but as a performance. "Hence, the indubitability of this sentence," says Hintikka, "is not strictly speaking perceived by *means* of thinking (in the way the indubitability of a demonstrable truth may be said to be); rather, it is indubitable *because* and *in so far as* it is actively thought of. . . . The indubitability of my own existence results from my thinking of it almost as the sound of music results from playing it or . . . light in the sense of illumination (*lux*) results from the presence of a source of light (*lumen*)."[9]

Marion and Hintikka thereby point to something important. If we understand the statement as a performance, then objections (1) and (2) no longer carry weight. Existentially, the status of "I am thinking, therefore I am" is different from the statement "I am moving, therefore I am," for I can *be* without moving but I cannot assert my existence without thinking it. To be sure, if I am walking, I am, but only as long as

> awareness of walking is a thought. The inference is certain only if applied to this awareness, and not to the movement of the body which sometimes—in the case of dreams—is not occurring at all, despite the fact that I seem to myself to be walking. Hence from the fact that I think I am walking I can very well infer the existence of a mind which has this thought, but not the existence of a body that walks. (Descartes, *AT*, VII, 352; also cited in *DMP*, 97)

What I *think* I am aware of may be refuted; it may well be that I think I am walking even though I am actually asleep. However, what cannot be refuted is that I am aware of something—that my "awareness of walking is a thought."

Descartes does not simply assume that in thinking he manifests his existence (2); rather, Hintikka believes that he dimly realizes the "performative contradiction" or "the *existential* inconsistency[10] of the sentence 'I don't exist.'"[11] "*I am, I exist* is necessarily true whenever it is put forward by me or conceived in my mind" (*AT,* VII, 25). It must be true whenever I utter it. My awareness is beyond doubt, even if the content of my awareness is not. It is impossible for me to deny the proposition "I am thinking, therefore I exist" without contradicting myself. This is existentially or "performatively" true. So long as we understand the proposition as a performance, Descartes is justified in claiming: "if I had merely ceased thinking, even if everything else I had ever imagined had been true, I should have had no reason to believe that I existed" (*AT,* VI, 32–33). As long as I am thinking, I am aware of existing; when I stop thinking, I stop existing, in the same vein as the music stops when the orchestra ceases playing.[12] Hintikka thus concludes that "Descartes could replace the word *cogito* by other words in the *cogito, ergo sum* [e.g., *velle* or *videre*], but he could not replace *performance,* which for him revealed the indubitability of any such sentence."[13] He was justified in claiming that the *ego cogito* holds the rank of a first principle.

Hintikka and Marion have thereby provided an answer to objections (1) and (2): I cannot think without being instantaneously aware that I am existing. Yet what about Kant's objection, (3)? While Kant might accept Hintikka and Marion's defense of Descartes's first principle, he would argue that Descartes's inference is nonetheless false, since Kant believes that Descartes fails to see that the equation between thinking and existence (*sum*) cannot be substantiated because thought is essentially reflexive. As soon as I am conscious of an object, including being conscious of myself, there must be a self that implicitly—as Kant puts it (using Leibnizian terminology)—"apperceives" my being thus conscious. In other words, there must be a self that is conscious of thus being conscious. Ludwig Wittgenstein illustrates this problem well. When I look into the mirror, I can see myself (as an object of reflection); however, I cannot see myself looking: "But really you do *not* see the eye,"[14] says Wittgenstein.

> Thus there really is a sense in which philosophy can talk about the self in a non-psychological way. What brings the self into philosophy is the fact that "the world is my world." The philo-

sophical self is not the human being, not the human body, or the human soul, which is the subject of psychology, but rather the metaphysical subject, the limit of the world—not a part of it.[15]

This metaphysical subject Kant calls the "transcendental unity of apperception" or "transcendental subject." It is distinct from the empirical psychological subject to the extent that it is nonphenomenal and can never become an *object* of reflection. It does not exist in this world. It is not part of it, but merely accompanies all my representations. In Kant's lights, once we realize that thought is essentially reflexive, Descartes's transition from the *cogito* to an actual *sum* can no longer be legitimate. Descartes, so Kant argues, fails to realize that we can never infer from the *formal* conditions of thought (which Kant regards as transcendental) to a *substance* of thought (empirical) (cf. *CPR*, A41, B399ff.). What can be known is only the self as a representation but not the pure spontaneity of the representing self.

Marion is keen to show that even this critique is not valid. When Kant says "it must be possible for the I think to accompany all my representations" (*CPR*, B131–32) (or later, when Husserl observes that "consciousness is essentially intentional"), he fails to realize that reflection is possible only on the basis of a prereflective consciousness. Philosophers from Kant to Heidegger, Marion claims,

> prove only the fundamental impotence of the common (representative or intentional) interpretation when it comes to thinking and repeating the Cartesian foundation of the first principle. They are beyond all doubt far from invalidating it. (*CQ*, 103)[16]

Their critique is valid only if we accept that thinking is essentially reflexive, yet Marion believes that Descartes clearly tells us that this is not so:

> My critic says that to enable a substance to be superior to matter and wholly spiritual (and he insists on using the term "mind" only in this restricted sense), it is not sufficient for it to think: it is further required that it should think that it is thinking, by means of a reflexive act, or that it should have awareness of its own thought. This is as deluded as our bricklayer's saying that a person who is skilled in architecture must employ a reflexive act to ponder on the fact that he has this skill before he can be an architect. (Descartes, *AT*, VII, 559; also cited in *CQ*, 104)

By *cogito* Descartes does not mean *cogito me cogitare*; rather, he refers to a thinking prior to reflection. There is an "internal awareness that always precedes reflective knowledge" (*AT*, VII, 422; also cited in *CQ*, 104). Kant's criticism is simply mistaken: not all my thinking is accompanied by my awareness that I am thinking.

For both Hintikka and Marion, it is important to note that Descartes argues not only that the *cogitare* is anterior to any reflection but, moreover, that we should not understand thinking in a limited way. It does not refer only to reason but can also be understood as a form of *sensing*:

> The fact that it is I who am doubting and understanding and willing is so evident that I see no way of making it any clearer. But it is also the case that the "I" who imagines is the same "I." For even if, as I have supposed, none of the objects of imagination are real, the power of imagination is something which really exists and is part of my thinking. Lastly, it is also the same "I" who has sensory perceptions, or is aware of bodily things as it were through the senses. For example, I am now seeing light, hearing a noise, feeling heat. But I am asleep, so all this is false. Yet I certainly *seem* to see, to hear, and to be warmed. This cannot be false; what is called "having a sensory perception" is strictly just this, and in this restricted sense of the term it is simply thinking. (Descartes, *AT*, VII, 29; also cited by Hintikka, "*Cogito, Ergo Sum,*" p. 138)

Or:

> By the term "thought" I understand everything which we are aware of as happening within us, insofar as we have awareness of it. Hence, *thinking* is to be identified here not merely with understanding, willing and imagining, but also with sensory awareness. (Descartes, *AT*, VIIIA, 8)

Thinking, for Descartes, is not only nonreflexive but also receptive. As Marion notes:

> consciousness does not at first think of itself by representation, because in general it does not think by representation, intentionality, or ecstasy, but by receptivity, in absolute immanence; therefore, it thinks at first in immanence to itself.... Before any other operation consciousness experiences itself, with an absolute immediacy, without which it could never experience anything else. (*CQ*, 105)[17]

There is an awareness or sensing that precedes self-consciousness. As we have shown above when Descartes says "I seem to myself" to be walking, to be dreaming, or to be warmed, he is claiming that even if all the appearances (walking, dreaming, the sensation of heat) may be false, what cannot be questioned is "the immediacy of *videor*, 'it seems to me'" (*CQ*, 106). I cannot doubt my awareness, though I can doubt that the content of my awareness is real (ontologically "in the world"). This awareness or sensing of having a thought is prior to reflection. With respect to (4), Heidegger's objection, we can thus argue that it is not that the *sum* precedes thinking but that there is thinking before there is reflective thought. Consciousness experiences itself in absolute immediacy. It *is* before any reflection enables us to conceptualize this. Descartes's first principle refers to a *capacity* of knowing, a sensing and doing that is distinct from reflexive consciousness. This sensing is always latent. It can never be turned into an object of reflection but accompanies all my representations. The certainty of my existence is not the outcome of some reflection or logical deduction; it is not something that we can only posit and never know, as Kant believes, but it has an existential basis: it refers to an awareness or sensing that cannot be questioned and that makes reflective consciousness possible in the first place. There is an awareness that precedes self-awareness. With the help of Marion and Hintikka, thus seems that we have invalidated the four objections raised above.

Existentially it is indubitable: to think is to exist. For Marion this proves the "protology of the ego" (*CQ*, 36), in which the "I" plays the role of a supreme being, since the awareness of "existence, like thinking, emerges only through the intermediary of an I" (*DMP*, 36). However, it seems that while we have said much about the status of thinking by defining it as a lived, felt, or sensed awareness, little has been said about the status of the *ego*. Indeed, contrary to Marion's observation, it appears to me that the analysis does not necessarily point to an "I" or a "protology of the Ego" but, to the contrary, to an egoless consciousness. What exists is the act or performance but not the "I."

This becomes apparent if we look at Sartre's depiction of prereflective consciousness, which we now realize in many ways resembles that of Descartes (though it was intended to provide a critique of Descartes's first principle):

> If I count the cigarettes which are in that case, I have the impression of disclosing an objective property of this collection of cigarettes: they are a dozen. This property appears to my con-

sciousness as a property existing in the world. It is very possible that I have no positional consciousness of counting them. Then I do not know myself as counting.... If anyone questioned me, indeed, if anyone should ask, "What are you doing?" there I should reply at once, "I am counting." This reply aims not only at the instantaneous consciousness which I can achieve by reflection... it is the non-reflective consciousness which renders the reflection possible; *there is a pre-reflective cogito which is the condition of the Cartesian cogito.*[18]

Unwittingly, Sartre is here saying something very similar to Descartes. We can do things without thinking about the fact that we are doing them—in the same way as we can be skilled in architecture without needing "to ponder first on the fact that we have this skill." Descartes would thus not necessarily object to Sartre's observation that the prereflective *cogito* is the condition of the *Cartesian cogito*, since we have seen that, as it may be argued, for Descartes, equally, the performative *cogitans* precedes the *cogito*.

However, what is important to me is that Sartre actually says more than this, since he believes that this prereflective consciousness no longer points to an intermediary or substantive "I," but to its loss. Let us take the following passage as an example:

When I run after a streetcar, when I look at the time, when I am absorbed in contemplating a portrait, there is no *I*. There is consciousness of *the street-car-having-to-be-overtaken*, etc., and non-positional consciousness of consciousness. In fact, I am then plunged into the world of objects; it is they which constitute the unity of consciousness; it is they which present themselves with values, with attractive and repellent qualities—but *me*, I have disappeared; I have annihilated myself. There is no place for me on this level. And this is not a matter of chance, due to a momentary lapse of attention, but happens because of the very structure of consciousness.[19]

The prereflective or nonpositional consciousness precedes (self-) awareness. As Sartre observes, one cannot even refer to a "non-positional consciousness of self," since the "'of self' still evokes the idea of knowledge.... This self-consciousness we ought to consider not as a new consciousness, but as *the only mode of existence which is possible for a consciousness of something.*"[20] It thus seems that Descartes's first principle actually points to a thinking in the wider sense of this term—indeed, an existing process of thinking—without the substantiality of a self.

The problem, however, is that such a reading is contrary to what Nietzsche calls our grammatical convention. The words "I" and "my" are mere adornments of speech. It is purely the "necessity of syntax"[21] that has compelled us to speak of a positional self. As Nietzsche argues:

> "There is thinking; therefore there is something that thinks (*ein Denkendes*)": this is the upshot of all Descartes' argumentation. But that means positing as "true *a priori*" our belief in the concept of substance—that when there is thought there has to be something "that thinks" is simply a formulation of our grammatical custom that adds a doer to every deed. In short, this is not merely the substantiation of a fact but a logical-metaphysical postulate. (Nietzsche, *Will to Power*, 268; cited by Marion, *DMP*, 145)

Not only does Sartre's observation contradict our grammatical convention but, moreover, it is without doubt that Descartes did not wish to envisage an egoless first principle. In fact, if we look at his seminal work *Meditations on First Philosophy*, it is curious to see that Descartes actually does not use the adage "I am thinking, therefore I exist," as he did in the *Discourse on Method*[22] four years earlier, but merely states *ego sum, ego existo*: "I am, I exist" (*AT*, VII, 25). What is at issue for him is precisely the substantiality of the "I" that Nietzsche questions in the quotation above. Not only is there no inference but, moreover, it seems that thought itself is excluded. Could that suggest that the *cogito* does not hold the rank of a first principle? Hintikka and Marion believe that no shift in thinking has taken place; rather, the statement merely takes for granted the proposition that as long as I am thinking, I exist. "'I am' ('I exist') is not by itself logically true," says Hintikka; rather, "Descartes realizes that its indubitability results from an act of thinking."[23] In the same vein Marion says that the exclusion of thought is valid only "if, and as long as a thinking thought thinks the formulation of existence" (*CQ*, 35). The *Second Meditation* thus in no way questions, but merely presupposes, the existential proposition "I am thinking, therefore I exist."

Yet our analysis suggests something more fundamental: If the observation "I am, I exist" presupposes a *cogitare* that exists prior to the constitution of an "I" as an object of theoretical reflection, then it is no longer evident why we should regard the ego as a first principle.

The novelty of Descartes's principle thus does not lie in the return to the substantiality of an "I" or "Ego," but in the return to a *felt* consciousness or awareness where the "I" has not yet made its appearance. As Sartre has shown us so clearly, on the prereflective level there is no place for an "I am, I exist." If this is the case, we cannot infer from the fact that "there is thinking" to the fact that "there is something that thinks (*ein Denkendes*)." Maybe it is to prevent such a move to an egoless consciousness—"where I have annihilated myself"—that Descartes replaced the "I am thinking, therefore I am" with the simple observation "'I am, I exist.'" The physicist and aphorist Georg Lichtenberg may not have been mistaken when he observed that the most Descartes could claim was "there is some thinking going on" (*es denkt*).[24]

3

Hubris and Humility
Husserl's Reduction and Givenness

Timothy Mooney

For more than a decade, Jean-Luc Marion has led us back to Husserl's writings. The shadow cast by his interpretation serves as a shade that delivers us from an earlier blindness, letting us discriminate much that lay in obscurity. He has helped us to understand Husserlian phenomenology anew, foregrounding as he does the breakthrough to givenness (*donation*). It may be possible, nonetheless, to show that his rendering is too severe in this or that instance, the very strength of its revelation having facilitated a certain occultation. Working in the other shadows of Merleau-Ponty and the early Derrida, we can look for still further thoughts of Husserl, fading in the margins and the main text of some old pages.[1]

I want to suggest that Husserl's investigations of reduction and givenness involve a hubris and a humility that are not precisely where Marion might look for them, were he to start with terms that bring the danger of ad hominem critique. In the first section of this chapter I set out the main points in Marion's reading of Husserl. I begin by outlining the broadening and breakthrough achieved in the early work, and then consider the shift that Marion sees presaged in the principle of all principles and announced in the reduction. On the latter's interpretation, appearing things are reduced to objects within the intentional immanence of consciousness. This process culminates in poor and flat phenomena that are modeled on the mathematizing horizons of the subject. I go on to give a short outline of Marion's alternative notions of the *interloqué* and the saturated phenomenon.

I commence the second section by looking briefly at what I call Husserl's philosophical hubris, brought out in some of his remarks concerning the subjective a priori. The hubris lies in the understanding of everything as a meaning for me, from God through to the world. It does not lie in the taking of beings as objects within horizons, for Husserl shows a notable humility toward the things themselves in their respective appearances. Such humility is not a rarity, but is threaded through the explications that follow on the procedures of *epochē* and reduction. In the rest of this section, my concern is to show that as Husserl's thought develops, he pays ever more attention to the original modes of givenness of transcendent things. In the third and final section, I suggest that Husserl also does justice to the character of the world as nonobjective ground and horizon. Philosophical hubris will in no way preclude empirical humility.

The Breakthrough and Givenness Lost

At the outset of *Reduction and Givenness*, Marion adverts to a broadening and a breakthrough in Husserl's early work. The last comprises the greatest achievement of Husserl's phenomenology.[2] It is often mentioned that Husserl seeks to go back to the things themselves. The referents of our word meanings must be rendered self-evident in full-fledged intuitions. Only by tracing knowledge back to adequate fulfillment in intuition can we uncover its pure forms and laws.[3] In the explication of intuition we encounter the first of three moves. There is the logically founding level of sensuous intuition, of thing-recognition. But intuition is broadened into a founded categorical level. Prior to ideational abstraction, there is the recognition of states of affairs in their instantiated being and Being instantiated. I apprehend, for example, that gold is yellow as whole to part, and along with this that the yellow gold *is*.[4]

Marion states that the second of the three moves pertains to meaning or signification. For Husserl, this realm involves a "surplus of meaning," for it shows itself to be wider still than the broadened realm of intuition.[5] An act of signification can be constituted without the need of a fulfilling or illustrative intuition. Signification therefore displays an autonomy to which intuition offers only an eventual complement.[6] The former can keep itself in presence without intuition, so that here, at least, Marion's Husserl does not succumb to the later

Derridean critique. An empty signification is not refused its truth, so presence triumphs as much in it as in intuition.[7] Yet intuition does not tolerate a remainder, for its respective modes seek to track down what is indicated or signified. It competes with signification for primacy.[8]

In the third move the breakthrough occurs. Marion already discerns it in the duality Husserl finds in the term "phenomenon." The word denotes the lived experience of appearing and its correlate, the thing that appears.[9] There is an experience—and indeed any experience—only if something is given. Givenness is not the given *of* consciousness, but givenness *to* consciousness. By virtue of givenness in general, the broadening of intuition implies the autonomy of signification instead of contradicting it. To broaden intuition is to broaden its fulfillment, which in turn depends on the givenness of meanings to be fulfilled.[10] Dynamic fulfillment (as opposed to coincident or static fulfillment, where an object suddenly "breaks in" to perceptual awareness without being expected) illustrates this perfectly: first there is given the meaning intention, and only afterward the corresponding intuition.[11]

Marion stresses that the phenomenological breakthrough does not consist in the broadening of intuition or in the autonomy of signification, "but solely in the unconditioned primacy of the givenness of the phenomenon."[12] Intuition and intention have sense only through the appearance of something that appears. The maintenance of the duality between appearing and what appears is Husserl's fundamental achievement. Givenness alone, as it functions in the correlation of appearance and appearing thing, gives semblance its seriousness, since "there is never an appearance without something that appears."[13] The same view is found in *Being Given*. Husserl's great discovery is that the evidence sees nothing unless it receives what does not belong to it. The origin of givenness remains the "self" of the phenomenon.[14] In Husserl's own formulation, "[a]bsolute givenness remains the last term."[15]

The inventory of givenness covers everything: the varieties of experience, the unity in flux, the thing exterior to it, the logical entity, and even absurdity and nonsense. Hence the conclusion that "givenness is everywhere."[16] In Husserl's words once more, "self-evidence (that petrified logical idol) is . . . freed from the privilege given to scientific evidence and broadened to mean original self-giving in general."[17] Having arrived at the generality of givenness, however, he grinds to a halt. Marion's explanation is as follows:

> Husserl, completely dazzled by unlimited givenness, seems not to realise the strangeness of such excessiveness, and simply manages its excess without questioning it. That is, unless bedazzlement doesn't betray—by covering over—a fear before the broadening of presence by givenness. It is here no doubt that there arises the question that Husserl could not answer, because he perhaps never heard it as an authentic question: What gives? Not only: What is that which gives itself, but more essentially: "What does giving mean, what is at play in the fact that all is given, how are we to think that all that is only is inasmuch as it is given?" It seems permissible to suppose that Husserl, submerged by the simultaneously threatening and jubilatory imperative to manage the superabundance of data in presence, does not at any moment (at least in the *Logical Investigations*) ask himself about the status, the scope, or even the identity of that givenness. This silence amounts to an admission (following Jacques Derrida's thesis) that Husserl, leaving unquestioned the givenness whose broadening he nonetheless accomplished, does not free it from the prison of presence, and thus keeps it in metaphysical detention. (*RG*, 38–39[18]/*RD*, 62)

As the story unfolds, detention turns into suppression. Marion's reading begins explicitly with Derrida's forefather Heidegger. The Heideggerian viewpoint lets him mark a scission between the return to the things themselves and Husserl's "principle of all principles."[19] On the principle, every originally given intuition is a legitimizing source of cognition. What is given in the flesh should be accepted simply as what it presents itself to be, and only within the limits in which it is there presented.[20] At first glance, this seems to reinforce the breakthrough of the *Logical Investigations*, in which "the only and uniquely determining thing here is the descriptive character of the phenomena, such as we experience them."[21]

It assuredly reinforces the breakthrough in that no right beyond intuition is required; the right to appear does not depend on a sufficient reason that makes selected phenomena well-founded. The price, however, is that intuition becomes an a priori.[22] There is a subtle shift from the receiving of the appearing thing to the self-standing immanence of the *Erlebnis*. But what is it that turns detention to suppression? It is the articulation of the "principle of all principles" by way of the reduction. This occurs in advance, and prevents the principle from being determinative for phenomenology. Intuition finally contradicts phenomenality, since in reduced immanence the latter is submitted to objectifying representation.[23] Marion traces the path toward this outcome in a reading that shows no little regret.

It is noted that the suppression is not simple or outright. Within the reduction, Husserl maintains the duality of phenomena. Immanence as reduced givenness in general is contrasted with the genuine immanence of lived experiences.[24] Transcendence is kept as a sense, so that the two sides of each phenomenon—the appearing and that which appears—can still arise in one and the same seeing.[25] In the reduction, nonetheless, genuine immanence is privileged. Only consciousness is given originally and absolutely, according to both its essence and existence. Such existence, moreover, is apodictic and necessary.[26] Phenomenality in the highest sense is interpreted as the certainty of self-presence. Everything else is characterized negatively in that it is consigned to being relative, contingent, and dubitable.

We need not conclude that transcendent things have only a negative characterization. In *Being Given*, Marion contends that Husserl assigns priority to logical and mathematical phenomena. They are models for other phenomena—including self-consciousness—by virtue of their certainty. They are distinguished from the others by the poverty of their intuition, by the sheer shortage of their givenness. A geometrical ideality, for instance, cannot find adequate fulfillment in actually experienced space.[27] Yet their very exemplarity is to a negative end. Husserl organizes empirical phenomena around these marginal cases. In so doing, he blocks access to extreme cases of givenness, and also to common-law phenomena such as the beings of nature and the living in general, and the face of the Other in particular. Such phenomena are characterized by the richness of their intuition, but Husserl neglects them.[28]

Nor, it seems, should givenness per se be characterized negatively by the certainty of reduced self-presence. One might contest Marion's claim that Husserl fails to examine the status, scope, and identity of givenness. Does he not write of its nearness and remoteness, its clarity and vagueness, its emptiness and fullness? It assuredly admits of degrees, for individuals as well as essences.[29] But Marion has a reply in waiting. If there are degrees of clarity (and there are), Husserl does not regard them as issuing from givenness. In the course of the reduction, things are presented as beings and, most crucially, as objects. To "[s]et forth the different modes of givenness in their essential sense," according to Husserl, is to equate them with "the constitution of the different modes of objectivity."[30]

Objectivity offers one mode of givenness, argues Marion, and does not entail that other modes be assimilated to it. But this is just what Husserl does. He submits givenness to the unquestioned paradigm of the object.[31] In his account also, the perception of a thing does not represent something nonpresent, but seizes upon a genuine presence in the flesh. What is not reducible to presence is excluded, that is to say, abandoned to imagination and memory.[32] As a consequence, nothing is left over. The Husserlian phenomenon is reduced without remainder to the evidence of presence. As such a perfect apparition of presence, it can be described as a "flat" phenomenon. It is rendered shallow and superficial, drained of its depth and color as it is delivered over to the sphere of immanence.[33]

Perhaps the notion of a horizon overcomes this flatness. We may recall that the sides of an object as simple as a cube are given in adumbrations or aspects. Two or three sides may be given directly to make up an aspect, but never more. The absent others are cointended as what remains unknown. There is always and in advance the horizon of determinable indeterminacy.[34] But in Marion's *Being Given*, the very notion of a horizon brings closure in its wake. We have noted that on the "principle of principles," the given should be accepted only within the limits in which it is presented. This de facto limitation is already inscribed in the de jure limits of a horizon. For Marion, furthermore:

> The exterior of experience is not equivalent to an experience of the exterior because the horizon in advance takes possession of the unknown, the unexperienced, and the not gazed upon, by supposing them to be always already compatible, compressible, and homogeneous with the already experienced, already gazed upon, and already interiorized by intuition. The intention always anticipates what it has not yet seen, the result being that the unseen has, from the start, the rank of a pre-seen, a merely belated visible, without fundamentally irreducible novelty, in short a pre-visible. Thus the horizon does not so much surround the visible with an *aura* of the nonvisible as it assigns in advance this nonvisible to this or that focal point (object) inscribed in the already seen. . . . Through a succession of lived experiences, intuition proceeds to fulfill its intentional aim at an object; it therefore stakes out a horizon within which it can retain (remember) them, compose them, and anticipate them around a noematic core. . . . Phenomenality is here grasped and included

in advance within a horizon of appearing always already seen, or at least visible—openness would be equivalent to a visual prison, a panopticon broadened to the dimensions of the world, a panorama without exterior, forbidding all genuinely new arising. (*BG*, 186–87/*ED*, 261–62)

What is meant by a broadening to the dimensions of the world? It is to *Reduction and Givenness* that we must return.[35] For Marion's Husserl, the task of bringing supposed objects to presence becomes programmatic because of the great breadth of the material delivered to constitution. A passage from *Phenomenological Psychology* is illustrative. Husserl contends that, imaginatively, we can bring more and more possible experiences into play to form a total intuition of the world. This would be a world picture, being "how it would look all in all and would have to look if we fill out the open indefinite horizons."[36] Marion comments that intuition does not just make worldly objects present; it makes the world itself present. Even the world is deposited into presence, without withdrawal, remainder, or restraint. The breakthrough is diverted into the completion of the metaphysics of presence, and he claims that we rediscover, by another route, the interpretation proposed by Derrida.[37]

As is well known, Marion seeks to reactivate the original breakthrough, to free it from the presence of objects in immanence. The Husserlian reduction gives the transcendental "I" its constituted objects. The Heideggerian reduction gives *Dasein* the Being of beings. Marion proposes a third reduction to givenness. Here the given constitutes an *interloqué*, a bedazzled interlocutor that is called in advance of its self-identity and deposed from autarky. An "I feel" or "I am affected" is more original than the "I think" accompanying representations. The constituting subject is already a passive receiver, its spontaneity of understanding yielding to the affection of sensibility.[38] If we take the example of *Experience and Judgment*, claims Marion, we find Husserl describing this already. He emphasizes the stimulus exercised by the intentional object over the ego, which is in turn abandoned to it.[39]

In *Reduction and Givenness*, Marion says relatively little of the given in general. Givenness is originally unconditional. It surprises and overcomes, and the call that it makes is absolute because it is indeterminate.[40] To gain some appreciation of its excess, however, a new phrase is required. It gives the title for the essay about it: "The Saturated Phenomenon."[41] It designates—no doubt in essentially occasional fashion—a givenness that surpasses intuition and signification beyond measure. Such givenness gives more than an intention could ever aim at, and in so doing overflows intuition as its surplus. Giving within its own limits, it can accord in this regard with the principle of principles. It is unforeseeable, unbearable, or bedazzling, unconditioned by horizons, and irreducible to the "I."[42]

What would a saturated phenomenon be like, at the very least as it appears to humans? For Marion, its excess of intuition would be seen but blurred, as if by the too narrow aperture, the too short lens, the too cramped frame that conspire to receive the quick and great and bright. To paraphrase Berkeley, it would blind us as if by an excess of light. Leaving its blurred traces, it would show our powerlessness to constitute it as an object, as something abandoned to and captured by the gaze of a subject.[43] It need not, for all this, be alien to synthesis or horizon. We have seen Marion write of the affection of sensibility. He holds that this can involve a passive synthesis coming from the activity of the phenomenon itself. Furthermore, its specificity can be recognized. If it does not depend on any horizon, this recognition of its uniqueness will prevent its being confused with other phenomena.[44]

It is part of our debt to Husserl, on Marion's reading, that his explication of internal time consciousness illustrates the distinctive characteristics of the saturated phenomenon.[45] Time is invisible and hence unforeseeable, for the flux admits of no homogeneous parts. Each phase already runs off from future to present to past in a continuous modification.[46] It is unbearable, since it does not admit of identifiable degrees. Between the primal impression and the first retention, nothing comes but an ideal limit. Time is unconditional in that it is the condition for an object without having to be one—it appears for itself in a horizontal rather than a transverse intentionality.[47] Finally, it is irreducible to the "I." It is the most original production that determines consciousness, which loses its status as an origin and discovers itself as originally determined and impressed and constituted.[48]

For all this, the phenomenon of internal time consciousness is taken as the sole exception to the transversal forcing of things and world into the flatness of objects without remainder, or whose vestigial remainder is determined in advance by totalizing horizons. And all this comes to pass because Husserl remains frozen before his own breakthrough.[49] He fails to define givenness and relapses into the Cartesian schema of a consciousness that determines transcendent things on the model of clarity and distinctness. The phenomenological method should provoke the indubitability of appearances, and not the certainty of objects. Givenness remains to be thought, says Marion, and so does the first reduction, but without returning to a pre-critical realism. It must still suspend absurd theories and the falsity of the natural attitude. Yet it must be done in order to undo it, to show what shows itself without it.[50]

Hubris, Humility, and the Things

It is clear that Marion's problem is not so much with the reduction as with how it is set up and what ensues from it. I have remarked that I hope to bring out Husserl's ultimate humility in the face of the world and worldly things. But first the hubris. It is in the subjective a priori brought out by the reduction that it rears its head. Husserl claims as much in his essay on the origin of the spatiality of nature. "Evidences for me" precede those of the natural sciences. In this, he states, one might find "the most unbelievable philosophical hubris." But we must not back down, he continues, from this consequence. Repeating the maxim of the fourth *Cartesian Meditation*, everything belongs to my ego, to my sense-giving.[51]

So far as I know, such hubris finds its most hyperbolical expression in *Formal and Transcendental Logic*. Before everything else is conceivable, I am, and the "I am" is—for the subject who says it in the right sense—the primordial intentional foundation for my world. The world for all of us is first this world of mine. And what holds for the actual world holds for an ideal one. Due to whatever prejudices (naturalistic or otherwise), the foregoing "may sound monstrous to me," remarks Husserl. Yet it is the basic matter-of-fact to which I must hold fast as a philosopher. "For children in philosophy," he goes on, "this may be the dark corner haunted by the specters of solipsism and, perhaps, of psychologism, of relativism. The true philosopher, instead of running away, will prefer to fill the dark corner with light."[52] Just a few pages later, the point is amplified, with God sharing the same fate as the world:

> Neither a world nor any other existent of any conceivable sort comes "from outdoors" into my ego, my life of consciousness. Everything outside is what it is in this inside, and gets its true being from the givings of it itself, and from the verifications, within this inside—its true being, which for that very reason is

something that itself belongs to this inside: as a pole of unity in my (and then, intersubjectively, in our) actual and possible multiplicities. . . . The relation of my consciousness to a world is not a matter of fact imposed on me either by a God, who adventitiously decides it thus, or by a world accidentally existing beforehand, and a causal regularity belonging thereto. On the contrary, the subjective a priori precedes the being of God and world, the being of everything, individually and collectively, for me, the thinking subject. Even God is for me what he is, in consequence of my own productivity of consciousness; here too I must not look aside lest I commit a supposed blasphemy, rather I must see the problem.[53]

Husserl quickly qualifies this passage. Here, as with the world and the alter ego, "productivity of consciousness will hardly signify that I invent and make this highest transcendency."[54] The very word "productivity" can be placed in parentheses. The early Derrida explains the relevant point as follows: God does not depend on me any more than the alter ego or the world, but He has meaning only for an ego in general, that is, for a transcendentally reduced *eidos*-ego whose meanings must be its own in any possible instantiation. Meaning needs an ego, not a neutral being-in-itself.[55] Husserlian hubris, then, is of a qualified variety.

If the hubris of ownness is circumscribed, there remains that of constitution. Behind the meanings for an ego is the ego's meaning-giving, to which everything else belongs. But Husserl might still be defended. I may give meaning, but not all the *determinants* of meaning need be attributed to me. They may be operative in their own way in the natural attitude, and come to the fore after the reduction. Certainly it is essential to the theory and practice of reduction that nothing be lost.[56] If Husserl shows that, in some notable respects, the meanings given by consciousness are themselves determined by the givenness of transcendent realities, he will have exploited his breakthrough instead of being frozen before it.

In his considerations of the meaning of the world, Husserl's humility comes to the fore. Phenomenology, he says, can do nothing but explicate the meaning that this world of natural experience has for us all, a meaning that can be uncovered but never altered.[57] Yet such humility may be of little benefit. Marion could retort that he still models mundane phenomena on logical and mathematical objects, with the world sharing an object's fate, stripped as it is of remainder.

But are these remainders so compliant? We can begin by inquiring after natural objects, especially the ones that are nonspiritual and nonliving. In *Ideas I*, they are posited as the "mere things" of the physical world, which supports the criticism that they are flattened without remainder on a theoretical template.

Even Husserl's starting points are unpromising. As Heidegger stresses, the very idea of a natural attitude is unnatural; an attitude is a stand that one takes up.[58] For his part, Marion notes that the regional ontologies of his objects are not only determined by the material funds and formal properties peculiar to them, but also by the empty form of any region, the form of an "object as such."[59] When he turns to the perception of "mere things," moreover, Husserl seems to privilege the ones closest to geometrical idealities. For the sake of simplicity, he remarks, we take as our example the thing that appears as unchanging. In *The Crisis*, he contends that when we privilege things at rest, the purpose is to bring out their bare bodily being, their extension and duration.[60] The *res extensa* of Descartes seems born again.

Appealing to things alive and of value might ameliorate the privilege of the example, but not remove it. Yet we are entitled to ask whether the extension and duration attributed to material things amount to logical or mathematical modeling. It is here that Husserl lays down an initial qualification. The terminology appropriate to physical things does not pick out objects that fall away from exact geometrical formations. The terms refer to things that are essentially and not accidentally inexact. They denote "anexact" morphological essences, not ideal ones.[61] We have to stress many times, he says, that each species of being has its own modes of givenness, and with them its own method of cognition. "It is countersensical," he adds, "to treat their essential peculiarities as deficiencies, let alone to count them among the sort of adventitious, factual deficiencies pertaining to 'our human' cognition."[62] Thus we find a humility in the face of the given. It is shown in itself and from itself, prior to the practical acts of straightening and sharpening that precede geometrical idealization.

Anexactitude does not preclude flatness, the shallowness and superficiality of a given that has been drained of its depth and color. But I would contend that few thinkers are as attentive as Husserl toward these other dimensions of the given. In treating of givenness through adumbrations, he is faithful to the things themselves, and to the injunction that nothing be lost in the reduction. It is true, as Marion notes, that perception does not represent something nonpresent, but seizes upon or heeds the thing in the flesh. Yet this holds only of the present adumbration. It is not represented, but the absent aspects are. They are cointended as also there. Just as the actual appearance is coordinated with an appearing thing, so the possible appearances are coordinated with more of that thing.[63]

It is also true that what is given indirectly pertains to memory and imagination. But Husserl would reply that this is a necessity of the physical thing, whose sense is determined by the data given in perception. There is nothing else, he claims, that could determine it.[64] As Jamie Smith observes, Husserl takes the inadequacy of sensuous perception seriously; inadequacy is due to the mode of givenness of the thing itself, and is not to be surmounted by abolishing the human standpoint.[65] Smith refers us to a familiar proposition considered by Husserl, namely, that God, the subject with an absolutely perfect knowledge, would have the adequate perception of the physical thing that is denied to us finite beings.[66]

This proposition is a countersense, in Husserl's eyes, for it implies that there is no essential difference between something immanent and something transcendent. If God had an adequate perception of the thing, it would be genuinely rather than intentionally immanent, a mere moment in the divine flow of consciousness. An omnipotent God may be capable of an all-in-all perception, but must first destroy the transcendency of the thing.[67] Which might suggest that God, no less than Husserl, takes physical things seriously. Remarkably, Husserl's argument prefigures the one he will use with regard to the alter ego: if I had perfect access to the Other's lived experiences, then he or she would be a moment of my own essence, and we would be the same. As Derrida has observed, respect extends through to the world at large; otherness already means something for the simplest of things.[68]

It is the character of the things that prescribes the ways they are given. We now encounter an argument that seems applicable to the panoptical world picture devoid of remainder. The multiplication of perspectives in imagination shows the irreducibility of the thing itself, not the ego's power. Yet even imagination has its limits. In the passive synthesis lectures, it is stated clearly that "[w]e cannot even imagine a mode of appearance in which the appearing object would be given completely."[69] We might conceivably have a thousand eyes that could apprehend all the thing's outer surfaces and inner depths, but we can only imagine our switching attention between them. Always and everywhere, perception pretends to accomplish more than it can.

It may be the case that we stay stripped of surprise, at least with the simpler things themselves. The essential inadequacy of their givenness may not allow them a remainder, in the sense of novelty and its possibility. Within the broad limits of manifestation in space and time, the appearances are capable of varying infinitely. The infinite, however, is not yet the indefinite, and there could be an infinity of narrower horizons that prescribe all the possible appearances for each type of object. We are certainly informed by Husserl that, in the theory of constitution, each type of object has its own horizon of predelineation.[70] The latter might chase down the relevant objects and foreclose novelty in each instance.

With none of these particular horizons, however, does Husserl suggest that we can ever complete the course toward the definite or fully determined, where nothing could delight or horrify us anymore. Absolute knowledge would collapse the tension between the object and the "how" of its determination, of which there is always a plus ultra.[71] Horizons do, of course, anticipate what we have not yet experienced. By their very nature they project the seen into the unseen, the touched into the untouched, and so on. To anticipate a determination in a thing or the thing itself, however, is not to shut off other ones. Horizons are prey to the new and its ability to shock. In the worldly realm of givenness and without exception, writes Husserl, there is the constantly open possibility that one experience will suddenly change into another, that a new givenness will explode the *noema* and cancel the object altogether.[72]

Marion might retort that novelty remains reducible to the relevant horizon, which converts it into a belated visible. Husserl would deny this claim outright. Novel aspects and things are irreducible to horizons as they stand. Horizons predelineate experience, but new and discordant experiences can alter a horizon or depose it altogether. From then on, things will never be the same again. Every transformation that consciousness undergoes is sedimented in its history and shows up in the relevant sense. For Husserl, "this is, so to speak, the destiny of consciousness."[73] We find an interplay of horizons and givens; in and through the latter, the former evolve and mutate. For everything inside the broad limits of appearance in space and time, "only the form of a possible future and the fact that something in general will undoubtedly arrive is incapable a priori of being crossed out."[74]

Far from closing down the new where it shocks or surprises, the Husserlian horizon serves to amplify it. A consciousness that expects the given to proceed in a certain way will be surprised all the more when it comes to frustrate or cancel the relevant expectation. Possibilities must in fact be expected (and not merely open) for surprise to counter them in the first place. If a consciousness had no horizons whatsoever, it might be startled, but not surprised. Put more precisely, it would be unable to gain the epiphanic awareness of otherness that transcends the immediate responses of the organism's nervous system. In such a mute and telescoped awareness, according to the Husserlian account, the radical novelty of the saturated phenomenon could never be received as such. One given would be as good or bad as another, the same for the indifferent subject whose lack of foresight makes it so.

Horizons allow for the shock of the new, and they also prefigure that more gentle novelty that is a frequent occurrence in everyday life, especially for the young. With the things that count as common-law phenomena, Husserl realizes that riches unseen are not anticipated in the invisible aspects alone. What is directly presented has its peculiar allure, and this—in Marion's language—makes the "I am affected" more original than the "I think." As early as *Ideas I*, it is stated that every property of a thing draws us into infinities of experience.[75] In later lectures, this allure of the given is set out a little more elegantly:

> It should be recognized that the division applying to what is genuinely perceived and what is only co-present entails a distinction between determinations with respect to the content of the object [a] that are actually there, appearing in the flesh, and [b] those that are still ambiguously prefigured in full emptiness. Let us also note that what actually appears, is, in itself, also laden with a similar distinction. Indeed, the call resounds as well with respect to the side that is already actually seen: "Draw closer, closer still; now fix your eyes upon me, changing your place, changing the position of your eyes, etc. You will get to see even more of me that is new, ever new partial colorings etc. You will get to see structures of the wood that were not visible just a moment ago, structures that were formerly only viewed indeterminately and generally," etc. Thus, even what is already seen is laden with an anticipatory intention. It—what is already seen—is constantly there as a framework prefiguring something new; it is an x to be determined more closely.[76]

Even the piece of wood calls out to me, giving itself in all its colors and contrasts; it summons me closer to it, so that I do not stride forward of myself alone. In Husserl's own phrasing, it intrudes. Knocking on the door of consciousness, it "wants" to be taken up.[77]

What can attract me, furthermore, is not just the detail or side foreshadowed. On Marion's account, the horizon assigns everything nonvisible to a focal point. But Husserl makes more of the phenomenon of a thing's breaking into awareness, and of the necessary distinction between the background of apprehension (the thing's hidden aspects) and the wider background of attention, the perceptual field of copresence or givenness-with. The object in the foreground is nothing without the background.[78] This outer horizon surrounds the object like a halo. It is from it that other things can break in, in their turn. We might recall his description from *Ideas I* of what lies outside his study, namely, the veranda that leads into the garden with children in its arbor.[79]

Occasions of breaking-in are more extreme examples of the affectivity of givenness in general. On Husserl's final view, every object given thematically is the derivative articulation of a process that begins in pregiving, or preobjective giving.[80] Marion refers to the stimulus exercised by the intentional object over the ego that is abandoned to it. But this is not what is primordial. The foreground of attention with its active synthesis of identification is built out of a passive synthesis of association. What is pregiven is neither an object nor a bare multiplicity of hyletic data, but a pattern in this or that perceptual field that exercises an allure on the ego. In gaining its prominence it motivates the associative ascription of a sense. Affectivity precedes the object of active constitution as well as following it.[81] The emergence of a foreground is not to be attributed to the spontaneous activity of an "I think."

In the outer horizons that serve as the fields for passive and active synthesis, we might find some of the features of Marion's saturated phenomenon, if indeed in rather literal ways. Does not each field of givenness show the cramped and narrow aperture of the foreground of attention? Does it not show our powerlessness to constitute it as an object? To be drawn to objectification by the background things—be they tables or chairs, rooftops in the Tuscan hills or children laughing in the garden—is to lose the currently focal thing. There is no outer horizon that can be comprehended in any possible gaze; of itself alone each one shows the pretension of perception to accomplish more than it is able.[82] And it is Husserl himself who draws an analogy between the thing in its spatial surroundings and the thing in the temporal world, the latter being revealed only in its passing through horizontal intentionality.[83]

Of course the saturated phenomenon of Marion carries its own peculiarities. Its excess of intuition overflows signification, which is tantamount to shutting signification down. Husserl might admit that signification stalls for the duration of the astonishment phase, but he would not admit of a sensuous phenomenon that would fail to motivate further prefigurings, however near it had come to saturation.[84] And one might wonder in passing whether Marion's saturated phenomenon is another formulation of the metaphysics of presence. Employing the Derridean register, we might describe it as a transcendental signified, as a terminus phenomenon whose total givenness in person brings it above and beyond the play of the sign.[85]

Leaving that question aside, however, Husserl may not have escaped finally the modeling of the simplest things on logical and mathematical phenomena. Horizons may leave open surprise and novelty and future riches, but only for actualization by a limited range of things. There may be founding objects that are poor in intuition, whose anexact and hidden aspects are monotonous in all their variations. If they are without inherent richness and allure, nothing can add these in. As we have seen, such objects are posited. The initial description of the natural attitude survives the reduction. It is of a world on hand with people and animals and objects of value that have as much immediacy as mere things.[86] As John Scanlon has noted, the materialism of Richard Avenarius' version of the natural attitude lives on when Husserl admits mere physical things without value, albeit constituted by the transcendental subject. These things compose the founding stratum to which all other being is related essentially.[87]

The natural attitude, in short, is telescoped into a naturalistic one. But as Scanlon goes on to observe, the method of reduction provides a means of escape that will be exploited to remarkable effect.[88] The educational worth of the reduction, remarks Husserl in *Ideas II*, is that it makes us sensitive to other and equal attitudes. On closer scrutiny, he adds that the naturalistic attitude is in fact subordinate to the personalistic one. The former gains a certain autonomy only "by means of an abstraction or, rather, by means of a kind of self-forgetfulness of the personal Ego."[89] The personalistic attitude is the one we are constantly in when we live together, meet, shake hands, talk, love, and act. We can also call it the practical attitude in very broad terms.⁹⁰ It includes the living and the useful and beautiful things that motivate us in need and desire: coal, hammers, vases, violins, paintings, and so on.⁹¹

What we have in this, according to Husserl, is an entirely natural attitude; it does not have to be achieved and preserved by artificial means. The naturalistic attitude is a derivation, a theoretical view, and its absolutizing of a bare physical nature is quite simply illegitimate. Husserl now gives us less of an attitude and more of the natural, unforced atmosphere of our lives. He comes to contend that there are no "mere things" without value in our basic experience. Thus the poor in intuition lose their immediacy and their founding status. Their givenness is recognized as founded, mediate, and highly abstract.⁹² The true world of the natural "attitude" has its being in the useful and beautiful things, in the people (and the animals, too) who are strange and familiar, who are friends and enemies and never just neutrally there.⁹³

Far from neglecting these givens or common-law phenomena, Husserl pays homage to their variety, and to the ways in which they help and delight and enrich us. Those things and people that have appeared to the ego have habitualized it from the outset—this is the destiny of consciousness that was referred to above. As personal egos we are brought against facticity, stresses Husserl, since we are dependent on a basis of motivations from society and culture and sensibility in general, all stretching into the obscurity of the past. We come upon this with the greatest force when we attempt to understand another person. Very much is already included in encountering others, and to meet them is not yet to know them. No matter how far we peer into the wondrous depths, they remain without fathom. Character makes up unsolved and unsolvable remainders, for oneself as well as for others.⁹⁴

Humility and the World as a Horizon

What of the world for Husserl? Does he show a humility toward it that goes beyond what is within it (to use provisionally a language of containment)? The entirely natural attitude comprises useful and beautiful and living things, the coal and violins and animals and people and so on. He tells us that it is also the prescientific nature that we experience together, namely, the common surrounding world of earth and sky and fields and woods.⁹⁵ For all these qualifications adduced in Husserl's defense, should we not still be disquieted by his hypothesis of a world picture? However derivative and artificial he finds the naturalistic attitude, it surely comes to pass in his work that the same attitude can reveal the world as it would look all in all.

Giving away too much to a theoretical view, in other words, Husserl may have forgotten his earlier argument against panopticism and his claim that we cannot even imagine an appearance in which the object would be given completely. When we read *Phenomenological Psychology*, however, we find that the possibility of an all-in-all view breaks down. For Husserl, it is true that we can form or explicate a total picture of the world, but it is also true for him that it is an openly progressing one; the totality of intuition does not amount to a panoptical vision in perception or imagination. Earlier in the same work, he is quite adamant that the visible world has no end, for every field of seeing has an inseparable outer horizon.[96]

This is confirmed when Husserl clarifies the forming of the all-in-all picture. When we try to fill out the open indefinite horizons, he says, "we would also see clearly that these horizons are infinitely indeterminate," and that whatever we imagine is "only a possibility to which we could very well juxtapose other optional possibilities."[97] What the process of free variation can produce is never a total picture, but the universal style of the world in the bare naturalistic sense: its structural forms of endurance in time, dispersal in space, and so on. Within these broad limits of manifestation, the appearances can vary infinitely.

In his 1935 essay on the origin of the spatiality of nature, Husserl moves even farther away from a characterization of the world as an object. Subtending the naturalistic conception of space as the place of places or outer horizons, he argues, is something more than the experiences of bodies at rest or in motion. Bodies make their contribution, since particular places are revealed in being occupied or passed through. But their motion or rest is relative, for it is experienced in relation to something that does not move or rest. This is the earth as ground. It is not a body at rest, since there is nothing further that it rests on. It is not a body in motion, since it does not itself arrive at or depart from somewhere. It is the primordial basis of movement and place that does not itself move or have a "where."[98]

The primordial earth is also the ground for the orientation of my own living body. Certainly, my body constitutes the "zero point" of spatial orientation, the "absolute here" in terms of which every other body is "there."[99] But if I cannot move away from my body, it is also the case that I cannot move away from the earth. It is the ground of my perceptual stability. In ordinary life I am always on it and always return to it, as even the birds must do.[100] Husserl envisages journeys of decades in which one is born on a spaceship. But even then the ship would be a fragment of the primordial earth, its structure building on the "root basis" (*Stammboden*) that provides us with our bodily orientation and concomitant habitualities. The primordial earth gives us an entire form of life. When we orbit the earth and take it as a homogeneous Copernican body, we have always already drawn on this root basis of prescientific experience.[101]

The meditation on the primordial earth deepens the account of the surrounding world. As early as *Ideas II*, this realm is interwoven internally with the sociocultural world of persons. And in a 1916/17 supplement they are taken to collectively constitute the life world (*Lebenswelt*), which is henceforth the title for the many-splendored world of the entirely natural attitude.[102] This account is taken up and reworked in *The Crisis*. The life world of nature and culture is characterized again as the subsoil for logical and theoretical truths. It demands an explication, but this does not uncover an object for any attitude whatsoever. Cognitions and truths applying to it emerge in the practical and personal projects of life. These cannot determine it more deeply as some kind of pretheoretical object, for it precedes all practical ends or purposes as well as theoretical perceptions.[103] Like the primordial earth that helps to make it up, it is a world that is lost from the natural scientific standpoint, but not well lost once this standpoint comes to be projected naturalistically into our everyday experience. For Husserl, the pregivenness of this original world is that of a grounding horizon:

> [T]he life world, for those of us who live in it wakingly, is always already there, existing in advance for us, the "ground" of all praxis, whether theoretical or extratheoretical. The world is pregiven to us, the waking and always somehow practically interested subjects, not occasionally but always and necessarily as the universal field of all actual and possible praxis, as horizon. To live is always to live-in-certainty-of-the-world. Waking life is being awake to the world, being constantly and directly "conscious" of the world and of oneself living in the world, actually experiencing and actually effecting the ontic certainty of the world. The world is pregiven thereby, in every case, in such a way that individual things are given. But there exists a fundamental difference between the way we are conscious of the

world and the way we are conscious of things as objects. . . . Every object has its varying possible modes of being valid, the modalizations of ontic certainty. The world, on the other hand, does not exist as an entity, as an object, but exists with such uniqueness that the plural makes no sense when applied to it. Every plural, and every singular drawn from it, presupposes the world horizon. This difference between the manner of being an object in the world and that of the world itself obviously prescribes fundamentally different correlative types of consciousness for them.[104]

Here, as ever, hubris accompanies humility: the sense of the world as a horizon is constituted by the ego as its own.[105] But what is important is that this sense follows the pregivenness of the world. And Husserl recommends eternal vigilance against the objectivism of naturalistic theories. We must take note, he writes in an appendix to his last major work, of "the dangers of a scientific life that is completely given over to logical activities." The dangers lie in the transformations of meaning that these activities drive one toward.[106] The transformations begin with the throwing of a garb of mathematical ideas over the life world. Through the garb the scientific method of prediction is eventually conflated with true being.[107]

In the remark about the dangers of a life given over to logical activities, one might discern a note of wistfulness and regret. But if this is so, the regret could be misplaced, the consequence of an overly harsh judgment that Husserl passes on his own philosophical career. The rejection of naturalistic objectivism is not an act subsequent to a late conversion. The spatiality and *Crisis* pieces are among the last in a path of investigations leading away from the object poor in intuition that is so rightly decried by Marion. The path begins with the broadening of evidence and the breakthrough to givenness. It moves on to admit a realm of phenomena as immediate as mere things, and quickly asserts the priority of the natural and sociocultural world over those objects modeled on logical and mathematical phenomena.

For Marion, the first reduction sets a limit on the given. It privileges immanence and the objective intentionality that intuition is to fulfill. These must themselves be reduced. More reduction will then mean more givenness.[108] But it is possible to see the first reduction in another way, as a limit that widens rather than constricts. It seems to me that it does indeed have an educational worth, making us sensitive to that deeper, natural atmosphere of our lives, which was in turn shown to presuppose the grounding world horizon that precedes any possible attitude whatsoever toward an object. In the world with its things we are immersed or absorbed, most often to the extent of forgetting our own constitutive accomplishments and those of others.[109]

Husserl could undoubtedly have exploited the breakthrough more fully, giving what cannot be objectified an even greater role. But the important point is that he did not remain frozen before givenness. While the early paradigm of the object may have slowed the evolution of his studies in the phenomenology of constitution, it did not thereby place a *ne plus ultra* in their path. Marion is well aware that Husserl constantly reworks the definition and procedures of the reduction, but he does not associate this with an explicit respect on the part of the latter for the ever-widening multiplicity of givens and pregivens that are admitted for description and constitutive explication.[110] It seems to me that, in Marion's interpretation, the operative separation of Husserl's reformulations of the reduction from his solicitous attention to givenness leaves us with a certain lacuna that is brought out in the following passage from *Being Given*:

> All the initial phenomenological concepts . . . had at the beginning the status of acts. Consequently, givenness, which the act of reduction makes manifest and by which it is ordered, must also be comprehensible as an act, no doubt the same as that of the reduction, or the recto of a single act whose verso is found in the reduction: the act of reconducting the *ego* to the given as given. That this act is not conceptually defined as a *quid* simply establishes that what is at issue is the concept of an act, and not of a quiddity, an object, or a theory. . . . Whatever the case may be, the lack of a definition of givenness remains patently obvious. Husserl did not conceptually determine givenness, which however determines the reduction and the phenomenon. He thinks on the basis of givenness, all the while leaving it for the most part unthought. We must admit this fact, less as an objection than as the precise definition of my own work and its justification: givenness remains to be thought explicitly there where Husserl accomplishes it without determining it as such. I do not pretend to begin where Husserl stopped, but simply to think what he accomplished perfectly without saying it.[111]

Yet how could Husserl ever have accomplished givenness perfectly without thinking and saying it, and without doing so in ways that are sufficiently determinate to transcend the poor in intuition? And what could have motivated him to rework the theory of constitution and the first reduction if not the sheer variety of givens that he forwarded for phenomenological elucidation?[112] The problems of reduction, as Merleau-Ponty suggested, are not for Husserl a prior step to phenomenology, but the very beginning of its inquiry, a beginning that turns out to be a perpetual one. Husserl should not be imagined hamstrung by vexatious obstacles, since "locating obstacles is the very meaning of his inquiry."[113] A meaning that is inspired by the motif of returning to the things themselves, given in its original contingency and empirical humility.

4

Glory, Idolatry, Kairos
Revelation, and the Ontological Difference in Marion

Felix Ó Murchadha

The terms of the title—glory, idolatry, kairos—are Christian, not Greek, if we understand Greek as the Greek of classical philosophy. Kairos is a Greek word meaning the opportune moment, but prior to Christianity it had little philosophical significance[1]; idolatry comes from *eidolon*, which in Plato means a deceiving image but in Christianity comes to mean false gods; glory—*gloria*—translates δόxa, a philosophical term that, however, is used in a new way to translate the Hebrew *kabod*. Thus, these very terms themselves point to a turning, a movement of thought that characterizes Christianity; one can say of them, as Heidegger does of the transformation of the meaning of *parousia*: "the otherness of the Christian life experience is evident in this conceptual transformation."[2] These terms refer to phenomena that are at the core of Christian revelation: to the appearance of God (glory), the danger of false appearances (idolatry), and the time of that appearance and of the history of salvation (kairos). The issue here is of an appearance that breaks into this world, so it is not *of* this world, but yet shows itself *in* this world. It is this concern that characterizes Marion's phenomenology of donation. His account of saturated phenomena—of *paradoxa*—concerns that irruption of strangeness in the world which both breaks with appearances (paradox) and yet gives itself as appearance (glory, δόxa).[3]

Against such critics as Janicaud[4] it must be insisted, however, that here what is at issue is not a blurring of the distinction between philosophy and theology as much as a recognition of the philosophical fruitfulness of traditionally theological phenomena (cf. *ED, 326/BG, 234*). Faced, therefore, with the terms glory, idolatry, and kairos, philosophy must insist on taking account of these phenomena in its own terms, that is, in relation to their compelling nature. This amounts to a question of authority. The claims of revelation to authority cannot be compelling in a philosophical sense; rather, the phenomenon of revelation needs to be taken up *as a phenomenon*.[5] At one stroke, the question of authority is displaced; the hermeneutics of Scripture must allow itself be justified by phenomenology. Once the phenomenological legitimacy of hermeneutics is posed, then Scripture is opened up to philosophical, and not solely theological, investigation.

At the same time the tension between Athens and Jerusalem—to give the two sides of this *polemos* their proper names—must not be covered over. This tension lies at the source of what is at issue in Marion's encounter with Heidegger's account of the ontological difference. To be clear: there can be no question of placing Heidegger in the "Athens camp" and Marion in the "Jerusalem camp": Heidegger was himself strongly influenced by Christianity, and Marion is still working within the parameters of Greek thought. Nevertheless, there are critical decisions—decisions that arise out of crises in thought—that color thinking so as to locate it in a certain position along the lines of tension between Athens and Jerusalem. The decision concerns nothing other than what counts as a phenomenon. Greek thought—in its classical form—posits a correspondence between the human mind and the principle of things, and even in the Hellenistic period the fallibility of this correspondence alone is at issue. The pathos of wonder immediately leads to the question of grounds, hence of that which is the *same* between thought and being. Christian thought calls such correspondence into question. The glory of God is precisely that to which no correspondence is possible, and that for a fundamental reason: because God reveals Himself in the world as beyond the world. Now, if that is so, does this not mean that the very unity of philosophy is threatened (i.e., that the principles of what *is* are challenged with an exception, one that concerns that which is most at issue in philosophy)? Or, to put the question in relation to Marion and Heidegger, can there be an *exception* to the ontological difference? If there can be, then the sameness of thought and being is superseded, thinking is liberated from being, and a place for faith is philosophically underscored by reference to phenomena that point beyond any account in terms of nature, understood in the widest sense.

This chapter can do no more than tease out some of these issues through an examination of, respectively, glory, idolatry, kairos.

Glory

Marion, in his reading of Romans 4:17–18 and 1 Corinthians 1:28–29, appeals directly to the notion of glory (*GWB*, 86–95/*DSE*, 128–40). The first passage concerns the faith of Abraham and, according to Paul, he is made "the father of us all, as it is written, 'I have made you the father of many nations'"—Abraham here "facing Him in whom he believed, the God who gives life to the dead and who calls the non-beings as beings, *kalountos ta mē onta hōs onta*" (quoted in *GWB*, 86/*DSE*, 228). This passage interests Marion because in it Paul uses the language of the philosophers—*onta*—but does so to surpass the distinction between being and nonbeing. For God, there is an indifference between being and nonbeing. Such indifference to the ontic difference between being and nonbeing can come only from another place, beyond being. That place is the place of faith, the call, the "as if" (*GWB*, 88/*DSE*, 130f.). The second passage goes as follows: "God chose the ignoble things of the world and the contemptible things and also the non-beings, in order to annul the beings (*kai ta mē onta, hina ta onto katargēsē*)—in order that no flesh should glorify itself before God" (quoted *GWB*, 89/*DSE*, 132). Here we are dealing not simply with an indifference to the ontic difference but an indifference to the ontological difference as well: here it is a question of the source of beingness itself. Now in fact—in the strict rigor of philosophical thinking—what is at issue here is not being and nonbeing at all. The dead *are*. Furthermore, when in 1 Corinthians Paul talks of nonbeing, he does so to refer to Christians, the lowest of the low, who, for all that, still *are*. One might want to call this a merely rhetorical exaggeration, hyperbole on Paul's part. Marion, however, sees precisely here the issue of glory as crucial in undermining the ontological difference. The world glorifies itself before God, and in so doing undermines the ontological difference by reducing to nothing that on which it cannot found itself in this glorification. Only what *is* can glorify itself before God (*GWB*, 93/*DSE*, 138).

The point here is that being and nonbeing, Being and beings, can be divided by something other than the ontological difference, namely, according to glorification. Nonbeing here is that which is of no importance, of no glory. What is of no glory does not appear, is not seen, is of no weight. This reduction to nonbeing is that which undermines the ontological difference by an inversion of the divine love: the world glorifies itself before God by viewing what is in terms not of being, but rather of the world. As Marion puts it: "Before the difference between beings, before the conjunction of being to Being, before the fold of the ontological difference, the "world" holds the discourse of the acquisition of funds—to glorify oneself before God" (*GWB*, 94/*DSE*, 138). In effect, what is at issue here are two glorifications, that of God and that of the world. To understand this, we must pause to examine what is meant by glory.

"Glory" translates *dōxa*—a word philosophically understood, in opposition to *epistēme*, as "opinion." An opinion is the statement of how things appear to someone. Indeed, *dokeō* has the meaning of "it appears so." What appears in a certain way must come to appearance, must shine forth in some way, must show itself. In shining forth it brings light on itself. Hence, *dōxa* has the meaning "fame." This has a wider political context: the one who states best how things appear, states it in such a way that it is then seen by us to be true, warranting our good opinion. He should be spoken of well of; and most importantly, remain in our memories. Hence, *dōxa* opens up a future. The opinions that we have are the making explicit of the appearance of things to us (*dokei moi;* it appears so to me). Those things and actions worthy of opinion are the higher things, the most worthy of things. The one who can give the worthiest opinion is the one who corresponds best to those appearances, and in so doing makes that which appears apparent, as if for the first time.

Now with the Septuagint translation of the Bible, the difficulty arose of translating the Hebrew term *kabod*.[6] This term has the meaning "weightiness." The person with *kabod* has "weight" in his community. The weightiness of the person is that which makes him stand out, be apparent in an emphatic sense. In that sense it can be a word for riches: the man with riches stands out, has a standing. In fact, in this original sense *kabod* approaches the prephilosophical meaning of *ousia*: it refers to the property owned by the person. Jacob's whole wealth is referred to as his *kabod* (Genesis 31:1). When used in reference to God, *kabod* refers to that which makes God apparent. While the difficulty is to think an invisible God, when He does reveal Himself, the appearance is referred to as *kabod*. The weightiness of God, however, is such that it cannot be seen. God can show Himself only by not appearing in person. For this reason, throughout the Old Testament (and this can be seen also in the account of the Ascension [cf. *PC*, 124–52]), the appearance of God is cloaked in a cloud. God shines too brightly for human eyes to see (cf. Exodus 24:16). There can be no correspondence with His appearance. His appearance is hidden because it breaks with the possibility of appearance in this world. That which is beyond the measure of this world reveals itself only as that which cannot be made apparent. As Karl Rahner puts it: "[I]n communicating himself as *deus relevetus* he becomes radically open to man as *deus absconditus*."⁷ To capture this meaning in Greek, the Septuagint translators of the Hebrew Scriptures used the word *dōxa*. The appearance of that which appears—*dōxa*—in the case of that which is invisible comes to mean the manifestation of that which does not show itself. It refers to the invisibility of God, invisible in the sense of being blinding to human vision, an excess of light.⁸ The glory of God lies precisely in the fact that no eye can see Him as He is. *Dōxa* comes to mean that which shows itself only by blinding, that of which there can be no opinion, because there can be no correspondence. Knowledge is not ruled out here, but rather is transformed into a knowing that cannot claim mastery over its object. The proper response to this glory is not thinking in the sense of seeking after wisdom.⁹ Glory calls not for opinion, not for discussion and argument, but rather for praise (*doxāzo*).¹⁰ The praise of God is a giving of glory. This giving of glory is tied up with the relation of creature and creator: all creatures give glory in reflecting—albeit imperfectly—the perfection of the Creator (this in Scholastic philosophy is termed "material glory"). A free being, on the other hand, is created with the possibility of giving glory as a free and loving acknowledgment of god ("formal glory").¹¹

This short excursus shows the complexities of glory as a term and the phenomena this term reflects. *Dōxa* means, between the classical and biblical senses, appearance and nonappearance, opinion and praise, worldly fame and that "which is not of this world." While the specific meaning of glory is not classical, that meaning indicates the transformation the word underwent in the encounter between the Greek and Judeo-Christian worlds. It also indicates the core of the conflict at the heart of the cross that "to the gentiles [is] foolishness" (1 Corinthians 1:23). That which is insignificant, indeed "less than nothing," for the world brings God to appearance in the world. The appearance of things is no longer simply that which arises in the opening of the world, but that which bears the trace of that which is not of this world but which calls from beyond it (cf. 1 Corinthians

1:26–29; *GWB*, 89f./*DSE*, 132f.). The conflict of glorifications that Marion finds in Paul, then, concerns the very worldliness of appearance.

It is important to note here that with Paul the term "world" (*cosmos*) takes on a negative meaning. *Cosmos*, the object par excellence of philosophical reflection, is that which distracts from the divine. This leads to the admonition that faith in Christ demands that the believer live in the world in such a manner as if not being in the world. The justification for this is the "glory of the cross": that which in the eyes of the world is as nothing becomes the manifestation of God's love. This, however, is excluded by the world's glorification of itself before God. The act of glorification there is an intuition of divine transcendence, which is acknowledged by the very exclusion of the cross that brings God to appearance. Thus the world undermines philosophical discourse itself, which, however, fails to acknowledge that which the world implicitly sees, namely, divine transcendence. Implicit in Marion's account is the idea that the philosophical critique of *dōxa* in fact sees the problem of glory. Philosophy in such an understanding attempts to block glory and glorification in its critique of the political *dōxa*. Indeed, one might go so far as to say that the world for Paul (and Marion) is the political world that grasps the divine in a way that philosophy cannot. What we see in John's gospel and in Paul's letters is a shift in the meaning of *cosmos*, from the world in a cosmological sense (in which case the heavenly bodies, and not the mere affairs of men, are of central importance) to the world an "anthropological" sense (in which the world refers to the affairs of men, what we might call the "worldly").[12] In this sense, Christianity launches a critique of the political, as does Greek philosophy, but from a different perspective: while philosophy subordinates *dōxa* to *epistēmē*, Christianity exploits the element of glory implicit in political *dōxa* in order to invert it.

It is with at this last point that we can turn to a pivotal text of Heidegger's, the *Introduction to Metaphysics*. Here Heidegger discusses the double meaning of *dōxa* as opinion and fame/glory. He says: "*Dōxa* is the regard in which a man stands . . . the regard [*An-sehen*, looking at, esteem] which every entity conceals and discloses in its appearance (*eidos*)."[13] Heidegger makes clear the political context here: the aspect in which one appears, differs from where one is seen; regard and esteem are political, they assume the place of the city (*pōlis*). But the city, in this understanding, "is" only through the ontological difference: the unconcealment of being happens in appearance in the glory of that which stands forth. Moreover, in the same passage Heidegger also talks of the "call" in the sense of reputation or fame (*Ruf*). The German word *Ruf*—from *rufen*, "to call"—means reputation: the reputation of a person depends on his or her calling. Entities are called into appearance, into sight. Called into appearance, entities *are*. The ontological difference cuts across any distinction between *dóxa* and *epistēme*. The glory of things is their appearance, and in this appearance unconcealment occurs. The possibility of appearance lies in the unconcealment of entities.

Truth in the sense of *aletheia* is gloriful and, if the Greeks did not think this basic experience of truth, it can be seen precisely in Plato's polemic against *dóxa*. If this is the case, then Heidegger may allow us to understand glory politically only as we understand it ontologically. Hence, against Marion one could say that what ultimately is at issue is not the glorification of the world in the face of the transcendent God, but rather the political foreshortening of ontological categories. In other words, for any entity to stand forth at all is for it to be glorified in the sight of those who perceive it, while politically the reduction of world to the worldly makes glorification a matter of the human affairs within the polis. But the plausibility of such a position gains from avoiding, as Heidegger does with simply a passing reference,[14] the whole later history of *dóxa* which I have outlined. By so doing he fails to account for how *dóxa* can undermine itself not ontologically but rather in terms of a higher instance. This higher instance for Marion is the gift.

In his interpretation of the prodigal son parable, Marion points to the importance of *ousia*. I have already noted the closeness of *kabod* and *ousia*. The prodigal son sees his inheritance as disposable property, unlike the father, who sees it in the interchange of gift. This is the crucial point: as gift, what *is*, is not understood in terms of its being but rather in terms of givenness (*donation*) itself. The gift comes from a love that is without ground. Now, it may seem here that the father is the giver of the gift, but that would suggest that he possessed—or saw himself as possessing—property that was in his gift. As Marion says:

> The father is not fixed on the *ousia* because with his gaze he transpierces all that is not inscribed in the rigor of a gift, giving, received, given: goods, common by definition and circulation, are presented as indifferent stakes of those who, through them, give themselves to each other in a circulation which is more essential than what it exchanges. (*GWB*, 99/ *DSE*, 145)

What does it mean to give oneself? In Marion's account it amounts to a giving oneself over to the crossing aims of love. This dispossession is ultimately that of *kenōsis*: an emptying of oneself as substance, as possessor, in favor of the very circulation of goods (*ID*, 89). It is a divesting of worldly glory, of weightiness, for the lightness of loving exchange. The gift, in other words, is unconditional; the condition of being (i.e., the ontological difference) is in fact itself given, through the loving gift.

According to Marion, "Being/being, like everything, can, if it is viewed as a giving, give therein the trace of another gift to be divined" (*GWB*, 105/*DSE*, 153). Now, while in the context of *God Without Being*, the gift here is the gift of God, clearly Marion intends this to be as much a philosophical as a theological claim. The trace, namely, of a gift, whoever the giver, can be seen in the Being/being. Hence, accepting Heidegger's understanding of Being as giving, this giving is not exhausted within Being, but rather points beyond it. This is the core of Marion's critique of *Ereignis* as a covering over of the gift by determining the giving in a way that negates the possibility of the gift (*ED*, 54–60/*BG*, 34–39). But where is that trace of another gift to be found? In that very entity where the ontological difference crosses *Dasein*. The trace is to be found in the one who is addressed (*interloqué*). For Heidegger, the gift of being is of that which affects and concerns us—the human is "concerned with and approached by presence" (*der von Anwesenheit angegangene*).[15] As is the case for the one who is addressed, the human being is not there as one pole of a relation; rather, it is only as the one concerned, as the one who receives, that the human being *is* at all.

Thus the issue here centers on the place of the human being. For Marion, the self is in the dative case: the self is the one to whom the address is made. Marion opposes this to the genitive case of *Dasein* (of Being). However, the later Heidegger moves away from such a "genitive" understanding of *Dasein*, to something approaching Marion's dative subject. This can be seen, in particular, in the notion of *Entsprechung*, correspondence.[16] For Heidegger, the human being's privilege is one of response. Responding to the claiming call of being (*Anspruch des Seins*), the human being is first addressed. The call is to him. The response that is called for is one of "corresponding to." The dative in this case works both ways. The human being is the one who responds to the claiming call of being by a stepping back, hence a distancing from being, which is received as given; and through that stepping back the human being enters into the language of that claiming call.

The difference between these two positions centers on the mood in which this gift is received, hence the mood that is fundamental to the self. Here, furthermore, the two glories/glorifications—of God and of the world—spoken of earlier reemerge in a different form.

For Heidegger it is above all in awe—*Scheu, aidōs*—that the gods appear.[17] This is a mood of modest restraint, of holding back before that which is. The gaze of awe is not one that fixes, but rather one that draws back, that is averted. The importance of this mood is that it responds to the mood of being. *Es gibt Sein*, it gives being, not in the sense of something that can be possessed, but in the sense of giving space and giving time in which things can be encountered. This is possible only through the restraining, holding back of being (*An sich halten*).[18] *Die Lichtung des Seins* is nothing other than the opening up of that space where such restraint is possible—indeed, called for. The claiming call of being (*Anspruch des Seins*) tells us nothing about what is, because it is a call to restraint. This is to say that it is a call into alterity, but an alterity immanent to being: the glory of the immanent.

Marion, on the other hand, sees the pure call in a radical boredom where both self and being are reduced to indifference.[19] He takes up Heidegger's analysis of boredom but presses it further: while for Heidegger beings (*Seiende*) are reduced to indifference, according to Marion, boredom can place *Dasein* beyond the call of Being itself. Drawing on Pascal, Marion sees boredom as a hatred: "the one who yields to boredom . . . hates (*est mihi in odio*) because nothing makes any difference for him (*nihil interest mihi*)" (RD, 287/RG, 191). Self and world disintegrate since, between them, nothing remains ("the dissolution of worldhood itself" [ibid.]). In this understanding, the ultimate mood is liberating. It is a liberation from self and from being. Such a liberation places the self beyond any concern with its own being or, for that matter, with any other. It brings the self to a transcendent alterity in which it becomes other than itself in response to a pure (i.e., indeterminate, in the sense of surprising) call. It is a call beyond being that I recognize only in admitting the claim, and hence myself as the one addressed. The liberation of boredom leads to a "compulsion to alterity" in which the *interloqué* discovers itself as a "subject without subjectivity": the glory of the transcendent.

This conflict of glories is at the same time a conflict of alterities. To defend that latter claim, I need to turn to the question of idolatry.

Idolatry

Marion sees the appearance of the divine under two aspects, idol and icon. He makes clear that these are not types of entities, but ways of being.[20] This is already to go a long way along the path of the ontological difference: a statue as entity comes to appearance through its way of being as icon or idol. However, as an icon, the entity brings to appearance that which goes beyond being, namely, the claim of love. "Only the icon shows the face" (*GWB*, 19/*DSE*, 31), Marion writes. Elsewhere, he distinguishes sharply between the façade and the face (*DS*, 93–96/*IE*, 76–80). The face is that which views me, which reverses my intentionality, which robs me of the "I" in giving a "me." The face summons the "invisible person," inviting us to "see the invisible" (*GWB*, 19/*DSE*, 32). The personal is opposed here to the thingly idol.

While, in Marion's theological writings, the opposition of idol and icon is stressed, in fact both fall under the category of "saturated phenomenon." It is important to stress here that this designation does not make either icon or idol an extreme phenomenon. On the contrary, a saturated phenomenon is that which fulfills most fully the definition of a phenomenon: "it alone truly appears as itself, of itself and starting from itself" (SP, 120). The allusion here is, of course, to Heidegger's definition of a phenomenon in *Being and Time*. The difference between the self-givenness of idol and icon lies, for Marion, in the subject who perceives them. The idol overwhelms vision to the point of collapse (*ED*, 432/*BG*, 315). It mirrors the capacity of the gaze. The icon, on the other hand, does not result from the gaze but summons it from an invisible source (*GWB*, 17f./*DSE*, 28f.). The icon is a face that, although visible and material, draws the one summoned into the depth of a gaze that is beyond the limits of his sight (*GWB*, 19/*DSE*, 31). "[E]very face is given as an icon" (ibid.) and, as such, breaks from the idolatry of things that reflect only the gaze of the viewer. In that sense the icon is the personal; it is that through which someone calls. Idolatry amounts, in this understanding, to reification, if not petrifaction. In that sense the icon defines the idol, and not the other way around. There is here a fundamental distinction between the givenness of persons and of things: while both the icon and the idol signal (*signa*) beyond themselves (*GWB*, 8f./*DSE*, 17f.), to apprehend something as an icon is to apprehend this signal as indicating a person drawing vision to a source beyond itself.

This drawing power is the call of love, in which the personal shows itself as itself. I shall return in the final section to the question of love. Here it is important to see that love is, for Marion, the self-giving of the personal, which is apprehended in the icon. To apprehend love is to apprehend the divine through the visibility of the icon. The idol is that which is apprehended as dazzling and mirroring the gaze, as allowing no room for the call of love. Its givenness returns me to myself, ending in an ineluctable solipsism (*ED*, 321/*BG*, 230).

It is precisely such a distinction that Heidegger attempts (especially in his later work) to overcome. While he does not engage in a phenomenology of the face, he does speak of the face-to-face of things:

> Yet being face-to-face with one another has a more distant origin [than human face-to-face relations]; it originates in that distance where earth and sky, the god and man reach one another. Goethe and Mörike, too, like to use the phrase "face-to-face with one another" not only with respect to human beings but also with respect to things of the world.[21]

The face-to-face relation Heidegger sees as originating in the fourfold of earth and sky, mortal and gods. In contrast to *Being and Time*, where *Dasein* opens up the world, here the world happens in the thing. The thing faces in the sense that it is a place from which the world is. Through the thing, that which characterizes the face-to-face, namely, distance and nearness, is manifest. When things are denied, as in calculative thinking that reduces things to objects (*Gegenstände*), the very possibility of the face-to-face disappears. Why? Because the face-to-face requires a world, an opening in which to happen. That opening happens in the thing, from which humans as mortals receive their being. In the face-to-face of things, human beings find their place and their measure. In *Being and Time* the thing as ready-to-hand is given free (*Freigabe*): it *is* only in the opening, the "free space" of the totality of relevance (*Bewandtnisganzheit*).[22] Its truth, though—that is, its unconcealment—is nothing other than its being allowed to be. The freedom of *Dasein* is not in its will, but rather in its response to this opening, a response that it is always already called to make; and thus freedom does not equate with spontaneity. This displacement of freedom from the subject to the world means that the human being is always first *in* freedom. Being in freedom is being in relation to things as things (i.e., as beings that *are*).[23] Heidegger returns to this notion of the free-giving when in the essay "The Thing," he says that the "appropriating mirroring gives free each of the four in its own." The four are given free—given space and time—in the happening of the thing. The thing sets free the space in which mortals and gods, sky and earth can be in their relation to one another.

The thing is in this sense not to be understood as an instrument of mere utility, nor as an aesthetic object of sensual pleasure, nor even as an object of knowledge. Rather, the thing is that which orients the world; it gives time and gives space. In his *Art and Space*, Heidegger talks of spacing (*Räumen*) as that which gives place. Place is where gods appear or from where they have flown. In this context, he introduces the distinction between sacred space (*sakraler Raum*) and profane space (*profaner Raum*). This is a central distinction to his concern here: it is only through a stepping back before the thing that the fourfold is revealed in it. This stepping back is in the face of that which withdraws from the objectifying—the idolatrous—gaze. It occurs in the face of a giving of space that appears only in privative form in profane space.[24] It is the sacredness in things to which Heidegger is pointing when he says that the "thing things world"[25]: the thing gives a world. The thing, in this sense, defeats the intentional gaze since it is, in Marion's terms, saturated with the invisible fourfold[26]; but it does so not as the icon does, by a counterintentionality, but rather by its emplacement.[27] The thing in its sacredness is in another place; it orients us, rather than us orienting it. While the phenomenality of the face, the heaviness of its glory weighing on me, inspires respect (*DS*, 143/*IE*, 119), the sacredness of things calls for reverence beyond sight and seeing[28]: sight is only through the sky that happens in the thing. The thing in this sense is neither idol nor icon, neither an invisible mirror because it repels the gaze, nor icon because it is impersonal; indeed, it gives the space for the personal. The glory of the thing lies in the opening up of the fourfold that happens in it.[29]

The face for Marion appears only through a liberation from the attraction to the earth; indeed, a release from the imprisonment of the cosmic is necessary. This reflects the contrasting emphasis on boredom and on awe that I noted above. The point for Marion is to lead the self back out of the world, in order to be open to a call that comes from beyond being. This phenomenological decision guides the conflicting understandings of the place of divine appearance: for Marion, to prepare a place for God is already idolatrous—"doubly idolatrous," as he puts it (cf. *GWB*, 25–52/*DSE*, 39–80), in the sense both of taking the measure of God from human predicates and in the sense of giving anteriority to being. This amounts to saying that Heidegger understands divine otherness on the basis of the sameness of being and thinking. To think God is to apprehend him from Being. Yet, according to Marion, revelation as phenomenon amounts to the interruption of the sameness of being. This interruption he understands as love, which requires no conditions of possibility in Being (*GWB*, 47/*DSE*, 73). It is the love of God that is other to Being, and that calls from a place beyond being.

The issue here is not one of alterity *tout court*, since alterity is already affirmed in the fourfold. The issue is, rather, whether alterity is to be thought from the sameness of being—sameness as the belonging together (*Zusammengehören*) of what is other,[30] or as that which suspends all such belonging together, as that which calls for a belonging beyond being (being in the world as if not of the world). The way in which God is to be understood depends on the answer to that question. The question, though, is in a sense misstated because a conflict of alterities is, strictly speaking, impossible: there can be no place from which both the thing and the face appear as other. Either the face is other as the thing is, or the thing is no other but an object to the gaze that finds no countergaze. There can be no question here of an overarching synthesis.

What is possible, however, is to see what motivates this divergence. The issue amounts to a question concerning the interruption of being. Such an interruption is thought of by Marion as difference: the differing, namely, between appeal and response. This difference is, for Marion, more fundamental than the ontological difference. I wish to explore what is at issue here, again somewhat obliquely, with reference to another difference, one that is crucial for understanding Revelation—namely, the difference between *chronos* and *kairos*, between the time of human affairs and the interruption of that time.

Kairos

If there is, between Marion and Heidegger, a conflict of "alterities," it is one that cannot be understood in terms of a difference between idol and icon. Rather, what is at issue here cuts across iconicity and idolatry. Idolatry has meaning only with reference to a transcendent instance. It is this, however, that Heidegger consistently rejects as philosophically (as opposed to theologically) impossible. In a sense, this impossibility is confirmed by Marion to the extent that, for him, the difference between the idol and the icon lies in the one perceiving it, and that difference is one of love. Love, however, requires faith

(PC, 101)—precisely that which Heidegger, in both his early and later work, placed outside philosophy/thought.[31]

While the nexus of faith and love is crucial for understanding the difference between icon and idol, this difference is itself indifferent in terms of that between appeal and response. Yet it remains the case that at the end of *Being Given* it is the question of love, which is opened up. This seems to be so for a fundamental reason: the reduction to givenness amounts to a fundamental openness to an alterity that is of another person. Love expresses not the extreme of such openness, but its fundamental nature. It is so because love is the most concrete expression of the difference of appeal and response.

To understand why this should be so, it is necessary to be clear on one thing: the reduction to givenness in effect means that ultimately phenomenological description must concern itself with the subject alone. While accepting that this is a dative subject, a "subject without subjectivity," it is nonetheless true that Marion can talk only from the subject, even if he does so in order to uncover "the immemorial originality of the one who calls over the one who is called."[32] Consequently, crucial to the understanding of difference in Marion is the affection of the subject as *interloqué*, or more radically as *adonné*—the devoted. This subject is taken by surprise; nothing can prepare him for the call, because there is no anteriority to the call or, at any rate, the anteriority is in the call itself. The temporality of this call is that of an immemorial past and an indefinite future. This is reflected in what Marion understands as the eventlike nature of phenomenality itself. In other words, all the regularities of experience point back to the irregular, the jarring, that which places the subject in the position of receiver, without mastery. But the subject, if called, is called upon to respond, and it is through that response that the call itself can be known. There must therefore be a "capacity" to respond that in some way is suitable to the givenness of the call. This capacity of receiving (reception) defines the *adonné*.

The capacity to respond is one which acknowledges that the initiative does not lie in the self, that the self is not original. Ultimately, it is a recognition of birth, of the natality of the self (cf. *DS*, 49–52/*IE*, 41–44). But crucially, the response differs from the call. This difference arises out of the delay (*le retard*) between appeal and response (see *ED*, 407f./*BG*, 295f.). The givenness of the self-giving is converted only through the prism of the *adonné* into the self-showing of the phenomena through the response. But there is no temporally prior appeal; rather, the appeal is only in the response, which then subsequently differs in the form of delay from the appeal. The difference here between donation and appearance is that which gives the ontological difference itself, to the extent to which it gives time.

The prism of the *adonné* is that of response. It is a response that places the subject in the position of the devoted one, of the follower. Indeed, more than anything, it places him in the position of lover in the sense of *agápe*. A hint of this idea is to be found in one of the basic texts of the philosophical tradition, the opening lines of Aristotle's *Metaphysics*, where Aristotle says: "By nature all men desire to know. An indication is the love [*agápesis*] they show for their senses" (*Metaphysics*, 981a1). In relation to his senses the human being is in a position of a lover—a devoted follower for whom the whole of reality is disclosed through them. Christianity, however, transforms such devotion into a selfless giving. In the Christian sense, *agápe* does not possess, but divests itself. We have already seen this kenotic idea with reference to the gift in Marion's account of the prodigal son. This love is not a mere affection but, Marion insists, is a form of knowledge. The knowledge involved here, then, is not one that tries to comprehend and possess, but one that gives space. But this divesting of myself requires faith. The move from object to other requires a leap, a confidence in the other's love that no facts of the matter will justify, which is in that sense beyond reason and grounds. This is the kind of knowledge to which St. Paul refers when he states, "Of times and moments [*kairos*] you know that the day of the Lord is going to come like a thief in the night" (1 Thessalonians 5:1–2). This is not a knowledge of what can be predicted, but rather a knowledge that has no object. It is, furthermore, a loving knowledge, since only love will give eyes to see the kairos as kairos.

While Marion claims the difference between appeal and response is prior to temporal difference, his descriptions of them have strong temporal elements, particularly with his emphasis on surprise. Surprise happens in a moment, and does so within horizons of expectation. Surprise suspends those horizons, but is impossible without reference to them. Surprise is that possibility which Greek metaphysics does not so much explain, as explain away.[33] Yet, it is surprise that characterizes above all the Christian experience of time. This is the importance of kairos. The kairos is the moment of an interruption of the world's horizons of that which is not of the world.

Conclusion

If Marion's understanding of the alterity of the icon leads him to a notion of loving knowledge with clear parallels to the knowledge of kairos in St. Paul, Heidegger's own reflections on Being owe much to readings of St. Paul on kairos.[34] The knowledge of the kairos is a knowing that is accomplished in life: the knowledge of the kairos, Heidegger states, is the knowledge of how to "live temporality."[35] This knowledge is no longer one that looks for first principles, because the future is precisely that which will reverse all such principles. The Second Coming of Christ involves the transformation of the world and is, as such, radically unpredictable. The *kairos* in this way is the action from without, from outside the world that will transform it. To live time means to live the constant newness of time, as a constant interruption of the daily concern with the world. To live temporality means to live in the glory of God, which both is and is to come. Understood in Aristotelian terms, this is doubly contradictory. First, either something is or is to come, and second, what is to come *is not*; hence the claim is being made that glory both is and is not. Heidegger's critique of being as presence begins with this "living futuricity": the future is that which is manifest already in the present, not as that which is not yet, but rather as that which is an absence in my present. In that sense, the "when" of the Second Coming—the kairos—is not something that can be fixed in some future time; instead, my knowledge of it is a knowledge of how to live and relate to the world in radical uncertainty. Hence, all time is kairological—not in the sense that at every moment the Second Coming occurs, but rather in the sense that living temporality is living in relation to the divine, and hence to that which is wholly other.[36]

It is here that one might expect Heidegger to turn, as Marion and, before him, Lévinas do, to the infinity of the other, to the glory of the face, the difference of appeal and response, perhaps even the loving gift. He might then have discovered *dōxa* as glory opening up a future not alone in the way fame does, but also in the sense of a promise of that which has no anteriority in being. Heidegger, however, attempts to think being as time—in other words, to think the kairos not as a break in being, but rather as the temporality, indeed historicity, of being. Here again Judeo-Christian and Greek themes are interwoven. Rémi Brague points out that Judeo-Christianity undermined nature in favor of history. We can see this in the very festivals that are celebrated to commemorate historical events rather than the cycles of nature.[37] This is so because God is manifest not in those natural cycles, but rather in temporally specific interventions in human history. We can see reflected here the transformation of "cosmos" from the cosmological to the sphere of human affairs. But far from thinking history as other than nature, Heidegger thinks nature as *phūsis*, as being, and being as historical. Indeed, for Heidegger, the history of being might be described as the epochally distinct ways in which nature has been understood.[38] Thought as such *alētheia* is kairological, which means that the kairos is not the temporality indifferent to being, but rather that of beings, of things to the extent to which they manifest the giving of Being. That giving, as a "letting be present," is responded to not in the will of faith, but rather with a letting-be, *Gelassenheit*. *Gelassenheit* responds to the alterity of things manifest in their temporality. The kairos places their future not as a now, but rather as that with which we come face-to-face.

Heidegger's question of Being can itself be understood as an attempt to understand the possibility of Revelation. He thinks Being as that which surprises, which is new, indeed is epochal. It is the transformative newness of Christ as the incarnate God that Greek metaphysics could not think. It is this that, for Heidegger, is the challenge of the phenomenon of Christian Revelation, but also that which gives phenomenological warranty to the thought of the ontological difference. Heidegger never leaves that initial impetus behind, and in his later thought the sacredness of the coming to presence of things in the gathering of the fourfold is understood by a letting-be that responds to kairological temporality by a preparedness for the sending of being. In such an understanding, the crucial distinction is not between things and persons, but between things (and persons) seen in their alterity and things (and persons) reduced to self-sameness (*Gleichheit*). The glory of things is their alterity, their (in each case) singular gathering of the fourfold such that Being is oriented from the thing in each case differently.

Marion, on the other hand, thinks the kairos from the loving gift of God. The conflict of glories and of alterities has its inner source in a phenomenology of love. This also points to that element of Judeo-Christian thought which Heidegger polemicizes against and reduces to the leveling metaphysics of production—namely, creation. Creation, an onto-theological concept par excellence for Heidegger, for Marion manifests that love which reveals the ultimate alterity of the other. As he puts it: "Love of the other repeats creation through the same withdrawal wherein God opens, to what is not, the right to be, and even the right to refuse him" (PC, 167). To think God from Being is, for Heidegger, to think God from the world, not as beyond the world. It is to think God without creation and things as glorifying the event of appearance and not the Creator. If this is idolatry, it is so only on Marion's terms, while if Marion is an onto-theologian, he is so only on Heidegger's terms. Despite their closeness, Marion and Heidegger are separated by a gulf that suggests an untranslatability not of so much of Greek and Christian, but of a phenomenology of the world and a phenomenology of transcendence.

5

Reduced Phenomena and Unreserved Debts in Marion's Reading of Heidegger

Brian Elliott

What Comes Before the Human?

In the question concerning the necessity of grace from Aquinas's *Summa theologiae* we find the following remark: "The free-will of man is moved by an external principle that stands above the human mind, that is, by God" (*quod liberum arbitrium hominis moveatur ab aliquo exteriori principio quod est supra mentem humanum, scilicet a Deo*; q. 109, art. 2).[1] If the ultimate motivator of human free will is God, then the highest object of man's desire, eternal life, must equally be solely within God's gift and never effected by human works. As Augustine says:

> Man cannot by virtue of his natural constitution produce works that stand in the right relation to eternal life. Rather, for this a higher power is needed that is the power of grace. Thus man cannot earn eternal life without grace. Yet he can realize works that lead to some good which is appropriate to man, such as "ploughing the field, drinking, eating, and having a friend." (q. 109, art. 5)

Here the highest human possibility is an impossibility for what is merely human. No matter what efforts of action or comprehension the individual makes, he or she will remain far from the ultimate goal unless something beyond human nature intervenes to grant supernatural aid. But this cannot mean that human works are utterly in vain, so that good deeds would be entirely dispensable. Rather, it is a matter of *what comes first*. The answer is unequivocal: God comes first, man follows.

The question that I wish to pose initially is this: To what extent does Heidegger's thought retain this basic thought of anti- or *ante*-humanism? This question is, I feel, decisive in light of the challenge Jean-Luc Marion has posed to Heidegger's thinking as a whole. The hypothesis I shall put forward to counter this challenge is the following: Heidegger's thought is, from the beginning, motivated by a basic experience analogous to that indicated by the Christian doctrine of divine grace.[2] I shall further argue that it was precisely to preserve this experience as a matter for thought that Heidegger sought an ostensively nontheological articulation of it.

If my hypothesis proves to be warranted, then Marion's reading of Heidegger as a phenomenologist who sought to reduce what he calls givenness to a horizon of being projected by human comprehension would be untenable. For it seems to me that what motivates Marion's ultimate and radical rejection of Heidegger's thought is a suspicion that for the latter, man remains the measure of all things. But this suspicion is one that, despite all of Marion's protestations to the contrary,[3] follows Husserl's rejection of Heidegger's project of fundamental ontology as set out in *Being and Time* (*BT*). According to Husserl, Heidegger was abandoning the true transcendental path of phenomenology in favor of a philosophical anthropology and its attendant relativisms. But to accuse Heidegger of putting man first is less excusable now than it was seventy-five years ago, when the broader context of his thinking both before and after the publication of *BT* remained obscure.

Thrownness and the Third Reduction

In *Reduction and Givenness* (*RG*), in the chapter titled "The Nothing and the Claim," Marion takes up his argument where it left off in a previous chapter dealing with the presence of the ontological difference in *BT*:

> In privileging an indirect path—through *Dasein*—toward Being, the enterprise of 1927 was not able to stage Being directly as a phenomenon, and thus to free the ontological difference as such. Indeed, here the question of Being is always

confused, in principle, with the question of the Being of *Dasein* alone. (*RG*, 167)

A number of responses to this putative confusion immediately suggest themselves. First, what was published as *BT* represents, as Heidegger himself makes clear at the end of the introductory section of that work, only the first two divisions of the first of two projected parts of the work as a whole. For our purposes the crucial unpublished text would have been the third division of part I, titled "Time and Being." Second, even if, as is eminently possible in the case of such an ambitious project, some lack of clarity remained in Heidegger's account of the relations of the different divisions of his projected work, this in no way justifies the claim that there is here a fundamental conceptual confusion "in principle." Finally, if there was indeed a confusion of the question of Being as such with the question of *Dasein*'s being, then in what sense could Heidegger have understood the analytic of *Dasein* as a *preparation*?

In the lecture series *Basic Problems of Phenomenology*,[4] which immediately followed the appearance of *BT*, Heidegger offers a recapitulation of the course of the *Daseinsanalytik* that puts an explication of the ontological difference in first place. Such an explication, he says, is necessary to show how any investigation of Being, as opposed to beings, is at all possible. He then explains why all ontological inquiry must be mediated by a foregoing analysis of *Dasein*:

> Grasping the understanding of Being [*Seinsverständnis*] means, however, understanding initially *that* being to whose ontological constitution the understanding of Being belongs, *Dasein*. The exposition of the basic constitution of *Dasein* is the task of the preparatory ontological analysis of the existential constitution of *Dasein*. (*GA*, 24, 322)

Here Heidegger clearly states that the analytic of *Dasein* is prior only in the sense of forming a necessary passageway through to a clarified understanding of Being as such. How can one assume here that there is a confusion of means and end? The exposition of *Dasein*'s particular way of being is never taken as the ultimate matter of thought by Heidegger; instead, this is Being itself.

Marion's insistence upon a confusion of Being as such with the being of *Dasein* can also be disputed with reference to the basic structure of thrownness (*Geworfenheit*) as this is set out in *BT* itself. It is telling that Marion's reading of *BT* makes no reference to this structure, the motivation for this absence being only too apparent.⁵ As Heidegger himself pointed out in the *Letter on "Humanism"* (1946), the origin of *Dasein*'s projective being is indicated in *BT* under the name of "thrownness":

> ... the project is essentially thrown. What projects in projection is not man, but rather Being itself that destines [*schickt*] man to the existence of *Dasein* as to his essence. This destiny [*Geschick*] realizes itself as the clearing of Being [*ereignet sich als die Lichtung des Seins*] which it is. This clearing provides the nearness of Being. In this nearness, in the clearing of the "there," man dwells as one who exists, without indeed being able today to experience and undertake this dwelling in any genuine way. (*GA*, 9, 337)⁶

The basic line of self-interpretation in 1946 insists that the text published twenty years before cannot be legitimately understood as a form of philosophical humanism where the first and last concern of thought is some isolated being of man. In *BT* itself the notion of thrownness is explicated within a section of the text that deals with the "being-in" of *Dasein*, that is, with the essential situatedness of human existence. The tone is set by the opening description of what Heidegger terms *Befindlichkeit*. After an initial reference to *Dasein*'s constant affective states or moods of various kinds as revealing the "burdensome character" of existence, the following remark is to be found:

> In affectivity [*Gestimmtheit*] *Dasein* is always and already revealed as *that* being to which *Dasein* in its being was given over, to the being which it has to be in the manner of existence. And precisely in the most indifferent and harmless everyday situation can the being of *Dasein* break forth as a naked "That it is and has to be." The pure "that it is" appears, the whence and whither remain in darkness. (*SZ*, 134)⁷

This radical passivity of *Dasein* in the face of the mode of existence that *is given to it to assume* is then referred explicitly to the notion of thrownness:

> This ontological character of *Dasein*, concealed in its whence and whither yet all the more immediately revealed, this "That it is" we term the *thrownness* [*Geworfenheit*] of this being into its there, in such a way that it is the there as Being-in-the-world.

The expression "thrownness" is meant to indicate the *facticity of being given over* [*Faktizität der Überantwortung*]. (*SZ*, 135)

What is noteworthy here in relation to Marion's interpretation in *RG* is that nothing positive is drawn from Heidegger's account of affectivity in relation to the theme of donation. In the passages cited, Heidegger clearly sets out how for him the being of *Dasein* should be viewed as something *given to be assumed*. By dwelling exclusively on the relation of *Dasein*'s constitutional affectivity to the essential nothingness of its being, Marion avoids recognition of the basic fact that *already in BT Heidegger thinks of human existence in terms of gift*. Thus, Marion can manage to render plausible his insistence on a basic confusion of Being with the being of *Dasein* only by focusing on the initial ontic prioritizing of *Dasein* in the preparatory working out of the project of fundamental ontology and then neglecting the central significance of that being's facticity.[8]

This second omission is all the more striking due to the fact that Marion subsequently takes up the very word — *Überantworten* (to be given over) — used by Heidegger in his explication of thrownness in *BT* to illustrate what he, Marion, takes to be "a decisive advance and new ambition" (*RG*, 168) or even a "reversal" (*RG*, 185) in relation to the position of *BT*,[9] this reversal supposedly being indicated by different accounts of nothingness offered by Heidegger in 1929 and 1943/49, respectively. The gloss on this putative reversal in Heidegger's thought, signaled for Marion by the term *Ereignis*, assumes all the more significance insofar as at this point Marion explicitly arrives at one of the key ideas of his later work *Being Given*, namely, the dynamic of claim and response he takes to be operative within all pure givenness:

> With the intervention of the *Ereignis*, the center of gravity shifts: the existential analytic, which claimed to go from beings back to Being, decidedly yields to the event of Being, which alone initiates its phenomenon — if there still is a phenomenon when the "there is" appears. The sole guiding thread for the interpretation of the Nothing as Being issues directly from Being, demands a response from Being, and is accomplished in the *Ereignis*. The passage to Being depends solely on the Being that claims.... Being expresses itself only by claiming, and it therefore gives itself only to a response. (*RG*, 186)

What remains essentially in question here is whether Marion understands himself to be revealing a fundamental dimension of phenomenality absent in Heidegger. The passage just cited indicates that he takes Heidegger to make good his previous sidelining of Being in favor of the being of *Dasein* in the mature period of his *Ereignisdenken*. However, an essential ambiguity with respect to this issue seems present in Marion's following announcement: "After the transcendental reduction and the existential reduction there intervenes the reduction to and of [the pure form of the] call" (*RG*, 197). This ambiguity is then dispelled in the account of the third reduction given in the concluding section of *RG*, according to which

> ... every *I* or even *Dasein* [is reduced] back to its pure and simple figure as an auditor preceded and instituted by the call which is still absolute because indeterminate. It gives the gift itself: the gift of rendering oneself to *or* of eluding the claim of the call. (*RG*, 204)

Here a question arises: In what sense does Marion's identification of a third reduction in truth move not only through but also beyond Heidegger?

The State of Debt and the Site of Givenness

In *Being Given* (*BG*) Marion attempts a revised and deepened account of pure givenness, again in dialogue with Husserl and Heidegger. Once again he takes as his guiding thread not the Husserlian determination of the phenomenon as present intuition but rather the Heideggerian concept of phenomenality as something's showing itself as itself *from itself* (see *BG*, 221). Similarly, Marion conspicuously passes over once again the key "achievement" of *Dasein* that Heidegger calls the "letting-be" (*Seinlassen*) of beings in their phenomenality.[10] Following the line of argument that sees a decisive breakthrough in thought where Being is recognized as absolute in the sense of absolved from all necessary ties to beings (see *RG*, 168), Marion pursues his idea of pure givenness as marked by a radical anteriority in relation to both the gift and that which may receive it. Failing to acknowledge the profound analogy between his idea of givenness and what Heidegger had already recognized in *BT* as the burdensome character of existence, Marion gives the following account of what he calls, after Mauss and Derrida, the debt:

> The debt designates not so much an act or a situation of the self as its state and its definition—possibly its way to be. This func-

tion of the debt is again named difference: the absence of the giver precedes all that he (or she) gives in such a way that the gift already bears as a shadow, in rising into visibility, the mark of its belatedness in relation to what gives it but is lacking from the outset: the giver. (*BG*, 99)

A debt is simply something had from something (*de-habere*), something owed (*de-hibere*). What Marion speaks of as a sense of self in the dative or ablative case (see *BG*, 269) is a state of being that recognizes its absolutely derivative, and thus nonoriginal, status. The origin of my being comes before me, and so my debt to what gives is absolute, without reservation. To grasp my own being as something given in such a way is, for Marion, to testify to the trace of a possible phenomenon that would exceed decisively the bounds of both Husserlian and Heideggerian phenomenology. What is in question here is nothing other than a redefinition of phenomenology in order to admit the phenomenological legitimacy of the revelation of God, and so avoid repeating "the absurd denegation on which metaphysics and the 'question of being' stubbornly insist" (*BG*, 242). Marion indicates the decisive either/or in the following manner:

> The debate is summed up in a simple alternative: Is it necessary to confine the possibility of the appearing of God to the uninterrogated and supposedly untouchable limits of one or the other figure of philosophy and phenomenology, or should we broaden phenomenological possibility to the measure of the possibility of manifestation demanded by the question of God? (*BG*, 242)

To admit the revelation of God as a genuine phenomenological possibility amounts, as the brief concluding section of *BG* states, to freeing phenomenality equally from the horizons of objectivity (Husserl) and of Being (Heidegger). The following conclusion is drawn:

> To let phenomena appear demands not imposing a horizon on them, whatever the horizon might be, since it would exclude some of them. The apparition of phenomena becomes unconditional only from the moment when they are admitted as what they give themselves—givens, purely. (*BG*, 320)

What does it mean to speak of phenomena without horizon, of absolute, unconditional, or unreserved givenness? In explicating the four marks of what he calls the "saturated phenomenon" (the result of what *RG* recognized as the third form of reduction), that is, its *invisibility, insupportability, absoluteness,* and *irregardability,*[11] everything indicates that the phenomenon in question is one not only lacking any horizon but also without any delimitation or definition whatever. Cut adrift from any anchoring in the world of concrete experience, the saturated phenomenon is, like the God of Augustine's *Confessions,* "before the beginning of all time and before everything of which it is even possible to say 'before'" (*quoniam ante primordial saeculorum et ante omne, quod vel ante dici potest*) (1:6, 9). Such anteriority signifies at once an *absence of place and measure,* something radically *alogos—*senseless.[12]

Whereas Heidegger thematizes what Marion would call the idol in the form of the sublime experience that removes us from the commonplace *within the concrete situation of earthly existence,* everything suggests that Marion is calling for recognition of a thoroughly utopic experience. In a line of argument already fully present in his much earlier work *God Without Being* (*GWB*), Marion rejects in principle Heidegger's insistence that the divine needs Being to grant it first of all a possible place of appearance. Marion determines what he calls Heidegger's postmetaphysical "idolatry" in the following way:

> In the beginning and in principle, there advenes neither God, nor a god, nor the *logos,* but the advent itself—Being, with an anteriority all the less shared in that it decides all the rest, since according to and starting from it there literally remains only beings, and nothing other than beings and the nothing. The very question of the ontic priority of "God" can be posed only at the heart of this advent. (*GWB,* 41/*DSE,* 65)

In this text it is already maintained that, for Heidegger, the anteriority of Being is grounded in the anteriority of *Dasein*'s being. But we have seen that this claim cannot be sustained even with respect to Heidegger's earlier thought. With the abandonment of the existential-horizonal perspective, Heidegger's thinking increasingly attests to the ontological dependency or transitivity of human existence. Thus it is not surprising that Marion can privilege the later *Ereignis-denken* over the earlier fundamental ontology. However, what comes to preoccupy Heidegger in the period of his later thought is precisely the issue of situatedness, of the place of human dwelling. The dwelling place becomes in the later Heidegger the situation of encounter where the divine may show itself *in the heart of everyday existence.*[13]

Not only is Marion not disposed to see the accentuation of place in the later Heidegger as a genuine advance in thought, but he also neglects almost entirely the correlative increase in importance accorded to language. Already in *BT,* Heidegger had insisted that all understanding of Being can take place only by means of linguistic articulation and interpretation. The determination of language as the "house of Being" in the *Letter on "Humanism"* two decades later marks the radicalization of this thought.[14] Such a determination, combined with the explicit ante-humanism of the later text, indicates that language here stands for nothing other than the place given to the human being for the encounter with Being and, consequently, the possible advent of the divine.

Through Phenomenology to . . . ?

Heidegger's later essays on language and poetry all indicate one thing: that the sense of human existence is made possible only through the donation of place through language. Marion is thus quite wrong to suggest that his notion of a pure form of givenness marks a genuine step beyond Heidegger's thought. As I see it, what really marks Marion's distance from Heidegger is the former's insistence on the saturated phenomenon as a revelation beyond all frames of reference, all horizons, and all language. The cogency of Marion's insistence on a form of phenomenality beyond all horizons is drawn from his rejection of the idea common to Kant and Husserl that all intuitive givenness requires an intention that constitutes in advance of such givenness an objective field of experience. But in the case of Heidegger such an idea of horizon is precisely *not* in play. For the sense of horizon in Heidegger is not that of predelineated objectivity, but instead that of radically singular finitude. Accordingly, critiques of Husserl's idea of the horizon on the grounds that it precludes phenomena characterized by absolute unpredictability or singularity do not hold for the Heideggerian notion.

Ultimately, therefore, the burden of proof lies with Marion. It is he who must offer a convincing account of the sense of positing a phenomenon beyond all horizons in the face of Heidegger's hermeneutic transvaluation of phenomenology. The main points of Heidegger's early critique of Husserl—rejecting the ideal of scientific presuppositionlessness; insisting on the historical dimension of all thought; affirming the impossibility of the transcendental reduction as a radical severance from factical existence—all this must be directly confronted if Marion's saturated phenomenon is to be accepted as a *phenomenological* phenomenon in any meaningful sense.

On the basis of what Marion has given us so far, this decisive confrontation remains to be realized.

In the absence of such a decisive philosophical engagement, I will return, finally, to the theological register with which I began. For in Marion's dialogue with Heidegger there is something akin to the older theological debates surrounding the relative authority of Scripture and direct revelation. Both thinkers grasp truth as a form of donation, but Heidegger alone recognizes that revelation can make sense only through the effort to attend and respond to what is given in and by language. Again, Heidegger alone acknowledges the need of a place where the truth of revelation would be preserved. The truth of Marion's saturated phenomenon, by contrast, comes like a thief in the silence of the night and is gone by the time light shines upon the earth.

Heidegger's Works Cited

GA: Martin Heidegger, *Gesamtausgabe* (Frankfurt: Klostermann, 1975ff).

GA 4: *Erläuterungen zu Hölderlins Dichtung*, 2nd ed. (1996).

GA 5: "Der Ursprung des Kunstwerkes," in *Holzwege*, 2nd ed. (2003); "The Origin of the Work of Art," in Heidegger's *Basic Writings*, trans. David F. Krell (London: Routledge, 1993).

GA 9: "Brief über den 'Humanismus,'" in *Wegmarken* (1976); "Letter on 'Humanism,'" in *Pathmarks*, trans. William McNeill (Cambridge: Cambridge University Press, 1998).

GA 24: *Grundprobleme der Phänomenologie* (1927/28, 1975); *Basic Problems of Phenomenology*, trans. Albert Hofstadter (Bloomington: Indiana University Press, 1982).

GA 26: *Metaphysische Anfangsgründe der Logik* (1928; 2nd ed., 1990); *The Metaphysical Foundations of Logic*, trans. Michael Heim (Bloomington: Indiana University Press, 1992).

GA 58: *Grundprobleme der Phänomenologie* (1919/20; 1992).

GA 60: *Phänomenologie des religiösen Lebens* (1920/21; 1996).

GA 61: *Phänomenologische Interpretationen zu Aristoteles* (1921; 2nd ed., 1994).

GA 65: *Beiträge zur Philosophie: Vom Ereignis* (1989).

PI: "Phänomenologische Interpretationen zu Aristoteles: Anzeige der hermeneutischen Situation" (Autumn 1922), *Dilthey-Jahrbuch* (1989), pp. 228–74 (also forthcoming as appendix to *Phänomenologische Interpretationen ausgewählter Abhandlungen des Aristoteles zur On-*

tologie und Logik, GA 62, and available edited by G. Neumann [Ditzingen: DeKlam, 2003]); "Phenomenological Interpretations of Aristotle: Indication of the Hermeneutical Situation," in *Supplements: From the Earliest Essays to Being and Time and Beyond*, ed. John van Buren (Albany: State University of New York Press, 2002).

SZ/BT: *Sein und Zeit*, 16th ed. (Tübingen: Niemeyer, 1993); *Being and Time*, trans. John Macquarrie and Edward Robinson (Oxford: Blackwell, 1973).

"Die Sprache," in *Unterwegs zur Sprache*, 10th ed. (Stuttgart: Günther Neske, 1993); "Language," in *Poetry, Language, Thought*, trans. Albert Hofstadter (New York: Harper & Row, 1971).

PART II

Marion: Gift and Reception

6

The Reason of the Gift

Jean-Luc Marion
Translated by Shane Mackinlay and Nicolas de Warren

A Contradiction in Terms

We give without account. We give without accounting, in every sense of the word. First, because we give *without ceasing*. We give in the same way we breathe, every moment, in every circumstance, from morning until evening. Not a single day passes without our having given, in one form or another, something to someone, even if we rarely, if ever, "give everything."[1] Also, we give without keeping account, *without measure,* because giving implies that one gives at a loss, or at least without taking into account either one's time or one's efforts: one simply does not keep account of what one gives. Finally, we give without account because, for lack of time and attention, most of the time we give *without* a clear *consciousness* of our giving, such that we give almost mechanically, automatically, and without knowing it.

The final version of this essay was prepared for the symposium "Givenness and God" (Mater Dei Institute, Dublin, Jan. 10–11, 2003). Since then, it has been published as "La raison du don," *Philosophie* 78 (June 2003): 3–32. Earlier versions were presented at Boston University ("The Consciousness of the Gift, Apr. 28, 2001, Dr. Nicolas de Warren), Université Paris VII ("Conférences Roland Barthes," Feb. 27, 2002, Prof. J. Kristeva), and Università degli Studi di Macerata ("La coscinza del dono," May 10, 2002, Prof. G. Ferretti). The current version has been substantially modified. (Trans.)

So, at first glance, the attitude of giving appears obvious enough, since its exercise is imperceptible; it happens without reflection and without concern. It could be that the gift's very evidence renders any consciousness of the gift and its giving almost superfluous. Thus, there would be nothing more to discuss about the gift, and no essence to interrogate; the gift would simply need to be made. The gift would not give something to reflect on, something of which one would need to become conscious. Instead, it would directly determine an ethical demand and a social obligation. If it still presented a difficulty, it would not be the difficulty of its definition, but of its exercise. For there would be nothing to say about the gift; instead, as with love, it would only be a question of making it.

Yet as soon as it seems to give us certitude, this evidence takes it back again. For these three ways of giving cannot be brought together without contradiction. Indeed, the third way of giving without account—to give without being conscious of it—manifestly cancels the preceding two ways. For if we truly give without ceasing and without measure, how could we not be conscious of it in the end? Reciprocally, if we give without being conscious of it, how could we know that we are giving without ceasing and without measure? More exactly, how can we be assured that this "without ceasing and without measure" makes our gift a true gift, if we are not conscious of it? In short, how can we give without account if we give without rendering an account of it?

But, beyond this formal contradiction, another contradiction takes shape that is incomparably more profound and that puts the gift as a whole in question. Indeed, the gift that claims to give without account in fact always accounts and even accounts too much. The gift gives in such a way that it loses nothing, and is never lost, but always finds its account and is recovered as at least equal to that which it would have remained had it never given anything. In fact and in principle, the gift does not give without account, because at the end of the account, it is always accounted for in one way or another. The gift gives cheaply (*à bon compte*) because it remains intact after having given—it recovers itself as it is. In short, it always finds its account and recovers itself. At the very least, we can always interpret a gift in such a way that it seems to collapse inescapably, not because of an obstacle that comes from elsewhere, but because of the simple fact that it occurs spontaneously and is brought about perfectly. It suffices to analyze its three dimensions—the giver (*le donateur*), the givee[2] (*le donataire*), and the given gift (*le don donné*) — to see how the gift is abolished in favor of its contrary: *the exchange*.

Let us first consider the giver. In fact, he never gives without receiving as much as he gave in return. If he gives and is acknowledged as the giver, he at least receives the givee's recognition, even if his gift is never rendered to him; and, even in the absence of any recognition from the givee, the giver still receives the esteem of those who witness his gift. If by chance he gives without anybody acknowledging him as the giver, perhaps because the gift remains a strictly private affair (without a witness), or perhaps because the beneficiary is unaware of the gift, or rejects it (ingratitude), the giver will still receive esteem from himself (for having been generous and having given freely). This esteem, which is in fact perfectly well deserved, will provide the giver with a sense of self-satisfaction, and thus with the sovereign independence of a wise man. He will feel — justly — that he is morally superior to the miser that he was able to avoid resembling. This gain will compensate in large part for his loss. But, suddenly, the giver has abolished his gift in favor of an exchange — and disappeared as a giver, to become the purchaser of his own esteem. To be sure, this happens at the price of an asset that is lost but then recovered. "A good deed is never wasted" (*Un bienfait n'est jamais perdu*), according to a French proverb.

Let us next consider the givee. In receiving, he receives not only an asset but, especially, a debt. He becomes indebted to his benefactor and therefore is obliged to render to him. If he immediately gives something back for the good received, he will be even — but precisely because he has canceled his debt by substituting an exchange in place of the gift, and thus canceled the gift, which disappears. If he cannot give something back immediately, he will remain obligated in the future, either provisionally or definitively. Throughout the course of his debt, he will have to express his gratitude and acknowledge his dependence. In this instance, he will bring about his release by repaying his debt with his indebted submission, even to the point of taking on the status of a servant before his master. If, perhaps, he denies having received a gift, at the price of a lie and a denial of justice, he will have to argue that it was only a matter of something that was due to him, or that he received nothing. In each of these cases, the givee erases the gift and establishes an exchange in its place — whether real or fictitious is of little importance, since it always ends up abolishing his status as a givee.

Finally, let us examine the given gift, which inexorably tends to erase in itself all trace and all memory of the gesture by which it was given. Indeed, as soon as it is given, that which is given, whatever it may be, imposes its presence, and this evidence obfuscates the act by which it is delivered. The given gift occupies the whole stage of the giving givenness, and relegates this givenness to the nonactuality of its past. If we must always remind ourselves to thank a benefactor before taking possession of the gift (as we constantly remind small children), this is less because of bad manners than because of phenomenological necessity. The gift captivates all our attention and thus annuls its provenance. As soon as it is possessed, as soon as its receipt is confirmed, the given gift is detached from its giver; in one blow, it loses its status of being given in givenness, appearing instead in its pure and naked market value. The gift is judged in terms of its price, cleansed of the giver's intention, becoming again an autonomous object endowed with its own exchange value: it is ready to return to the commercial circuit (to be resold, exchanged, "cashed in"). As soon as it is given, the gift disappears as a given gift, to be solidified in its value as an object for possible—and hence almost inevitable—exchange.

How can one not conclude that the gift, as soon as it becomes actual and appears in the cold light of day, is inescapably transformed into its contrary, according to a threefold assimilation to exchange and commerce? How can one not conclude that this self-suppression implies a radical phenomenal instability that gives the gift the appearance of a phenomenon but leaves it incapable of being constituted as an objective phenomenon? The gift contradicts itself by a contradiction in terms—a contradiction in terms of exchange.

Either the gift appears as actual but disappears as a gift, or it remains a pure gift but becomes unapparent, nonactual, excluded from the instance of things, a pure idea of reason, a simple noumenon incompatible with the conditions of experience. That which appears according to the real conditions of actual experience must, from the gift that it was, be cashed in as an exchange. Either the gift remains true to givenness but never appears or it does appear, but in the economy of an exchange, where it is transformed into its contrary—to be precise, into an exchange, a given that is returned (*do ut des* [I give so that you will give]), something given for a return and returned for a given, part of the trade and management of goods. Exchange is imposed as the truth of the gift, and cancels it. By submitting itself to an economy, the gift exchanges its essence as gift for an actuality that denies it—precisely in exchange. For an economy economizes the gift.[3]

The Economy

Does this critique of the gift—perhaps so effective because so abstract—in turn escape criticism? Obviously, it is open to a counterattack, since it rests on at least one unexamined presupposition: namely, that the gift implies a perfect and pure gratuity, in which it is necessary to give for nothing, without there ever being a return.

However, the postulate of gratuity is debatable. First, because for both the giver and for the givee, to receive or to grant a reward that is moral (esteem or recognition), symbolic (obligation), and therefore unreal (not a thing, nothing to do with value or a price) is not purely and simply equivalent to a real reimbursement (an amount, a thing, an asset). Indeed, to confuse the two kinds of gains—received or given—implies annulling all difference between the real and the unreal, and between the thing and the symbol. Suspended between cynicism (which realizes the unreal) and idealism (which dismisses the thing), such a description simplifies the specificity of the phenomena that are at stake here to the point where it annihilates them.

Moreover, it is not evident that the gift disappears as soon as the least satisfaction accompanies it. One may very well be satisfied as a result of a gift, without that satisfaction having been foreseen and preceding the gift as its motivation, or anticipating it as its prior intention. It is entirely possible to discover that we are happy to have given or received, without that giving or receiving having been done solely with the aim of being happy. It could even be that we receive this satisfaction only because we have *not* looked for it, nor forecast it, nor foreseen it—in short, it could be that satisfaction engulfs us precisely because it happens to us unexpectedly, as a bonus (*par surcroît*). The joy of a gift does not motivate the gift any more than it precedes it; rather, it is added to it each time, as a grace that is unexpected, unforeseeable, and in a sense undeserved.

Finally, how is one to avoid suspecting that to require such a strict purity of the gift would imply its absolute independence from every possible other (*autrui*)? This purity would finally lead to a total independence in which not only exchanges and gifts are prohibited, but also alterity in general. Also, how can one not have the feeling that such gratuity would put in question, along with the alterity of the gift's other (*l'altérité de l'autre du don*), the very selfhood of the ego, which I put at stake as giver or givee? In the end, to give with full gratuity, without desire, would we not have to annul our selfhood — or, on the contrary, claim to be a god? At the very least, wouldn't this so-called gratuity be reduced to a pure and simple indifference that, with eyes closed, gave nothing to anyone and received nothing from anyone?[4]

The aporias of gratuity seem so obvious that we should never have been ignorant of them: if the gift contradicts itself when we impose gratuity on it, why have we made that imposition? Of course, there is an excellent reason to do so: because gratuity seems to be — and, in a sense yet to be determined, actually is — the best defense against the economic process of exchange, its absolute contrary. But in what way is gratuity exempted from the economy? To this first question, a second must be added: Why must the gift disappear as soon as it satisfies the conditions of gratuity, as if being exempted from the economy were the equivalent of being excluded also from experience in general? What could the requirements of exchange and of the economy have in common with the conditions of possibility of experience? In fact, they end up coinciding, provided that we reconstitute several stages of their convergence.

First of all, an economic process presupposes and produces an equality of exchange:

> In exchanging, it is necessary that each party should agree to the quantity and quality of each of the things exchanged. In this agreement it is natural that each should desire to receive as much, and to give as little, as he can.[5]

It remains to be understood where the power of this equality comes from and how it almost inevitably extends its empire. It is, of course, not only an issue that concerns formal rigor, nor even the requirements of honesty. Rather, it is an issue of a theoretical possibility. According to Cournot:

> Whatever man can measure, calculate, and systematise, ultimately becomes the object of measurement, calculation, and system. Wherever fixed relations can replace indeterminate, the substitution finally takes place. It is thus that the sciences and all human institutions are organised.

Thus, he continues, "as the abstract idea of wealth . . . constitutes a perfectly determinate relation, like all precise conceptions it can become the object of theoretical deductions."[6] Measure (mathematical quantification) makes equality possible, and therefore also makes exchange possible. In these conditions, the gift becomes an object by the exchange that "equalizes" it—an object of exchange, and therefore an object of commerce, according to "the abstract idea of *value in exchange*, which supposes that the objects to which such value is attributed *are in commercial circulation*."[7] Commerce allows the exchange of goods only by fixing a measure of equality between objects of value. However, it fixes these measures of equality in terms of value only because it has already determined the gift in terms of exchange. Now, these terms of exchange are in turn constituted as objects by a measure that arranges them according to equalities and equivalents, and thus puts them in an order. Consequently, the gift enters into exchange and commerce because it is transcribed in terms of an economic exchange and thereby transposed in terms of an object.

We thus understand how the economy can fix the conditions of possibility of experience for objects of exchange: it deploys and puts directly into play the requirements of the *mathesis universalis*, according to its strictest Cartesian definition. Order imposes exchange, and measure guarantees equality in the field of the gift, which thereby becomes problematic as such, even aporetic, insofar as it is converted into an exchange. Either the gift arrives at its concept—exchange—and satisfies its proper conditions of possibility, or it remains gratuitous—that is, without order or measure—and thus contradicts the conditions of its possibility. The gift can be thought only by being transposed into an exchange—in accordance with the properly metaphysical requirements of rationality.[8]

The abolition of the gift, such that it passes into the (measured) equality of exchange, also defines the conditions of possibility of its appearance in experience. For the equality of exchange matters only to the extent that it renders a reason (*rend raison*)[9] for its possibility and its actuality in experience. The economy thus claims to measure exchange on the level of reason, and to render reason to it. Every exchange will have its reason, for no longer will anything be exchanged in vain. In fact, the "economy strives not to consume anything in vain," since what is at issue in "political economics," as in every other science (even human sciences), is a "way of connecting effects to causes"—in this case by means of exchange, which alone defines value.[10] In an economy, just as elsewhere, to render reason allows one to render account, because reason calculates, restores equality, and provides self-identity—which in this instance is value.

The Reason of the Gift ■ *107*

Reason renders reason because it identifies the conditions of exchange, and therefore assigns conditions to possibility and justifies wealth (as with so many other phenomena) as an effect, by attributing adequate causes to it.

That the equality of exchange renders reason to the economy was in fact confirmed by Marx *a contrario*. Marx objects to the "jurist's consciousness [that] recognises in this [comparison between exchanges involving labour and all other exchanges], at most, a material difference, expressed in the juridically equivalent formulae: *Do ut des, do ut facias, facio ut des, facio ut facias* [I give so that you will give, I give so that you will act, I act so that you will give, I act so that you will act]" and insists on a contrary view:

> Capital, therefore, is not only, as Adam Smith says, the command over labour. It is essentially the command over *unpaid labour* . . . a definite quantity of other people's unpaid labour.

In so doing, Marx not only unveils the mechanism of "the secret of profit making" but also, by denying the supposed equality in the exchange between salary and labor, destroys the whole "political economy."[11] Thus, the economy as such consists in restoring equality between the terms of exchange in order to provide this phenomenon—the exchange—with the means of satisfying the conditions of its possibility and thereby actually appearing.[12]

Thus, exchange suffices for rendering reason—rendering its due to the gift (in the economy) and rendering its cause to the effect (in experience). Reason always suffices, and its sufficiency restores equality, intelligibility, and justice. In principle, nothing has the right to exempt itself from the demand of reason. Every pronouncement, every action, every event, every fact, every object, and every being[13] must furnish a response to the question that asks it why? διότι? *cur*? Even the very simplest of ideas must do this, even God[14]; therefore, even—especially—the gift. On the contrary, if the gift rests on gratuity, sufficient reason cannot but economize it, precisely in the name of the economy in which reason carries on. Consequently, sufficient reason owes it to itself to exclude the gift from experience, and therefore from phenomenality: one must render invisible everything for which one cannot render reason—and first of all the gift.

In this way, one can understand the annulment of gratuity by the economy. Rendering reason to the gift means demonstrating that no one gives without rendering account, nor without rendering an account for it—thus, without being reimbursed, in either real or symbolic terms. In short, it means demonstrating that one gives only with an account, and for the sake of satisfaction. Sufficient reason can indeed always seize the gift by assigning a reason of exchange to each of its moments. The gift's self-contradiction, which I have formally indicated above, can then be repeated more concretely, in the form of a threefold response to the demand of sufficient reason. To arrive at this interpretation, it suffices to distinguish between external reasons (or causes) and internal reasons (or motives).

The giver does not give gratuitously because, as we have seen, he is always reimbursed, either in real or in symbolic terms. But most of all, one can cancel the giver's merit by arguing that he has given only what he was able to give, and thus that he has given from his surplus. By definition, he was able to dispose of this surplus, and therefore it did not really belong to him. By giving it, he has merely redistributed an excess of property that he had unjustly confiscated. In principle, the duty of justice obliged the giver to distribute that which—in all justice—did not belong to him. In claiming to give, he has done nothing more than fulfill his duty of justice. Justice, which is the motive (internal reason) for the apparent gift, explains it and commands it as a simple duty. Consequently, the giver's claim to gratuity, and even the gift's entitlement to be called such, collapse in the face of a simple duty of justice—the duty to render to each his account, his due.

Reciprocally, the givee can put forward sound motives for receiving an asset as part of a simple exchange and denying that he is the beneficiary of a gift. It suffices for him to maintain that this supposed gift has come about simply as his due. Consider the case where I find that I am impoverished and in real need—I am destitute. This means not only that I am in need, but that I need that which I lack because my condition as a human being requires it—necessarily and by right. On the basis of human rights, I have the right (and not simply the need) to nourishment, to clothing, to housing, and even to earn a salary. Therefore, that which public or private assistance might give me is delivered as my due, and no longer as a gift. Not only would there not be a question of gratuity, but gratuity would do me injury and an injustice. I claim my due in virtue of a right, and those who give me my due owe it to me by virtue of a duty that is imposed on them in accordance with an objective right. In fact, if they abandon me to my misery, they would put at risk not only my life but also my humanity, which they would debase to animality.

By the same token, they would lose their own humanity by abolishing mine. They must render reason to the humanity that is in me, but also in themselves. If they do not come to my rescue (by simple solidarity among fellow human beings), they put at risk their own status as human beings and their ethical dignity as subjects with rights. Thus, by giving me what I need in order to remain a human being, others only fulfill their duty. They do not give me a gift, but render to me what is due, which in return guarantees their own human dignity. It is a question of an exchange—symbolic, to be sure—between my humanity and theirs. However, the symbol is here infused with the highest possible reality, for it reunites us in the same equality, the same humanity. The gift is abolished in that which is due, and gratuity is abolished in solidarity. All that is operative is the symbolic exchange of sociality—the ultimate economy.

If we now consider, beyond motives (internal reasons), the causes (external reasons), we can in the same way draw the given gift (the object itself, the thing) back into the economy. Let us take a banal example: when a "humanitarian" organization (to avoid calling it "charitable") or a local community association "gives" (let us accept this problematic term for the moment) food, clothing, housing, or employment ("social" or reserved jobs), that organization certainly distributes these goods gratuitously, without payment or an economic transaction. However, this does not mean that these goods have no value for exchange, no market price. On the contrary, to dispense these goods gratuitously, they must be produced and distributed; that is, procured. How? Obviously, by means of gifts: the surplus of individuals, the unsold stock of businesses, or subsidies from community funds. In each case, it is a matter of consumable goods and equipment, with a market value that is calculable with precision and already inscribed in the economic sphere.

These goods and values are removed from the economic sphere by those who, having acquired or produced them within the economy, part with them at an economic loss (pure gratuity, or gratuity mixed with realism—these goods having become useless, unsalable, depreciated in value, etc.). During the period of time in which they are under the control of "humanitarian" associations—that is, until their redistribution—these goods remain outside the economy, with their exchange value neutralized. However, as soon as they are given, they recover this value; and it is precisely for this reason that they are a real assistance to those in need, in that these people are provided with goods for which they do not have to pay a price, but which nevertheless have an exchange value, a value in the economy. The advantage of the "humanitarian" stage of this process obviously does not lie in a definitive suspension of the exchange cycle, nor in an illusory escape from the economy. On the contrary, the advantage lies in the goods finally being reinscribed in the economy, almost gratuitously, in what is close to a neutralization of the exchange. The short moment in which the exchange is suspended (the gift in a strict sense) is directed solely toward finally reinscribing the gift in the economy, and thus making it *disappear* as a gift.

Moreover, the moment of the gift—which is now to be regarded as provisional—is not the first to suspend the economy. On the contrary, the first to do this is the poverty of the one who is poor, which excludes him from entering into exchange, thus canceling the economy, because it does not operate here (*annulait par défaut l'économie*). Therefore, the gift suspends (in a second and positive way) only the initial suspension (the poverty of the first instance); then, by paying on behalf of the one who is insolvent, it reinstates him in the cycle of exchange. The gift is therefore not a gift, in two senses: first, because in the end it restores the economy; second, because it "buys back" (so to speak) poverty and need by providing them with the means for paying, buying, and exchanging anew. Hence, the gift labors for the economy's reinstatement, and not at all for its suppression. The gift restores the poor person's former unbalanced accounts in order to allow him to render accounts anew—in short, to render reason for future exchanges. Thus we often speak of these "humanitarian" associations not only as an associative *economy* but also as vehicles for integration. Integration into what, if not into the economy? The moment of the gift not only is provisional, but appears in the end as a wayward economic agent—a cause or reason, and so powerful that it restores the economy at the very point where it was blocked.

The gift, in its three figures, can and even must (by virtue of a simple care for social functioning) either allow itself to be drawn back into an exchange (justice between giver and givee) or work toward reinstating exchange (insertion by the gift). Hence, it must be abolished in the economy that it restores, rather than being exempted from it. There is therefore always a motive or cause for submitting the gift to an economic interpretation and rendering it reason according to exchange. Either the gift remains provisional and a simple appearance, or it appears, but as an object and according to an exchange, by satisfying sufficient reason, which assimilates it into the economy. The economy economizes the gift because it renders it reason sufficiently.

Reducing the Gift to Givenness

After all this, is it possible to understand the gift as it is given and spoken—that is, as a gift—without in the end rendering it to economic reason or dissipating it in the phantom of an empty gratuity? Such an understanding would demand, at the very least, preserving the gift from the logic that demands not that it give what it claims to give, but instead that it give *reasons* for giving (or, rather, for *not* giving). In other words: How is it possible to avoid compelling the gift to render itself to a reason that authorizes it only by canceling it? The gift is unthinkable in the economy because it is interpreted there as necessarily being a relationship of giving–giving, like an exchange of gifts, where the first gift is recovered in the gift that is returned for it, and where the returned gift is registered as the return on the initial gift (*do ut des*). Paradoxically, the gift is lost here because it does not manage really to give at a loss—in short, it is lost because it has lost the freedom to be lost. Consequently, how is one to conceive of a gift as such: a lost gift that has lost its head, a loss without return—and nevertheless not without a thinkable meaning, even a certain reason adapted to it?

Evidently, we will not arrive at an answer to this question as long as we investigate the gift in terms of exchange and describe it on the economic horizon. We will succeed only if we stop approaching the gift as a concealed exchange that is yet to be interpreted according to economic reason—either as an unconscious exchange or as a supposedly gratuitous exchange (presuming that this is not a contradiction in terms). In short, we will succeed only if we think the gift as such, irreducible to exchange and economy. However, if the gift is not related to exchange, even as an exception to it, we would have to be able to think it starting from precisely that which exchange abolishes—that is, excess and loss, which are in fact the same thing. But we can do justice to excess and loss, and therefore to the gift as such, only by leaving the horizon of exchange and economy.

But is there any other horizon than this, and how is one to identify it? This other horizon could be discovered—if that is to be done without illusion or arbitrariness—only starting from the gift itself, or rather from the point where its phenomenon wells up just before it is dissolved into exchange, during the fragile moment where its three moments are not yet rendered to the economy's sufficient reason. We can discover this other horizon only by restraining the phenomenon of the gift from sliding down into an exchange, and by maintaining it in itself; that is, by reducing the gift to itself, hence to givenness, which is the gift's own proper horizon.

Givenness is opened as a horizon only to the extent that we reduce the gift to it, in the double sense of drawing the gift back to givenness and of submitting the gift to a phenomenological reduction by establishing it in givenness. Yet, givenness is not self-evident and, because it always precedes the gift, it seems to us that it is even less accessible than is the gift. Nevertheless, we can presume that if givenness opens a horizon for the gift, it will testify to itself at least by not immediately assigning the gift to a social process or an ethical behavior (even if it eventually does this), but rather by allowing the gift to appear without requiring that it be dissolved into exchange. In order to appear, the gift reduced to givenness would only have to be given—no more and no less—without having to render reason for itself by coming back to a revenue and making the least return on investment. That would mean describing the gift without reconstituting the terms of exchange; that is, without the two terms that are the minimum basis for any exchange. For, if the giver were to give without a givee to acknowledge this, or if the givee were to receive without any giver to honor, or even if both the giver and the givee were to exchange no given thing, then in each case one of the conditions of possibility of an exchange would be missing, and the gift would be brought about absolutely and as such. Let us attempt such a threefold description of a gift that is liberated from the terms of exchange.

First, a gift can be brought about as a gift without any giver being rewarded (in either real or symbolic terms), because it can be brought about without any giver at all. To see this, it suffices to analyze the hypothesis of a gift that is received from an anonymous or even nonexistent giver. These two conditions in fact coincide in the case of an inheritance, where death steals the giver, forbidding that anything at all be rendered to him. By definition, I am so much unable to render anything to him that this very impossibility constitutes the condition of the gift that is made to me. Indeed, it needs the testator's death for the will to come into effect; thus, it is necessary that I have no one to thank if I am to be able to receive the gift he gives me. The testator will not receive recognition from me (nor recognition of a debt), since he will no longer be here to enjoy it; and, if I declare my recognition, this will be before precisely that social group that knew him, yet of which he is no longer part. It could even happen that I receive the gift of this inheritance without the testator having wanted that, and even against his intentions, because either he was completely unknown to me up until that point, or I to him, with only a genealogical inquiry having led his executor to me. In each of these cases, the giver is lacking, thus excluding recognition and reimbursement. Nevertheless, the gift is brought about perfectly. Therefore, it appears fully, even though it is unexpected, undeserved, unpaid, without recognition or return. On the contrary, it takes on its full meaning in the very absence of motive and sufficient reason.

Second, the gift can be brought about as a gift without a givee of any sort. To establish this, would it not suffice to take the argument from anonymity again, this time applying it to the givee? Indeed, in the vast majority of cases, when we contribute to a "humanitarian" organization, we do not know the individual person who is going to benefit from our help. The organization mediates our gift, such that we remain anonymous to the givee, who in turn is anonymous to us. The gift is carried out even though no givee is made known, such that, by definition, he or she can never render anything to me. However, this argument from anonymity could be contested by arguing that here, in the final instance, it is not a question of a gift, because the intermediary (the association)—even if it does its work scrupulously (distributing contributions, helping efficiently)—precisely refuses to make a gift by rendering the recipients anonymous and merging them into the crowd of those who are helped. As we have seen in the preceding section, here it is more a question of solidarity and what is due by right than it is a question of a gift.

There is still another case where a gift is brought about perfectly, with a clearly identified givee, without, however, any risk that he will be able to make a reimbursement and thus transform the gift into an exchange: the case where I give to an enemy. Whether an enemy is private or public matters little, since in either case the hate he bears toward me will make him return my gift with an insult, and every claim to generosity with additional humiliation. Not only will he not render a gift in return for mine; not only will he deny that there is even a gift at issue; but he will also foster a still greater hate for me. He will return the favor I give him (*il me rendra la monnaie de ma pièce*), inverting the debt a hundredfold. I will deserve to be even more hated by him, because I have wanted to make him benefit from my wealth, to render him slave to my protection, to overpower him by my generosity, and so on.[15] He will therefore take vengeance on me in order to free himself from the least obligation of recognition. He will kill me rather than acknowledge that he owes me the least recognition. Even so, is my gift compromised by this? Not at all, for a gift that is scorned and denied, even transformed into an affront, nonetheless remains perfectly and definitively given; this desolation even makes it appear with a more sovereign force. It is only to an enemy that I can make a gift without risk of finding it taken up in an exchange or trapped in reciprocity. Paradoxically, only my enemy takes care of the gift by protecting it from a relationship of giving–giving. Whoever gives to his enemy does so without return, without anything coming back, and without sufficient reason—incontestably.

Third, the gift can be brought about without giving any object that can be brought back to an exchange value. Indeed, what can I give that is more precious than such a gift? Without doubt, there is nothing more precious than my attention, my care, my time, my faith, or even my life. And, in the end, the other person expects nothing less and can hope for nothing more. Nor I from him. For in giving these nonobjective gifts, which elude being either understood or possessed, which supply no gain or assignable return, and which really provide *nothing* (*nothing real; ne rem*), I in fact give myself in my most complete selfhood. In giving this *nothing*, I give all that I have, because I am not giving something that I possess apart from myself, but rather that which I am. Hence, the paradox that I give (myself) more, the more I give nothing: the given gift does not consist in a substrate or a real predicate. Therefore, from here on, I am giving outside the horizon of possession (and dispossession) of anything whatever, and therefore outside both objectness (*objectité*) and the reason that could render an account for the gift.

It should not be objected that by giving no object, I would give less, or would even dispense with actually giving at all. On the contrary (and here the argument repeats itself), I am excused from really giving—that is, from giving *myself*, me in person—when I settle for giving an object in place of myself. Thus, I give money in order to be excused from giving my time and attention. I pay into an annuity in order to be excused from having to love, and so regain my liberty. What happens, for example, when I give a woman a magnificent piece of jewelry? Two hypotheses: Either I give her this object alone, but in order to admit to her that I am leaving her or that I do not really love her (i.e., to settle accounts); or I give it to her as an indication that I love her irrevocably, thus simply as a sign of the true gift, which remains nonobjectifiable and invaluable—the gift of my time, my attention, my faith, my life—in short, the gift of myself. This is a gift that I can give only symbolically now, since it will require the entire duration of my lifetime to carry it out in reality.[16] In summary, either the object that is given remains alone and signifies the denial of the full gift (the gift of self), or it is presented as a simple indication and marks the promise of the full gift (this same gift of self), which is always still unaccomplished. Every gift that is given—insofar as it implies more than actuality—must become unreal, nonobjectifiable, and invaluable.

Thus, the gift, in its three moments, can be reduced to the givenness in it and can dispense with itself—and it can do this all the better when it lacks one of the terms of reciprocity and is freed from that to which the economy attempts to debase it in each instance: the giving-giving relation of exchange. The gift is given more perfectly the more it is ignorant either of the giver who is compensated by his (good) conscience, or of the givee who is freed from all consciousness (of debt), or of the given that is recoverable as an exchange value by a (commercial) consciousness. The gift is reduced to givenness by being brought about without any consciousness of giving (*conscience*[17] *de don*)—without the self-consciousness that would make it render reason of its accounts and multiply reciprocity. The gift reduced to givenness has no consciousness of what it does; it has hands to do it with, but it does it only on condition that the right hand does not know what the left hand is doing.

The Case of the Gift: Fatherhood

However, this result may still raise a concern. Does it not prove too much, and too quickly, for it to offer a rational argument—is it not simply a question of a polemical response? Does not bracketing each term of the exchange, aside from avoiding reciprocal exchange, come at the price of the disappearance of all of the gift's real process? Does not suspending the exchange's sufficient reason also entail the abolition of all rationality of the gift itself? For we have arrived at an outright contradiction: instead of being defined in relation to the givee, the giver would give all the better by disappearing (as unknown or deceased) from the givee's view; the givee, far from appearing by dealing with his debt, would appear all the better by denying it (as anonymous or an enemy); and that which is given, far from being concretized in a manifest object, would appear all the better by evaporating into the unreal or the symbolic (as an indication). Under the pretext of clarifying the gift in light of its givenness alone, have we not, rather, dissolved phenomenality? In short, does not the would-be phenomenological reduction of the gift to its givenness in the end prohibit it from even having the dignity of a phenomenon?

This difficulty cannot be dodged, but neither should it be overestimated, for it is the consequence, essentially, of beginning the examination at the wrong point. We began our inquiry into the gift by starting with its contrary—exchange—and we recovered proper access to it only by disqualifying that which prevented it—reciprocity. Having left the economic point of view, and making our way through the debris of exchange, we continue to be entangled there at the very moment when we are doing our best to free ourselves from it. Thus, we may need to attempt a direct description, starting from itself, of a phenomenon of the same kind as the gift, but this time inscribed from the outset on the horizon of givenness: a phenomenon that could never allow itself to be recaptured by the economic horizon, a gift that is always already reduced and drawn back to givenness, free of any degradation into economy, born free of sufficient reason. In short, a gift that is naturally reduced to givenness, an exceptional case where the difficulty would not consist in overcoming the natural attitude so as to carry out the reduction but, rather, in face of a phenomenon that is already (naturally) reduced, in reconstituting it (so to speak), starting from that to which it is reduced. Which phenomenon would be able to satisfy this inverted description of appearing *only as always already reduced?* Let me suggest one: *fatherhood*.

Fatherhood is undeniably a phenomenon, since it appears wherever people live; it is a phenomenon that is regularly observable, since it stretches over the duration of each lifetime; finally, it is unchallengeable, since no human being can claim not to have experienced it. No one can deny it, least of all those who themselves are either fatherless or childless, since the phenomenon is even more apparent in such absences, as we shall see. Fatherhood (provided that we do not bring it down to exchange straightaway) never puts itself forward as a simple biological product of procreation, nor as a primary interest group, nor as an elementary political category. Doubtless, fatherhood is connected to all of these things, but only after the fact, once it is subjected to an economic interpretation in terms of exchange, according to which it is a first stage in a series of increasingly complex communities that lead, in principle, up to the state. However, no matter how powerful and widely accepted this interpretation might be, it still belongs to metaphysics and, above all, it conceals the determinations of the gift, in the form in which it appears on the horizon of givenness.

First of all, as with every phenomenon, fatherhood appears insofar as it gives itself. But it gives *itself*, unlike most other phenomena, *insofar as it gives*.[18] Fatherhood manifests all the given phenomenon's characteristics, though they are exhibited not only in the mode of a given but also in the mode of a giving. For if fatherhood did not give, neither would it give itself as a phenomenon that shows itself. Thus, it gives, but with a style that is absolutely remarkable and proper to it.

Fatherhood does indeed give, but *without being able to be foreseen*; for the intention to procreate is never enough for procreation to happen, any more than the intention not to procreate is a guarantee against its happening. Again, fatherhood gives, but *without cause* and without any univocally assignable reason. This is proved by the inability of demographic science to calculate the evolution of the fertility rate or to anticipate long-term population growth or decline. This inability is so pronounced that demographic science resorts to the unquantifiable consideration of psychological, cultural, and even religious factors that at best allow a simple intelligibility a posteriori but never a serious forecast. Thus, fatherhood produces—or, rather, produces itself—as an *event* and not as a simple fact: welling up from pure possibility, it does not produce a finished result, determined and concluded once it is delivered, but rather brings about a possibility (the child), whose future, in turn, cannot be foreseen, nor deduced from causes, nor anticipated, but must be waited for.

All these determinations also characterize the phenomenon in general, considered as given,[19] except for one decisive difference. Here, the phenomenon that is given also gives, and thus lays claim to an exemplary role among all given phenomena: that of the given that itself gives (*donné donnant*). That the given gives not only itself, but also a given other than itself, implies the opening of an uncontrollable excess, growth, and negative entropy, which misery, death, and fear are not enough to extinguish (on the contrary, in fact). Simply put, here the given always and necessarily gives something other than itself, and thus more than itself; it proves to be uncontrollable and inexhaustible, irrepressible and impossible (in other words, it makes possible the impossible), having neither master nor god. But there is more, for the given gives insofar as it phenomenalizes both itself and that which it gives. This means that the visible itself—in fact, nothing less than the sum of all the phenomena visible up until this point—

will also grow, with an irrepressible, incalculable, and inexhaustible excess that nothing will conquer. By giving itself and showing itself, fatherhood in principle gives and manifests more than itself; the event of its arrival in the visible thus provokes a phenomenal event that is endless by right. Nowhere else does the given's character (*Gegebenheit*)—in other words, the character of appearing in the mode of the given (which would almost deserve the neologism "givenence" [*donnéité*][20])—announce itself as clearly as here, thus conferring on fatherhood an exceptional phenomenological privilege.

However, this exceptional privilege (the highest form of givenness) is echoed or balanced by another characteristic, which can only be conceived negatively, at least upon first glance. This very phenomenon that gives itself in giving cannot, for its part, give itself without first having been given to itself—that is, received from elsewhere; namely, from a(nother) father. But the father's gift brings about anew the threefold paradox of the gift reduced to givenness.

First, the giver remains essentially absent and bracketed here. For *the father is missing*. To start with, the father is missing because he procreates in only a moment and, having become useless, withdraws immediately—in contrast to the mother, who remains, and in whom the child remains. The mother's immanence to the child stigmatizes the father's unfortunate transcendence. The father is also missing later because he leaves (must leave), and attracts the child's attention by—in principle—being lacking to him. Not that he always leaves like a paradoxical thief, forcibly abandoning mother and child. Rather, he is lacking because he can never merge with the given child (in contrast to the mother, who can, and even must, do this for a time), since he can remain united with the child only by taking leave—precisely so as then to pass on his help: as extroverted provider, hunter, warrior, or traveler; in short, as one who constantly returns, coming back to the hearth from which he must distance himself if he wants to maintain it. In order to live there, the father must be missing, and thus shine by his absence. He appears insofar as he disappears.[21] Finally, and most of all, the father is missing because (in consequence of the previous two absences) his fatherhood can never rely on an immediate empirical confirmation. Even a genetic identification is mediated (since it requires time, instruments, and study), and still results in a juridical process of recognition (or denial) of paternity: inevitably, the father remains putative. This does not mean that he conceals or disavows himself as father, but rather that he can declare himself only by recognizing—necessarily after the fact—the child whom he could, by definition, never know from the outset. He can claim the child as his (therefore also deny him) only with a delay, through a mediate word and a juridical declaration. He can really give a father to his child only by giving to him again—after the gift of biological life that is always somewhat random—this time, a status and a name: in short, an identity. This symbolic identity must be constantly given again, endlessly, in every moment, and can be made secure only by repeating it until the end. The father must spend his whole lifetime giving and regiving identity to his child; this identity is his child's status as gift without return, but also without certainty. Fatherhood, or the redundancy of the gift that lacks. For these three reasons—withdrawal, departure, and redundancy—the father appears as the giver who is perfectly reduced to givenness: the bracketed giver.

Second, the gift reduced to givenness is further confirmed in the phenomenon of fatherhood in that the child, however much he appears to be a givee (par excellence, since he receives not only a gift but also himself as the gift of a possibility), by definition cannot make good on the least consciousness of a debt. Indeed, no matter how deeply he is moved by the feeling of indebtedness, nor how earnestly filial piety is sometimes at work in him, nor how seriously he strives to correspond to the father's gift, an obstacle always stands in the way. It is not a question here of subjective ingratitude or of empirical hate, though these are always possible and at least looming. It is a more radical question of an in principle impossibility. Whether he wants to or not, whether he feels bound to it or not, the child can never "render," and will remain ungrateful, inadequate, and inconsiderate, because it will never be given to him to render to his father what he has received from him—life. The child can render him time, care, and attention (watching over his advanced years, ensuring that he is lacking nothing, surrounding him with affection, etc.), possibly until the very end; but the child will never be able to give him life in return at the hour of his death. At best, the child will render a peaceful death to his father, but he will never give back (or render) him life.

It should not be objected that the child will be able to give life in turn. True, the child may be able to do this, but whomever he may give it to, it will not be to his father. For he, too, will give it to those who, by the same principle, will be able to give it only to their own children, and never to their father. These children will, in turn, be exposed as givees who are absent and, in turn, installed as givers who are missing. This is how the arrow of time is pointed, with a genuinely original differance (from which even the differance of the delay of intuition also derives). The child responds adequately, even justly, to the father—the giver who is missing—only by avowing himself to be a givee who defaults. Genealogy extends onward by virtue of these ineluctable impossibilities of rendering the gift, of closing the gift that is reduced to givenness back into the loop of exchange.

As for the gift that is given in fatherhood, at this point it goes without saying that it can in no way be converted into an object or a being (whether a subsistent being or a utensil being does not matter). The father gives nothing to the child other than life (and a name that sanctions this). The given gift is reduced here precisely to life, which, exactly because it renders possible—and potentially actual—every being and every object, itself belongs neither to beingness (*l'étantité*) nor to objectness (*l'objectité*). Life is not, since nothing is without it; it is not seen, or defined, or grasped as something real—as one thing among others. A corpse lacks nothing real that would allow it to be distinguished from the living—"he almost looks like he could talk" (*il ne lui manque que la parole*), as one says of someone who has just died. But speech is not one real thing among others; it triggers things by naming them and, making them appear, it never itself appears as a thing. Life that is given does not appear, is not, and is not possessed. It gives us our appearing, our being, and our possessing of ourselves. In it, the gift is perfectly reduced to givenness—that nothing which tears everything away from nothingness.

Fatherhood thus lays out, in fact and by right, the whole phenomenality of a gift reduced to pure givenness. With fatherhood, the giver is manifested even insofar as he is absent, the givee insofar as he defaults, and the gift in direct proportion to its unreality. Not only do the phenomenological requirements of a reduction of the given to givenness not contradict the description of the gift as a phenomenon in its own right (*de plein droit*); not only are these demands fulfilled, here at least, almost perfectly; but above all, fatherhood appears as a phenomenon in its own right (given) and even privileged (the given that itself gives [*donné donnant*]) only if the phenomenological view interprets (*déchiffre*) it as always already naturally reduced, by reconstituting (so to speak) that on the basis of which it is discovered as reduced, and in the face of which the models of exchange, procreation, and production definitively show themselves to be impotent (*impuissants*) and inadequate. The contemporary difficulty with conceiving fatherhood follows directly from an incapacity (*impuissance*) to reduce the gift to the givenness in it.

The Gift Without the Principle of Identity

Thus reduced without remainder to givenness, the given and giving phenomenon of fatherhood opens new domains to the phenomenality of givenness (or givenence [*donnéité*]) in general, which we cannot explore here. But we can at least emphasize a characteristic of the gift's phenomenality in the strict sense, which is brought into clear light here.

Fatherhood is clearly distinguished in that it is unfolded without reciprocity and with excess. What importance is to be accorded to these two particularities? It is without reciprocity because the father can give (life) as father only on the express condition of never being able to receive it in return from the one to whom he has given it. The father cannot give in order to receive in return—and is singled out precisely by this privilege. The privilege becomes paradoxical only if one persists in envisaging it on the economic horizon, where it seems to arise from a lost exchange and a disappointed reciprocity; but this privilege is easily demonstrated, on the contrary, as soon as analysis takes the chance to transgress the economic horizon for good and enter onto the horizon of givenness. The father appears without contest as he for whom I, as the child, can do nothing, as he to whom I can render nothing, as he whom I will allow to die alone. However, the neglect in which I must finally abandon him, regardless of what may happen and what my filial sentiments may be, has nothing to do with a bitter impotence or a harsh injustice. For, before all else, it marks the sole indisputable transcendence that all human life can and must recognize in its own immanence; with the result that if we ever have to name God with a name, it is very appropriate to call Him "Father"—and Him alone: "Call no one on earth your father, for you have only one Father, and He is in heaven" (Matthew 23:9).

The father—as him to whom we can render nothing, precisely because we owe him our inscription in the given—makes evident the son, he who could not give to himself that which he has nonetheless received as most his own—and vice versa. For we do not experience ourselves solely as given, like every other phenomenon, but as gifted (*adonné*)—as those who receive themselves in the reception of the given, far from waiting for this given in the position of a receiver who is already available and secure in itself. To what extent does the experience of oneself as a gifted also imply the recognition of filiation in myself? The response to this question perhaps (and no more than perhaps) exceeds the scope of philosophy and possibly touches on a domain that is already theological; but the phenomenology of the reduced gift leads one inevitably at least to pose it as a question.[22]

Beyond the transcendence that it unveils in the gifted's intimate immanence, fatherhood also and especially imposes a strictly phenomenal determination: the invalidation of reciprocity. For if the reduced gift attests to itself as irreducible to exchange, that depends, as has just been seen, on the fact that it has no need to rest on the two (or three) terms of the exchange in order to be brought about; it can give its all, as money thrown away, to receive without being able to render, and to be realized without transferring any reality susceptible of being possessed. Consequently, not only can fatherhood, like every other reduced gift, be dispensed of reciprocity, but it cannot even tolerate it nor give it the least right. The reduced gift gives (and receives) without return or revenue, even on condition of having nothing in common with these.

What does this abandonment of reciprocity signify? This question does not concern ethics, whose operations (altruism, justice, generosity, disinterestedness, etc.) themselves become intelligible and determinant only once reciprocity is overcome, and on the basis of this overcoming. Therefore, this overcoming, coming before ethics, goes back to the fundamental determination of metaphysics, of which it puts a radical principle in question: the principle of identity. This principle supposes that nothing can be, at the same moment and in the same respect, other than itself; in other words, possibility is founded on logical noncontradiction: "We judge to be false that which contains contradiction, and to be true that which is opposed or contradictory to the false."[23] Logical noncontradiction, which founds the formal possibility of each thing on its thinkability, hence on its essence, rests on self-equality. In consequence, reciprocity in exchange reproduces between two beings and their two (or more) essences the single requirement of noncontradiction. The economy extends and applies this requirement to the relations of production, possession, and consumption of objects, which are woven by societies and which support their cohesion. Inversely, not to respect this requirement provokes contradiction, and therefore in the end prevents exchanges and societies. The political ideals of equality and solidarity take up the same requirement at a higher level of complexity.

Under all its figures, reciprocity generalizes the same principle of identity and the same requirement of noncontradiction.

Henceforth, if the reduced gift attests to itself only in subverting reciprocity—and thus the self-equality of things—not only does it contradict the economy and its conditions of possibility for experience, but it also and especially contradicts the principle of noncontradiction itself. As the case of fatherhood proves, the reduced gift allows for a thing not being left equal to itself, but becoming (or, rather, giving) more than itself, or as much as it loses in the exchange of being accomplished as gift. The reduced gift always gives (or receives) more (or less) than itself, for if the balance stayed equal, the gift would not actually take place—but, in its place, an exchange. For exchange respects the principle of identity, and so it offers only an elementary variant on the case of a relation between two terms. The father, for example, loses himself in giving a life, which will never be rendered to him; and he contradicts himself in renouncing an equal exchange, precisely to fulfill the office of father; but, moreover, he gives much more than he possesses, in giving a life that in one sense he does not have (in and of) himself, because it is not identified with him, who himself remains the son of another father. Fatherhood manifests the nonidentity of each self with itself, this contradiction of self to self then being unfolded in all the figures of inequality. In general, the gift is produced only by provoking this nonidentity with itself, then in releasing an inequality without end: that of the giver with the gift, of the givee with the gift, and of the gift with itself. These nonidentical inequalities can be described successively and even alternatively as a loss, as an excess, or as an equivocation—but they can never be understood on the model of self-identity.

This essential and polysemous nonidentity, which liberates the gift everywhere it operates, in the end imposes nothing less than a new definition of possibility. Henceforth, it must no longer be conceived as bare noncontradiction—namely, the self-identity of an essence, which attests to its rationality in posing no contradiction for the understanding—but as the excess (or, just as well, the deficit) of the self over the self, which, in giving without return, gives more than itself and provokes an other different from the first self (and hence itself also different from itself). Possibility does not consist in self-identity with the self, but in the self's excess over itself. Following the paradoxical logic of the gift, which excludes exchange and reciprocity, everything always ends up as much more (or less) than itself, without any impossibility being opposed to this. For the impossibility that would have to be opposed to this would remain a simple nonpossibility, in the sense of non–self-identity and the principle of identity, the contradiction of which defines *precisely* the new acceptance of possibility that is set to work by the gift—which, far from perishing from its nonidentity and its inequality with itself, wells up only if these latter are unfolded to their end. This means that no impossibility can prevent the new possibility of the gift, since it is fed on impossibility and on the very contradiction of self-identity, self-equality, and the reciprocity of exchange. To that which gains itself only in losing itself—namely, the gift, which gives itself in abandoning itself—nothing is impossible any longer. Not only does that which does not give itself lose itself, but nothing can ruin (*perdre*, lose) the gift, since it consists in the contradiction even of its possibility.

The Horizon Proper to the Gift: Unconditioned Possibility

Such as we have just reestablished it on its own terms under the figure of fatherhood, the phenomenon of the gift unfolds only by eliminating in itself the terms of exchange, to the point of contradicting the principle of (non)contradiction. This result, supposing that it is admitted, far from solidly establishing the phenomenality of the gift and illuminating its logic, could lead to a reinforced difficulty. First, because the exception made to the principle of identity seems to reinforce the tendency to marginalize the gift, with this extreme case of phenomenality being a contrast that makes clear the common regularity of exchange, which is left conforming to identity and noncontradiction. After all, if the gift in general is exemplified principally by the case of fatherhood, would it not be necessary to confine to this indisputable phenomenal exception (a gift naturally reduced to givenness, a gift responding to the gifted) the possibility of contradicting (non)contradiction, indeed the possibility of impossibility? Only the exemplary gift—fatherhood (hence also the gifted)—could be an exception to the principle of identity, which, for remaining phenomena and even for other gifts, would continue to be the rule. But as reasonable as this evasion may seem, it fixes nothing.

First, because *all* gifts without exception are brought about by contradicting the identity in themselves, because they contradict the equality between their terms. Fatherhood offers an example only because it manifests precisely this contradiction of identity not only in itself but in all possible gifts. Next, because the gift as such (in other words, all gifts) exempts itself not only from the first principle of metaphysics—the principle of identity and noncontradiction—but also from the second: "that of Sufficient Reason, in virtue of which we consider that no fact can be real or actual, and no proposition true, without there being a sufficient reason for its being so and not otherwise."[24] For this principle posits that everything—facts, propositions, and hence (especially) phenomena—must have a reason that justifies its actuality. In other words, for a phenomenon to be brought about, it is not sufficient that the possibility of its essence (noncontradiction) be shown; it is also necessary to justify the actuality of its existence, and that can happen only if a term other than it comes, as cause or reason, to render intelligible this transition. But can we always assign a reason or a cause to the phenomenon that gives itself?

I have shown elsewhere the phenomenological fragility of this claim: the phenomenon, in the strict sense, has the essential property of showing itself in itself and on the basis of itself—hence of not becoming manifest in the way an effect becomes actual, namely, by means of another cause or reason than itself. A phenomenon shows *itself* all the more as itself, in that it gives *itself* on the basis of itself.[25] Is the particular case where the given phenomenon takes the figure of the gift, one in which we could more readily assign to its phenomenalization another *self* than itself? Merely formulating the question is sufficient to see that the gift, even less than any other phenomenon, permits another instance to preside at its phenomenalization. The gift shows itself on the basis of itself because, like every other phenomenon, it gives *itself* on the basis of itself, but also because, more radically than every other phenomenon, it gives its *self* on the basis of *itself*. The gift that gives (itself) gives only on the basis of itself, hence without owing anything to another reason (or cause) than itself. One need only return to the precise description of the gift to verify that this phenomenon manifests itself and gives itself as it gives—*of itself*, on the basis of itself alone, without any other reason than itself.

Let us suppose the simple illustrative case where a gift appears to its giver before he gives it (the givee remaining bracketed here). How does the reduced gift come (*advient*) to this giver so that it becomes an actual gift? Let us consider first the uncritical answer: the gift passes to actuality when this same giver decides to give it and lays claim to establishing himself as its efficient cause and last reason. But this response is not valid, for the decision itself remains an appearance. More essentially, we must understand how the giver himself comes to the decision of actually giving this gift, hence how (the decision of) taking the decision happens (*advient*) to him. And the response to this question is not as easily established as one might expect.

For, evidently, the giver does not decide to give some gift because of the object that he is giving. First, because an object as such can decide nothing, in particular it cannot decide between itself and all the other objects susceptible of being considered as what one might give. Next, because the reasons for preferring to give one object rather than another could not result from calculations, which in any case the object would suffer, without producing them or justifying them. Neither does the giver decide on some gift because of some potential beneficiary, who could have begged for it more than the others—the number of needy discourages, and the impudence of the claims disgusts, without allowing one to decide. It must therefore be that the giver alone decides to give, by himself. But he must still decide to *give* and not only to part with an available object following rules that include a benefit for him, nor only to share it out by calculation (even by justice, which is itself an equality), nor to distribute it following economic laws (an exchange). It must be, here again, that a gift gives itself, reduced purely to the givenness in it. And that can happen only if the gift wells up from itself and imposes itself as such on its giver. It can do this only by coming (*advenant*) to this giver as something to give, as that which demands that one give it (*donandum est*)—by appearing among many other objects or beings like itself, in the midst of which the gift imposes itself of itself: as so useful for a distress close to its actual (and provisional) proprietor, that henceforth he or she must become the leaseholder whose time has expired, and finally the giver; or as so beautiful that it is only fitting for a beauty greater than that of its possessor, who is obliged to pay homage with it; or finally as so rare that its finder feels constrained to convey it to a jewel box more exceptional than himself. The examples of this silent constraint—political (devolutions: Lear to his daughters), moral (renunciations: the Princess of Cleves), religious (consecrations: the stripping of Francis of Assisi), or others—abound to the point of dispensing us from describing them further.

Here, before being given, the gift comes (*advient*) to this point on the basis of itself, on the basis of a *self* that imposes itself doubly. First, it imposes itself as that which must be given—a phenomenon distinguished among other phenomena by a prominence such that no one can legitimately proclaim himself its possessor, as a phenomenon that burns the fingers, and of which the very excellence demands that one be rid of it. Next, the gift imposes itself in imposing on its initial possessor that it be let go to a recipient who is always other; for the gift makes the possessor's decision about to whom it is to be given, hence also demands of this possessor that he make himself the giver and dispossess himself of it (in this order, and not the inverse). Thus the gift reduced to givenness is brought about in virtue of nothing other than its own *givability*: in appearing as givable, it transforms its reality as a being or an object and thus convinces its possessor to be rid of it, so as to allow it to appear precisely according to a perfect givability. The gift decides its givenness by itself and decides its giver by itself, in appearing indisputably as givable and making itself be given. And this phenomenality comes to it from nothing other than itself. It has no recourse to any cause, nor to any reason, other than the pure demand of givenness that it show itself as it gives itself—namely, in itself and of itself. It comes (*advient*) on the basis of its own possibility, such that it gives this possibility originarily to itself.

Inversely, let us suppose the illustrative case where a gift appears to its givee, who receives it (the giver remaining bracketed here). How does the reduced gift come (*advient*) to this givee as an actual gift? Because this same givee decides to receive it and lays claim to establishing himself as its final cause and initial reason. But it still remains to be understood how the givee comes to accept this gift as gift, hence first to decide by himself to accept it. Now the difficulties mount up. First, it is necessary that the final beneficiary accepts the receiving of a gift; but this acceptance implies a prior renunciation—and a considerable renunciation—since it is a matter of abandoning the posture of self-sufficiency and calm possession of oneself and one's world; in short, renunciation of that most powerful of fantasies, which is the foundation of the whole economy and every calculation of interest in an exchange, that fantasy of the self-identity of the "I" (contradicting the principle of identity). Before accepting a gift—which would nevertheless seem easy, since it appears to be a matter of gain, pure and simple—it is necessary first to accept to accept, which implies recognizing that one no longer increases oneself by oneself, but rather by a dependence on that which one is not, more exactly on that which the "I" in one is not.

And this consent supposes that one abandons self-equality; hence, not only that which morality would label egoism, but above all that which the reduction to givenness has stigmatized as exchange and economy. It is a matter of nothing less than abandoning one logic to let oneself take up another, which no sufficient reason governs and no cause controls. Next, it is necessary to distinguish between that which it is appropriate to accept and that which one cannot or should not accept; for not every good is offered as a gift that is to be received—whether it remains the possession of an absent or unknown proprietor (desire for a lost object, abandoned and then found, that belongs by right to another), or whether it can in no way become an appropriable good for the enjoyment of whomsoever (such as environmental goods, which belong to nobody), or whether what appears as a gift ends up proving to be an evil in reality (the horse abandoned to the Trojans by the Greeks), and so on. Whence this conclusion: to discern if and when it is a matter of a gift, it is first of all necessary that the gift itself appear given as such; namely, as given to be received.

The beneficiary cannot, as such, satisfy these two requirements— accepting to accept and knowing what to accept—since he himself becomes a givee only at the moment when they are satisfied in his eyes, and hence before him. Therefore, there remains only a sole hypothesis: the gift itself must make itself accepted by the one who accepts it, and that it must declare itself from itself as a gift to be received. And the gift succeeds in this precisely when, from the innumerable crowd of beings and objects that are available, but undistinguished or ruled by possession, one detaches itself and imposes itself by appearing as the one that I must accept (*accipiendum est*). It appears then as a phenomenon that has welled up under the aspect of *acceptability*. It appears in designating itself as to be received, and in making itself accepted by the one who, at first and most of the time, neither sees it as a gift nor conceives of himself as the givee. Such an acceptability is exerted on the one who, without it, would not recognize himself as a givee; and it is not exerted solely, nor at first, in the manner of a moral pressure or a sensual seduction, but in virtue of a privileged aspect of phenomenality—the phenomenality of that which in itself and by itself gives itself to be received. The gift phenomenalizes itself of itself insofar as it shows itself as it gives itself—as that which none can begin to see without first receiving it. The gift thus received refers back to no cause, nor to any reason, other than its pure logic of givenness, appearing in its own right (*de plein droit*). Presupposing neither its givee nor its giver, it comes (*advient*) on the basis of its own possibility, such that it gives this possibility originarily to itself: it shows itself in itself because it gives itself in itself.[26]

At the end of this inchoate description, we arrive at the outline of a result: if one seriously undertakes to reduce the gift to givenness, the gift gives itself on the basis of itself alone; not only can it be described by bracketing its givee, its giver, or its objectness, but above all it gives rise to them all under the two aspects of its own phenomenality—givability and acceptability. Therefore, the reduced gift comes to pass (*advient*) with no cause or reason that would suffice for rendering account of it, other than itself—not that it renders an account to itself, but because it renders itself (reason) inasmuch as it gives itself in and by itself. Actually, it renders itself in multiple senses. It renders itself in that it abandons itself to its givee, to allow him the act of acceptance. It also renders itself to its giver, in that it puts itself at his disposal to allow the act of giving. Finally, it renders itself to itself in that it is perfectly accomplished in dissipating itself without return, as a pure abandoned gift, possible in all impossibility.

Thus, the reduced gift—which is illustrated with the phenomenon of the gift giving itself and making itself received—accomplishes the *self* of the full phenomenon (*phénomène plénier*). That which appears, appears as that which shows itself (Heidegger); but that which shows itself, shows itself and can show itself only in itself, hence on the basis of itself. But once again, it can do this showing of itself on the basis of itself only if, in showing itself, it puts its self in play (which, in short, can happen only if it gives itself in itself). A phenomenon shows itself in itself only if it gives its *self*.[27] And giving itself here signifies giving itself in the visible, without reserve or retreat, hence without condition or measure, hence without cause or reason. Unless it is said that the real reason for appearing, like that for givenness, consists in not having a reason. The gift gives itself of itself without borrowing anything from a possibility that comes from elsewhere, such as the parsimonious calculation of sufficient reason—in short, without any other possibility than its own. The gift reduced to givenness requires no (privileged) rights ([*passe-*]*droit*) in order to give itself or to show itself as it gives itself. It requires no possibility from anything, but gives possibility to all on the basis of that which it opens in and by itself.

The Gift Without Principle of Sufficient Reason

Whence it follows that, in exceeding the requirement for a cause and a reason, not only does the gift not lack rationality but, completely to the contrary, it could also be able to constitute itself as a "greater reason" than the tight *ratio reddenda* of metaphysics. Or again: Could it not be that the gift provides the nonmetaphysical figure of possibility par excellence, and that the possibility that is "higher than actuality" opens itself first of all as gift? In other words, if the phenomenon in the strict sense opens itself in itself and on the basis of itself, welling up from a possibility that is absolutely its own, unforeseeable, and new, then could not the gift offer itself as the privileged phenomenon — more exactly, as the figure of all phenomenality?[28]

That the gift reduced to givenness, and — on its basis — the phenomenon as pure given arise from no other cause or reason, but only from themselves, in no way implies that they lack rationality or that they have a conceptual deficiency. For nothing proves that the highest rationality of a phenomenon is defined by the requirement to render reason for its phenomenality to an instance other than itself. It could be that such a figure of reason — a metaphysical figure of heteronomous reason — suffers from an immeasurable deficiency, and that it compromises and even censures the phenomenality of all phenomena, to the point that, in these nihilistic times, it could be that the only phenomena that can still burst forth into broad daylight are those whose intuitive saturation frees them from the grasp of the principle of reason. And to contest the primacy of the principle of reason over the phenomenon — or, what here amounts to the same, of the economy over the gift — is in no way a misguided undertaking, since one and the other, in their respective formulations, spell out a fundamental contradiction precisely from the point of view of givenness.

For the economy, which is founded on exchange, requires equality and its justice, since it is itself defined thus: "Proprius actus justitiae nihil aliud est quam reddere unicuique quod suum est (The proper act of justice is none other than to *render* to each his own)."[29] But what does *reddere* signify here, if not "render" (that is, "regive," hence first of all "give")? Justice would therefore consist in giving to each, possibly (but not necessarily) in return and by reaction, what is due to him. But then justice is no longer based on exchange, since exchange itself is understood here as a particular (moreover, devalued) mode of the gift! Hence, on the contrary, like exchange itself, justice would presume an original intervention, however dissimulated, of the gift itself. Could the reason of exchange and justice lie hidden in the gift, and not at all the inverse? To be sure, the economy could neither reduce the gift nor be reduced to it, but it could arise from it by simplification and neutralization; in short, it could in the end require it and attest to it as its real reason.

Is it the same for the principle of reason? Actually, Leibniz constantly bases it—the "great metaphysical principle" that he proclaims it to be—on the same surrender to *reddere*: "Axioma magnum./Nihil est sine ratione./Sive, quod idem est, nihil existit quin aliqua ratio reddi possit (saltem ab omniscio) cur sit potius quam non sit et cur sic sit potius quam aliter" (The great axiom./Nothing is without reason./Or, what amounts to the same: Nothing exists without it being possible [(at least for (one who has) omniscience] to *render* some reason why it is rather than is not and why it is so rather than otherwise).[30] One can render a reason for everything—but how is one to render a reason for it being necessary to *render* this very reason? Though the solidity of the principle of reason has nothing to fear from attempts to submit it to, for example, the principles of contradiction or identity, and though it can resist the quietist pretensions of gratuity or indeterminism, it nevertheless wavers before the immanence of *reddere* in it. For to provide a sufficient reason, it is necessary that a mind (an omniscient mind, as it turns out, for contingent statements) renders it. But rendering it (*re-dare*) implies that one regives it, that one gives it in return, hence essentially that one gives it. For the French *rendre* (render) derives from the colloquial Latin *rendere*, formed from *reddere* in relation to *prendre* (take).[31]

In the end, it may also be possible to translate "render reason" by "re-presentation" (Heidegger); but this re-presentation neither exhausts nor replaces givenness, from which it arises, and which allows it as one of its derived operations. That even (sufficient) reason— which is so foreign to the gift—needs to be given is plainly no longer justified by the principle of rendering reason, which in this instance is capable of nothing and understands nothing. Since it is even necessary to render reason, it, too, rests on the gift, and not at all on itself. Therefore reason, which does not know how to give, never suffices for *giving* this other "reason" for rendering reason—hence the gift alone can give it. Reason becomes truly sufficient only if the gift (reduced to givenness) gives it (and renders it) to itself. Reason suffices no more for thinking itself than for thinking the gift. In short, if it is necessary to regive reason, this implies that the *ratio* remains, in itself, secondary and derivative from a more originary instance—the givenness that puts it in the position of operating as a complete reason and a final argument. Givenness governs the *ratio reddenda* more intimately than exchange rules the gift, because no reason can be dispensed from being rendered (that is, from a gift putting it on the stage and preceding it). The gift alone renders reason to itself, for it alone suffices for giving it. This time the gift no longer waits for its good standing by right (*bon droit*) of reason, but on the contrary justifies reason, because it precedes reason, as a "greater reason" than reason.

The gift alone gives reason and renders reason to itself. It thus challenges the second principle of metaphysics, just as it contradicted the first. How, precisely, is this privilege of the gift's metaphysical extraterritoriality to be understood, and how is it to be extended to phenomenality in general?

The gift gives reason, and gives it to reason itself; in other words, it renders to reason its full validity, because it gives itself reason, without any condition or exception. In fact, the characteristic of a gift consists in its never being wrong and always being right (literally, having reason): it depends on no due or duty, hence it never appears owing or in debt. Having no presupposition (not even the justice of equality or the equality of exchange), no prior condition, no requisite, the gift gives (itself) absolutely freely. For it always comes (*advient*) unhoped-for and unexpectedly, in excess and without being weighed on a balance. It can never be refused or declined; or, if it is refused (and we have clearly seen that this can often be done), it can never be refused with legitimate reason nor, above all, can it be refused the right to give itself, since it gives itself without price, without salary, without requirement or condition. Always coming in excess, it demands nothing, removes nothing, and takes nothing from anybody. The gift is never wrong, because it never does wrong. Never being wrong, it is always right (literally, has reason). Therefore, it delivers its reason at the same time as itself—reason that it gives in giving itself and without asking any other authority than its own advent. The gift coincides with its reason, because its mere givenness suffices as reason for it. Reason sufficing for itself, the gift gives itself reason in giving itself.

But isn't it the same for the phenomenon in general, at least provided that it truly shows itself in and on the basis of itself, because it gives itself of itself in an accomplished givenness (according to the anamorphosis, the unpredictable landing [*arrivage*], the fait accompli, the incident and eventness [*événementalité*])?[32] Isn't it clearer still if first of all one considers saturated phenomena (the event, the idol, the flesh, and the icon or the face)?[33] When it shows itself on the basis of itself and in itself, the phenomenon comes to pass (*parvient*) only in giving itself, hence in coming (*advenant*), without any other condition than its sovereign possibility. It shows itself in that it imposes itself in visibility, without cause or principle that would precede it (for if they are found, they will come only after its coming, reconstituted a posteriori). Moreover, it does not simply show itself in the visible, such that its horizon defines it *ne varietur* (without anything changing); it adds itself there at the same time as each new instant; and it adds itself there because it adds a new visible that until then had remained unseen and that would have remained so without this unexpected event. Hence, it redefines the horizon to the measure of its own new dimensions, pushing back its limits. Every painter knows perfectly well that in bringing about a painting, he reproduces nothing in the world, but produces a new visible, introduces a new phenomenon, and makes it an irrevocable gift. The phenomenon is never wrong, but always right (literally, has reason), a reason that appears with its gift—its sole and intrinsic reason.

7

The Gift
A Trojan Horse in the Citadel of Phenomenology?

Joseph S. O'Leary

Theologians ruminate among inherited concepts and images, seeking to clarify their history and judge it critically. To establish a perspective in which even a single such concept can be brought into question or deconstructed is no easy matter. To bring the entire tradition into perspective and retrieve it in a well-founded way, as Heidegger aimed to retrieve the tradition of Western metaphysics, is a prodigious task. Recently, a larger context for that task has emerged as Christians have learned that their entire tradition is only one fiber in the texture of the human religious quest. The old closures of identity have become inoperative, and at the same time the security of our origins has been withdrawn. Foundational notions such as "creation," "election" (chosen people), "kingdom of God" (promised land), "divinity of Christ," and "resurrection" have become increasingly nebulous as they have been put under erasure by the scientific, evolutionist worldview, on one side, and the critical, historical study of Scripture, on the other. Metaphysical definitions of these notions have yielded to the "softer" language of "phenomenon," "event," or "process." Faith may still use the old terms, suitably reinterpreted, to open itself to a gracious ultimate reality, but the texture of the net of faith has become looser (since a tighter net can no longer succeed in holding our minds).

One concept that seems to be surviving well, and that seems rather to increase in vividness as the others withdraw, is the notion of grace.

Indeed, grace—as phenomenon, event, process—could fill in for all the other notions that have become so elusive, or could provide the key for their postmetaphysical retrieval. Instead of talking of an omnipotent, omniscient Creator, one could speak of a gracious drawing that brought the universe into being according to laws inscribed within it (Teilhard). Incarnation, redemption, and resurrection could all be "reduced" (in something like a phenomenological reduction) to an event of grace (and of course the entire vocabulary of the Spirit feeds into this reading). It is against the background of this phenomenological turn in theology that "the theological turn in French phenomenology" (Dominique Janicaud) has had such an electrifying impact, promising a new alliance between faith and philosophy. Jean-Luc Marion's theological writings do not fuss about ontological claims of classical dogma but initiate the reader into a space, an enveloping event, something like Teilhard's *milieu divin*. In this space it makes little sense to define ontological foundations. Rather, one discerns its dimensions from within the space itself. Marion's discussions of the divine distance—a gracious withdrawal to which we are oriented by the icon or by the Cross—and of the call and the gift as fundamental existentials that relate us to God are aspects of this total event, which could be considered a transcription of Heidegger's *Ereignis* into the key of grace.

The space that Heidegger explores is that of the togetherness of thinking and Being, that in which mortals stand forth in the openness of the world, and the condition of that space is identified as the "quiet power of the possible" that lovingly grants Being. Being is discerned, in its *Jeweiligkeit*, its constant temporal arising, to be essentially a gracious event, a gift. In *Zeit und Sein* (1962), Heidegger spoke of the "it" that grants being, the "Es" in "Es gibt Sein" (There is Being), which is his equivalent of Parmenides' *esti gar einai*: "*Esti gar einai*—'For there is Being.' In this saying lies concealed the initial mystery for all thought."[1] Heidegger had been drawn to the Parmenidean dictum as early as 1922.[2] The Parmenidean resonances in the 1962 lecture not only steer the career of his thinking to end where it had begun, but also might be seen as closing the entire Western career of the thinking of being with a recall of its origin. For the vocabulary of being is receding in later Heidegger, and still more in Lévinas, Derrida, and Marion, as well as among thinkers inspired by Neoplatonism, such as Jean Trouillard, Joseph Combès, and Stanislas Breton, for whom Being would be merely the "trace" of an ineffable ultimate, as in Plotinus. The phenomenological exploration of the given is no longer enveloped by the notion of Being.

If in theology the notion of grace has expanded to envelop and surpass the solid substantiality and sharp definitions of traditional dogma, in phenomenology the notion of givenness (*donation*) has expanded to embrace and surpass Being. The notions of grace and givenness share certain strengths. They are unitary notions: all the other key notions of theology and phenomenology, respectively, can be parsed and ordered in reference to them. They are critical notions: they serve to dismantle reifications and dissolve metaphysical blockages. They are charged with immediacy: led back to grace and givenness, theological and phenomenological thought is set in a fresh relationship to its theme and converted away from the merely theoretical to an existential engagement with the given in its givenness.

But the objection that immediately arises is that these notions are convenient abstractions, and that the unity they impose on the vast pluralism of activities and languages of giving or of grace is a metaphysical construction, in fact opposed to the spirit of phenomenology. Marion's admiring critics—Janicaud, Derrida, Jean-Louis Schlegel, Jocelyn Benoist—find here a basic problem. Since the publication of *L'idole et la distance* in 1977, theologians have found in Marion a resource for the overcoming of metaphysics in Christian tradition, but his own vision could also be seen as restoring metaphysics in the key of phenomenology. His *donation* is as comprehensive as *esse* is for St. Thomas: the analogy of being is retrieved as an analogy of donation. As in neo-scholasticism, philosophy has a rapport of mutual reinforcement with theology, with no prejudice to the autonomy of the two disciplines.

A questionable feature, again redolent of the metaphysical, is the omnicompetence implicitly claimed for the phenomenological approach. In theology, it would be impracticable to reduce the entire content of Christian teaching to a set of phenomenological data. The events attested in Scripture are indeed a *Sache selbst* to which one may appeal to overthrow inappropriate theoretical perspectives of later theology. But the questions posed to theological judgment cannot all be answered simply by pointing to "the phenomena." Critical theology reassesses the various strands in the web of tradition, using various methods of critical reason, phenomenological reduction, or deconstructive reading, as the issues require. To privilege phenomenology as the sole or even as the primary path of thinking is a metaphysical decision that can turn against phenomenology itself, and that in theology can actually lead to a distortion of the biblical phenomena. Phenomenology is a method at the service of theological judgment, but it cannot preempt the role of judgment as a free and responsible activity of the reflective mind.

The history of metaphysics can be told as the story of Being, and a rich phenomenology of Being can be construed by reading that history against its grain, as Heidegger does. Similarly, the history of theology can be told as the story of grace, and a rich phenomenology of grace can be construed by reading that history against its grain, as Lutheran theologians might attempt to do. The great moments in the history of philosophy are those in which Being is remembered anew, and the great moments in the history of theology are those in which grace is remembered anew, whatever the limits or deviations of the remembrance in both cases. But if we step back from these histories, we meet the suspicion that both Being and grace as unitary phenomena are in fact fictional constructs, and that, moreover, no discourse of grace or of Being has been or can be purely phenomenological, but all are necessarily imbued with doctrinal presuppositions.

Being is what all things have in common—*koinon pasi to on estin*.[3] When one tries to give more concrete content to this notion, as in theories of the analogy of Being that introduce varieties or degrees of Being, the suspicion arises that one is no longer talking about Being as such but simply about different kinds of reality. Only where there is a firm metaphysical framework that is first agreed on can one proceed to differentiate humans, animals, angels, and God in terms of their degrees or kinds of Being. Phenomenology offers no evident support for such a framework. When phenomenologists draft something like it, they seem to be drawing on the expired account of metaphysical habits of thought. Whether the same must be said of Marion's project is a basic question, the answer to which should not be given a priori but on the basis of close frequentation of his oeuvre, and especially of the central work, *Étant donné*. Even if the overall structure of Marion's arguments shows up as a cryptometaphysics, one may still draw on their rich texture for a postmetaphysical mapping of the contours of reality in a more pluralistic mode than Marion would himself be ready to countenance. (I understand "postmetaphysical" to mean not that metaphysics or onto-theology is dead or untrue, but that it no longer provides the governing horizon of all thought. The "step back" to prior and more comprehensive phenomenal and linguistic contexts inaugurates a thinking that cannot be fully retrieved by metaphysical reason.)

Givenness: A Problematic Category

Just as ontologists cannot talk for long about Being in itself, but need to refer to concrete beings to flesh out their discourse, so Marion cannot talk for long about givenness in itself, but needs to bring in concrete phenomena—not only ordinary, everyday phenomena in general but also particular phenomena of a higher order, such as the "event," the "call," or the "gift." He interrogates the gift in view of its givenness just as the ontologist interrogates beings in view of their being. To do so, he must construct a unitary theory not only of givenness but of the gift as well, as we shall see.

Granel argues that in order to speak of time consciousness, Husserl is obliged to invoke elements from the banished realm of perception and intentionality (other than the immanent intentionality of pure time consciousness in its retentions and its stretching forward). Marion's discourse of pure givenness may face a similar dilemma. Givenness and phenomenality are one and the same, but phenomenality is more concretely focused and more fruitfully parsed when conceived as givenness, which Marion sees as the pure process of phenomenality, unencumbered by Being. But when one starts to differentiate degrees of givenness, recognizing that not all objects are given in the same mode, univocally, there arises the temptation to consign ordinary phenomena to a lower realm, leaving pure givenness to emerge only at the exalted level of saturated phenomena. Such phenomena instantiate givenness "without the mediation of objecthood or beingness (as, for example, the painting)" (*ED*, 252). The world becomes transparent to its own givenness; the gift is entirely absorbed in its gifthood. Alternatively, if one says that pure givenness is already realized in common phenomena, must not the higher phenomena then introduce some new factor that cannot be brought under the rubric of givenness? If this new factor is described as givenness raised to a higher power, there is a danger that the unitary, analogical conception of givenness will break down into equivocity (a merely homonymous relationship between the different usages of the word "given").

A unitary notion of grace faces the same tensions. It fares well if one presupposes a metaphysics of creation. All that God has created is His gift, so all is grace. The first theorist of grace was Philo of Alexandria. Grasping Being itself and every human capacity as a gift of the "One Who Is," he identified grace as the supreme *archē*, determining the nature of God Himself and the functions of His powers.

His sense of dependence on God, and of creation as a gift, is rather dulled by the wooden metaphysical explanation that all things have God as their supreme Cause (*On Noah's Work as a Planter*, 31), and the modern reader might wish that Philo had followed through on his insight in a more consistently existential style. "All things are a grace of God. . . . All things in the world and the world itself is a free gift and act of kindness and grace on God's part" (*On the Special Laws*, 3, 78). "God gives not only the gifts, but in them gives the recipients to themselves. For he has given myself to me and everything that is, to itself" (*On Dreams*, 2, 224). Even ordinary perception and thought are impossible unless God opens up the senses: "It is God who showers conceptions on the mind and perceptions on sense, and what comes into being is no gift of any part of ourselves, but all are bestowed by him, through whom we too have been made" (*On the Cherubim*, 127; cf. Proverbs 20:12). Thinking of grace has also been supported by a metaphysical anthropology: humans are finite and can act beyond what their finite resources allow only with a supplement of power coming from God, an ontological boost we call grace; humans are also wounded by sin, and can be freed from it and healed only by the intervention of grace.

All of this is luminously evident within the metaphysical framework of classical theology. It lies at the base of Augustine's consistent thinking through of the doctrine of grace, a doctrine closely interlinked with his ontology in his earlier writings, though becoming more tautly and narrowly biblical in the anti-Pelagian tracts. The Reformation shifted the emphasis to a situation of encounter with grace, which is marked by paradoxes not immediately reducible to the classical ontology, notably the idea of an extrinsic justification conferred on the sinner, who is mantled with Christ's righteousness that remains *extra nos*. This undercuts the ontological unity of the subject, replacing it with a situational or dialectical identity; the believer is *simul iustus et peccator*, at each moment condemned by the Law and forgiven by the Gospel, a sinner when he looks to self, righteous when he looks to Christ. Grace is no longer a universal ontological principle, but simply (in the exegesis of Erasmus and Melanchthon) the event of the divine *favor*, experienced by sinners in existential contexts. The universal principle of grace has become as much an abstraction as talk of being in general. In both cases, the traditional metaphysical account is transformed into and replaced by a plurality of situational discourses. Marion's phenomenology of a divine call that dislodges the ego, that locates one as a "me" before one is able to say "I," has much in common with the Protestant dialectic of grace, though the more exclusive regime of "givenness" in his recent writings may have diluted this.[4]

"What have you that you have not received?" (1 Corinthians 4:7). It is attractive to enlarge this question to the most universal level and to make it the basic principle of being. The Japanese begin every meal (and accept money) with the word *itadakimasu* (we receive). It could be claimed that grateful consciousness of receiving lights up a universal feature of all being. But a phenomenology of receiving and its attendant metaphysics court the danger of essentialism. Can one really formulate it as a simple, universal ontological law on which to build a philosophy of givenness or a theology of grace? To do so seems to override the contributions of interpretation and of faith to this construction of reality. One chooses to interpret the world as gift or to see everything as grace. And each culture develops that act of faith according to its own style of interpretation. If the Japanese, in Shinto mode, interpret the rice as a gift of the gods, when they put on their Zen Buddhist thinking cap, they may interpret the rice as an impermanent phenomenon revelatory of emptiness. Eating the rice as a meditative exercise is no doubt a way of living the moment as a gift. But if a language of gifthood is developed here, it is quite different from and irreducible to the Shintoist one. Christians might claim that their language of gifthood, of thanking the Creator, is the only fully true language, and the phenomenologist might claim to have isolated the essence of gifthood and the correct phenomenological disposition of receiving (perhaps in a *Denken* that is a *Danken*) within or beyond all these religious languages. Even if all these languages stake a claim to transcendental comprehensiveness, the mere fact of their particularity and plurality suggests that they are all culture-bound interpretive constructions. Just as we have different kinds of music and poetry, so we have different cultures of giving and receiving that secrete different ways of projecting a sense of transcendental givenness or gifthood.

"God is the giver of all that is." Yes, our experience of receiving grounds this utterance and makes it a useful and convincing one. One can reformulate it rigorously as a metaphysical theory of the communication of being; but this, too, is a culture-bound way of speaking that may also be useful and convincing on occasion. It is a wholesome exercise to thank God for all that comes from God's hand, but we less and less understand the meaning of this idea. If the reception of a gift is as difficult or more so than the granting of a gift, as Ricoeur has remarked, the same is true of the reception of life and the world as a gift from God's hands. To correctly adopt the posture of receiving involves reflections just as complex as those involved in the gracious conferring of a gift, and when the donor is God, the reflections take on a theological character that need not make for simplification—witness the immense controversies about grace, in which it is not at all clear that those who simply throw themselves into the role of pure receivers hit quite the right note. Sometimes we may adopt an alternative approach and allow the things of the world to confront us in their enigmatic thereness, suspending the idea of God as the one who creates and grants them. Our dominant religious vision may need to be supplemented and qualified by rival ones for its own sake, for it risks becoming a convenient simplification, cutting us off from the diversity of the empirical.

I cannot determine here the extent to which Marion's thought does justice to these perspectives of a historicizing, pluralistic, and relativizing hermeneutics, or the extent to which he effectively counters them. My impression is that they represent a real threat to any phenomenology that aims to uncover fundamental structures for which universal validity is claimed. This impression is intensified as I examine Marion's recent discussion of the gift, for this theme, which at first promises to enrich and anchor the meditation on phenomenality as givenness, turns out to have an irreducible quirkiness that makes it a treacherous guest within the citadel of phenomenology.

The Pluralism of the Gift

A phenomenologist is likely to intuit the essence of the gift, as if the gift were a reality that presents itself to the mind in its pure form, rather than a complex institution that has no pure form. What anthropologists report is messier: "We know almost nothing of the system of the gift, because we have failed to apprehend it in appropriate models."[5] To be sure, Marion's chief theme is the ethical gift, a private and interior matter, to be distinguished not only from the economy but also from the public institutions of ritual giving, whether the tribal practices studied by Boas, Malinowski, and Mauss or their modern avatars—reciprocal invitations to dinner, wedding gifts, and so on.[6] But even in the ethical realm there may be a historical and cultural variety of styles and conventions of giving, and of imagining the act of giving, so that its essence is not easily isolated.

We have no difficulty with the idea that money—buying and selling—is an institution. Only capitalist ideologists talk of economics as a product of human nature. Of course, it has some roots in human nature, but to identify these is a difficult task, one likely to remain a matter of pluralistic debate. Economic arrangements vary greatly from epoch to epoch and from culture to culture. To say that giving, in contrast, is something immediate and natural would be a mystification. Indeed, in our culture many people are more at ease in economic relationships than in relationships of giving and receiving. To step out of the role of being consumers or employees and into the role of being givers or receivers is not experienced by them as a welcome return to something more basic and natural, but as a disturbance of a habit that has become second nature. Giving transcends the calculations of finance, but it demands equally refined reflection on another order of implications. It is not a release into unaccountability. Marion's "giving without counting" is by no means as natural as breathing; it is in fact an apotropaic gesture calculated to keep calculation at bay. It is because the accountability of the gift is greater than that of the sanitized financial exchange that the figure of the beggar is a troubling presence on the landscape of a consumer society. "Beggary should be abolished," Nietzsche thought. "You feel guilty if you don't give them anything and you feel guilty if you do."

We may resent paying a bill, but necessity spares us having to think about it. We may not resent our lavish expenditure on a gift, our subscription to the other order of exchange, but that is not because of some blanket "unaccountability"; rather, it is because of the affection we feel for the recipient and that we do not feel for the payee of bills, or because we respond to the socioethical imperative of generosity as a nobler form of "investment" than merely complying with the rules of the financial system, or for the apotropaic or cathartic motive mentioned above. To give is to invest something of oneself, whereas to pay is a vulgar action excluding individual creative initiative. To give is ennobling; to pay, debasing. Sometimes there is an ethical tinge to one's decision to pay as an act of honesty or not to pay as an act of protest, but the measure of the action is still the cold quantity of the coin of the realm, whereas the measure of a gift has only a tangential relation to the price paid for it.

One could argue, then, that the institution of the gift is in fact more complex and elaborate than the economy. But is it not at least clear that there is a qualitative distinction between the two orders? The order of the gift, centered on mutual recognition, and the order of commerce, centered on commodities, have different and contrasting functions. This would appear to provide a solid platform for a philosophy that would unveil the values implicit in the gift and oppose them, point by point, to those of the economy. However, I wonder if the distinction is sufficiently radical and sufficiently waterproof to serve as a foundation in first philosophy. The frontier between the economy and the gift shows signs of being quite porous. Some say that the expression "free gift" or "gratuitous gift" is a pleonasm. But giving is not a purposeless activity; it seeks to achieve something, and this of itself limits purist claims to utter gratuity. Moreover, we often speak of people giving themselves in service, even though they are paid for it. For the gifts that the apostles receive from the faithful, Jesus uses an economic metaphor: "the laborer is worthy of his hire" (Luke 10:7). The "honorarium" is a form of payment that marks the porous frontier between the mercenary and the gratuitous. Marion would reply that these mundane considerations are eclipsed when the pure gift "happens"; it eventuates itself spontaneously, suspending the web of calculation that may have been spun about it. An example would be the forgiveness that Tolstoy's Karenin, otherwise a calculating soul, spontaneously grants to his wife and even her lover (*Anna Karenina*, IV, 17). If we reserve the term "gift" for such graced phenomena, then we can find only traces or elements of gifthood in what are commonly called gifts.

Derrida uses the "impossibility" of pure giving as yet another deconstructionist argument against essentialism. Just as "meaning" and "truth" never constitute themselves purely but are produced within a linguistic milieu characterized by dissemination or *différance* (so that their pure presence is forever deferred), so the "gift" is produced in a system of exchanges that abolishes its pure constitution and dooms it to remain undecidable. As in the case of meaning and truth, the phenomenological status of the gift is ephemeral; it disappears in the very act of appearing. A broader and more concrete view of the culture of giving might avoid these strenuous paradoxes, and simply trust in the processes of giving and receiving, in all their unpredictability and in their occasional interaction with ordinary economic exchange.

In Marion, far from being reduced to a provisional moment in the web of *différance*, phenomenology is a stable procedure, establishing basic structures of phenomenality and extending its writ to everything without exception, since everything is given as a phenomenon.

Phenomenology, he is confident, can discern the essence of gifthood and thence clarify the essence of being or phenomenality as givenness. The emphasis on the purity of the gift cuts off interest in the impure forms of giving that abound on every side. These invite the attention of an applied hermeneutical phenomenonology but do not offer much encouragement to a refoundation of phenomenology as a science of essences. Without attempting to master the phenomena of giving by reducing them to a single essence, such an applied phenomenology could draw on the various idiosyncrasies and paradoxes of giving to open up paths of thought contrasting with those suggested by the varieties of economic behavior. It could explore a variety of hints concerning a gracious reality and the possibilities of using the language of givenness in order to speak of it. But such a phenomenology would never get around to constructing anything like a ladder of analogy between the homely and the transcendental or transcendent usages of the word "gift." The pluralism of the everyday practices and language of giving carries over to the use of this language when speaking of Being or of God. It is a language or a cluster of metaphors that we find useful for orienting ourselves in relation to ultimate realities, but it does not provide a metaphysical map of these realities.

Yet if the theme of the gift complicates the task of phenomenology by forcing it to think pluralistically, its phenomenological promise is such that the phenomenologist cannot afford to neglect it. If it is a treacherous guest in the household of phenomenology, it is also a guest who cannot be sent away, a gift that cannot be given back. Anthropologists and philosophers are fascinated by the theme, because the activities of giving and receiving open up a realm that is not reducible to technological or utilitarian rationality. Hence the gift is the showpiece of the MAUSS group (Mouvement Anti-Utilitariste dans les Sciences Sociales). In the midst of the everyday, with no religious overtones, people continue to give and receive according to an economy (in the wider sense of the word) that cannot be reduced to calculations of profit and loss. Gifts entail and sustain relationships of an order different from those of rationalized urban life. Financial transactions are objective and quantitative, and oriented to an equal balance; giving and receiving are personal and qualitative interactions, with an element of spontaneity and asymmetry that aims not at a return to equality but at a constant spiraling of the process in an ever widening network of relationships. A traveler in Crete relates how he wanted to repay a man who had gone out of his way to help him. "Look at the wheel!" he was told; "you will give to someone else in turn." The wheel of giving is not a closed circle, but forward movement on an open road. "The pleasure of the gift includes the possibility and sometimes the hope of a return, but no guarantee, and certainly no control of the subject over the operation."[7]

Commodity exchange is the machinery of society, but gift exchange is the language of community. Archaic societies may have a merchant class, and be well aware of economics. But "the order of merchandise is deliberately prevented from becoming autonomous in relation to its total social context."[8] Even in advanced societies such a containment and contextualization of the economic order may be found. An admirable feature of Japanese life is that the rituals of giving and receiving are so carefully cultivated. They involve a certain strain, but the Japanese evidently cling to them in order to preserve communal bonds against the devastation of a totally capitalistic society. The homeostasis of giving is not achieved by a once-for-all leveling of accounts, but by a sustained, agonistic game of give-and-take: "It is understood that one must neither make the return gift too quickly, for it is elegant to remain obliged to the giver for a certain time, nor to return too much, for this would imply breaking off the relationship, and consequently deciding to extinguish debt and suspend the play of giving."[9] Consciousness of giving and receiving is heightened reflexively in ritual: the tea ceremony is an enactment of giving and receiving in all its dimensions; hospitality and the appreciation of hospitality are set in a context that allows an attunement to the harmony of the cosmos and a deep gratitude for such humble things as tea and tea utensils. Elements drawn from different religious and artistic traditions serve to bring out these wider resonances, and to allow the everyday activities of giving and receiving to intimate a higher plane of being. This is not a return from the complexity of economics to the simplicity of an older order. What the tea ceremony suggests, rather, is that the art of giving, like any art, is endlessly inventive. Thus the new field it provides for anthropological exploration is as complex as the field of standard economics or, more so, just as poetic language offers a field of exploration as complex as that of standard linguistics, or more so. Rituals of giving reveal

> the imaginary of the gift as such, that which posits that the entire world, the social world as well as the animal world and the cosmos, can be engendered and organized only on the basis of

the gifts that people give one another, vital principles or powers in themselves antagonistic, but which the gift has the function of transforming into allies.[10]

A well-based phenomenology of the gift should surely center on the intersubjective theme of mutual recognition (Hegel's *Anerkennung*). This recognition is not established by gestures of friendship alone:

> A supplementary element is needed, this material element, this pledge of good faith, offered as substitute for the one who offers to be associated with it. . . . The ceremonial presentations of gifts reveal a fundamental structure of reciprocity as condition of all social life in the human species.[11]

The purely ethical conception of giving is a modern construct, possible only after the breakdown of public rituals of giving, including sacrifice:

> It is because symbolic control by means of ritual is no longer possible that the gift becomes the moral problem of generosity—including unconditional generosity—and that there remains of sacrifice only the ethical element: renunciation. . . . The internalization of the gesture signals the loss of its social function.[12]

The modern fear of letting the economy be perverted by irrational elements of giving goes hand in hand with the equally modern fear of letting the world of giving be perverted by economic calculation; one seeks "to think these bonds and the market in isolation as two impermeable worlds, of which the first, when it comes in contact with the second, is always contaminated and finally dominated by it."[13] In contrast, even the early Christian texts on which Marion draws, emerge from a context of communal practices of giving and receiving. These survive in part in the Christian liturgy today, which, although no longer a "total social fact" or "that symbolic operator in which the totality of the social and cultural life of a group is involved,"[14] continues to give a ritual and public dimension to the Christian ethics of giving (underestimated by Hénaff). Marion would no doubt see the Eucharist as a supreme instantiation of *la donation*, but the ethical purism of his conception of giving might undercut the give-and-take of the Eucharist as a sacrifice and as communal sharing. Sacrifice is an extension of ritual giving beyond the creation of mutual recognition between humans to a quest to win such recognition from invisible powers. The sacrificer offers the victim the opportunity to win something from the invisible divinity, in a *do ut des* (I give so that you will give) exchange that Marion would consider to contradict the very essence of giving.[15] The offering of a ritual gift or a sacrifice is a risk and a challenge that certainly seeks a response, consisting basically in the recognition of the other party. This dynamic carries over even to the highest ethical forms of giving and does not taint them or reduce them to merely economic exchange, as Marion and Derrida fear.

The empirical study of giving and receiving reveals that gifts follow a quirky trajectory, more spiral than circle, opening up complex networks of relationships and resisting the rational closure that various economic, psychoanalytical, or structuralist theories have sought to impose.[16] Marion's reduction of "the gift" to its essence seems a bid for metaphysical closure at the expense of the social and cultural complexity of giving. Derrida and others object that there is no semantic continuity between the givenness of the given in phenomenology and the activity of giving gifts.[17] If Marion's essentializing account of the gift unravels, then a "first philosophy" based on the essential, reduced notion of the gift will prove impracticable. Analogously, Wittgenstein's essentialist early philosophy unraveled in his later thought, which took more account of the quirky pluralistic texture of language. Perhaps the next wave of French philosophy will similarly come to terms with the factors that frustrate or complicate the drive to foundational insight that has characterized the present generation of phenomenologists.

A Hegelian approach would survey all the historical forms of gifthood, ordered in a dialectic that would at the end produce an integral vision. But even this laborious alternative to the shortcut of phenomenological purism may be thwarted by the initial complexity and undecidability of the movement of the gift. Beyond Hegel lies a still more open-ended and pluralist texture of inquiry. The step back to basic phenomena that Marion attempts, in the wake of Husserl and Heidegger, can be a check on the broad sweep of historical reason, imposing a pause for meditation on matters it has overlooked, especially on the ethical ideals of giving and receiving. But can phenomenology impose itself as surpassing Hegel and his successors, as providing the higher vantage that exceeds and integrates all that modern rationality has achieved? Husserl and Heidegger thought so, and Marion shares their faith. It may be, however, that it is not the destiny of phenomenology to be a first philosophy. If it opens up paths of thinking that elude the recuperative grasp of metaphysical reason, it may be at the price of never itself being able to constitute a comprehensive form of thought enjoying a metaphysical sweep. Faced with this limit, phenomenology needs to put itself back in dialogue with the human sciences, including the neurosciences, and with forms of philosophical reasoning informed by historical and anthropological inquiry, from Hegel on. A pure phenomenology that would banish the hybridized and dialogical exercises of Sartre, Merleau-Ponty, Ricoeur, and Derrida may no longer be possible.

Aporiai: "The Reason of the Gift," §§ 1–2

Marion's starting point in "La raison du don" is not the sociological one but a quasi-Cartesian focus on what he calls elsewhere the *ego amans et non cogitans (seu calculans)*. We give "without counting," for we give ceaselessly, without measure, and unconsciously. This seems a quite abstract description, unless it is to be taken as shorthand for some more detailed phenomenology developed elsewhere by Marion, or possibly by Lévinas. It also seems to focus on the subjectivity of the giver, at the expense of the cardinal function of giving: to establish and sustain human relationships. One could take it that this constant activity of giving is a constant responding and relating, but this is not made explicit. The quasi-Cartesian point of departure makes it difficult to bring giving into view as an act of love or a practice intimately imbricated with loving.

The Cartesian model also hinders easy access to the phenomenology of eros in *Le phénomène érotique*. It tends to present giving and loving first as solitary oblations of the being of the ego rather than something created between two parties. A more Hegelian approach that would bring in the milieu of interpersonal recognition might relieve the discussion of paradoxes and problems that are perhaps more a product of the point of departure than of the topic itself. Even Platonic Eros is relational from the outset, in that the lover is taken outside himself in ecstatic contemplation of the beautiful form; and this is a fortiori the case with Christian agape. Marion's refusal to acknowledge the distinction between eros and agape, or to examine the rich historical traditions of these two understandings of love in their tension and their amalgamation (as studied notably by Anders Nygren), does not prevent him from constructing a luminous phenomenology of being in love; but it is one that eschews all the differentiations that literature, anthropology, and psychoanalysis bring to light. (Interestingly, Nygren scolded Marion's admired Pseudo-Dionysius for identifying eros and agape.)

If we read the opening statement of "La raison du don" as a concrete phenomenology, it would apply best to the Neoplatonic One, which overflows without cease, without measure, and without consciousness. Perhaps Marion would say that humans practice a sovereign generosity in the image of the divine. But the striking "without" clauses are problematic in a manner reminiscent of his early work on the notion of "God without being," and of a love that does not need to be. "Without ceasing": normally we think of giving as a matter of individual acts rather than a constant state. The idea of giving as a constant state certainly chimes with the desire to make *la donation* a fundamental, universal principle, like grace or like being. If we conceive of some people as constant givers—such as mothers dedicated to their children, persons consecrated to a religious life, people whose entire existence takes the form of a gift—it is probable that a concrete phenomenology of such life projects would reveal a history of discrete acts and renewed and changing choices rather than a general pattern of semiunconscious giving. And in extending such a pattern to people in general, Marion seems to reduce giving to something more elementary, to the common energy one puts forth in living. "Without measure": we may measure less carefully in giving than in buying—though "big spenders" do not measure in either case. But giving, like buying, has an inbuilt limit—the limit of "what we can afford." A person who gave without any precautions or limits would hardly be performing the human act of giving, but would have fallen into some kind of pathology. "Without consciousness": the idea that giving is unconscious, like breathing, is counterintuitive. Plotinus, rejecting the idea of an Intellect that thinks without knowing that it thinks, remarks: "If such occurred in us, who are ever aware of our drives and reflections, if we are even moderately wise, it would be a cause of lunacy" (*Enneads*, II.9.1).

Surely, in making a gift one consciously adopts a certain attitude, just as one adopts another attitude when making a purchase. One casts oneself in the role of giver exactly as consciously as one casts oneself in the role of buyer. Indeed, giving is a more self-conscious act, for one has to calculate the appropriateness of a gift, the pleasure it is likely to bring, the nature of one's relationship to the recipient, whether one can afford it, whether one's time, energy, or money might not be more wisely invested. The first three of these considerations are eliminated in transactions of buying and selling. In any case, can unawareness add to the value of a human act, or awareness subtract from it? As the tea ceremony shows, giving and receiving become deeper and more spiritual acts when we deepen awareness of what we are doing. A paralyzing self-consciousness may indeed inhibit gestures of affection or movements of passion. But the spontaneity of the gift is not of this order. It is the spontaneity of a creative act, which cannot be begun without a deliberate and conscious choice, though it ought to be carried through with unself-conscious grace.

The act of giving is a specific event that does not seem to have the universal reach Marion ascribes to it. It follows on receiving: "Freely you have received, freely give" (Matthew 10:8); "It is more blessed to give than to receive" (Acts 20:35). Gratitude is a conscious motivation, and generosity based on gratitude is a duty we learn. There is an infinite asymmetry between giving and receiving. I receive everything—the world, my very existence, every grace and blessing—but I give very little in return. One might say that giving sets the seal on one's awareness of receiving, and attests eloquently to universal givenness. But to claim that giving is as universal and permanent an activity as receiving would be to identify all our activities with giving, dissolving the concrete contours of the gift. Or perhaps one might say that the capacity for giving is as constant as the capacity for receiving. Just as the sporadic quality of our grateful reception does not diminish the reality that all that we are and have is received, so the sporadic quality of our giving does not diminish the reality that our being, just as it is inherently received, is also inherently given—to live is to give, and refusal to give is a futile resistance to the movement of life itself. Marion seems to claim a convertibility of giving and being even at the level of everyday experience. Others might say that "to exist is to pray" and that prayer is merely the coming to awareness of the basic character of being as dependence. But such views are not phenomenological. They are metaphysical constructions. Taking the completely opposite tack, one could say that giving and prayer, even as practiced in secret, are institutions, activities based on established conventions, that do not offer their "essence" to direct phenomenological inspection.

The abstract and problematic aspects of Marion's starting point carry over into the series of aporiai that he goes on to derive from it:

> If we give without thinking, how are we to know that we are giving incessantly and without measure? More exactly, how

> can we be assured that "incessantly and without measure" sufficiently characterizes our gift as a veritable gift, if we have no consciousness of it? . . . The third way of giving without counting—to give without being aware of it—manifestly annuls the two preceding ones; for if we really give ceaselessly and without measure, how could we not in the end be aware of it? (RdD, 4)

The chief aporia of the gift is that it appears, only to disappear. The giver is always rewarded in some way, the recipient is indebted, and the gift itself occludes its gift character and becomes a mere object of exchange:

> Either the gift remains true to givenness, but never appears, or the gift does appear, but in so doing, enters into an economic process of exchange, and is transformed into its opposite—into an exchange: the given that is given back (*do ut des*) . . . , the commerce and management of goods. (RdD, 5)

This dilemma rests on an attempt to establish a paradigm of pure giving, which requires total exclusion of any involvement of gift with exchange. Marion's Husserlian watchword, "the more reduction, the more donation," does not work very well here, for in reducing the gift to a rarefied ideal, he cuts off the intriguing but impure shapes that giving actually takes. He tends to dismiss naturalistic accounts as products of the "natural attitude" (an attitude that is surely quite legitimate outside the rarefied context of Husserlian methodology). If he is claiming that the saturated phenomenon of the pure gift lights up the more discreet phenomenon of our constant unconscious giving, so that the grace of gifthood is revealed to be everywhere at work, then would he not be distilling from the phenomena something like a Platonic Form of the gift, which is in turn lit up by givenness as the Idea of ideas (in the manner of the Good as read by Heidegger)? Similar treatment of the "event" or the "moment" also works on two registers, in that singular moments and events reveal a trait of the phenomenality of being at all times. However, when the ideal form of the gift, the moment, or the event meets the actual plurality and complexity of human experience of time, eventhood, and giving, its mastery over them is not necessarily acclaimed. The phenomenologist's construction of the singular pure experience may illuminate many aspects of the complex reality without being accepted as the essential key to its meaning. The entire account of being or of phenomenality built on the basis of such constructions is likely to find itself enjoying the status of just one story among others.

The stress on the purity of the gift has more to do with philosophical construction than with the empirical realities of giving. Giving happens in a wide context of "give-and-take." To give is to loosen the hold of economic control and self-possession and to enter a different network of relations, in which one becomes a more vulnerable subject linked to others in a more vibrant and unpredictable way. The Gospel's injunctions to give without seeking a reward are fulfilled in a practice of more generous giving; they are not invitations to an examination of conscience that goes back over every act of giving to discern whether it was truly disinterested or not. The Gospel is quite happy to accept that most giving is not purely disinterested, and even when it calls to more selfless giving, it adds that this will bring a heavenly reward. "The gift is a boomerang."[18] This is particularly true of the gift of an apology or the gift of forgiveness: "Forgiveness is a fundamental gift, a gift of passage (as we say 'rites of passage') from the system of violence to the system of the gift, a foundational social and psychological act, which has given rise to astonishingly few studies by researchers in the human sciences."[19] Forgiving, like giving, can be caricatured as a self-interested gesture, performed for the peace it brings to the forgiver or to disarm a dangerous enemy. But the dynamics of forgiveness need not fear recuperation by such motives, for it sets something in motion that transcends the initial motives.

Marion admits that the demand of pure gratuity is rather rarefied. He asks:

> Does this critique of the gift—so efficacious, because so abstract—itself escape all criticism? It clearly lies exposed to a counterattack, since it rests on at least one unexamined presupposition: that the gift entails a perfect and pure gratuity, that it should give for nothing with no return ever. (RdD, 6)

He points out that the moral reward of giving is not of the same order as commercial reimbursement; that the reward may follow the gift rather than being the motive that precedes and disqualifies it; and, above all, that "the severe purity thus asked of the gift would even entail its absolute independence from any possible other; it would lead in the end to a complete autarchy prohibiting not only the exchange and the gift, but otherness in general" (RdD, 6). Moreover, this gratuity also puts in question

> the very ipseity of the ego, which is involved as giver or receiver. Would we not have to annul our ipseities or, rather, pre-

tend to be a god so as to give in complete gratuity, "without envy"? Unless this pretended gratuity is merely a pure indifference which, with closed eyes, gives nothing to anyone and receives nothing from anyone? (RdD, 7)

A Buddhist would query the "ipseity of the ego" as a delusive fixation. There is no immunity or autonomy of a transcendental ego, an "I think" surveying the process of giving. "The subject cannot be grasped independently of its action."[20] An "I" that precedes its action is merely a scholastic entity. In relational give-and-take, both self and other come alive in a new situation, and this situation dissolves the artificial attempt to fix the bounds of the self and its property. An individual who offers an apology or words of forgiveness gives something of himself and exposes it vulnerably to the other. If the apology is refused or the forgiveness condemned, his peace may return on his own head (cf. Matthew 10:13; Luke 10:6), but if it is accepted, it initiates a new order of relationships in which the identity of both self and other is redefined.

At this point, one might expect Marion to explore the intersubjective phenomenality of giving. Giving is always a messy business, involving us with untrustworthy flesh-and-blood others—the Bible ascribes that experience even to the divine giver. Giving, apart from the surrender of control on the part of the giver, is never without consequences—it evokes a reaction far more involving than the signing of a commercial receipt. Concern with pure giving wraps the act of giving in a protective shield and thwarts its natural and usual consequences. What people fear in giving is often less the expense than the relationship it initiates. But instead of exploring this line of reflection, Marion upholds the postulate of gratuity, despite its problems:

> If the gift contradicts itself when one imposes gratuity on it, why do so? No doubt for an excellent reason: because gratuity seems—and in a sense to be carefully determined actually is—the best defence against exchange and the economy, its absolute contrary. (RdD, 7)

As with Derrida, the contradiction lodged in the gift becomes the key to its special status. But the contradiction arises not from gratuity as such but from the demand for an absolutely pure gratuity and from the absolute opposition between gift and commerce as two essences that cannot communicate. (In the Boston version of the text Marion associates these scruples with quietism and Jansenism!)

However, Marion goes on to exhibit the aporia of the gift anew in a more objective style. Equality of exchange is essential to the economy, he points out, citing Turgot, Cournot, Say, and Marx. Rationalism seeks to impose this postulate of equality on giving as well, as its sufficient reason. The self-contradiction of the gift "can now be repeated more positively in the form of a triple reply to the demand of sufficient reason" (RdD, 10). The internal and external reasons of giving are now reviewed, and we see that they apparently reduce gifthood to a rational exchange that contributes to the reinforcement rather than the suppression of the economic order. Giving becomes an activity of resistance to the enveloping claims of metaphysical reason, and at this point of the argument it seems to be struggling heroically against overwhelming odds.

The Triple Reduction (§§ 3–4)

To free giving from the domination of commercial logic, Marion interrogates the gift "beginning at the point whence its phenomenon arises, just before it is dissolved in exchange, during the fragile moment in which its three moments have not yet yielded to the sufficient reason of the economy" (RdD,13). There is perhaps something mythical or even mystical about this pure phenomenological moment. Marion has whittled gifthood down to so pure a form that its actual phenomenological apparition is condemned to be a rare and fleeting event.

The means by which Marion seeks to establish the horizon of gifthood are paradoxical. Giver, receiver, and gift must disappear so that gifthood can manifest itself. Just as, for Husserl, in order to study the pure form of time perception we need to take the most exiguous percept possible—a simple tone, for example—so Marion first isolates the form of gifthood in exiguous forms of giving: a dead or anonymous benefactor, an ungrateful or indifferent recipient, a gift that may consist only in an invisible inner attitude. Here the gift is alienated from the social bond that is usually regarded as primary:

> Alms, as a unilateral gift to an unknown person, is a bizarre case. . . . Logically, it is a gift that excludes, affirms a domination, of which the chief sense is to reveal the impossibility for the recipient of returning the gift. The spiritual dimension can neutralize the perverse effects of the unilateral gift to an unknown person incapable of returning it (but this does not happen necessarily).[21]

Even if the reduction is thought to reveal the essential structure of giving, rather than producing a perversion of it, it is hard to keep such a rarefied structure in view for long. In his analysis of time consciousness, Husserl stepped beneath the level of perception and intentionality to study the hyletic level of consciousness as a mute, naked sensing of impressions. Granel asks why he did not go a step farther and put sensation and impression out of play, in order to reach a still more ineffable presence![22] Marion's givenness is just as much an ultimate absolute as Husserl's time consciousness and is established by just as radical a despoliation, recalling the *aphairesis* of negative theology. But just as in Husserl the exiguous perceived temporal object, such as the tone, is still a distraction from the pure awareness of time, so in Marion the residual presence of giver, recipient, and gift is a distraction from the pure horizon of gifthood. In both cases the radical reduction risks becoming a "phenomenology without phenomenon."[23]

"First, the gift can be constituted as a gift without any compensation of the giver (either in real or symbolic terms), because the gift can be constituted without any giver at all" (RdD, 14)—as seen in the example of an anonymous benefactor. But anonymous donations to individuals or to public charities, though meritorious, are hardly the primary style of giving. Paul's fund-raising for the Jerusalem community maximized the personal bonds it would create between donors and recipients (Romans 15:25–28; 2 Corinthians 8–9—texts that might be worth a fresh exegesis in light of current concerns with the gift). "Second, the gift can also be constituted as a gift without a recipient" (RdD, 14)—as in the case where I give to an enemy. But would it not be better that the gift affects the enemy, perhaps turning him into a friend? Would not such a dissolution and transformation of fixated identity testify to the power of the gift? Christianity itself turns on a gift that transforms enemies into friends (the gift of divine forgiveness enacted in the self-giving of Christ). "Third, the gift can be accomplished without giving any object susceptible to being returned into the fold of exchange value" (RdD, 15)—as in the gift of my attention, my care, my time. I note that psychoanalysts and others do subject the latter gifts to financial measurement, precisely so as not to make them enslaving of the recipient, a situation that again relativizes the sharp disjunction between gift and economic exchange. Regulated commercial exchange can be a blessed release from the crushing obligations incurred by receiving gifts. Again, is a gift with no object not also a deficient kind of gift? While it may be "the intention" that counts, the giver usually tries to incarnate the intention by offering flowers, an embrace, or some other concrete token. The gift of grace in Christianity is massively embodied in the corporeality of Christ and the sacraments.

A problem with all three illustrations is that they show not the nonexistence of giver, recipient, or gift, but their concealment or nonapparency. Also, there is no "reduction" of the ego of the giver; rather, "I give myself in my most complete ipseity" (RdD, 16) — the unconscious giver, far from being non-self, is more purely and intensely self. "The gift reduced to givenness has no awareness of what it is doing; it has hands to do it, but the right ignores what the left does — and it does it only on this condition" (RdD, 16).[24] Could we say that in this regime of giving, the self is protected by being concealed, even from its own observation?

This suspension of giver, receiver, and gift risks avoiding the grasp of economic rationalism only by "the disappearance of all the real process of the gift" (RdD, 17). Now Marion concedes that the point of departure was incorrect: "We began the inquiry on the gift from its contrary, exchange, and found a correct access to it in disqualifying what hindered it, reciprocity" (RdD, 17). Marion still does not think of beginning the inquiry with the intersubjective process of give-and-take, in which giver, receiver, and gift themselves lose their fixated identities. Indeed, he equates reciprocity with economic exchange, as if the potential for reciprocity and the quest for reciprocity inscribed in every gift were a degradation. Giving to others whose nonresponse is assured is a method of disinfecting the gift of economic besmirchment, and indeed, paradoxically, of bringing it under economic control. One puts the gift in an account that is pleasingly unambiguous, in that the "expenditure" column is regularly filled by the free choice of the ego, while the column for "returns or recompense" is a pure blank.

This transparent asymmetry carries over to Marion's study of fatherhood, as "a gift always already reduced and brought back to givenness, free of all decline into the economy, born free of sufficient reason" (RdD, 17). The exposition of this positive phenomenon is intended to correct the too abstract point of departure that defined the gift over against economic exchange by the triple "without," and thus to replace the antinomies to which that led with paradoxes that bring out the full phenomenality of giving. Fatherhood is not an ordinary *donnée* but a given that is itself a giving, a *donné donnant* (RdD, 18).

Though fatherhood, as a kind of contract, has a social and political significance that varies from place to place, Marion claims that there is a fundamental phenomenon that arises before these social aspects, which are ascribed to "the economic interpretation in terms of exchange," that "belongs to metaphysics" and "obscures the determinations of this gift, as it appears in the horizon of givenness" (RdD, 18). But it may be suspected that, like all the other institutions of giving, fatherhood does not have a pure essence that lies open to immediate phenomenological inspection. In discrediting as "metaphysical" whatever empirical insight into fatherhood the human sciences may yield, Marion turns the tables in advance on anyone who would object that his own abstraction of an essence of fatherhood is quintessentially metaphysical. Fatherhood gives new vividness to the triple reduction:

> First, the giver remains essentially absent and suspended, for *the father is lacking*. . . . He leaves (must leave) and makes himself noticed by the child in that he is lacking to him, and this on principle. . . . In order to remain, the father must be lacking and shine by his absence. He appears insofar as he disappears. (RdD, 19)

This chimes with Marion's reconceiving of God the Father as the divine distance, a separation that unites. Marion here deals with a theme that is central in psychoanalysis, but does not draw on the insights of Freud or Lacan to provide his phenomenological *Wesensschau* with an empirical footing. Similarly, he discusses self-love with no reference to the psychoanalytical theory of narcissism.[25] This is not simply a matter of ignoring empirical research, for psychoanalysis affects the very essence of such matters, that is, it has direct philosophical consequences.

"Secondly: . . . the child, though appearing to be a recipient (and par excellence, because he receives not only a gift but receives himself as the gift of a possibility), cannot by definition make good on the least consciousness of a debt" (RdD, 20). But could not one say, with equal plausibility, that it is one's relation to one's father that determines one's lifelong conceptions of debt and duty? Can that be written off as a secondary and "metaphysical" social or economic interpretation? Marion speaks of filial duty as barred by an impossibility in principle, the impossibility of returning the gift received—life itself. The child gives life to another, keeping open the spiral of the gift, which Marion sees reflected in genealogical tables. Marion follows up this clue to the logic of the "wheel" of giving, noting how time's arrow relates parents to children in a chain of givers and receivers whose giving and receiving are predicated on a radical nonreciprocation. Emptiness is built into the process.

Finally,

> the gift given in fatherhood . . . can in no way become an object or an entity. . . . The father gives to the child only life (and a name which sanctions it) . . . which, precisely because it makes possible . . . every entity and every object, itself belongs neither to beingness nor to objecthood. (RdD, 21)

One thinks of the mother as the one who gives life, and the father as the one who gives a name and identity to the child, breaking the mother–child symbiosis to establish for the child the objectivity of the symbolic order. If the category of "gift" is central to paternity, it is in quite a different form than in the case of maternity, and the eventual return of the gift will take a different form as well. The son returns the gift by continuing the father's work, defending the father's name—notions that make little sense in the case of the mother. But perhaps *paternité* in this discussion should be translated as "parenthood" rather than "fatherhood."

Paternity, Marion concludes, deploys "the entire phenomenality of the gift reduced to pure givenness" (RdD, 21). Whether it really does so remains doubtful to this reader—first, because the philosophical structures set forth seem as much a formal construction, in a constantly paradoxical style, as the fruit of actual phenomenological study, and would need to be fleshed out more fully to carry complete conviction; and second, because it remains unclear whether this structure is capable of taking the abundance of anthropological discourse on paternity into account.

Marion's Buddhist Affinities

Marion's triple reduction has a very interesting analogue in Mahayana Buddhism. In the Perfection of Wisdom sutra, the virtue of giving is seen as perfect when one realizes that neither giver, nor gift, nor recipient has any real existence. Giving (*dāna*) is the first of the six (or ten) virtues of a bodhisattva, and the sixth is wisdom (*prajñā*), the wisdom that apprehends the emptiness of all entities. Perfect giving is rooted in wisdom and in awareness that neither the giver, nor the recipient, nor the gift itself has any inherent existence. Hence no enslaving attachment to any of the three can arise. The idea of seeking a reward for such giving also loses any possible ground. "When he has given a gift, he does not make it into a basis or support. And he does never expect any reward from it."[26] The act of giving remains a free act, not impeding the openness of wisdom, because it does not fixate on giver, gift, or recipient. This is less a philosophical purism than a charter for spiritual advance.

In the long account of *dāna* given in the *Mahā-prajñāpāramitā-śāstra* (extant only in Chinese), an encyclopedic commentary, apocryphally attributed to Nāgārjuna, on the Perfection of Wisdom SUTRA in 8,000 LINES, the lofty doctrine of empty giving is embedded among homelier preaching that stresses the moral benefits of giving: that the gift consists essentially in the will to give, independent of benefit to the recipient, and that an impure gift is one motivated by self-interest, insolence, aversion, fear, desire to seduce, and such factors.[27] The good giver gives with faith and respect, from his hand, at the right time, without harming anyone. Only the gift made in view of the way of nirvana is pure, as opposed to a gift seeking happiness in this or the next life. Giving destroys passions of avarice, envy, hypocrisy, dissipation, regret, and lack of respect, among others. A *śravaka* gives in order to escape from rebirth, but a bodhisattva gives for all beings, or to know the true character of the dharma and to acquire Buddhahood.

Even at the highest point, *do ut des* (I give that you may give) thinking is not eliminated: "When one knows that the thing given is absolutely empty, the same as nirvana, and one gives alms to beings in that spirit, the recompense of the gift is inexhaustible."[28] It is almost as if the reward structure were built into the idea of the gift. The bodhisattva "gives indifferently at all times,"[29] not discriminating among recipients of what he gives, but practicing the detachment that accords with the nonduality and sameness (*samatā*) of empty reality. Such giving is without marks (*animitta*). The three obstacles to it are found in the thought that "it is *I* who give *this thing to this recipient*."[30] Such notions are characteristic of discriminative thinking, which makes much of the solid identity of things and has forgotten the merely conventional character of their being. The nonexistence of giver, gift, and recipient abolishes the distinctions between them. "The great bodhisattva who resides in the perfection of wisdom by the method of nonresiding should fulfill the virtue of the gift by the method of refusal, abstaining from the distinction between giver, beneficiary, and the thing given."[31]

The Buddhist vision has no need to find paradoxical aspects of the gift, as Marion does. The practice of giving in all its empirical diversity is taken on board. The bodhisattva's perfection of giving realizes the inner nature of all giving, as a transaction between a giver and a receiver involving a gift, all three of which are empty of substantial being. To tune into this emptiness is to be able to take part in the play of giving and receiving with spiritual freedom, fixated on neither oneself, nor the other, nor the gift. Applying this to paternity, one could say that father and son play well their roles in bequeathing and receiving the name (the symbolic order) when neither clings to the delusive reification of ego nor lends to the name itself an imaginary grandiose status (as happens in chauvinism or in insular patriotism).

The Gift beyond Reason (§§ 5–7)

Within the gift there are levels of excellence, and the higher forms of gifthood illuminate the others—this method of thinking is central to Marion's architectonic. Thus "fatherhood is distinguished clearly in that it is deployed without reciprocity and with excess" (R∂D, 21). It would be better to say that the relationship is asymmetrical. Reciprocity between Father and Son and even between God and His people is central to Scripture; to talk of fatherhood as "invalidating reciprocity" and "not according it the slightest rights" (RdD, 22) seems somewhat stilted. When this is taken as a cue to the essence of gifthood, one again feels that the insistence on phenomenality risks short-circuiting forms of relationality that phenomenology cannot master. Linked with this is a similar short circuit in the relations of phenomenology and rationality. Marion not only reduces the order of signification to that of phenomenality;[32] reason itself must be reduced to givenness! "This surpassing [of reciprocity], anterior to ethics, itself reaches back to the basic determination of metaphysics, putting in question its root-principle, the principle of identity; this principle supposes that nothing can be, at the same moment and in the same respect, other than itself" (RdD, 23). "The relations of production, possession, and consumption that weave societies and sustain their cohesion," "the political ideals of equality and solidarity"—

> reciprocity generalizes under all these forms the same principle of identity and the same demand for non-contradiction. Hence, if the reduced gift is attested only in subverting reciprocity, and thus the equality of things with themselves, not only does it con-

tradict the economy and its conditions of possibilities of experience, but also and above all it contradicts the principle of noncontradiction itself. (RdD, 23)

Ironically, this radical claim flirts with bad logic: "A is based on B. C subverts A. Therefore C subverts B." Marion would say that social solidarity is not merely based on noncontradiction (what isn't?). It is, rather, a generalization of the principle of noncontradiction. But can one generalize a principle that is already absolutely universal?

How does the gift undermine the principle of noncontradiction?

> The reduced gift allows a thing not to remain equal to itself but to become (or rather to give) more than itself, or again it allows a thing to lose in the exchange in being accomplished as gift. The reduced gift gives (or receives) always more (or less) than itself, for if the balance remained equal, the gift would simply not have taken place—but in place of it, an exchange. (RdD, 23)

The father

> contradicts himself in renouncing an equal exchange, precisely to fill his role of father; but as well he gives far more than he possesses in giving a life that in a sense he does not have (in and of) himself. . . . Fatherhood manifests the non-identity of every self to itself. (RdD, 23)

All this means is that gifts are intrinsically asymmetrical and set up a process of exchanges that can never be closed in final equalization of accounts (a point made by Godbout). The logic of this is something like Hegelian dialectic—more open-ended, if one likes, in accord with Bataille's notions of gratuitous expenditure, taken up by Derrida. To say that it rattles the principle of contradiction, however, goes too far. Or, if it does, one might by the same token argue that everything does so, as Marion indeed suggests: "This essential and polysemic nonidentity, which the gift frees wherever it is practiced, ultimately imposes nothing less than a new definition of possibility"—that is, "possibility consists not in the identity of self with self but in an excess of self over self" (RdD, 24). The self-identity of everything is undermined by its possibility. Whether such a dialectical account of possibility is sufficient to track the dynamics of the gift may be doubted. In any case, Marion again makes this logic tributary to the phenomenal, and even its claimed polysemy comes within the bourne of a phenomenological overview. Rather than pursue the logic of the gift,

Marion, inspired by Heidegger's liberation of the thinking of being from the dominance of the principle of sufficient reason (in *Der Satz vom Grund*, 1956), wants the logic of the gift to be so paradoxical that the claim of logic is broken and the gift can come into view in its authentic phenomenality, like the rose that is "without why."

In Buddhism, entities have a merely momentary existence, and cease to be as soon as they arise. Nāgārjuna gives logical bite to the emptiness-teaching of the Perfection of Wisdom sutra by his dialectical refutations that show all entities to be empty of inherent existence and to enjoy only a provisional or conventional manner of being that collapses on its inner contradiction as soon as one tests it by analysis. This is the "middle way" between substantialism and nihilism; "emptiness" signifies the nonsubstantiality of all phenomena due to their dependent co-arising:

> Each of the terms of the causal process has no more existence than the stitches of a jersey. To think causality, conditionality, in depth, is to admit that nothing is itself. Nowhere is there any identity, any ipseity. Everything holds together, finds itself in interdependence, *Esse* = *interesse*. In Sanskrit, *śūnyatā*, emptiness.[33]

Nāgārjuna takes a series of items that could be put forward as claimants to real existence—including the self, time, motion, and various Buddhist truths—and in each case shows logical contradictions implied in this claim to real existence, which undermine the claim. But far from overthrowing the principle of noncontradiction, it is by this very principle that he reveals that "nothing is itself"—that everything is empty of own-being. A thing cannot be both of two contraries, but it may be neither, if it is "devoid of a sense or a reference."[34] If the gift is at one and the same time two contraries, then the suspicion is that the notion of gift is devoid of sense or reference, or has a merely functional existence, as a provisional designation.

Where Madhyamaka Buddhism uses the principle of contradiction to undermine the claim of apparently self-evident phenomena, Marion uses the phenomenon to undermine the claim of the principle of contradiction. But, as in his reduction of giver, gift, and recipient, Marion offers an example that does not go as far as he wishes it to. Spontaneous, creative giving may elude the claim of the principle of sufficient reason. Fatherhood may have a paradoxical relation to that principle, for if the father stands for the symbolic order, his authority also has a contingent character; to the child, the authority of the father is linked with that of the symbolic order, but as a personal claim on the child, it introduces him into a realm of interpersonal freedom that is not covered by logical principles. The indulgent father abrogates for the child the principle of sufficient reason, much as the God of the New Testament abrogates the primacy of the Law. But when this freedom reaches the point where the father or his gift is experienced as an unresolved contradiction, the consequences are disturbing.

The gift gives itself of itself from itself. It cannot be made answerable to a principle of reason above it. Without the self-manifestation of the gift, the activities of giving and receiving remain impossible:

> The giver does not decide for such and such a gift because of such and such a potential beneficiary, who would have solicited him more than the others; the number of the needy discourages and the impudence of the demands disgusts as well, without allowing one to decide. (RdD, 26)

One might object that, against such Hamletism, the Good Samaritan simply decides to adopt, or recognize, someone as a neighbor, by taking pity on one person in need, *solvitur donando*. But for Marion, as for Derrida, nothing is this simple. Giving has a condition:

> This is not possible unless the gift arises of itself and imposes itself as such on the giver. It can do so only in coming to him as something to be given, as that which demands that one give it: *donandum est*. (RdD, 26)

The Samaritan may have made rational calculations about how to help the man fallen among thieves, but the core event is that the necessity of his act of giving imposed itself as a revelation or inspiration. This is a very pure or "saturated" phenomenon of giving, reminding me of Augustine's account of grace as *delectatio victrix* (victorious delectation), made much of by the Jansenists. Indeed, the self-manifestation of gifthood is a miracle of grace. Again, one can query the phenomenological plausibility of this self-manifesting gift. Rather than the gift, is it not the other, the potential beneficiary, who elicits the response of giving? Also, the more ordinary rational bases of a free choice of giving are played down by Marion. In giving such unique authority to the self-manifestation of the gift, he may undercut the importance of creative initiative in fulfilling the command of charity. To see the entire order of giving, receiving, and return giving as launched and steered by the phenomenon of the gift, itself imposes a nondialectical stability on the processes of interpersonal exchange in order to secure givenness as such as the universal law of all phenomenality. Yet his language does bring into view an aspect of giving, which founds its disinterested graciousness, an aspect celebrated in religious rituals or the tea ceremony.

"The gift decides by itself about its donation and decides by itself its giver in appearing incontestably as givable and in making itself be given" (RdD, 27). The sole reason of the gift is its inherent self-destination to be given and received. All phenomena reveal themselves as given, but this special phenomenon reveals itself as gift and commands the giver and receiver to adopt their respective positions. Both giver and receiver are dislodged from their self-centered security by the power of the gift. They forgo "the most powerful of phantasms, which founds every economy and every calculation of interests in exchange, namely, that of the self-identity of the 'I' (contradicting the principle of identity)" (RdD, 27). Phenomenality is not something passively contemplated, but something that at its highest imposes itself as an authority demanding the obedient responses of giving and receiving. "The reduced gift . . . achieves the *self* of the full phenomenon" (RdD, 29). It has the power of something beautiful, which exacts the homage of a creative recognition. One can turn one's back on the gift, but to do so is to alienate oneself from phenomenality, that is, from the way things truly are. Does this undercut the freedom of the gift, the idea that to give and to receive is a project realized by two people together? The grace of the gift is that it grants the possibility of such a free exchange. To say that the gift phenomenalizes itself on its own accord, without reference to any prior cause or reason other than its own pure logic of givenness, would be more graphic if one spelled out how the gift enables a situation of freedom, a breakthrough beyond calculation, achieved by giver and receiver together in obedience to the spirit of the gift. The gift creates the giver and the receiver, but equally the giver and receiver create the gift, just as the work of art creates the artist but the artist equally creates the work, even if in some sense the work brings itself into existence, *causa sui*.

Marion concludes with an ingenious reduction of the principle of sufficient reason to the register of givenness. "In exceeding the demand for a cause and a reason, not only is the gift not doomed condemn itself to lack rationality, but to the contrary it may be able to constitute a 'larger reason' than the narrow *ratio reddenda* of metaphysics" (RdD, 29). Reason itself is given:

> To assure sufficient reason, it is needful that a mind (specifically, in the case of contingent propositions, an omniscient mind) render it. But to render (*re-dare*) implies that one gives it again, that one gives it in return, thus essentially that one gives it. . . . Since reason must thus be rendered, since even it must be given, it rests on the gift, not at all on itself. (RdD, 31)
>
> *Ratio* remains in itself secondary and as if derived from a more originary instance—givenness, which places it in the situation of figuring as a complete reason and as a last argument. Givenness controls more intimately the *ratio reddenda* than exchange controls the gift, for no reason can dispense itself from being rendered, that is, from being staged and preceded by a gift. (RdD, 31)

This echoes Heidegger's idea that a primordial phenomenological openness necessarily precedes and in some sense grounds the "merely" rational matters with which metaphysics is concerned; thus *a-lētheia* as unconcealment would be the condition of possibility of truth as accuracy or correspondence, and the latter would have secondary if not epiphenomenal status. To say that the gift, or the giftedness of being, eludes the principle of sufficient reason is plausible; to say that it founds that principle as the *principium reddendae rationis*, the principle that demands that reasons be *given*, is less so. It looks as if there is merely a verbal connection between the givenness of phenomena and the giving of reasons for them.

I conclude that Marion's phenomenology remains rather tangential to the empirical realities of giving and receiving as human relational activities that follow laws more complex than those of the economy. While awaiting further clarification of these laws, has philosophy nothing to say? Must phenomenology resign itself to providing merely auxiliary clarifications to a naturalistic account of giving? In articulating the claims of phenomenology in their most consequent and far-reaching form, Marion has sharpened and highlighted the fundamental question facing the phenomenological movement since its origins, the question of its status and scope. In studying how phenomenology deals with the gift, we see again and again how the gift slips out of the phenomenologist's sight, and how phenomenology tends to overreach itself in its efforts to retrieve the territories subtracted from its sway. Perhaps the gift is only one of innumerable cases in which the focus on phenomenality does not suffice to bring us to grips with the matter itself.

8

Phenomenality in the Middle
Marion, Romano, and the Hermeneutics of the Event

Shane Mackinlay

"The Reason of the Gift"[1] is part of Jean-Luc Marion's broader phenomenological project, which begins from his critique of the traces of a constituting subject retained by Husserl and Heidegger. While Marion's phenomenology of givenness (*donation*) eliminates these traces, it does so only by reducing the subject to a passive recipient on whom phenomena impose themselves. In contrast, Claude Romano (another contemporary French phenomenologist) responds to the same concerns about *Dasein*'s subjective character without limiting the subject to pure receptivity.[2] By comparing these two responses to the issue of a constituting subject, I will draw attention to some of the limitations in Marion's account, and highlight the importance of hermeneutics in phenomenology.

Marion argues that neither Husserl nor Heidegger breaks free of certain fundamental presuppositions that undermine the Husserlian project, and that belong to a line of thought running back to Kant and Descartes. In Marion's view, both Husserl and Heidegger reduce phenomena within limits dictated by and for a sovereign subject: "Metaphysical (in fact, Cartesian) egology is a paradigm that always haunts the I, even reduced, even phenomenological" (*BG*, 187/*ED*, 262; cf. *BG/ED*, §§1–3, §19, §25). Thus, in Heidegger's *Being and Time (BT)*,[3] *Dasein*'s projection and possibility take on an increasingly dominant position. As a result, the world is more a characteristic of *Dasein*'s own self-projection than the referential totality in which *Dasein* finds itself always already disposed and thrown (*BT*, §14, 92/64; cf. *BT*, §18, 119/86; *BT*, §18, 121/88). In *Reduction and Givenness* (*RG*), Marion concludes that while *Dasein* is in many respects a "destruction" of the ego, it depends on an implicit "I am" that is an "heir" of the cogito's "I think" (*RG*, 106/*RD*, 160; *BG*, 261/*ED*, 360).

Marion's response to the shortcomings he sees in Husserl and Heidegger is to center his own phenomenology on the givenness of phenomena. He insists that phenomena must be seen as *given* rather than as constituted in any way, and consistently applies his principle of givenness to exclude any suggestion of phenomena appearing under conditions imposed on them by a subject. Instead of the appearing of phenomena being conditioned, Marion asserts that a phenomenon *gives itself* of itself (*BG*, 138/*ED*, 196), and appears by *imposing itself* on a recipient (*BG*, 201/*ED*, 282).

Thus, in "The Reason of the Gift" Marion uses gifts as a paradigm for phenomena in general, and argues that no reason can be given to account for a gift apart from the gift itself. If a gift is explained as the effect of a cause, then it is either given in response to something that has been received or given to achieve an end. In either case, it is no longer simply gratuitous; the gift is assigned a value in an economy and becomes an object of exchange. Marion maintains that a gift is possible only beyond the metaphysical domain that is ruled by the principles of causality and of sufficient reason. His phenomenology of givenness sets out this nonmetaphysical domain, within which a phenomenon appears purely as given and on its own horizon—a phenomenon reduced to givenness.

At one point in *BG*, Marion suggests that *Dasein*'s facticity should be understood in a "middle voice where I am neither the author nor the spectator of the phenomenon" (*BG*, 147/*ED*, 207). Here, he is echoing the introduction to *BT*, where Heidegger situates phenomenality in the context of the middle-voiced verb φαίνεσθαι, indicating that phenomena cannot be understood either as the activity of a subject or as a purely passive experience of that which happens to us (*BT*, §7, 51/*SZ*, 29). Marion's critique of the traces of subjectivity and agency retained in *Dasein* supports a conclusion that the subtle nuance of this middle voice eludes Heidegger (at least in *BT*). However, the same assessment can be made of Marion himself—though in his case the emphasis is on the "self" of the phenomenon, and therefore the passive voice dominates.

In this chapter, I highlight Marion's failure to sustain a middle voice by comparing him with Romano. Romano shares Marion's concerns about Husserl and Heidegger, concluding that consciousness has an "absolute priority" for Husserl,[4] and that because *Dasein* "remains the measure of all phenomenality" for Heidegger, it conserves "the prerogatives conferred on the modern subject since Descartes" (*L'événement et le monde* [*EM*], 30). Romano responds to these concerns by developing an account of the event, which is one of the phenomena also considered at length by Marion.[5] However, unlike Marion, whose account of the event marginalizes hermeneutics, Romano makes hermeneutics central to his account. I contend that Romano's focus on hermeneutics allows him to describe the appearing of phenomena as a genuine encounter between the perceiver and the perceived. That is to say, he comes closer to a "middle voice" than does Marion, although Romano himself does not describe his project in exactly these terms.

Before directly comparing Marion and Romano, I set out the account of the event given by each of them, with particular emphasis on the place they assign to hermeneutics, and on their account of the subject as the *adonné*[6] and the *advenant*, respectively.

Marion's Phenomenology of the Event

Events fascinate Marion because, rather than persisting in presence as objects do, they *happen*. Events well up in appearing, and impose themselves as a fait accompli. They cannot be planned, produced, or foreseen. Marion uses the happening of events to support his insistence that phenomenology must attribute the initiative in appearing to phenomena—and not to any cause that might explain them metaphysically, nor to any consciousness for which they appear. Marion emphasizes this initiative by inverting the normal understanding of both causality and intentionality in the appearing of events. Thus, rather than events being dependent on a cause, he presents them as phenomenological facts that have priority over any cause, and are even uncaused. Likewise, rather than events being the "objects" of a subject's intentional act of consciousness, he proposes that they impose themselves on a perceiver, and thus reveal the "self" of a phenomenon. Marion's emphasis on this "self" of a phenomenon leads him to redefine the subject as the *adonné*, who is defined by receptivity. After outlining these two inversions, I argue that they make the *adonné*'s role essentially passive, and that this passive receptivity is reflected in Marion's restriction of hermeneutics to acts of interpretation *after* an event has actually happened.

Marion makes a sharp distinction between the "facticity" of the event and the "actuality" (*effectivité*) of an effect, which can be reduced to the predictable product of known causes. In doing this, he argues for the phenomenological priority of the effect (that appears) over its cause (whose presence he relegates to metaphysics). He argues that an inquiry into the causes of an effect relies on metaphysical presuppositions that are inadmissible in phenomenology. Therefore, to remove phenomena from the metaphysical domain, they should not be considered as effects, but simply as "faits accomplis."

Marion's key argument for the phenomenological priority of facts is that it is possible to ask about what caused a phenomenon only *after* it has already happened. So, even though a cause might have a *metaphysical* priority over its effect, the fact of a phenomenon's appearing has a *phenomenological* priority over whatever may have produced it.[7] On the basis of this temporal priority, Marion inverts the normal relationship between cause and effect, so as to "construe the cause as the effect of the effect" (*BG*, 165*[8]/*ED*, 232). He argues that, considered phenomenologically, "the event *precedes its cause*[9] (or causes)" because any knowledge of its cause *as cause* can come only after the event has happened, as an effect (*BG*, 165/*ED*, 233).

Marion is aware that giving the effect (as event) priority over its cause contradicts the principle of causality, and he reinforces this contradiction by comparing the event of the given phenomenon to God, who is the classic exception to the principle of causality. As an event, a phenomenon is a "quasi (non-)cause (*causa sui*)" that shares the divine privilege of "not having to respond to the question that enjoins all other beings to offer a reason [*rendre raison*] for their existence and their appearance" (*BG*, 160f./*ED*, 227). Therefore, if phenomena are to be understood as "event[s] without cause or reason," then the universality of the principle of causality must itself be put into question (*BG*, 161/*ED*, 227). Describing phenomena as events rather than objects is part of Marion's strategy to remove them from the metaphysical domain in which the principle of causality is valid.

Arguing for the event as a phenomenological *causa sui* allows Marion to emphasize the "*self* of the phenomenon" (*BG*, 159/*ED*, 226). Some such concept of self is implied by his recurring language about "that which shows *itself*" and "that which gives *itself*."[10] However, beyond describing it as "original" (*IE*, 31/*DS*, 36), Marion never specifies exactly what this self is. His concern is not so much with the phenomenon's self per se, but rather with his claim that "in the appearing, the initiative belongs in principle to the phenomenon, not the gaze" (*BG*, 159/*ED*, 225; cf. *IE*, 30/*DS*, 35). He insists that the appearing of phenomena is not a metaphysical actuality produced by something else that acts as cause or constituting agent. Rather, the appearing of a phenomenon is a phenomenological fact in which "the *self* of the phenomenon . . . comes, does its thing [*survient*], and leaves on its own; showing *itself*, it also shows the *self* that takes (or removes) the initiative of giving *itself*" (*BG*, 159f./*ED*, 226). Far from being constituted, the phenomenon "*imposes*" itself (*BG*, 201/*ED*, 282; emphasis added), so that "the gaze receives its impression of the phenomenon before any attempt at constituting it" (*BG*, 159/*ED*, 225).

By ascribing a "self" to phenomena, Marion seeks to add credibility to his claim that the event of a phenomenon's appearing does not result from a perceiving subject's action: "If the phenomenon really gives *itself*, then it obligatorily confiscates the function and the role of the *self*, and therefore can concede to the ego only a *me* of second rank, by derivation" (*IE*, 45*/*DS*, 53f.). If there must be a "self" in order for there to be action in the world, then Marion believes this self must belong to the phenomenon. Thus, if one of the roles of a "self" is to be the source of an intentional act of consciousness, he contends that, in the fact of an event, "intentionality is inverted: I become the objective of the object" (*BG*, 146/*ED*, 207). Instead of making the phenomenon, I am made by it; as a fait accompli, it accomplishes not only itself but me as well. To indicate that I receive myself in receiving the phenomenon, Marion designates this recipient the *adonné*—the one who is given over in the giving (*BG*, 322/*ED*, 441f.).

Marion maintains that the receptivity of the *adonné* "mediates" or "goes beyond" passivity and activity (*BG*, 264/*ED*, 364; *IE*, 48/*DS*, 57)—a claim that supports his view that *Dasein*'s facticity should be understood in the middle voice (*BG*, 147/*ED*, 207). Moreover, he ascribes great significance to the *adonné*'s receptivity, in its role as that which transforms the given into the shown, and thus makes it a phenomenon (*BG*, 264f./*ED*, 364; *IE*, 49f./*DS*, 58f.). However, Marion is so concerned to avoid producing another heir to the Cartesian ego that the balance of his thought tends strongly toward depicting the *adonné* as passive. In both the instances where he proposes a receptivity that is beyond activity and passivity (*BG*, 264/*ED*, 364; *IE*, 48/*DS*, 57), Marion immediately elaborates that receptivity by describing the *adonné* as a "screen" on which the given "crashes" in order to manifest itself (*BG*, 265/*ED*, 365; *IE*, 50/*DS*, 59). In this image, there is no sense of activity in the reception, nor even of "mediation"—the *adonné* seems to be simply passive.

The passivity of the *adonné* corresponds to the emphasis Marion places on the "self" of the phenomenon. He repeatedly insists that the phenomenon gives *itself* and shows *itself* on the basis of *itself*—the phenomenon of the gift even "decides *itself*" (*BG*, 112/*ED*, 161). One of the risks in placing such an emphasis on a "self" of the phenomenon is that, far from overcoming or mediating the distinction between passivity and activity, the distinction is simply repeated in an inverted form. Indeed, Marion often describes phenomena in terms that ascribe to them something very close to the active role previously assigned to the subject. Thus, in place of phenomena being constituted by a subject, he sees phenomena as imposing themselves on a subject, who is in turn constituted as receiver by this imposition.[11] Marion's phenomena often seem to be acting as agents, imposing themselves on the passive recipient of consciousness into which they crash. There is no question that the primacy Marion accords to givenness[12] removes the vestiges of Cartesian or Kantian sovereignty from the subject. However, in many instances this dethroning seems to be accomplished simply by enthroning a new sovereign rather than by overturning the dominion of sovereignty as such.

Marion's insistence on the initiative and selfhood of phenomena prevents him from finding a middle way between the active and passive voices—though where Heidegger is inclined to the active, Marion is inclined to the passive. Consistent with this restriction of the recipient to a passive role, Marion excludes acts of interpretation from the actual happening of events. In place of Heidegger's ontological (or existential) sense of hermeneutics,[13] where hermeneutics is intrinsic to the actual appearing of phenomena, Marion confines hermeneutics to a marginal and derivative sense of "subsequent interpretation"—after phenomena have already appeared.

Marion responds to critics of the place he gives to hermeneutics by protesting that his "interpretation of the phenomenon as given, not only does not forbid hermeneutics but demands it" (*IE*, 33n/*DS*, 39n).[14] However, this protestation of innocence is somewhat disingenuous, because although he proposes "a hermeneutic without an end in time" (*BG*, 229/*ED*, 319), this is only hermeneutics in its derivative sense. On the two occasions where he specifies a role for hermeneutics in relation to events, Marion describes a future series of epistemic acts that interpret an event subsequent to its happening (*BG*, 229/*ED*, 319; *IE*, 33/*DS*, 39). At no point does he make any concession to the more fundamental ontological sense of hermeneutics that Heidegger proposes as primary.

Marion concludes his protest by correctly identifying that the point at issue is not the necessity of hermeneutics but its "phenomenological legitimacies" (*IE*, 33n/*DS*, 39n). However, he does not actually discuss this key issue, which determines the place hermeneutics is assigned in phenomenology. In short, does the phenomenological domain limit hermeneutics to epistemic acts in the way Marion suggests? Alternatively, as I am arguing, is not all phenomenology necessarily hermeneutic, because of the hermeneutic character of phenomenality itself?

A condition of possibility for any act of cognition or consciousness (including the epistemic type of hermeneutic interpretations admitted by Marion) is that there be some relation between consciousness and whatever is given to it as phenomena. Because this relation shapes the ways we interpret the meaning of both consciousness and phenomena, it can properly be referred to as hermeneutic—and, if it is hermeneutic, it is hermeneutic in a fundamental sense.

Romano's Evential Hermeneutics

Romano agrees with Heidegger that the fundamental phenomenological structure of the subject's encounter with phenomena is itself hermeneutic (in the primary sense). Thus, Romano describes the "subject" (which he calls the *advenant*) as a self-projecting agent who acts, makes decisions, and exercises freedom in a hermeneutic structure of possibilities (*EM*, 51). Likewise, he designates the interpretation of this *advenant* as "evential hermeneutics [*herméneutique événementiale*]" (*EM*, 34). However, Romano avoids the subjectivist aspects of *Dasein*, and does justice to Marion's concern for the genuine transcendence and otherness of phenomena that give themselves *as themselves*. In Romano's account, the *advenant* has a "passibility . . . [that] precedes the distinction of active and passive" (*EM*, 99), and that could equally be described as a "middle voice."

Romano's principal critique of Heidegger is that in insisting on everything that happens to *Dasein* being understood as one of *Dasein*'s own possibilities, Heidegger reduces phenomena to "modalities" of the Being of *Dasein*. By doing this, Heidegger restricts his account to one single event—"the *sole event that is* Dasein *itself, the event of its Being*" (*EM*, 27). There is no Other, and therefore no possibility of becoming other, because everything that happens is a possibility of *Dasein*, which it always already *is*.

Romano views *Dasein* as limited to an empty playing out of its own already existing possibilities, and introduces the possibility of the genuinely new by distinguishing between two types of events. Understood in the ordinary "evental [*événementiel*]" sense, events happen as an actualizing or factualizing of a possibility that is already present in the world, and are described by Romano as "innerworldly facts." Essentially different from these are "events in a properly event*ial* [*événemential*] sense," whose happening is a radical arriving (*advenir*) that upends the preexisting possibilities and thus reconfigures the world. Romano's distinction has some parallels to Heidegger's ontological difference, in that innerworldly facts are very much ontic actualities, while evential events not only reveal the fundamental significance of the happening of events, but also are the origin of the structures within which innerworldly facts can themselves arise.[15]

Romano singles out four key phenomenological differences between innerworldly facts and evential events. Innerworldly facts (1) are impersonal, (2) happen within a world, (3) are subject to causal explanation, and (4) are inscribed in a datable present. By contrast, evential events (1) are addressed to particular entities, (2) reconfigure the world, (3) cannot be explained by causes, and (4) occur with a "structural delay" that opens a future.

(1) Innerworldly facts, such as a bolt of lightning, are fundamentally impersonal events that do not affect any entity in particular (*EM*, 37). An evential event, on the other hand, such as grief, is always "addressed" to a particular entity, so that "I am in play myself" in its happening (*EM*, 44).

(2) Innerworldly facts always appear within the horizon of a preexisting world. Romano understands this "world" in a very Heideggerian sense, as a hermeneutic network of possibilities within which human subjects interpret meaning, understand themselves, and project their own possibilities in action (*EM*, 51). Evential events differ from innerworldly facts in that they do not happen *within* the already established horizon of a preexisting world, but rather *reconfigure* the world by upending (*bouleversant*) its possibilities, and thus appearing on their own horizon. Far from being innerworldy, these events are "*world-installing* [*instaurateur du monde*] for the *advenant*" (*EM*, 56). When an evential event happens to me, my world is "reconfigured"

and made "new"; none of my possibilities and projects remain unaffected.[16] In fact, "the event *is* [emphasis added] this metamorphosis of the world in which *the very meaning of the world is in play [se joue]*" (*EM*, 95). Importantly, while the world opened by the event is genuinely new, it results from a reconfiguration of the existing world rather than from a radically new creation.

(3) Because an innerworldly fact is an actualization of a preexisting possibility in an already established horizon, it is foreseeable within this horizon and subject to causal explanation (*EM*, 64). Eventual events, on the other hand, do not appear within any preexisting horizon, and are therefore not explicable as the effects of causes within such a horizon. Thus, Romano characterizes their welling up as "an-archic"—a "pure beginning on the basis of nothing [*pur commencement à partir de rien*]" (*EM*, 58). To illustrate this, he discusses the event of the first meeting that begins a relationship between two people. As a fact, its actualization is entirely explicable, in terms of how the two people came to cross paths, and even in terms of personality characteristics that might dispose them toward friendship. However, as the event in which a new relationship opens up in my life, a meeting "radically transcends its own actualisation, it reconfigures my possibles articulated in a world, and introduces in my own adventure a radically new *meaning*, which makes my adventure tremble, upends it from top to bottom, and thus modifies all my previous projects" (*EM*, 59). From this perspective, events are radically *inexplicable*. Indeed, far from being explained as the effect of a cause, an event is its own origin: "It is pure bursting out from itself into itself, unforeseeable in its radical novelty, and retrospectively installing a rupture [*scission*] with all the past" (*EM*, 60). This bursting forth establishes a new horizon of meaning, with a different range of possibilities on which I can project myself. The event "retransfigures my world" (*EM*, 61), "obliging the *advenant* to understand otherwise both himself and his world" (*EM*, 62). Because this shift in understanding takes place within the new horizon that an event opens, it becomes possible only *after* an event has already happened. Consequently, eventual events have a "structural delay," such that they are encountered only retrospectively (*EM*, 64), and thereby open me to the past (*EM*, 69).

(4) The final phenomenological difference between facts and events arises from this structural delay, and concerns temporality. An innerworldly fact is a "fait accompli"[17] that "is produced in a datable present, a definitive present where all is accomplished" (*EM*, 64). It

is simply a fact, with no unactualized potential, and is therefore located at a specific time. An event, on the other hand, is not datable for Romano: "It does not so much inscribe itself *in* time as *open* time, or *temporalise* it" (*EM*, 65). An eventual event is never encountered in the present of its happening, but only retrospectively, from the future that it opens.

Like Marion (and Heidegger), Romano gives the "subject" a new name—"the *advenant*," reflecting his understanding of how subjectivity arises and is reshaped in the happening of the event. Basic elements of Romano's concept of subjectivity are comparable with Heidegger's account of *Dasein* in *Being and Time*. Thus, Romano understands selfhood as the capacity to appropriate possibilities in a world.[18] However, in a crucial departure from Heidegger, there is no sense in which Romano's "subject" is itself the origin of its possibilities; rather, its possibilities are *opened to it* in the opening of a world that is the happening of an eventual event. For Romano, subjectivity is coming to (*ad-vient*) oneself in the happening (*advenant*) of an event in which one is implicated.[19]

This perpetual coming to (*a-venture*) myself of the *advenant* precludes any possibility of claiming sovereignty, either over myself or over the world of possibilities in which I project myself. Romano insists that I always come to myself from an origin other than myself, and that this is true from the very beginning of my existence. This insistence is reflected in the central place that he gives to birth in his analysis[20]: it is the event "that opens the world of the *advenant* for the first time" and that, "before any project of his and before any understanding . . . makes possible [*possibilise*] all his possibles and the world" (*EM*, 96). Though my birth happens to a "to whom [*à qui*]," strictly speaking, "I" am not present until after I am born. I am never the origin of that which I am, and which I am from my very beginning (i.e., originally).[21] Birth thus establishes a structural delay at my very origin; according to this delay, I can project myself only into future possibilities that have been opened by an event that itself always lies in the past. Romano's account of this delay allows him to describe the *advenant* as being born into a dynamic that makes it essentially temporal while precluding any suggestion that the *advenant* is itself the origin of this dynamic.

Romano's insistence that the *advenant* is not the origin of itself, nor of the world in which it projects its possibilities, leads him to introduce what he calls an "*eventual* possibility [*possibilité éventuel*]," which is the opening of a world, with its horizon of projectual possibilities, in the happening of an eventual event (*EM*, 117; emphasis added). As the opening of a world, eventual possibility is that which makes these projectual possibilities *possible,* and in which a future is opened that is not limited to an ultimately sterile playing out of the "dead possibilities" of my present (*EM*, 119). Eventual possibility reconfigures my world, and opens me to a possibility for myself *that I have not myself projected*, and that is therefore genuinely *other* than what I already am (*EM*, 121f.).

Marion in Light of Romano

Marion and Romano make similar critiques of the priority Husserl gives to consciousness, and of Heidegger's understanding of *Dasein* as self-projecting Being-in-the-world—especially with respect to the Cartesian tendency that survives in some of Heidegger's analyses. For both Marion and Romano, Heidegger does not do justice to the appearing of phenomena in their own right, but reduces them to a projection of the subject. This leads both thinkers to place a strong emphasis on the appearance of phenomena *as themselves*, imposing themselves *within their own horizon* rather than on a preexisting horizon established by a subject. Much of Romano's description of evential events closely parallels Marion's description of events: an evential event "*is produced on the basis of itself*" (*EM*, 42; cf. *BG*, 138/*ED*, 196); it appears as "*its own origin*" and on "*its own horizon*" (*EM*, 60; cf. *BG*, 229/*ED*, 318f.); it cannot be explained as the effect of any preceding cause, and is therefore "an-archic" (*EM*, 58; cf. *BG*, 160f./*ED*, 227), "unforeseeable" (*EM* 60; cf. *BG*, 199f./*ED*, 280f.; *IE*, 33/*DS*, 38), and even "im-possible" (*EM*, 122; cf. *BG*, 172f./*ED*, 243f.).

However, despite their many similarities, there are significant differences. Most significantly, Romano is far more cautious than Marion in attributing selfhood to events. While both ascribe the initiative of its happening to the event itself, and speak of its occurring "on the basis of itself," only Marion directly refers to "the self of the phenomenon" (e.g., *BG*, 159/*ED*, 226; *IE*, 34–38/*DS*, 40–45). In contrast, Romano takes great pains to distance himself from any suggestion of the event's having selfhood as such by situating it firmly in the context of its happening to a human subject: "The event, in the eventual sense, *is rightly [justement] nothing other* than this reconfiguration of my possibles, by which it is given to me to understand myself otherwise" (*EM*, 75). The "new world" that is installed by this reconfiguration remains "*my* world" (e.g., *EM*, 61; emphasis added). For Romano, the new horizon of possibility opened by the event is always a horizon for the understanding and projection of the *advenant* to whom the event happens (*EM*, 60–62). The event brings an excess of meaning and of possibility into my world, but these are clearly meaning *for me* and possibilities *for me* (*EM*, 61).

Marion's concern to exclude any suggestion of a constituting subject prevents him from admitting any great significance for the one to whom a phenomenon appears. He describes the appearing of a phenomenon as its "imposing" itself on a receiver (*BG*, 138/*ED*, 196), whose receiving shows the phenomenon simply as it gives itself (like an image on a screen [*BG*, 265/*ED*, 365] or the illumination of an indicator lamp [*BG*, 217/*ED*, 303]), and who even receives himself in this receiving—and is therefore the *adonné* (*BG*, 282/*ED*, 390). Not only does the subject have no constituting role, but the phenomenon is received as an already completed package—a "fait accompli" (*BG*, §15). The *adonné*'s reception of this already accomplished fact has no significance for the phenomenon other than allowing it to be shown. This implies that, in Marion's account, nothing about the *adonné* affects phenomena other than this capacity to transform givenness into manifestation, and that therefore a phenomenon can appear indifferently to any *adonné* whatsoever, while remaining essentially the same phenomenon. For Marion, there is no sense of an *encounter* between the *adonné* and that which is given, but simply a *transfer* of a predetermined package.

At first sight, Romano gives a similar impression, especially when he says that the event "has opened a *new* world" (*EM*, 55; emphasis added). However, he is clear that this world is "new" only in that "it is no longer, properly speaking, the *same* world" (*EM*, 55). More often, he describes the event as that which "*upends*" (*EM*, 45; emphasis added) and "*reconfigures* my possibles articulated in a world" (*EM*, 59; emphasis added), and leads to a "*metamorphosis* of the world and its meaning" (*EM*, 93; emphasis added), a "*mutation* of meaning" (*EM*, 95; emphasis added), or even a "*transition* from one sense of the world [evental] to the other [evential]" (*EM*, 94; emphasis added). All of these descriptions make clear that while the event brings something genuinely new for the *advenant*, it is not a creation ex nihilo that is received on a blank screen, and to which the particular *advenant* is irrelevant. Rather, the event happens in the context of an already existing totality of possibilities for meaning and projection, and its happening is the upending and reconfiguring of this very totality. The result of such an upending or reconfiguring depends fundamentally on the particularities of what is upended and reconfigured. In Romano's account, the world opened by the event is genuinely new, but not a radical origin.

This fundamental interrelatedness of the *advenant*, the world, and the event is central to Romano's thought, and means that each of these concepts can be understood only in terms of the others. The *advenant* is the one who is always arriving in the events that open his world; the world opened by events is the totality of possibility for the *advenant*; and events themselves are the reconfiguring of the *advenant*'s world.

One point in Marion's account where the lack of interrelatedness between the *adonné* and the world is particularly striking is in his description of birth. Here, Marion is very close to Romano, describing birth as the event that "is accomplished without me and even, strictly speaking, before me" (*IE*, 42/*DS*, 49), and that "happens [*advient*] only insofar as it has given me a future [*advenir*]" (*IE*, 42*/*DS*, 50). However, for Marion, birth is simply about *me*, understood in a very narrow sense: it "determines me, defines my *ego*, even produces it" (*IE*, 42/*DS*, 50). Even though he describes this ego as one "that receives itself from what it receives" (*IE*, 43*/*DS*, 51) and for whom birth opens "innumerable temporal intuitions" (*IE*, 43/*DS*, 52), Marion makes no acknowledgment that my being born is the opening of a world in which I play myself out as an event of projecting toward meaning-filled possibilities. In the absence of this fundamental and constitutive interrelatedness between me and my world, the *adonné* remains separated from the world by a gulf that he is unable to bridge—the passive and isolated recipient of the intuitions that are imposed on him.

On the other hand, Romano presents birth precisely as the original opening of a world of possible meaning and projection. In his view, from its very beginning, the "I" who is born can be understood only in terms of an interrelatedness with my world (*EM*, 97f). This mutual interrelation between the *advenant* and the world in which he arrives at (*ad-vient*) himself, which is almost completely absent in Marion, is critical for Romano: "The world only opens *for* an *advenant*, who only happens *through and on the basis* of the world [*j'advient par et à partir du monde*], who only takes place there where the event wells up, who is the 'place' of the taking-place of the world as such" (*EM*, 95).

On the basis of this interrelatedness, Romano succeeds in understanding the *advenant* as actively implicated in the way an event happens, without placing him in a constituting role, and while still ascribing the initiative for their happening to events themselves. The lack of such an interrelatedness in Marion's thought leaves him with the essentially adversarial structure of a subject *over against* an object. To remove the constituting role from the subject, he inverts this structure by ascribing a quasi selfhood to phenomena and relegating the *adonné* to being the passive recipient of whatever already accomplished object might happen to crash into him.

Romano's description of the *advenant* is far closer to our experience of ourselves than Marion's description of the *adonné* or, indeed, Heidegger's description of *Dasein*. Romano's account of the *advenant*'s adventure is a thoroughly human story, built around my striving to realize possibilities by means of action, decision, projection, and understanding in my world. One of the features of Romano's account that assures this humanness is the central place he assigns to meaning. From the outset, he designates the horizon of the world as "a hermeneutic structure"—a horizon of possible meanings that can be understood and interpreted, and thus provide a basis for meaningful projection and action (*EM*, 51). For Romano, an original characteristic of the *advenant*, opened in birth, is the endeavor "to understand the meaning of one's adventure" (*EM*, 96). Consequently, the *advenant*'s adventure in a world is itself hermeneutic, and Romano's account of the *advenant* is fundamentally (or even ontologically) hermeneutic. Unlike Marion, Romano does not view hermeneutics as a subsequent interpretation of what has already happened. Rather, the very happening of the event reveals a fundamental and *hermeneutic* interrelatedness of event, world, and the one who comes to himself in that happening. Moreover, Romano is faithful to this very Heideggerian sense of hermeneutics while consistently avoiding Heidegger's tendency (in *Being and Time*) to establish *Dasein* as a self-originating self-projection.

Conclusion

Marion and Romano succeed in decisively moving phenomenology away from the Cartesian and Kantian legacy of constitution by a subject. By placing events at the center of their account of phenomena, they emphasize that phenomena do not persist in presence, as objects do, but *appear* as something that happens.

I have argued that Marion's account of events overlooks a fundamental hermeneutic dimension, and have highlighted this by contrasting Marion's understanding with that offered by Romano in his evential hermeneutics. Because of his appreciation of the importance of this hermeneutic dimension, Romano comes closer than Marion to a middle voice for describing the encounter between the immanence of consciousness and the transcendence of the objects of experience. By recovering some of the features of *Dasein* as Being-in-the-world, without repeating Heidegger's tendency to reduce the world to the subject's own self-projection, Romano can describe the *advenant* in very human terms of projection toward meaningful possibility. By contrast, Marion's insistence that the initiative of a phenomenon's givenness and appearing belong to it alone leads him to present the appearing of phenomena as more of a forceful imposition on the *adonné*, who passively receives them.

However, Marion's phenomenology of givenness is far broader than Romano's evential hermeneutics in two respects. First, while Marion's account is clearly concerned with phenomenality in general, Romano makes a sharp distinction between evential events and innerworldly facts. This distinction could be conceived as a "swinging middle," in which an essentially Heideggerian account of self-projection is occasionally interrupted by the self-imposition of evential events reconfiguring my world. Second, while Romano considers only one type of phenomenon (events), and then moves on to focus on temporality, Marion considers the particularities of an extraordinarily broad range of phenomena. It would be especially interesting to apply Romano's evential hermeneutics to some of the other phenomena already analyzed by Marion, such as works of art, the face, and revelation.

The Dative Subject (and the "Principle of Principles")

Ian Leask

Jean-Luc Marion's philosophical project is largely about being true to phenomenology's supreme principle—the principle that every originary intuition is a legitimizing source of cognition, that everything originarily offered in intuition be accepted as it presents itself.[1] It is by interrogating this "principle of principles," by unfolding its full consequences, that Marion can posit his "third reduction"—beyond both Husserl and Heidegger—and so unveil the primacy of sheer givenness. In doing so, Marion would claim, any autarchic subjectivity (whether transcendental or existential) is dethroned and dismantled in one and the same act that givenness (*donation*) is "set free": accepting givenness without horizons means accepting a subject that cannot posit itself or its substratum.

In what follows, I shall outline the remarkable series of moves Marion makes that allows him to posit *Gegebenheit* without horizons; this may not amount to much more than an adumbration, but it should still allow us to situate Marion's specific consideration of givenness and subjectivity. And it is this specific consideration that raises the central issue to be addressed here—namely, whether the "purged" subjectivity that emerges from Marion's "third reduction" might present a fundamental, structural difficulty for the full unfolding of the "third reduction." In other words, I want to ask whether the dative subject disrupts the efficacy of the "principle of principles" and, thus, whether one requirement of Marion's project works against another.

Situating the Saturated Phenomenon

Marion's phenomenology aims to treat phenomena as phenomenality, without the kind of assumption (ranging from *ousia* to noetic primacy) that has traditionally framed them. His contention is that if intuition is freed from its enforced (and ultimately nonphenomenological) subservience to the realm of intentional legitimation—if, that is, intuition is no longer subject to the ideals of adequation or objectifying representation—then sheer givenness might appear on its own terms, as originary, unconditioned, and without a priori or presupposition.

Thus Marion suggests that—in addition to the "poor" phenomenon (of, for example, mathematics or logic), in which certainty requires little intuitive content, and in addition to the "common law" phenomenon (of, for example, scientific investigation or technological production), in which there is an equivalence of concept and fulfillment, of intention and intuition—we should consider the possibility that the phenomenon might exceed the limits of any metaphysical regime. Here, Categories must give way to giving; the principle of sufficient reason is overcome by both "a principle of sufficient intuition" (*un principe d'intuition suffisante*; SP, 105/*PS*, 84) and a principle of *insufficient* reason; and intentionality is overwhelmed by an unforeseeable, "bedazzling" excess. In such cases—the historical event, for example, or autoaffection, or my experience of the icon, or, indeed, revelation—we have (or are given) *excess*, para-dox, phenomenality without boundaries; in short, we have *saturated* phenomena. Now, Marion suggests:

> [t]he intention (the concept or the signification) can never reach adequation with the intuition (fulfillment), not because the latter is lacking but because it exceeds what the concept can receive, expose, and comprehend. . . . According to this thesis, the impossibility of attaining knowledge of an object, comprehension in the strict sense, does not come from a deficiency in the giving intuition, but from its surplus, which neither concept, signification, nor intention can foresee, organize, or contain. (ITN, 37)

The concept here is no longer the measure of intuition. Rather, phenomena are treated as absolutely irreducible: the only terms and conditions that apply are those of phenomenality itself; ultimately, there is no a priori. Thus, to cite various texts: "givenness alone indicates that the phenomenon ensures, in a single gesture, both its visibility and the full right [*bon droit*] of that visibility, both its appearance and the reason for that appearance" (SP, 105/*PS*, 85); "the excess of intuition overcomes, submerges, exceeds, in short saturates, the measure of each and every concept" (ITN, 40); "givenness does not subject the given to a transcendent condition, rather it frees the given from such conditioning" (OFP, 11); "[t]o let phenomena appear demands not imposing a theme on them, whatever the horizon might be, since it would exclude some of them" (*BG*, 320/ *ED*, 439).

And so, with this full adherence to the "principle of principles," we break through to what was always latent in phenomenology: the primacy of *Gegebenheit*. Or, rather, we break through to the hinterland of modern metaphysics itself. For the ambiguity that characterizes previous phenomenological treatment of givenness is, in a sense, only the most intensified example of a profound ambivalence stretching back through modern thought as a whole: alongside noetic primacy and constitution, we also find, in Husserl, delineation of the nonhomogeneous, excessive flux of inner temporality; alongside the transcendental unity of apperception we also find, in Kant (or, more specifically, in his "aesthetic idea"), recognition of "an intuition . . . for which no adequate concept can ever be found"[2]; alongside the *cogito* we also find, in the case of the Cartesian infinite, an *ideatum* that surpasses an idea. The history of philosophy is saturated with saturated phenomena ("even if it rarely does them justice"; *BG*, 219/ *ED*, 305). Marion can claim, therefore, that there is nothing arbitrary in his project; he has "merely" made plain modern philosophy's concealed yet irrepressible root system.

The "Principle of Principles" Without Egology

With this general background sketched out, we can begin to look more specifically at the question of the subject. What we find is that the result of Marion's "third reduction" is a reciprocal, even isomorphic, "unsaying": questions of cause, origin, antecedent, and transcendent condition fall away as sheer givenness is set free; meanwhile, the "I," losing its priority and dominance, finds itself as passive recipient of an excessive givenness beyond its control, as an interlocuted "me" that is *subject to* before it is subject. ("[T]he I experiences itself as . . . constituted and no longer constituting because it no longer has at its disposal any dominant point of view over the intuition that overwhelms it [*l'intuion qui le submerge*]"; SP, 119/*PS*, 121). The ego is undone by the unsayable *plus ultra*, the nonpresent excess, of sheer givenness; the self is stripped of its privileges. "The receiver [*L'attributaire*] is thus imposed in the place of and counter to the 'subject' as a strict consequence of the givenness of the phenomenon" (*BG*, 252/*ED*, 348). What Husserl's genetic reevaluation had touched upon is now fully articulated. We are presented with, we are given, the basic truth of phenomenology.

In order better to understand this "unsaying" of the subject, we need to elucidate how Marion's undertaking involves three crucial steps in relation to his phenomenological forebears. The first, as we have seen, is to think more thoroughly, to think in a "truly phenomenological way," phenomenology's "principle of principles"—and thus to take this fundamental principle beyond its initial Husserlian domain. The second is to achieve this "thorough thinking," and thus to get beyond Husserl, in the light of Heidegger's insight that, although Husserl interprets phenomenality as givenness, transcendental subjectivity has already been presupposed as the matter of philosophy[3]—and that "givenness itself is interpreted in turn as the givenness of an actual presence for consciousness with a view to certitude" (*RG*, 51/*RD*, 81). But, of course, Marion's project is in no sense a straightforward restatement of Heidegger's; it also involves a serious reserve regarding Heidegger's own ontological preoccupations. For Marion, Heideggerian Being too easily obscures and enframes the givenness that remains the phenomenological kernel of Husserl's principle. (Because, for Heidegger, the "phenomenon of Being" can be manifested only in terms of beings, "'destinal' *Dasein* is privileged in a way that mirrors Husserl's privileging of intention,[4] and in a way that thus blocks full phenomenological access to 'the phenomena themselves.'"[5]) Thus, it is by rethinking (1) the "principle of principles," in the light of (2) Heidegger's critique, but also by rethinking both in the light of (3) a "refusal" of Heideggerian ontology, that Marion can arrive at his reformulated ego—interlocuted (and no longer nominative), passive, beyond Being, "truly open" to givenness. An apparently circuitous route: from Husserl's givenness, to the critique of its resident egology, to the critique of the presuppositions of that critique, to a givenness fully purged in the course of this odyssey.

With this three-step process, Marion can maintain that he has rethought the "principle of principles" without assuming any fundamental egology, that he has extracted the phenomenological kernel from its autarchic shell. The claimed result: givenness without the privileged Ego—but also without Being. For Marion, phenomenology breaks "decisively" (*décidément*) with metaphysics when it thinks the phenomenon without any horizon—either epistemological or ontological (*BG*, 320/*ED*, 439). There is no a priori; there is "only" givenness.

If it is the case that "there is no a priori," that phenomenality can be removed from what Marion has termed "the imperial rule [*l'impérialisme*] of the a priori conditions of knowledge" (*BG*, 69/*ED*, 101), then, of course, Marion's phenomenology has enormous implications not just for philosophy but also for theology. Kantian (and, indeed, all broadly Protestant) objections to so much natural theology are largely undone if we accept that there are no a priori determinations for experience—that, for example, impossibility (treated as givenness without horizon) might be "part of" our experience, or that what gives itself does not always show itself. God's immanence (although not, of course, His transcendence) might become open to rational, phenomenological description.

Nonetheless, however fascinating these issues might be, I want to restrict my consideration here to the question(s) of subjectivity and the extent to which Marion's "third reduction" does indeed remove all horizons, all "preconditions of experience." More specifically, what I want to consider here is whether reception, although by no means constitution, remains in any sense residually egological. Certainly, Marion has left autarchic subjectivity unfolded on itself, reconfigured as the passive recipient of an antecedent givenness; but, in floating free from any ontological reference, does this interlocuted "I" retain certain privileges *qua* beneficiary of givenness?

Marion would maintain, of course, that the "principle of sufficient givenness" rules out any a priori primacy of (or for) reception; he insists that it is possible to bracket all three elements within the triad that constitutes "performative" givenness. Thus he tells us that there can be givenness (a) without any "thing" being given (when, for example, I give time, or my word, or a blessing, or a curse); (b) without a giver (in the case of a found object); but also (c) without a "receiver" (a gift to a charity is to nobody I know; my love for an enemy may not be accepted; the ingrate can "undo" his own receiving; the target of seduction can remain oblivious to all advances).[6] Phenomenologically, these bracketings seem irrefutable; formally, there can be no reasonable opposition to the demonstration that we still have givenness beyond the economy of the gift given and received. Nonetheless, despite this formal veracity, it seems equally undeniable that Marion's schema still requires a certain priority afforded the recipient. And it is this requirement that I should like to interrogate further.

The Priority of the Dative Subject

As we have seen, there is a necessary isomorphism in Marion's project, whereby "so much givenness" means, *pari passu*, "so little constitution." It is not just that "[a]s long as the ego remains, the givenness stops . . . [and] only appears once the ego is bracketed" (SPCG, 126); it is also that the principle of givenness "withdraws primacy from the I" (OFP, 12); that, in the face of the saturated phenomenon, "[t]he 'I' loses its anteriority and finds itself, so to speak, deprived of the duties of constitution, and thus itself constituted: a 'me' rather than an 'I'" (SP, 119/*PS*, 121); that "the I is [now] experienced . . . as claimed, assigned, and convoked in the accusative, deprived of its right to the nominative" (*RG*, 199/*RD*, 298); and so on. In other words, the aim is not just to think "givenness in itself" but, equally, to think of the "I" as constituted rather than constituting; the one aim is central to the other. (As Marion puts it, "subjectivity is not the actor, but the receiver. . . . [S]uch an original passivity of subjectivity is a way, I think a radical way, to deconstruct the transcendental ambition of the ego"; OTG, 70). And it is precisely for this reason that reception must be a necessary operative assumption here (however "bracketable" it may be in general terms): if the *interloqué* is to be more than just another deconstructed subject, if it is to be reconfigured in terms of and in relation to sheer givenness,[7] then, quite apart from its accusative and locative formations, a further, dative aspect is crucial and unavoidable. Givenness seems to require a dative subject *to whom* the phenomenon shows itself inasmuch as it gives itself.

Of course, there is no question that this dative subject remains either unrecognized or hidden ("behind the curtain") in Marion's project. On the contrary, Marion is wholly explicit about this "to whom": book 5 of *Being Given* states unambiguously not only that the third reduction inverts the nominative subject into "a more original dative" (*un datif plus original*; BG, 249/ED, 344), but also that the receiver of phenomena—"the gifted," *l'adonné*—must be recognized as a primary point of reference vis-à-vis givenness, as a kind of lodestone offering the only possible indication of the antecedent "force" of givenness.

Thus we are told that it is the "precise situation" of the recipient (rather than, for example, the giver) that provides the "resolute and essential" description of phenomena; that phenomena show themselves intrinsically *qua* received (rather than *qua* possessed, produced, constituted, etc.); that the gifted, the dative subject, is more originary—that is, phenomenologically ultimate—"as a strict consequence [*en stricte conséquence*] of the givenness of the phenomenon" (*BG*, 252/*ED*, 348). As beneficiary of a givenness that is beyond the terms and domain of Being, that is outside of any ontological matrix, the dative self is a necessary medium for givenness; if givenness cannot be said to be, it can be manifest only in its (sometimes saturated) appearing to me.

Having established this point, we should also be quite clear that while Marion's dative self (or "the gifted") might enjoy a certain epistemic priority, it is by no means some transcendental ego of old; it has no interiority prior to reception, no expectation before accepting, it is not "older" than the phenomena it receives. (Crucially, it receives itself, like "any other phenomenon," in receiving as such.) In short, the "priority" of the dative subject is in no sense a priori; "the gifted" always does its work—including the work of producing itself—after givenness gives itself. We might say, with a nod toward Lévinas, that Marion's subject is always a latecomer. Thus, whatever the significance or priority of the recipient, we are no longer dealing here with metaphysical "substance" or "a priori conditions"; there can be no reasonable contention that Marion's project somehow or other confirms Husserlian egology, or that a transcendental, "nominative" ego can be inferred in Marion, just as it is explicit in Husserl. And yet, despite urging this hermeneutical caution, I want to raise what I take to be a central question here, about whether Marion avoids the very aporia of the dative subject that he himself identifies in phenomenology's "principle of principles." The question is this: Once subjectivity is reformulated "in the dative case," and once givenness is necessarily *given to*, do we end up revisiting what Marion has termed the "classic ambiguity" (*SP*, 106/*PS*, 87) of Husserl's *Ideen*?

Husserl's "principle of principles," we can recall, stated that "every originary presentive intuition [*gebende Anschauung*] is a legitimizing source of cognition [*eine Rechtsquelle der Erkenntnis*], that everything originarily . . . offered to us in 'intuition' is to be accepted simply as what is presented as being. . . ."⁸ As Marion is the first to recognize, it is the "to us" that is such a stumbling block here; what it implies is that "the givenness of the phenomenon on the basis of itself to an "I" can at every instant veer [*virer*] toward a constitution" (SP, 106/PS, 87; see also BG, 187/ED, 262). The dative, in other words, can too easily undo the effect of the Heideggerian critique of Husserlian egology; there is now a threat that, as Marion puts it:

> givenness, precisely because it keeps its originary and justifying function [*fonction originaire et justificatrice*], can give and justify nothing except before the tribunal of the "I" [*le tribunal du Je*]; transcendental or not, the phenomenological "I" remains the beneficiary . . . it falls to the "I" to measure what does and does not give itself intuitively, within what limits, according to what horizon, following what intention, essence and signification. Even if it shows itself on the basis of itself, the phenomenon can do so only by allowing it to be led back, and therefore reduced, to the "I." (SP, 106/PS, 87–88)⁹

All of which takes us to my central point: to ask, as I have already indicated, whether Marion fully avoids the risk he identifies here—whether, that is, the necessary priority afforded the recipient threatens the efficacy of any "third reduction." When Marion tells us, in *Being Given*, that "givenness is marked only in the very experience of the given" (BG, 60/ED, 89), or that "[only our] lived experience makes the phenomenon possible" (BG 125/ED, 178), or that "phenomena are given only if I let them come upon me" (BG, 128/ED, 181), or that it is only through the gifted's "will to see" that givenness might show itself (BG, 306–7/ED, 421–23), or, indeed, that "the gifted . . . has nothing less than the charge of opening or closing the entire flux of phenomenality" (BG, 307/ED, 422)¹⁰—do such formulations not suggest that the "classic ambiguity" of the *Ideen* remains unresolved? Despite Marion's magisterial labors, might it be that we still have to negotiate Lévinas's suggestion, in *Otherwise Than Being*, that a certain "presence of mind" (*la "présence d'esprit"*) is "necessary for the reception of a given [*nécessaire à la réception d'une donnée*],"¹¹ and that "the a priori . . . cannot be excluded [from reception]"?¹²

Perhaps any effort to answer these questions needs to bear in mind Marion's own dictum, in *Being Given*, that "[m]etaphysical (in fact, Cartesian) egology is a paradigm that always haunts the I, even reduced, even phenomenological" (BG, 187/ED, 262).

Marion's Ambition of Transcendence

Mark Dooley

The essay that best encapsulates the recent thought of Jean-Luc Marion is, in my opinion, "The Saturated Phenomenon" (SP). Here the author gives an account of what he calls the paradox of an "impossible" phenomenon, one that bedazzles the ego through an excess of intuition over intention. Although this idea has generated a good deal of fairly robust criticism,[1] most of the essay's readers are nevertheless impressed by the way in which Marion uses it not only to enlarge upon the project of *God Without Being*, but also to convey a sense of where his latest work, developed in texts such as *Reduction and Givenness*, is taking him. I am one of those readers who think that this essay is one of the most daring and original to have appeared in recent Continental thought, and I also believe that it has earned Marion his reputation as the leading Catholic theologian of his generation.

This admiration notwithstanding, I nevertheless have some reservations regarding the efficacy of Marion's argument in SP, believing as I do that it leaves itself open to justified criticism at a number of levels. In what follows, my aim is to challenge its central metaphenomenological claim—that "we have to establish that an unconditioned and irreducible phenomenon, with neither delimiting horizon nor constituting *I*, offers a true possibility and does not amount to 'telling tales'" (SP, 185). On my view, the history of philosophy bears witness to a plethora of failed attempts to get at such an unconditioned and irreducible phenomenon, and to try and resuscitate this idea is simply to ignore much of the profitable work that has been done over the past two centuries to convince us of the futility of this endeavor.

Ever since Nietzsche declared, circa 1886, that

> . . . even supposing there were an in-itself, an unconditioned thing, it would for that very reason be unknowable! Something unconditioned cannot be known; otherwise it would not be unconditioned! Coming to know, however, is always "placing oneself in a conditional relation to something. . . ."[2]

Philosophers on both sides of the Atlantic have lost confidence in the claim that the central aim of philosophy should be to get in touch with mind or language-independent reality.

Those, however, who continue to subscribe to the foundational assumptions of realism and representationalism follow Thomas Nagel in suggesting that the anti-essentialist impulses of people such as Nietzsche, James, Wittgenstein, Derrida, and Rorty devalue the philosophical enterprise to the point of parody. For, as Nagel argues,

> [p]hilosophy cannot take refuge in reduced ambitions. It is after eternal and nonlocal truth.

This in turn suggests that

> . . . [it] is not like a particular language. Its sources are preverbal and often precultural, and one of its most difficult tasks is to express unformed but intuitively felt problems in language without losing them.[3]

For Nagel, thus, objects have an intrinsic character over and above the way they are described by us, and the aspiration of philosophy should be to go as far as one can in transcending all subjective determinations, so as to experience the object in its unconditioned and prelinguistic state. This project he has labeled the "ambition of transcendence." The principal contention of this chapter is that Marion shares with people such as Nagel this metaphilosophical ambition, and that what Marion calls the "saturated phenomenon" is but one more attempt to breathe life into the Nietzschean unconditioned, something that I think is beyond the scope of human inquiry.[4]

One of the main reasons why Marion considers the ambition of transcendence to be worthy of phenomenology is because for him, the primary aim of all reflection should be to fight free of the ego, or the "I," to the point where it no longer constitutes the phenomenon but experiences itself as constituted by it. This implies that, once constituted, the ego "no longer has at its disposal any dominant point of view over the intuition that overwhelms it." Hence the "I" becomes a "me" insofar as it is "deprived [*destitué*] of the duties of constitution" (SP, 210–11). The "me" comes after the subject of metaphysics, transcendental phenomenology, and even goes beyond Heideggerian *Dasein*. It is what Marion terms "the subject on its last appeal" (SP, 211)—an interlocuted (*interloqué*) "me" that is summoned by an excess of pure "unconditioned givenness [*donation*]."[5] The question for phenomenology is, thus, why it prefers to "compromise the return to the things themselves by qualifying evidence and truth with ideality" (SP, 187) when it has a genuine—albeit radical—possibility of envisaging "a type of phenomenon that would reverse the condition of a horizon (by surpassing it, instead of being inscribed within it) and that would reverse the reduction (by leading the *I* back to itself, instead of being reduced to the *I*)" (SP, 184).

The problem, as I see it, for this idea of a "phenomenon that is saturated with intuition" (SP, 195), one that prohibits "that any language ever reach it completely and render it intelligible,"[6] thereby giving "reality without any limitation" (SP, 200), is that it seems to be predicated on a form of intuitive realism that has long since survived its sell-by date. That is, it appears to accept uncritically the basic presuppositions of phenomenology and, as stated at the outset, to ignore the many useful attempts, in the philosophy of language and elsewhere, to disabuse us of the belief that we can reach the unconditioned through an act of self-abnegation. For those of us who subscribe to the anti-essentialist dictum that, to paraphrase William James, "the trail of the human serpent is over everything," such self-sacrifice is, however, neither possible nor desirable. In the remainder of the chapter, I shall attempt to defend why I believe this to be the case.

In response to Nietzsche's claim that something unconditioned cannot be known, Marion might insist, as he argues in "The Saturated Phenomenon," that it is entirely possible that "the phenomena that really arise" do so "without being inscribed, at least at first, in the relational network that ensures experience its unity, and that they matter precisely because one could not assign them any substratum, any cause, or any communion" (SP, 203–4). Marion's belief in a nonrelational phenomenon, one that "maintains its absoluteness and, at the same time, dissolves its danger when one recognizes it without confusing it with other phenomena" (SP, 207), bears witness to a type of Neoplatonic hyperrealism that privileges and presupposes a distinction between *language* and *fact*, one that I don't believe can be made. Of course, it is true to say (pace linguistic idealism) that there is much in the environment that human beings cannot dominate. But it does not follow from this that there is a *way* things are, irrespective of *the way they are described*, as Marion seems to imply. To appreciate why this is so, one has to concede, as Kierkegaard maintains, that language and thought are two sides of the same coin, or that there is, in other words, no sharp divide between what Nagel calls the "content" of thoughts and the "form they take in the human mind." Stated otherwise, it is to concede Rorty's point that "we shall never be able to step outside of language, never be able to grasp reality unmediated by a linguistic description."[7]

The upshot of such a concession is to adopt the anti-essentialist line that "there is nothing to be known about anything save what is caught in sentences describing it."[8] Moreover, there is no way of determining which of our infinite number of descriptions more accurately represents the way the world is than any other. To follow Wittgenstein in believing that there is no way to come between an object and its word is to take for granted Hilary Putnam's point that "elements of what we call 'language' or 'mind' penetrate so deeply into reality that the very project of representing ourselves as being 'mappers' of something 'language-independent' is fatally compromised from the start."[9] Hence anti-essentialists react to Marion's claim that the saturated phenomenon "truly appears as itself, of itself, and starting from itself, since it alone appears without the limits of a horizon and without the reduction to an 'I'" (SP, 212–13) by pointing out that there is simply no way of separating the contribution made by the inquirer from the object of his inquiry—no way of determining, in other words, where subjectivity stops and objectivity begins.

To defend the idea of an "absolute" and "irreducible" phenomenon that somehow avoids being described is analogous to the epistemological skeptic's claim that there are indeed intrinsic, nonrelational properties of things that are neither knowable nor describable. The obvious anti-essentialist rejoinder to such a suggestion is "Give us an example of some of them." If the skeptic gives such an account, then it turns out that those properties were describable and knowable after all. If, on the other hand, he reiterates that he cannot, because they are unknowable and ineffable, then it is important to inquire how he came to know of them to begin with. All of this is just a way of trying to convince those who are committed to the idea of an unconditioned phenomenon that such an idea may be no more than an *intuition* (not in the sense of phenomenological perception, but qua feeling or hunch), one that owes its currency to the force of the language game currently being played in a particular community.

This, in turn, suggests that the anti-essentialist is not as averse to humanism as people such as Marion or Lévinas, to take the most obvious examples. For to argue, as do Sellars and Rorty, that *all* awareness is a linguistic affair is to subscribe to Robert Brandom's Heideggerian view that "all matters of authority or privilege, in particular epistemic authority, are matters of social practice, and not matters of fact."[10] As such, those of us who do subscribe to this view are inclined to privilege sociological explanations about what we believe above the explanations traditionally afforded by either orthodox theology or transcendental philosophy. Hence, for followers of Brandom, as for followers of the Heidegger of division I of *Being and Time*, the idea of prelinguistic experience of anything does not derive from an ability to compare language and fact, but rather is a product of the adoption of certain social practices by a society on the basis of its particular needs and interests—practices that have been formed in part by the tradition of Greek metaphysics and medieval theology.

Philosophers such as Marion and Nagel usually respond to arguments in favor of the ontological priority of the social by saying that to reduce the ontological or the phenomenological to the social is, to quote Nagel, a crude "attempt to cut the universe down to size."[11] It displays an unjustifiable lack of wonder and humility in the face of a world that stands over and above the human, a world that is full of surprise, strangeness, and bedazzlement. Marion eloquently describes this experience of bedazzlement when he asks, "What, then, does this eye without a look [*cet oeil sans regard*] actually see?" In response, he says that

> [i]t sees the overabundance of intuitive *donation*, not, however, as such, but as it is blurred by the overly short lens, the overly restricted aperture, the overly narrow frame that receives it—or rather, no longer accommodates it. The eye apperceives not so much the appearance of the saturated phenomenon as the blur, the fog, and the over-exposure that it imposes on its normal conditions of experience. (SP, 210)

The saturated phenomenon, that is, "gives itself to be seen, each time, only according to one perspective, which is total as well as partial"

(SP, 207). Hence, in fully saturating all horizons, this absolute phenomenon imposes itself in defiance of all subjective conditions of possibility. But, as Marion insists, "this very disfiguration remains a manifestation" (SP, 208).

One could draw an analogy here with the traditional monotheistic God of Western theology, one who is both known and unknown, one who reveals Himself and yet remains hidden. In this case also, knowledge of God is lacking, not because of an inherent deficiency but because He saturates and overflows all horizons of possibility. What we know of Him is in and through the paradox of an excess of intuition that "overcomes, submerges, exceeds, in short saturates the measure of each and every concept." Indeed, in his article "In the Name," Marion argues as much when he says that

> [a]ccess to the divine phenomenality is not forbidden to man; in contrast, it is precisely when he becomes entirely open to it that man finds himself forbidden from it—frozen, submerged, he is by himself forbidden from advancing and likewise from resting. In the mode of interdiction, terror attests to the insistent and unbearable excess in the intuition of God. (ITN, 41)

Once again, however, those of us who share a belief in what Richard Rorty nicely terms the "ubiquity of language"[12] are still unconvinced that there are any prelinguistic starting points to thought other than, as Donald Davidson suggests, causal pressures from the surrounding environment. To repeat, it is one thing to say that there were objects before there were humans, but it is quite another thing to suggest that *there is a way* such objects exist *independently of the way they are described*. Presumably, a phenomenon that exceeds and floods all epistemological horizons is supposed to denote reality as it is intrinsically, insofar as it "is purely of itself and starting from itself," one "that does not subject its possibility to any preliminary determination, a *revelation*" (SP, 213). If so, Marion is one of those who believe that there are indeed "starting points which are prior to and independent of the way some culture speaks or spoke."[13] But unless Marion can tell us a little more about the nature of the saturated phenomenon, the suspicion will always be that he is in the same dilemma as the skeptic—one who, when asked about *what* it is that may be unknowable or ineffable, replies simply that it is ineffable. If, however, he continues to insist on its ineffability, it will be quite justifiable to suspect that an appeal to a phenomenon of this type is rooted merely in a personal intuition.

To trust the claim that language is all-pervasive and ubiquitous requires us, however, to fall back on Brandom's contention that epistemic authority is a matter of social practice. Due to the fact that anti-essentialists and linguistic historicists see no way to come between objects and their words, they also dispute the claim that appeal to unmediated experience allows us to "drive a wedge between the cultural-political question of what we should talk about and the question of what really exists."[14] This is so because *all* statements about everything—from trees to saturated phenomena—must be made in a particular language, the language of one community or another. Hence, to say that something exists is, from this point of view, equivalent to saying that it satisfies our current purposes to talk of such a thing in such terms.

So when Marion says that it is through the experience of bedazzlement and paradox that the unconditioned becomes manifest in its givenness, the anti-essentialist is inclined to rejoin that the feeling of "stupor, indeed of the terror which the incomprehensibility resulting from excess imposes upon us" (ITN, 41), can be understood not by talking about a saturated phenomenon, but by talking about how our current repertoire of descriptions may need to be enhanced and enlarged in order to cope with some previously unencountered problem. Just because something appears to us as being beyond the scope of our current linguistic practices, it does not follow that it may not at some future point be described in terms that are familiar to a possible future audience.

It does not follow, in other words, that the feeling of something unfamiliar denotes an experience of the wholly unconditioned. Perhaps what Marion thinks is a "religious" phenomenon is simply a new causal pressure exerted by the environment that has yet to be put into words, in much the same way that what was once described as the work of demons and extraterrestrial forces is now described as a fall in serotonin levels. The point is, however, that what determines how you describe something is not a result of the degree to which that thing exceeds intention, but rather a result of the ends and purposes that you or the larger community have in mind. For example, I may choose to describe an early sunrise as a religious phenomenon, if my purposes are what I call "spiritual." On the other hand, I may choose to describe it as something "uplifting," on the basis that it replenishes my vitamin D resources—the purpose here being to improve my health. Either way, what decides how I will choose to describe the sunrise will not be based on the sunrise-in-itself, but on my particular needs, interests, purposes, and desires.

All this can be summed up by saying that I doubt that Marion's third reduction is any more successful in getting us in touch with the unconditioned than Husserl's reduction of the natural attitude or Heidegger's *Gelassenheit*. From an anti-essentialist viewpoint, all that is happening in each case is a movement from using one set of terms to describe a piece of space-time to the use or employment of an alternative set. As such, anti-essentialists see no sharp break between the description of the world as employed by those in the natural attitude and those who believe themselves to be in the position of an interlocuted "me." Whereas Marion would see Heidegger's analytic of *Dasein* as a failure of phenomenology to reach its full potential—that is, "to give reality without any limitation" (SP, 200)—I, on the other hand, see *Dasein* as being neither more nor less in touch with things than Marion's "interlocuted" self. This is because, as I have been suggesting, I don't believe that merely by the adoption of a more disinterested stance, such as that proposed by Marion's reduction of the "I" to the "me," one is somehow enabled to lessen the impact of one's interpretive horizon. Stated otherwise, I don't believe it gives you the capacity to escape a network of social practices so as to see the world in a purely disinterested fashion.

The only difference, as I see it, between *Dasein* and the *interloqué* is simply one of degree. That is, the former describes the world with the use of a set of metaphors that emphasizes commitment, while the latter deploys a second set that emphasizes detachment. From an anti-essentialist's perspective, there is, of course, no way to determine which of the two sets more accurately represents reality qua the unconditioned. For this would presuppose, to quote Rorty, "the impossible attempt to step outside our skins—the traditions, linguistic and other, within which we do our thinking and self-criticism—and compare ourselves with something absolute."[15] Neither phenomenology, natural science, Aristotelian cosmology, postmodernism, nor Hegelian historicism has ever succeeded in providing a neutral backdrop against which to judge the efficacy of its truth claims regarding what it believes is intrinsic to the world. To say that any one of these has succeeded in so doing would be tantamount to declaring that you have some independent, transcultural test by virtue of which you can clearly demonstrate that a particular set of descriptions is somehow made true by extralinguistic reality. As far as I am aware, no such test has been shown to exist.

The obvious consequence for anti-essentialism, or the anti-essentialist line that I have been pushing throughout this chapter, is that those of us who subscribe to it are not in a position to say that we have discovered a truth about the world that Marion's phenomenology has failed to grasp. Anti-essentialists are, in other words, just as susceptible to the claim that their views about language and reality are just more intuitions made plausible by certain social practices. That acknowledged, therefore, I think that in the final analysis the debate between the anti-essentialist and the hyperphenomenologist comes down to the issue of rival intuitions regarding what social practices it is wise for us to adopt, given our current needs and interests. What will decide between such competing intuitions can be determined, I suggest, only on the basis of arguing about the relative advantages and disadvantages of holding those intuitions and having the purposes that first gave rise to them. I believe the world that has come into being since we lost the urge to seek "the unconditioned" is certainly better than that which held sway prior to that change of direction. But as I have been arguing, that is not because I can prove to you that there is no such thing as the unconditioned—just as I don't believe Marion has any knockdown arguments to prove that there is such a thing. Rather, it is based simply on the hunch that the world would be a better place if anti-essentialist impulses won out over the ambition of transcendence. Once again, this is because I can see no reason to dispute Brandom's and Heidegger's claim that "all matters of authority or privilege, in particular epistemic authority, are matters of social practice, and not of objective fact."

In closing, let me say that, notwithstanding all the reservations expressed here regarding the saturated phenomenon, I nevertheless have the highest admiration and respect for what Jean-Luc Marion has achieved and will, no doubt, continue to achieve. As intimated at the outset, we are all the better for his scholarship, erudition, and originality. Even if my own desire is to encourage people to abandon the ambition of transcendence, I am nonetheless grateful for Marion's unrelenting drive to realize that ambition. For in so doing, he forces the anti-essentialist to the brink by making him doubt his own deeply held intuitions. Even though the anti-essentialist usually responds by restating those intuitions, he is glad, in my case at least, that he has been forced to confront the possibility that there may indeed be more to life than is dreamed of in philosophy books, even of the anti-essentialist variety.

PART III

Marion and Beyond

Le phénomène érotique:
Augustinian Resonances in Marion's Phenomenology of Love

Eoin Cassidy

Jean-Luc Marion's *Le phénomène érotique* (*PE*)[1] is not only the culmination of an ongoing and long-standing concern[2] but, as such, is also the most explicit statement in his oeuvre to date about the sheer primacy of love. Specifically, *PE* suggests that only in the *phénomène croisé*, only in erotic love, can one receive the gift of significance that is capable of contesting the ultimate challenge of nihilism—namely, the challenge of "What's the use?" or "to what end?" (*à quoi bon?*). As we shall see here, Marion's suggestions resonate profoundly with those of a classical philosopher unmatched in his sustained analysis of love and his conviction that the promise of loving and being loved defines the person: Augustine—despite the latter's well-publicized reservations concerning the erotic character of love.[3] Indeed, given these reservations, it may seem that such a reflection will be condemned to futility. As I hope to show here, however, many of the themes characteristic of Marion's analysis of love show a remarkable affinity to those in the *Confessions* and, indeed, to those throughout the Augustinian corpus. This affinity is most evident with the treatment of love as desire, as "the restless heart." But it is also demonstrated in the significance that both Marion and Augustine attach to the person as a lover; in the motif of immortality reflected in the juxtaposition of "adieu" with "à Dieu"; and in their shared insistence on the unity of love.

I should stress that in what follows, there is no attempt either to offer a sustained analysis of Marion's *PE* or to critique his phenomenology of love from an Augustinian perspective. Rather, the aim is more modest: to allow for a fruitful juxtaposition that might (a) illuminate the historical depth of Marion's meditation and (b) remind us, in this context, of the perennial value of Augustine's reflections.

Love in Order to Understand (*Ama Ut Intelligas*)

Under the heading "The Silence of Love," Marion opens *PE* with a critique of the metaphysical tradition that has failed to attend to "what is philosophy"—specifically, to the significance of love in the explication of philosophy as "the love of wisdom." As Marion puts it:

> Philosophy defines itself as "the love of wisdom" because, in effect, it ought to begin by loving before claiming to know. In order to achieve understanding, one must first desire it. (*PE*, 10)[4]

For Marion, it is not just that a critique of the history of the divorce between philosophy and love merits at least as much attention as that devoted to a critique of the history of metaphysics; it is also that the two critiques are intimately related.[5] The world of metaphysics cannot truly understand desire because it misconstrues the focus of desire. In presuming that the desire to know is satisfied in attaining certitude about objects that exist, it fails to grasp the seriousness of the challenge posed to philosophical discourse by the universal experience of the desire for certitude. As Marion recognizes, desire reveals a subject that is in search of certitude about itself—a subject who seeks that which will certify the "I" of "I am." The world of metaphysics fails to recognize that desire draws us inexorably to question the subject who desires. Even where it offers the certitude of myself as a thinker, metaphysics can never give me certitude of myself that is anything other than the certitude of an object—a being that exists. It passes over in silence the only certitude that is important—that which concerns the "I," the human subject.[6]

Thus, for Marion, the failure of metaphysics is compounded by the fact that the existential self-doubt that desire reveals is not one that can be answered satisfactorily by establishing the certitude of my existence—it is not solved by the *cogito* that gives me the certitude of a thinking being, because it fails to hear the most simple and yet most penetrating of all questions—"so what?" (*et alors?*) or "to what end?" (*à quoi bon?*). As he recognizes, the certitude that results from either an epistemological or an ontological reduction is totally exposed to the question "to what end?" or, more simply, "What's the use?":

> I can clearly acknowledge with certainty "I think therefore I am"—only to have this certitude immediately annulled in asking myself "to what end?" The certitude of my existence can never suffice to render it just, nor good, nor beautiful, nor desirable—in sum, it will never suffice to assure it. (*PE*, 42)[7]

Taking his theme from the opening lines of Ecclesiastes,[8] Marion acknowledges that the possibility that all questions are futile cannot be ignored—the ultimate nihilistic challenge posed by the suggestion that "all is vanity" cannot be sidestepped. Furthermore, if Marion is correct, this challenge can never be met by any assurance that I might be able to give to myself. Rather, it is one that I can receive only from another, because it is only the other that can address the challenge of the preacher in Ecclesiastes; it is only in and from the other that I might receive a response to the question "Does anyone love me?" (*M'aime-t-on?*).

Augustine would never have doubted the truth of Marion's insight that in order to understand, one must first desire to understand. Indeed, given the centrality of desire in Augustine's psychology of the person, the phrase " believe in order that you may understand" (*crede ut intelligas*) could just as easily have read "love in order that you may understand" (ama ut intelligas).[9]

To anyone familiar with the *Confessions*, one of the most striking features of Augustine's biographical narrative is the detailed nature of the account of his search for wisdom and the manner in which that search became narrowed into the relentless pursuit of certitude. From his earliest encounter with Cicero's *Hortensius* there awakened in Augustine "a longing for wisdom and its immortality." As he tells us:

> How I burned, my God, how, indeed, to fly back from earthly things to you, but I did not know what you would do with me. For with you is wisdom. Love of wisdom is in Greek "philosophy," with which that book fired me.[10]

Through the long years as a follower of the Manichaean cult, Augustine was preoccupied with the belief that the attainment of certain truth could be achieved only by the unaided use of human reason. In this context, we should not underestimate the reality of the despair he felt on losing confidence in the attainability of this goal, a loss of confidence that was made all the more real by his contact with the skepticism of the New Academy.[11] A key moment in the process of Augustine's celebrated conversion is his letting go of the belief that the self can possess certitude and that the self can possess it through its own unaided efforts. Instead, Augustine comes to replace this conviction with an acceptance of his status as a lover—a lover of wisdom—and the acknowledgment that this love of wisdom is received as a gift only from the one who is loved.

Famously, Augustine describes this conversion as a journey from pride to humility: the relentless drive for certitude is replaced by the acceptance, in faith, of the assurance that comes from another (God). The point of Isaiah 7:9—"Unless you believe, you will not understand"[12]—becomes clear to him; it becomes a constant refrain in Augustine's writings that only faith heals the proud heart. Furthermore, this faith can never simply or even primarily be conceived as an intellectual assent. It is nothing less than a movement of the heart that is synonymous with love[13]—or, more precisely, an enlargement of the heart that is engendered by desire. Hence "ama ut intelligas"!

One of most striking aspects of Augustine's writings is his belief that it is only by nurturing the gift of desire that we can foster a right relationship to ourselves, to God, and to our fellow human beings.[14] This insight is expressed repeatedly during the course of a series of commentaries on passages from the gospel of John,[15] in which Augustine emphasizes (a) the need to recognize that desire is the condition of human life as it is lived in this life,[16] (b) the need to purify desire,[17] and (c) the importance of expanding desire.[18] He reminds his listeners that Christ leads by encouraging desire and that Christ as Physician heals the sickness caused by sin by nourishing desire.[19]

The most detailed treatment of desire in these homilies is found in homily 26. In the opening verse we find the following passage:

> These men were far from the bread of heaven and they did not know how to hunger for it. They had weak jaws of the heart; they were deaf with open ears; they saw and stood blind. For indeed, this bread searches out the hunger of the interior man.[20]

The imagery reveals a number of related themes. What Augustine so successfully evokes in this passage is the sense of interior or spiritual paralysis that affects those unable to desire God's love. The focus of Augustine's reflections is on understanding the reasons why there are those who reject Christ's overtures. They do not know how to hunger for it—they have lost the ability to desire God's love. It is not just disordered desire but, even more important, the failure to desire that ultimately destroys the human potential, because it constricts the soul.

Augustine goes to some lengths to contrast those who hunger for God's justice (grace) and those who hunger for their own justice (self-sufficiency). It is his abiding conviction that it is possible to lose the knowledge of desire if and only if one believes oneself to be self-sufficient. If he is correct, there are only two categories of people who cannot desire: those in despair and those whose lives are shaped by pride. The former are fixated on the futility of desire; the latter, on its irrelevance. From Augustine's point of view the most destructive effect of pride is that it prevents one from even commencing on the way to Christ because it kills the desire to make that journey.[21] As suggested by the opening lines of the *Confessions*,[22] Augustine is in no doubt about the importance of the gift of a restless heart. For him, it opens the path of desire that alone can lead both to self-understanding and to God. As the above suggests, it is a path trodden only by those who are humble.

The following incident, recounted in the *Confessions*, brings this insight into focus. Augustine, who is in the company of some friends, hears a story of a conversion to Christianity and gives us his reaction:

> But while he [Ponticianus] was speaking, O Lord, you were turning me around to look at myself. For I had placed myself behind my own back, refusing to see myself—If I tried to turn my eyes away they fell on Ponticianus, still telling his tale, and in this way you brought me face to face with myself, once more forcing me upon my own sight so that I should see my wickedness and loathe it. I had known it all along, but I had always pretended that it was something different. I had turned a blind eye and forgotten it.[23]

The passage is a reminder of the lengths to which the proud person will go to avoid the Socratic dictate "know thyself." Furthermore, it reveals that self-understanding is received as a gift—a gift that heals the proud heart. What did Augustine see? He saw himself as a sinner—as unlovable—and in the moment of his acceptance of this gift of self-recognition, he was healed and in turn became lovable. He

Le phénomène érotique ■ 205

suggests that the conversion of the heart, which prompts the desire for self-understanding, is received through the gift of another's love. As Augustine recognizes, it is possible to listen to oneself only to the extent that one listens to a friend; it is not possible truly to look at a friend without at the same time being forced to look at oneself.

The Person as a Lover

One of the most striking aspects of Marion's "réduction érotique" is the fact that it is situated within a sustained critique of the Cartesian turn to the subject, a turn that heralded an era excessively preoccupied with the link between being and knowing.[24] Through an analysis of the nature of the challenge posed by "vanity," Marion contrasts the desire for the certitude of a knower with an alternative focus for desire. This alternative focus alone acknowledges that self-understanding is possible only insofar as one recognizes the possibility that one is presently loved or lovable, or could be at some time in the future. In his pursuit of this analysis, one of Marion's most valuable insights is that the "who" that is desired is different in the two. One desires to know with certitude the autonomous self who is the font of all certitude—the coming together of the absolute desire to know and to be. But the other desire is for the assurance that one is loved—an acknowledgment that situates the focus of desire far from the autonomous, independent *cogito*. From Marion's point of view, the only *telos* that does justice to the understanding of love as desire, and that alone is capable of meeting the challenge posed by "vanity" (*à quoi bon*), is that which is placed under the rubric of the "réduction érotique"—namely, one that acknowledges that the person is first and foremost a lover. The quest for certitude is replaced by the search for assurance because, as Marion recognizes, one can have certitude only of *things*, and there is no thing that escapes the critique of vanity.[25] If his analysis is correct, the only appropriate subject for desire is the person as a "lover," or as one who is loved, rather than as one who "is" or one who "thinks."

In a sustained analysis of the challenge posed by "vanity" (*à quoi bon*), Marion both scotches the notion that one can confer significance on oneself and acknowledges that this challenge can be met only if one can address not only the question "Does anyone love me?" (*M'aime-t-on?*), but also the more radical question "Can I initiate love—can I be a lover?" (*Puis-je aimer, moi le premier—comme un amant?*). It is not the certainty of my existence that I require; rather, it is the assurance of my significance or my value. Thus Marion's contention is that only in the intimacy of erotic love, or in the promise of this intimacy, can one receive the assurance of significance. I can love myself because I receive assurance from somewhere else—I discover myself lovable through the gift or the call of another.[26] In a reflection that also looks toward Lévinas, Marion draws a phrase from Isaiah 6:8, "Here I am" (*me voici*), to highlight the manner in which significance is mutually given in word or in silence.[27] The only assurance that I want or need is love—the assurance of my dignity as a lover. This assurance is both received and given in the "me voici" that surges forth as a pledge of eternal love.[28] In and through this pledge or covenant, the "I" or the ego is actually reborn as lover and beloved.[29] In a manner of speaking, I receive my significance the moment that the other consecrates me as a lover—a consecration that finds its articulation in the exclamation, "Come!"

The questions that this issue brings to the surface are nothing less than those of self-identity—How do I perceive myself? What questions define me? Marion contends that the great Kantian questions I can ask—"Who am I?" "What can I know?" "What ought I to do?" "What permits me to hope?"—will not suffice to penetrate the mystery of self-identity because even they do not meet the challenge posed by the question "to what end?" (*à quoi bon?*). Only a question that is not chosen, but rather is experienced at the core of one's being—one that brings to the surface issues of value and purpose—is adequate to sketch the appropriate contours of self-identity. Such a question is "Does anyone love me?"[30] Thus Marion concurs with Augustine that only within the framework of love can one legitimately ask, "Who am I?"

In placing emphasis on the other and, indeed, the otherness of the other,[31] this question exposes the vulnerability, the lack of certainty, that marks the human situation, and acknowledges the truth of the insight that self-identity and, indeed, self-love is something that is received rather than achieved.[32] Paradoxically, it is only in the abandonment of the epistemological and ontological claims to certitude that one can counter the claims of "vanity" and validate the claims of desire: it is not I, but rather the other, who is the ultimate guardian of my identity. This "other" cannot be reduced to me but nevertheless is not a stranger to me. In a passage that has profound Augustinian resonances, Marion reflects upon the source of the assurance that alone can address the question of my identity:

> The assurance never comes from an "ontic" other who would conserve me in my "beingness," but from another who is closer to me than I am to myself. (*PE*, 122)[33]

As Marion sees it, I receive the assurance of myself as a lover in the very act of making love—I receive the assurance from love itself, which is ultimately received as a gift from the other who accepts my love. In that sense, it is the pledge or the covenant of love or the other who loves me that is closer to me than I am to myself.

Thus Marion's *réduction érotique* situates self-identity under the rubric of love as desire: the gift of erotic love reveals me to myself in my individuality—as a lover. As Marion puts it:

> I become myself and recognize myself in my singularity when I discover and admit in the end the one that I desire; the one who alone shows me my most secret centre—the one whom I miss and the one who misses me. (*PE*, 172)[34]

Over a long period in and through attending to the desire for the other that is missed, I become less . . . obscure to myself. "My desire tells me about myself in showing me that which excites me."[35] In thus attending to the rationality of desire I come to see myself not only as one who is loved but, just as important, as a lover.[36]

All of which has clearly Augustinian resonances. In a celebrated phrase from the *Confessions*, "*pondus meum amor meus*,"[37] Augustine discloses an acute sensitivity to the way that love/desire defines the human person. It is no accident that this phrase has come to be viewed as the touchstone of Augustinian anthropology: the conviction that human beings are first and foremost lovers is one from which Augustine would never deviate.

In many respects the *Confessions* can be read as Augustine's portrayal of the universal search for self-identity, one that reveals the person as a profound puzzle to himself or herself. The restlessness of the human heart, as portrayed in the *Confessions*, testifies to the difficulties that humans experience in their quest to find anchor points within which to assure their identity. Similarly, the detailed analysis of the psychology of moral evil that one finds in the *Confessions*[38] and the often tortuous detail that Augustine uses to describe his own struggle ("my inner self was a house divided against itself"[39]) is eloquent testimony to his recognition of the struggles facing all who seek some assurance about their very existence.

As mentioned above, from the moment of reading Cicero's *Hortensius*, Augustine was left in no doubt that it is the quest for truth that defines the person. No other theme comes near to matching in detail and intensity this "bewildering passion for the wisdom of eternal truth"[40] that is etched into the pages of the *Confessions*. However, the key insight that for so long eluded Augustine's grasp was the correct manner in which to understand this quest. As he says:

> Truth! Truth! How the very marrow of my soul within me yearned for it as they dinned it in my ears over and over again! To them it was no more than a name to be voiced or a word to be read in their libraries of huge books—But my hunger and thirst were not even for the greatest of your works, but for you, my God, because you are Truth itself with whom there can be no change, no swerving from your course.[41]

The focus of Augustine's love for truth is upon the one who *is* truth rather than some abstract mastery of an intellectual cosmic puzzle. Fifteen years of dalliance with the Manichaeans had taught Augustine a hard-won lesson: that the quest for truth can never be satisfied unless one is conscious of the difference between an obsessive curiosity (*curiositas*) and true or holy desire.[42] It is nothing less than the difference between the desire to appropriate knowledge, as one would appropriate an object, and the desire to know the person who is the subject of one's love—to know that, and only that, which love reveals. The insight that marks Augustine's conversion, as recounted in the *Confessions*, is that the only appropriate focus for the quest for truth is a *person*, in and through whom I receive the gift of truth. Augustine was in no doubt that this person is God—it is God as truth who is the true focus of Augustine's love or desire. Thus Augustine would no doubt concur with Marion that the only question capable of making sense of desire is the question of whether there is someone who loves me, and who in turn ensures that I am capable of being a lover. The phrase "to love and to be loved was sweet to me" acts almost as a refrain that shapes the early books of the *Confessions*.[43] It is a reminder that for Augustine, the only way to understand the restless heart that shapes human nature is to see it in the context of the desire to love and to be loved.

The distinction between *curiositas* and desire has another focus that draws attention to the direction of the path illuminated by desire. A central premise of the *Confessions* that is shaped by Augustine's emphasis on interiority is that *curiositas* or disordered desire is marked by a love that is both directed at that which is lower rather than higher and, most important, is "inflated with desire for things outside the self."[44] The whole structure of the *Confessions* is modeled on the imagery of the biblical account of the Prodigal Son[45]—a structure that finds its most celebrated expression in the following passage:

> You were within me, and I was in the world outside myself. I searched for you outside myself and, disfigured as I was, I fell upon the lovely things of your creation. You were with me, but I was not with you.—You called me, you cried aloud to me; you broke my barrier of deafness. You shone upon me; your radiance enveloped me; you put my blindness to flight. You shed your fragrance about me; I drew breath and now I gasp for your sweet odour. I tasted you, and now I hunger and thirst for you. You touched me, and I am inflamed with love of your peace.[46]

It is a passage that highlights a number of key themes that mark Augustine's anthropology. First, in the emphasis on interiority reflected in the motif of the return to the self, we have the central insight that shapes Augustine's understanding of the divine–human relationship: the one who is loved, God, although infinitely above me, is also closer to me than I am to myself.[47] Second, in that sustained evocation of the motif of "calling," Augustine reminds his readers in no uncertain manner that the possibility of seeking God is dependent upon God seeking us first[48]—one can desire God only because He has first desired us.[49] It was Augustine's abiding conviction that one cannot confer significance on oneself. The person as a lover can love only because he or she is loved first. One is drawn to desire by the profoundly affective character of the gift of one who is beautiful—the one in whom I delight. Finally, the passage offers us an evocative portrayal of the person as a lover—the passionate desire of a lover for God. In the constellation of these three themes, we see clearly the Augustinian understanding of the person as a lover; we can also see, without doubt, the way in which Augustine's understanding converges remarkably with Marion's.

Love and the Desire for Eternity

One of the most significant aspects of Marion's analysis is his focus on the moment when the "I" becomes visible to itself as a lover—for, as he suggests, this self-recognition has the mark (or at least the promise) of eternity etched onto its identity. As Marion puts it, "In the moment of love, the lover is only able to believe that what he says and does is both said and done under a sign of eternity" (*PE*, 173).[50] It is a theme that, as we have already observed, he returns to frequently, making the point that the act of loving is comprehensible only insofar as it includes the promise that this moment is *for all time*.[51] Whether or not the promise is fulfilled is another matter, but this does not invalidate the conviction that my identity as a lover is in some way marked by this desire for eternity.

The desire for eternity reemerges with particular force as Marion reflects upon the significance of fidelity in defining the past, present, and future of the erotic phenomenon. Under the heading "La Fidélité comme temporalité érotique,"[52] Marion notes that the boundaries to erotic love are not set by anything other than fidelity to the covenant; furthermore, the interior logic of erotic love presupposes "a long and profound fidelity—nothing less than eternity" (*PE*, 286).[53] And so, in a clear critique of the core Heideggerian thesis that the anticipation of death is the ultimate possibility, Marion proposes a more radical last anticipation—one that does not anticipate death but, instead, the last love. It is not death that provides the final boundary to love; it is fidelity, and any fidelity to the covenant presupposes eternity. From the beginning, the lover anticipates eternity. He does not so much desire it as presuppose it; anticipation anticipates not just the possibility of the covenant but, even more important, its fulfillment.

But is this covenant ever capable of being fulfilled? By its very nature, Marion argues, erotic love is in constant need of re-creation—a characteristic that seems to contradict the intrinsic rationality of the covenant, the desire for a relationship that is durable.[54] Thus Marion first suggests that this need for durability/visibility can be met only by a third person—the infant who gives witness to this covenant. Even so, in time this witness can still depart. Accordingly, Marion reintroduces the concept of anticipation as a way of addressing this difficulty—what he describes as the eschatological character of the pledge. In that context, I am able to fulfill myself as a lover, but only "because I am able to love at each moment as if it is for eternity" (*PE*, 322),[55] in the light of eternity (*sub specie aeternitatis*).

In this respect, Marion disagrees with those who believe that the promise of eternity is not intrinsic to the very nature of covenant love. From his viewpoint there is nothing purely aspirational about the desire for eternity; rather, eternity surges up from the very nature

Le phénomène érotique ■ 211

of the pledge of love. Only eternity satisfies the strict demands of the rationality of erotic love.[56] Hence his evocative reflection on the word "adieu": Marion suggests that lovers ought to live in the light of eschatological anticipation—they ought to live in the light of the end (*l'adieu*) or, as the words suggest, in the light of their passage "to God." As *PE* has it:

> The lovers fulfill their covenant in the *adieu*—in the passage to God, whom they summon as their last witness, their first witness, the one who never leaves and never lies. Thus, for the first time, they themselves say *"adieu"*: next year in Jerusalem—the next time in God. To think in the direction of God is possible, erotically, in this *"adieu."* (*PE*, 326)[57]

For Marion, it is God who, as that eternally faithful witness to the covenant of love, saves the pledge by rendering it durable and definitively visible.

Perhaps, as the above quotation suggests, Marion might also be prepared to explore the Augustinian idea that in the *à Dieu*, the lovers' love is in God or toward God: for Augustine, only a love that is in God or toward God is eternal; love can be fulfilled only within such a horizon.

One of the most memorable sections in the *Confessions* is that in which Augustine describes the death of a close friend whom he had known since early childhood. Not only does this section mark the moment, at the age of nineteen, that he first became conscious of his own mortality; in the course of this section, Augustine also offers his most extended treatment of the nature of love and the significance of friendship.[58] Indeed, there are few passages in classical literature that offer the reader either a greater sensitivity to the intimacy that constitutes the love between friends or a more profound acknowledgment of the significance of this love for the life of each human being. In recounting this moment of awakening to his own mortality, occasioned by the death of his friend, Augustine offers the following comment:

> I wondered that other men should live when he was dead, for I had loved him as though he would never die. Still more I wondered that he should die and I remain alive, for I was his second self. How well the poet [Horace] put it when he called his friend the half of his soul! I felt that our two souls had been as

one, living in two bodies, and life to me was fearful because I did not want to live with only half a soul. Perhaps this, too, is why I shrank from death for fear that one whom I had loved so well might then be wholly dead.[59]

It is an evocative passage that demonstrates the profoundly interpersonal character of Augustine's anthropology. His philosophy of interiority—the return to the "heart"—is not to be confused with introspection; love of the other for his or her own sake, whether described as neighbor or friend or lover, is at the core of his understanding of the human person.[60] Instead, the turn to interiority concerns the direction in which one should travel in order to find one's brother or sister, "who is closer to me than I am to myself."

The above passage not only shows Augustine's familiarity with the classical understanding of friendship but also, and more important for our purposes, it reveals the true nature of the challenge to the "self" posed by the reality of death. For Augustine, death is not something that poses the ultimate challenge to my being as one who exists or that reminds me of my radical aloneness before being. On the contrary, death is experienced in the context of the challenge that it poses to love. It is the loss of a friend rather than my own mortality that provides the lens through which death is viewed. The phrase quoted above, "for I had loved him as though he would never die," is one that will deeply preoccupy Augustine. As he says in another passage, "What madness to love a man as something more than human"[61]; and again, in another passage, "I had poured out my soul upon him, like water upon sand, loving a man who was mortal as though he were never to die."[62] Augustine was never in any doubt that at some foundational level, the intimacy of love demands to be eternal and resists all rational attempts to constrain it within the boundaries set by death. He could easily say, with Marion, that "the lover from the beginning anticipates eternity; he does not desire it, rather he presupposes it" (*PE*, 299).[63] How, then, does Augustine attempt to address this paradox posed by the fact of human mortality? He does so in and through his reflections on the nature of true love. As he suggests:

Blessed are those who love you, O God, and love their friends in you and their enemies for your sake. They alone will never lose those who are dear to them for they love them in one who is never lost, in God.[64]

One of the hallmarks of the distinction that Augustine makes between ordered and disordered love hinges upon the difference between a love that is exclusive and one that is inclusive—a love that generously includes a "third." In the faith perspective of Augustine, this openness to the generosity of love is always described as a love that is "in God."[65] As we can see from the above quotation, the touchstone of the inclusiveness of the love of true friendship is that it even includes the love of enemies.[66]

For Augustine, in the context of his faith perspective, it is this love that is "in God"—or, as he will increasingly emphasize in his later life, a love that is "towards God"—which is eternal.[67] It is the love that extends even to enemies that is eternal, because all love participates in the life of the eternal God who is love, and God's love is all-embracing. In this profession of faith lies the hope that challenges both pride and despair; it is the confident assurance or prophetic hope that love is eternal.[68]

The Unity of Love

One of the most important theses to emerge from Marion's phenomenology of erotic love is that there is a unity to love and that, furthermore, this unity is founded on the template of erotic love.[69] Given the wide range of experiences associated with love and reflected in the three words that the Greeks needed to describe love—*erōs*, *philia*, and *agapē*—it seems at the outset to be a rather improbable thesis. Furthermore, the idea that the unity of love could be founded upon the intimacy of erotic love that is born of desire would seem difficult to reconcile with the very different experiences suggested by *philia* (friendship) and *agapē* (disinterested or benevolent love). Nevertheless, Marion's arguments here are highly persuasive and worth pursuing.

The key to grasping the possibility that erotic love might provide a template for the unity of love is to be found in a close examination of what Marion means by erotic love. In the course of an earlier discussion on those factors that can destroy the covenant of love, Marion makes a telling distinction between erotic love and what could be called an erotic impulse: only the former flows from the interior freedom of the person, he suggests.[70] He then develops this theme by suggesting that we can even love erotically without physical contact. Primacy is here given to the word—that special word that speaks of that which is between us—the word that, in respecting distance, can nevertheless touch the heart and offer the intimacy of love. As examples of such love he lists parent to child, friend to friend—and, of course, person to God.

In the final section of *PE*, Marion confronts the apparently equivocal character of love by drawing attention to the truth of the intuition that not only erotic love, but all forms of love, share a common context that is created by the challenge that "vanity" poses to self-identity. It is a bold assertion that allows Marion not only to highlight the manner in which his phenomenological analysis of erotic love has the potential to uncover the deepest roots of human questioning; it also convincingly situates a very different form of love, such as friendship, in the context of this overall vision of the unity of love.[71] Furthermore, it is not only *philia* but also the two classical poles of love, described by *erōs* and *agapē*, that are reconciled under the template of erotic love—one that, as we have seen, combines the desire for intimacy with the recognition that the intimacy that is born of love is received as a gift from the "other." Marion is in no doubt that this template provides a way of reconciling the two very different forms of love: just as it is not only *agapē* but also *erōs* that is revealed through an offering or a gift, so, likewise, *agapē* shares with *erōs* the characteristics of the passionate love of the lover.[72]

Marion concludes with a brief but convincing reflection on the Christian belief that God is love and on the significance of viewing His incarnate revelation from the perspective of a phenomenology of erotic love.[73] In this scenario, God's revelation provides the Christian believer with a model for comprehending the unity of love that does justice to the importance of intimacy. Marion creates an evocative portrait of a God who is both immanent and transcendent—a God who is close to us and like us in that He loves as we do, and a God whose love infinitely transcends our limited capacity. As Marion puts it:

> God precedes us and transcends us, but in the first place and above all in that He loves us infinitely more than we love and are loving Him. God surpasses us in being a better lover.[74]

Here, Marion's phenomenology of love has the very real potential to allow for discovering in the Christian revelation of God a way of responding definitively to the critical challenge of nihilism. For it is the God who loves (before He "is") who might answer the challenge posed to human meaning and value by the nihilistic character of the opening words from Ecclesiastes—that all is vanity. God is revealed as the first and definitive other who, in loving me, enables me in turn to love and, in so doing, offers me the assurance that only love can provide. Once again, the convergence with Augustine is remarkable: Augustine was never in any doubt of the truth of that phrase from the first epistle of St. John: "This is the love I mean; not our love for God, but God's love for us."[75]

If Augustine's writings are, in so many respects, an attempt to create a bridge between Jerusalem and Athens, then this is nowhere more evident than in his treatment of love—a motif that would forever remain central in his philosophical and theological writings. The deep challenge for Augustine's attempt to reconcile the Greek and Christian notions of love is twofold. First, he had to account for the apparent diversity of the experience of love, as reflected in the variety of words used to describe it. Second, there are critical differences between the Greek and Christian ways of viewing love that highlight the originality of the Christian insistence on the centrality of both the "grace dimension" of love and the idea that love ought to be extended to enemies.

In many respects, the Latin distinctions among *amor, amicitia,* and *caritas/ dilectio* replicated those between *erōs, philia,* and *agapē* that shaped the classical culture, although the significance attached to them would vary considerably.[76] No one familiar with the traditions of Platonism and Neoplatonism could doubt the significance of the motif of *erōs* in providing a way of understanding the human psyche. Clearly, the Neoplatonic background of Augustine's philosophy contributed to his understanding of love as desire and to the emphasis that he would place on the significance of *amor*. A similar ease in according the same significance to *philia* and *amicitia* is not so clear-cut. The Greeks placed an extremely high premium on friendship: the love of friendship is valued as an end in itself; Aristotle would even proclaim that it is only in and through friendship that we become like the gods, capable of attaining the ultimate goal of all human striving—*eudaimonia*.[77] The question for Augustine is whether it is possible to accord to friendship the same significance as in the Greek world, or even to reconcile it with a love, such as *caritas*, that places emphasis on the benevolence of love, the grace or gift dimension of love, and the idea that love ought to be extended to enemies. More generally, the question for Augustine, writing from a Christian perspective, is whether it is possible to argue for a unified theory of love that does justice to its complexity as reflected in the different forms of love.[78] As we shall see, Augustine goes to some lengths to reconcile these different forms of love within a unified perspective. The reason for this effort is quite simple: the cornerstone of Augustine's reflections on love is his belief in the unity of this concept, a unity based on his conviction of the correctness of the Christian standpoint that God is love, and that therefore all forms of love come from this source and share the critical characteristics of the divine life that is love.

What is most evident in Augustine's treatment of love as desire—for the most part reflected in his use of the word *amor*—is his insistence on both the benevolent character of desire and the fact that desire is received as a gift. On both counts this stress places Augustine at some distance from classical Platonism and Neoplatonism. As he puts it:

> All love, even the love we call carnal—for which the more usual Latin word is not *dilectio* but *amor*, *dilectio* being commonly used and understood in a higher sense—all love, my dear brother, implies necessarily an element of goodwill towards those who are loved.—Men are not to be loved as things to be consumed, but in the manner of friendship and goodwill, leading us to do things for the benefit of those we love. And if there is nothing we can do, goodwill alone is enough for the lover.[79]

The emphasis Augustine places on the benevolent character of love, no matter how it is described, could hardly be clearer. What is particularly significant is that he not only emphasizes the benevolent character of love as desire, but that he also uses the example of friendship as a model to describe benevolent love. This is crucially important in the context of a supposed contrast between the desire for reciprocity in friendship and the benevolent and/or disinterested character of love. For Augustine, this is a false contrast: he will always insist on the benevolent character of friendship, and he will question whether even benevolent love can ever be disinterested. As far as Augustine is concerned, all love should be interested; at the very least, it should be interested in the well-being of the one who is loved. The spurious ideal of disinterestedness, which is used to denigrate forms of love that reflect a desire to be loved, would have no part in Augustine's anthropology. There is nothing disinterested about the person described in the light of the motif of "a restless heart"; but that in no way compromises the benevolent character of "ordered love." In fact, Augustine will criticize the disordered desire of his early life precisely on this ground:

> I was so blind that I could not discern the light of virtue and of beauty that is loved for its own sake—I could not find happiness, even in the sense in which I then conceived of it, unless I had these friends. And yet I certainly loved them for their own sakes, and I felt that they loved me for my sake in return.[80]

To love others for their own sake is the touchstone of "ordered love," whether understood as *amicitia* or *caritas*.

Closely allied to the motif of the benevolence of love is the issue of the graced dimension of love—a core feature of the Christian understanding that all love is first and foremost received as a gift. As mentioned above, Augustine would never lose sight of the truth of the Johannine insight "This is the love I mean: not our love for God, but God's love for us."[81] The gift of love in turn enables me to love.

Although the motif of *caritas* most obviously gives expression to this dimension of love, it is also present in Augustine's deliberations on both desire and friendship—both experienced as gift. Augustine was always conscious of the origins of desire. Desire grows in and through the gift of God's love—a gift that instills delight and engenders desire.[82] Likewise, friendship is seen in the context of a gift that awakens desire.[83]

Certainly, a very obvious difference between friendship and *caritas* is that only the former is founded upon the experience of the attractiveness of a shared likeness in respect of virtue, whereas the latter extends even to enemies. It is a difference that reveals a critical culture gap between the worlds of Athens and Jerusalem. And yet it is characteristic of Augustine that he seeks to interpret both in the light of a unified vision of love. As his life progresses, he will increasingly place the emphasis in friendship not on the present enjoyment of virtue but rather on the role that friendship plays in encouraging both partners on the road to virtue. The friend is seen as the spiritual guide who frequently reminds the other of the need to be healed or who provides indispensable support on the journey to God:

> We are commanded to love this Good with all our heart, with all our soul, with all our strength; and to this Good we must be led by those who love us, and to it we must lead those whom we love.[84]

The question of the universal extension of all forms of love, including friendship, must also be seen in this light. As Augustine puts it:

> ... friendship is not confined by narrow limits; it includes all those to whom love and affection are due, although it goes out more readily to some, more slowly to others, but it reaches even our enemies, for whom we are commanded to pray.[85]

In the last analysis, Augustine's vision of the unity of love is based on his recognition that just as God is love, so also love is of God: "love is God."[86] It may be *caritas* rather than erotic love that provides the template for this love, but what Augustine emphasizes above all is the *inclusivity* of ordered love. Again, the convergence with Marion's *PE* is remarkable.

Conclusion

Without wishing to exaggerate the similarities that might be suggested through a juxtaposition of Marion's phenomenology of erotic love and Augustine's reflections on the character and significance of love, we can see, nevertheless, some striking parallels. Both understand that the question posed by Ecclesiastes has the potential to render desire stillborn in the human soul—it carries the potential to destroy the human spirit. Both are in no doubt that the gift of love is the only way in which that nihilistic critique can be addressed. Both stress the unity of love. Both are acutely conscious that human nature is shaped by love and that it is only by attending to the voice of love that one recognizes where one's fulfillment is to be found—in and through the gift of the one "who is closer to me than I am to myself."

This convergence says as much for the perennial value of Augustine's anthropology as it does for Marion's very obvious familiarity with the late classical world. Far more importantly than either of these points, however, it reminds us that without love, all is vanity and we are nothing.

Hermeneutics of the Possible God

Richard Kearney

> I come in the little things, saith the Lord.
>
> —Evelyn Underhill

God, if God exists, exists not just for God but also for us. And the manner in which God comes to us, comes to mind, comes to be, and comes to dwell as flesh among us, is deeply informed by the manner in which we think about God—in short, how we interpret, narrate, symbolize, and imagine God. This, I suggest, calls for a philosophical hermeneutics instructed by the various and essential ways in which God "appears" to us in and through "phenomena," and "signals" to us in and through "signs." It is my wager in this chapter that one of the main ways in which the infinite comes to be experienced and imagined by finite minds is as *possibility*—that is, as *the ability to be*. Even, and especially, when such possibility seems impossible to us. I am not saying this is the only way, or even the most primordial way; just that it is a very telling way, and one that has been largely neglected in the history of Western metaphysics and theology in favor of categories such as substance, cause, actuality, absolute spirit, and sufficient reason.

In the first part of this chapter I propose briefly to explore ways in which phenomenology—as first developed by Edmund Husserl and Martin Heidegger—helped to open up a new path for thinking about

God in terms of the possible. In the second part, I will chart a further itinerary through three hermeneutic circles of reading—*scriptural*, *testimonial*, and *literary*—that, I believe, disclose rich textual resources for reimagining God as *posse*.

The Way of Phenomenology

Husserl

Edmund Husserl inaugurated the phenomenological method. One of the primary purposes of this method was to open our minds to the realm of "pure possibility," thereby liberating us from our habitual attachments to mere facts and opinions. Husserl identified five basic steps in the method: (1) the *epochē* (bracketing or suspension) of the presuppositions and prejudices of our so-called natural attitude; (2) the "reduction" of our attention back to "the things themselves," as revealed in the intentional life of consciousness; (3) the "free variation in imagination" of any topic of inquiry across all its variants—actual and virtual, real or imaginary—until an invariant structure or essence (*eidos*) appears; (4) the "intuition" of this essential meaning in the pure immanence of consciousness; and (5) the "description" of essential meaning by transcendental subjectivities extending toward a telos of absolute reason.

Though most of Husserl's mainstream work appeared to bracket out the theological or confessional question of God, there are a number of fascinating conjectures about a phenomenological approach to the divine in several of his later and posthumously published lectures, letters, and manuscripts. In some texts Husserl's God approximates to a "transcendental ideal" in Kant's sense, that is, an Idea situated at infinity that directs the various intentions of consciousness asymptotically. As such, it operates regulatively as a sort of teleological idea of Reason.[1] In other passages, such as paragraph 35 of *The Crisis*, Husserl compares the phenomenological method to a "religious conversion" that triggers an "existential metamorphosis of humanity."[2] In short, the phenomenological *epochē* and reduction effect a change of attitude in the human subject that Husserl considers analogous to that brought about by a religious transformation of the "natural" self. He even goes so far as to speak of the *Idea Christi* as "the archetypal idea of the Man-God" that mobilizes human striving toward a universal humanity.[3] Moreover, we have it on the testimony of Sister Adelgundis Jaegerschmidt, who nursed Husserl in his final years, that Husserl confessed that "human life was nothing less than a journey towards God," even though the philosophical vocation was, strictly speaking, a "path to God without God."[4]

The basic postulate of a phenomenology of religion is this: religious consciousness is a distinct, sui generis mode of intentionality that aims at a transcendent meaning—called God—without being in a position (after the methodical bracketing of the question of transcendence) to verify or falsify its truth claims. While Husserl construes the religious mode of intentionality as one of "faith," he is also wont to link this same intentionality with an inherent tendency of "phenomenological reason" itself directed toward an absolute goal of meaning.[5] On occasion, these two seemingly incompatible claims—for faith and for reason—lead to some conflict, as when Husserl argues that "religious intuition presupposes the most universal intuition of absolute givens" and, as such, requires an approach transgressing the normal limits of transcendental subjectivity.[6] (Husserl might be said to anticipate here Jean-Luc Marion's disclosure of the "saturated phenomenon" that, Marion argues, finds its apogee in the "saturated phenomenon par excellence"—Christ.[7]) To address this tension, Husserl sought to distinguish between two senses of the word "religion." On the one hand, writes Husserl, we have "religion as a progressive myth, as an authentic and unilateral intuition of religious ideals, surrounded by an horizon of presentiments whose infinite dimensions remain impenetrable, compelling us to kneel before the unfathomable." On the other hand, we have "religion as a metaphysics of religion, as the ultimate fulfillment of a science of universal understanding, in the sense of the norm of all intuitive myths and symbols, regulating all the figures and transformations of its imaginary."[8] The tension between these two approaches was, I believe, never fully resolved.

Husserl's own instinct, it seems, was to move in the direction of a generous phenomenology of comparative religion. This would acknowledge the valuable resources of both monotheistic and nonmonotheistic religions (such as Buddhism) as respective approximations to the "teleological idea of reason," guided by a universal entelechy and striving toward ever more perfect freedom. But even as Husserl appeared to subordinate faith to reason in this universalist gesture, he was still prepared to speak of this entelechy as a kind of unconditional "absolute obligation" (*absolutes Soll*) whose quality was not only moral but also "mystical."[9] Similarly, in a famous passage in *Ideas*, book 1, Husserl makes the telling concession that when he speaks of the divine, he is referring to an "'Absolute' in a completely different sense than that of the absolute of consciousness" and to a "transcendent in a completely different sense than the transcendence of world."[10] It is not, Husserl insists, a human subject that "invents or produces this supreme transcendence."[11] Little wonder, then, that Husserl could write in a letter to the young Roman Ingarden that there was no problem more important than that of God![12]—adding that it was an essential task to rediscover "the meaning of divine being and of the divine creation of the world."[13]

In the light of all this evidence, Jean Greisch does not hesitate to affirm that we find in Husserl the "lineaments of a theological philosophy associated with the teleological idea of reason."[14] By all accounts, we are moving here from transcendental egology to transcendental theology. But that does not mean that we can ever fully disentangle the use of the terms *theology* and *teleology* in Husserl. From beginning to end, God appears as a term for "absolute entelechy"—the progressive actualizing of divine potential as "infinite life, infinite love, infinite will."[15] Moreover, I suspect that one of the reasons that Husserl's God is not just an Idea of Reason but a gift of life is that this Absolute "entelechy of entelechies" constitutes itself for us in and through the "free variation of possibles" that imagination provides both in (a) the great texts of Scripture and literature and in (b) the third step of the phenomenological method—namely, "imaginative variation"—which seeks formally to revisit these texts in the eidetic realm of "pure possibility." Indeed, it might be said that for Husserl it is this exploratory and intuitive use of imagination that seeks to bring together the otherwise opposed worlds of eidetic reason and experiential faith. As he confesses in *Ideas:* "If anyone loves a paradox, he can readily say, and say with strict truth if he will allow for ambiguity, that the element which makes up the life of phenomenology, as of all eidetical sciences, is 'fiction,' that fiction is the source whence the knowledge of eternal truths draws its sustenance."[16]

The God of Husserl's phenomenology is not just an abstraction of rationalist deism nor a glorified Monad of Sufficient Reason—it is also a God of an intuition so deep that it surpasses and overflows all our intentions. This latter is a God of testimony and empathy, of suffering and action, of passion and compassion. As Husserl himself concedes: "God experiences in himself [*lebt in sich nach*] every suffering . . . and it is only by suffering with in this manner that he can surmount his finitude, his not-having-to-be in infinite harmony in light of which he exists."[17] That is also why for Husserl the self of spirit is one that not only "receives itself from another but is also capable of losing itself for another."[18] Here, arguably, we find the phenomenological roots of what Ricoeur calls the "sujet convoqué" and what Marion calls the "interloqué." The phenomenologically purged self discovers its originary existence as one that is inextricably tied to others in a series of intersubjective transversals that lead ultimately to God. "In myself," writes Husserl, "passing through the other selves with whom I find myself tied, all the ways ... lead to the same pole, God, who transcends both man and world."[19]

It is this kind of thinking that enables Jean Greisch to conclude his highly illuminating investigation of Husserl's phenomenology of religion by declaring that since, for Husserl, "every life only becomes conscious accompanied by love,"[20] the acute awareness that Husserl has of the "absolute vocation of the subject, places him on the road to a God whose true name is Love."[21]

Moreover, the fact that Husserl approaches the question of God, after the reduction, in a manner that is radically open to every possible variation of meaning and manifestation means that this is the most nondogmatic divinity one could imagine. One might even say that for Husserl a certain methodical agnosticism or atheism is a necessary prelude to the disclosure of neglected aspects of divinity. It certainly keeps the doors open to dialogue between the great religions of the world, resisting the temptation to impose the confessional presuppositions of any one faith. A phenomenology of religion in this sense is the contrary of apologetics. Its attentiveness to the realm of "pure possibility" marks a refusal of exclusionary dogmatism and throws down a challenge to the old metaphysical notions of God as impassive actuality or *ens causa sui*.

An insurmountable tension remains, however. Husserl's uncompromising adherence to a rigorous science of transcendental reason—with God representing the ultimate universal pole—cannot be easily squared with the mystical or personal God of confessional revelation. The God of Reason and the God of Faith remain, it seems, on separate, if parallel, tracks in Husserl's phenomenology. But both Gods hint, in their respective ways, toward a divinity fueled by "the passion of the possible"—a special passion accessible through the "free variation of imagination."

Heidegger

Martin Heidegger took the phenomenological inquiry about God and the Possible in new directions. His basic insight that for phenomenology "possibility stands higher than actuality" (formulated in his introduction to *Being and Time*) was to prove of crucial significance. It offered a new ontological meaning to Husserl's claim that it is the realm of possibility, opened up by the phenomenological method of reduction and free variation, that leads us to an essential intuition of truth. Heidegger gave Husserl's argument a more existential articulation, however, when he showed how "*Dasein* is its possibilities," from its everday concerns and projects to its most ultimate and ownmost possibility of all—the possibility that is the impossibility of any further possibility: one's being toward death (*Sein-zum-Tode*).

Heidegger was also borrowing here from Kierkegaard's original suggestion in *Sickness unto Death* that divine existence should be conceived of in terms of the "possible." "For prayer," writes Kierkegaard, "there must be a God, a self—and possibility—or a self and possibility in a pregnant sense, because the being of God means that everything is possible [*mulig*], or that everything is possible means the being of God; only he whose being has been so shaken that he has become spirit by understanding that everything is possible, only he has anything to do with God. That God's will is the possible makes me able to pray; if there is nothing but necessity, man is essentially as inarticulate as the animals."[22] What, exactly, Kierkegaard means by "possibility in a pregnant sense" is something that Heidegger sought to clarify when he identified the truth of Being with "the quiet power of the possible," in his conclusion to *Being and Time*. The fact that Heidegger described Kierkegaard as neither a pure philosopher nor a pure theologian, but a law unto himself,[23] is also of interest as we seek to identify the exact status of Heidegger's own contribution to a depth hermeneutics of the Possible.

Given Heidegger's phenomenological analysis of *Dasein*'s different categories of possibility in *Being and Time*—as *Seinkonnen*, *Möglichkeit*, *ermöglichen*—one might be forgiven for supposing that the "power of the possible" refers to an essentially *human* property.[24] However, in the *Letter on Humanism* (1947), Heidegger claims that such a humanist supposition is mistaken. In a pivotal if much neglected passage in this postwar letter to Jean Beaufret, Heidegger revisits this exact reference to the "quiet power of the possible," redefining it this time as an unambiguous gift of Being itself. Theological connotations abound, albeit elusively. And we are tempted to ask, What, if anything, does this "quiet power" of Being have to do with God?

The passage in question opens as follows: "Being as the element is the 'quiet power' of the loving potency [*Vermögens*], i.e. of the possible [*des Möglichen*]." Already the interpolation of the new term *Vermögen*, to qualify the standard term for the possible in *Being and Time*—namely, *das Mögliche*—signals a shift from an existential-transcendental perspective (easily confused with humanism) to a more unequivocally Being-centered one. This new assignation for Being's own power of possibilizing is more topological than anthropological. It marks a clear departure from the transcendental residues of "possibility" still evident in the existential analytic of *Dasein* in *Being and Time*. Determined now to avoid any further humanist misreadings, Heidegger is emphatic on this point. "Our words 'possible' and 'possibility' are," he explains, "under the domination of 'logic' and 'metaphysics,' taken only in contrast to 'actuality,' i.e. they are conceived with reference to a determined—viz. the metaphysical— interpretation of Being as *actus* and *potentia*, the distinction of which is identified with that of *existentia* and *essentia*." But Heidegger explains that when he speaks of the "quiet power of the possible," he means neither (1) the "possible of a merely represented *possibilitas*" (a Leibnizian-Kantian category of modal logic) nor (2) "the *potentia* as *essentia* of an *actus* of the *existentia*" (an Aristotelian-scholastic category of metaphysics). He means, as he states here, "Being itself, which in its loving potency [*das Mögend*] possibilizes [*vermag*] thought and thus also the essence of man, which means in turn his relationship to Being." Heidegger concludes this decisive passage thus: "To possibilise [*vermögen*] something is to sustain it in its essence, to retain it in its element."[25]

The significance of this pronouncement on the "possible" cannot be underestimated. It offers a unique insight into the famous "Turn" in Heidegger's thought from "phenomenology" (with its residual transcendental, existential, *Dasein*-centered idioms) to "thought" (with its shift of emphasis to Being-as-Being, *Sein als Sein*).[26] Heidegger I's humanist-sounding idioms of Being as temporality and historicality are now replaced with a more sacred-sounding language of love and grace, consistent with Heidegger II's rethinking of Being as Gift (*Es gibt*). Playing on the latent etymological affinities between the German verbs for loving (*mögen*) and making possible (*vermögen*), Heidegger invites us to rethink Being itself as the power that possibilizes the authentic being of things:

> It is on the strength of this loving potency or possibilization of love [*das Vermögen des Mögens*] that something is possibilized [*vermag*] in its authentic [*eigentlich*] being. This possibilization

[*Vermögen*] is the authentic "possible" [*das eigentlich "mögliche"*], that whose essence rests on loving.[27]

The proper response of human beings to such loving-possibilizing is, Heidegger suggests, to love-possibilize Being in return. How? By thinking things and selves in their authentic essence. "Thought is . . . to concern oneself about the essence of a 'thing' or a 'person,' that means to like or to love them."[28] The possibilizing of Being may thus be understood in terms of a double genitive referring both to Being's loving-possibilizing of thought and thought's loving-possibilizing of Being. Thus we might translate Heidegger's phrase—"Aus diesem Mögen vermag das Sein das Denken"—as "Being possibilizes thought which possibilizes Being." The sense of this translation is confirmed, it seems, in Heidegger's subsequent sentences:

> The one renders the other possible. Being as the loving-possibilizing is the "*posse-ible*" (*Jenes ermöglichte dieses. Das Sein als Vermögend-Mögende ist das "Mög-liche"*).[29]

By choosing to translate the operative term *Mög-liche* as *posse*-ible, I am suggesting that the shared semantic sense of *mögen* (to love) and *vermögen* (to be able/to make possible) is perhaps best captured by the Latin term *posse*—a word that, according to Nicholas of Cusa, lies at the very heart of divine being, qua God's power to love. Nicholas coined the word *Possest* to capture this double belonging of possiblity and being that he identified with God. "God alone," he wrote, "is all that he is able to be."[30]

Heidegger does not go so far. There is no mention of Nicholas of Cusa. Yet much of his language is deeply resonant with the religious language of Christian eschatology. Indeed, in a related passage in the 1947 letter to Beaufret, Heidegger actually equates the essence of Being with the "sacred" and the "divine."[31] This, in conjunction with his *Der Spiegel* claim that "only a god can save us now" and his *Beiträge* allusion to Schelling's equation of the God of Exodus 3:14 with the "possibility of being" (*seyn wird/Seyn-könnende*) certainly solicits the surmise that *some* rapport might exist between the "possibilizing" power of Being and the *Possest* of God.[32] Moreover, Heidegger's liberal borrowings from Christian mystical theology—for example, Eckhart's *Gelassenheit*, Angelus Silesius's "rose-that-blooms-without-why," and Paul's eschatological *kairos*—all suggest a deep, residual affinity with the author's early fascination with Catholic and Lutheran theology. And even if it is probably more the "god of the poets" (than of revelation) that the later Heidegger has in mind when he invokes a "saving god," one cannot gainsay some kind of relation between ontological and theological readings of the "loving possible." Indeed, in the *Introduction to Metaphysics*, Heidegger had already hinted that the ontology/theology relationship might take the form of an *analogy of proper proportionality*: namely, the believer is to God what *Dasein* is to Being.[33]

Thus, when Heidegger speaks of poetic dwelling as an invitation to abide in "that which has a loving for man and therefore needs his presence" (*was selber den Menschen mag und darum sein Wesen braucht*), one has reason to suspect that some kind of deity is hovering in the vicinity.[34] And this surmise is substantiated when one observes how several of Heidegger's last writings recast the Husserlian notion of teleological possibility in terms of a quasi-eschatological drama. A typical example is *The End of Philosophy*, where Heidegger claims that the "end of philosophy is the place in which the whole of philosophy's history is gathered in its most ultimate possibility"—a final possibility that is also the "first possibility" from which all genuine thought originates.[35] Such a possibility is clearly beyond all human powers of determination, for "its contours remain obscure and its coming uncertain."[36] So we are back once again, it seems, with that possibilizing-appropriating of human thinking by Being itself: a form of happening (*Ereignis*) and giving (*Es gibt*) that remains beyond our ken and control. Being is thus rendered as "that which is capable of being," the *esti gar einai* of Parmenides now rethought by Heidegger as the "possibility of Being." From a human point of view this means, quite simply, letting things be what they *can be*.[37]

But whatever this "possibility of Being" may be, it is certainly *not* the mere *potentia* of some metaphysical substance, nor the *possibilitas* of some representational logic (alongside reality and necessity).[38] The loving-possible is for Heidegger something that surpasses the understanding of both metaphysics and logic. It is nothing less than the giving of Being itself.

The Eschatological Way

In this second part, I will proceed by means of three concentric hermeneutic circles—scriptural, testimonial, and literary. By traversing this threefold "variation of imagination," I hope to identify some key characteristics of the God of the Possible. In what follows, I would like to address two main questions: (1) How might a hermeneutics of God as *posse* benefit from a mode of thinking that takes its cue from "poetical" rather than "metaphysical" thinking? (2) How might such a hermeneutics of *posse* enable us to avoid theodicy—the claim that if *all* things are possible to God, this must also include *evil* things (a position I will vigorously contest)?

The Scriptural Circle

My efforts to rethink God as *posse* rather than *esse* draw primarily from the biblical message that what is impossible for man is possible for God. This latter notion of messianic possibility is evident in many scriptural passages. In Mark 10, for example, we are told that while entry to the Kingdom seems impossible for humans, all things are made possible by God. The exact text reads: "For humans it is impossible but not for God; because for God everything is possible" (*panta gar dunata para to theo*) (Mark 10:27). In similar vein, we are told in St. John's prologue that our ability to become sons of God in the Kingdom is something made possible by God: "Light shone in darkness and to all who received it was given the possibility [*dunamis*] to become sons of God" (John 1:5; my translation). The word *dunamis* is crucial and can be translated as either "power" or "possibility"—a semantic ambivalence to which we shall return below. Further evocations of the possibilizing power (*dunamis pneumatos*) of the Spirit are evidenced in Paul's letters to the Corinthians and Romans; but perhaps most dramatically of all in the Annunciation scene, where Mary is told by the angel that the *dunamis* of God will overshadow her and that she will bear the son of God—"for nothing is impossible [*a-dunaton*] with God" (Luke 1:37).

In all these examples, divinity—as Father, Son, or Spirit—is described as a possibilizing of divine love and logos in the order of human history where it would otherwise have been impossible. In other words, the divine reveals itself here as the possibility of the Kingdom—or, if you prefer to cite a *via negativa*, as the *impossibility of impossibility*.

A hermeutical poetics of the Kingdom looks to some of the recurring *figures*—metaphors, parables, images, symbols—deployed in the Gospels to communicate the eschatological promise. The first thing one notes is that these figures almost invariably refer to a God of "small things"—to borrow from the wonderful title of Arundhati Roy's novel. Not only do we have the association of the Kingdom with the vulnerable openness and trust of "little children," as in Matthew, but we also have the images of the yeast in the flour (Luke 13), the tiny pearl of great price (Matthew 13), and, perhaps most suggestive and telling of all, the mustard seed (Mark 4)—a minuscule grain that blooms and flourishes into a spreading tree. The kingdom of God, this last text tells us, is

> ... like a mustard seed that, when it is sown in the ground, is the smallest of all the seeds on the earth. But once it is sown, it springs up and becomes the largest of plants and puts forth large branches, so that the birds of the sky can dwell in its shade.

One might be tempted to call this recurring motif of the Kingdom as the last or least or littlest of things a *micro-eschatology* to the extent that it resists the standard macro-eschatology of the Kingdom as emblem of sovereignty, omnipotence, and ecclesiastical triumph. The frequent reference in the Gospels to the judgment of the Kingdom being related to how we respond in history, here and now, to the "least of these" (*elachistos*) (e.g., Matthew 25:40) is crucial. The loving renunciation of absolute power by Christ's empyting (*kenosis*) of the Godhead, so as to assume the most humble form of humanity (the last and least of beings), is echoed by the eschatological reminder that it is easier for the defenseless and powerless to enter the Kingdom than it is for the rich and mighty. And I think it is telling—as Dostoyevsky reminds us in the Grand Inquisitor episode of the *Brothers Karamazov*—that the greatest temptation that Christ must overcome, after His forty days in the desert, is the will to become master and possessor of the universe. This is a temptation He faces again and again, right up to His transfiguration on Mount Tabor, when his disciples want to apotheosize and crown Him by building a cult temple there on the mountain (Luke 9). Instead, Christ proceeds to a second kenotic act of giving, refusing the short route to immediate triumph and embracing the *via crucis*, which demonstrates what it means for the seed to die before it is reborn as a flowering tree that hosts all living creatures. As "King" he enters Jerusalem, not with conquering armies but "seated upon an ass's colt" (John 12). He upturns the inherited hierarchies of power, fulfilling the prophecy of Isaiah that he would bring justice to the world, not by "shouting aloud in the street" but as a "bruised reed that shall not break, a smouldering wick that shall not quench" (Isaiah 42:2–3).

But in addition to these *spatial* metaphors of the Kingdom exemplified by little things—yeast, a mustard seed, a pearl, a reed, an infant, the "least of these"—a hermeneutic poetics of the Kingdom might also look to the *temporal* figures of eschatology. These invariably take the form of a certain *achronicity*. I am thinking here of the numerous references to the fact that even though the Kingdom has *already come*—and is incarnate *here and now* in the loving gestures of Christ and all those who give, or receive, a cup of water; it still always remains a possibility *yet to come*. This is what Emmanuel Lévinas calls the "paradox of posterior anteriority"; and it is cogently illustrated in an aphorism of Walter Benjamin that combines the spatial figure of the portal with the eschatological figure of futurity: "This future does not correspond to homogenous empty time; because at the heart of every moment of the future is contained the little door through which the Messiah may enter."[39]

As "eternal," the Kingdom transcends all chronologies of time. Christ indicates this when He affirms that "before Abraham was, I am" (John 8:58) and when He promises a Second Coming when he will return again. In short, the Kingdom is both (a) *already* there as historical possibility and (b) *not yet* there as a historically realized kingdom "come on earth." This is why we choose to translate the canonical theophany of God to Moses on Mount Sinai (*esher ayeh esher*) not as "I am who am" (*ego sum qui sum*) but as "I am who may be." God is saying something like this: "I will show up as promised, but I cannot *be* in time and history, I cannot become fully embodied in the flesh of the world, unless you show up and answer my call 'Where are you?' with the response 'Here I am.'" (I explore this eschatological enigma of time in further detail in the conclusion, below).

The Testimonial Circle

Our second hermeneutic circle explores a poetics of the Kingdom in light of a number of testimonies recorded by religious writers down through the ages. This we might call the *testimonial* or *confessional* genre. Unlike "metaphysical" thinkers, who presuppose an ontological priority of actuality over possibility, these more "poetical" minds reverse the traditional priority and point to a new category of possibility—divine possibility—*beyond* the traditional opposition between the possible and the impossible.

Let me begin with the pregnant maxim of Angelus Silesius: "God is possible as the more than impossible." Here Angelus—a German mystical thinker often cited by Heidegger and Derrida—points toward an eschatological notion of possibility that might be said to transcend the three conventional concepts of the possible: (1) as an epistemological category of modal logic, along with necessity and actuality (Kant); (2) as a substantialist category of *potentia* lacking its fulfillment as *actus* (Aristotle and the scholastics); and (3) as a rationalist category of *possibilitas* conceived as a represention of the mind (Leibniz and the idealists). All such categories fall within the old metaphysical dualism of possibility versus impossibility. But Angelus intimates a new role for the possible as a ludic and liberal outpouring of divine play: "God is possible as the more than impossible ... God plays with Creation/All that is play that the deity gives itself/It has imagined the creature for its pleasure." Creation here is depicted as an endless giving of possibility that calls us toward the Kingdom.

I think the early medieval Jewish commentator Rashi also had something like this in mind when interpreting Isaiah's God calling to his creatures—"I cannot be God unless you are my witnesses." He takes this to mean "I am the God who will be whenever you bear witness to love and justice in the world."[40] And I believe that the Holocaust victim Etty Hillesum was gesturing toward a similar notion when, just weeks before her death in a concentration camp, she wrote: "You, God, cannot help us but we must help you and defend your dwelling place inside us to the last."[41] Both Rashi and Hillesum were witnessing to the *dunamis* of God as *the power of the powerless*. This, clearly, is not the imperial power of a sovereign; it is a dynamic call to love that possibilizes and enables humans to transform their world—by giving themselves to the "least of these," by empathizing with the disinherited and the dispossessed, by refusing the path of might and violence, by transfiguring the mustard seed into the Kingdom, each moment at a time, one act after another, each step of the way. This is the path heralded by the Pauline God of "nothings and nobodies" (*ta me onta*) excluded from the triumphal preeminence of totality (*ta onta*)—a kenotic, self-emptying, crucified God whose "weakness is stronger than human strength" (1 Corinthians 1:25). It signals the option for the poor, for nonviolent resistance and revolution taken by peacemakers and dissenting "holy fools" from ancient to modern times. It is the message of suffering rather than doing evil, of loving one's adversaries, of "no enemies," of "soul force" (*satyagraha*). One thinks of a long heritage ranging from Isaiah, Jesus, Siddartha, and Socrates to such contemporary figures as Gandhi, Havel, Dorothy Day, Jean Vanier, Ernesto Cardinal, Thich Nhat Hanh, and Martin Luther King, among others. The God witnessed here goes beyond the will-to-power.

Nicholas of Cusa, as already mentioned, offers some interesting insights into this eschatological God when he declares that "God alone is all he is able to be" (*Trialogus de Possest*).[42] Unlike the God of metaphysical omnipotence, underlying the perverse logic of theodicy that seeks to justify evil as part of the divine Will, this notion of God as an "abling to be" (*posse* or *possest*) points in a radically different direction.

Let us pause for a moment to unpack the phrase "God is all he is able to be." Since God is all good, God is not able to be nongood (that is, non-God)—defect or evil. In other words, God is *not* omnipotent in the traditional metaphysical sense understood by Leibniz and Hegel. He is not a being able to be all good *and* evil things. That is why God could not help Etty Hillesum and other victims of evil. God is not responsible for evil. And Hillesum understood this all too well when she turned the old hierarchies on their head and declared that it is *we* who must help God to be God. Was she not in fact subscribing here to a long—if often neglected—biblical heritage? After all, if Elijah had not heard the "still, small voice" of God in his cave, we would never have received the wisdom of his prophecy. If a young woman from Nazareth had said "no" to the angel of the Annunciation, the Word would not have become flesh. If certain fishermen, tax collectors, and prostitutes had not heard the call to follow the Son of Man, there would have been no Son of God—and no Gospel witness. So, too, if Hillesum and others like her had not let God be God by defending his dwelling place of *caritas* within them, even in those hellish moments of Holocaust horror, there would have been no measure of love—albeit as tiny as the mustard seed—to defy the hate of the Gestapo. For if God's loving is indeed unconditional, the realization of that loving *posse* in this world is conditional upon our response. If we are waiting for God, God is waiting for us. Waiting for us to say "yes," to hear the call and to act, to bear witness, to answer the *posse* with *esse*, to make the Word flesh—even in the darkest moments.

I think Pseudo-Dionysius the Areopagite could be said to add to our understanding of this great enigma when he speaks, in book 7 of the *Divine Names*, of a "possibility beyond being" (*hyperousias dunameos*) that engenders our desire to live more abundantly and seek the good. "Being itself," he writes, "only has the possibility to be from the possibility beyond being." And he adds that it is "from the infinitely good *posse* [*dunamis*] of what it sends to them [that] they have received their power *dunamis*]."⁴³ I am tempted to relate this notion of an infinitely good possibilizing of God to another extraordinary passage in the *Divine Names*—this time book 9, section 3—where Dionysius writes of the God of little things:

> God is said to be small as leaving every mass and distance behind and proceeding unhindered through all. Indeed, the small is the cause of all the elements, for you will find none of these that have not participated in the form of smallness. Thus, smallness is to be interpreted with respect to God as its wandering and operating in all and through all without hindrance, "penetrating down to the division of the soul, spirit, joint and marrow," and discerning thoughts and "intentions of the heart," and indeed of all beings. "For there is no creation which is invisible to its face" (Hebrews 4:12). This smallness is without quantity, without quality, without restraint; unlimited, undefined, and all-embracing, although it is unembraced.⁴⁴

Is this extraordinary passage by Dionysius not a passionate invitation to embrace a micro-eschatology of the Kingdom? Is it not a solicitation to embrace an eschatology of little things—mustard seeds, grains of yeast, tiny pearls, cups of water, infinitesimal, everyday acts of love and witness? It appears so.

Moreover, I think it is just this kind of microeschatology that Gerard Manley Hopkins had in mind when he recorded God's grace in small and scattered epiphanies of the quotidian—when he speaks, for example, of God's "pied beauty" being manifest in various "dappled things," from "finches wings" and "rose-moles all in stipple upon trout that swim" to "all things counter, original, spare, strange;/ Whatever is fickle, freckled—who knows how?" ("Pied Beauty"). For Hopkins, it is not the mighty and triumphant Monarch that epitomizes the pearl of the Kingdom ("immortal diamond") but, contrariwise, the court fool, the joker in the pack, the least and last of these. Here is Hopkins's take on the eschatological kingdom:

> In a flash, at a trumpet crash,
> I am all at once what Christ is, since he was what I am,
> And
> This Jack, Joke, poor potsherd, patch, matchwood,
> Immortal diamond,
> Is immortal diamond.

Hopkins's deity is one of transfiguration rather than coercion, of *posse* rather than power, of little rather than large things.[45] An echo, perhaps, of Dante's deity in the "Paradiso," who is described as a tiny, indivisible point of light in contrast to the towering figure of Lucifer in the final canto of the "Inferno." But in our shift of registers from theology to poetry, we are already embarking on our next circle of readings.

The Literary Circle

In our third and final hermeneutic circle—the literary—I include a number of passages that offer more explicitly poetic epiphanies of the possible. This amplification of our investigation to embrace a literary poetics extends the range of reference to take in soundings of *posse* that transcend the confessional limits of theism or atheism, enjoying as they do a special liberty of imagination—a "poetic license" to entertain an unlimited variation of experience. As Emily Dickinson rightly observed, "possibility is a fuse lit by imagination," a belief that informs her imaging of the eschatological possible:

> I dwell in possibility—
> A fairer house than prose—
> More numerous of windows—
> Superior—for doors . . .
> Of visitors—the fairest—
> For Occupation—This—
> The spreading wide my narrow Hands
> To gather Paradise—

The French author Rabelais had his eye on a similar paradise when he affirmed the possibility of life through death, yea-saying to his last moments as he jubilantly declared: "J'avance vers le grand possible!" In his remarkable novel *The Man Without Qualities*, the Austrian writer Robert Musil offers a further perspective on the eschatological *posse* when he claims that "possibility is the dormant design of God in man"—a design waiting to be awakened by our poetic dwelling in the world. Our true vocation in history, for Musil, is one of utopian invention. It involves an audacious surpassing of given reality toward imagined possibility. Here is the passage in full:

> One might define the meaning of the possible as the faculty of thinking all that *might be* just as much as what is. . . . The implications of such a creative disposition are huge. . . . The possible

consists of much more than the dreams of neurasthenics; it also involves the still dormant plans of God. A possible event or truth is not just the real event or truth minus the "reality"; rather it signals something very divine, a flame, a burning, a will to construct a utopia which, far from fearing reality, treats it simply as a perpetual task and invention. The earth is not so spent, after all, and never has it seemed so fascinating.[46]

The metaphor of fire—with its allusions to both the burning bush (Exodus 3:14) and the Pentecostal flame of speaking tongues—is explored by Wallace Stevens in a poem addressed to the philosopher George Santayana titled "To an Old Philosopher in Rome." Here again the correspondence between the simple (indigent, small, inconsequential) and the eschatological (the Kingdom) is conveyed by the figure of a candle flame that illumines the real in the light of the "celestial possible." The pneumatological call to speak in tongues commits itself here to a poetics of the poor and unremembered. Stevens writes:

> A light on the candle tearing against the wick
> To join a hovering excellence, to escape
> From fire and be part of that of which
> Fire is the symbol: the celestial possible ...
> Be orator but with an accurate tongue
> And without eloquence, O, half-asleep,
> Of the pity that is the memorial of this room,
> So that we feel, in this illumined large,
> The veritable small ...
> Impatient for the grandeur that you need
> In so much misery, and yet finding it
> Only in misery, the afflatus of ruin,
> Profound poetry of the poor ...
> It is poverty's speech that seeks us out the most.

But it is doubtless the Prague poet Rainer Maria Rilke who has composed one of the most inspiring invocations of the gracious power of *posse* in the conclusion to his *Letters to a Young Poet*. Here the eschatological promise of a coming God is combined with the erotic expectancy of a waiting lover. "Why don't you think of Him [God] as the one who is coming?" he asks his youthful correspondent—as

> one who has been approaching from all eternity, the one who will someday arrive, the ultimate fruit of a tree whose leaves we are? What keeps you from projecting his birth into the ages that

are coming into existence, and living your life as a painful and lovely day in the history of a great pregnancy? Don't you see how everything that happens is again and again a beginning, and couldn't it be *His* [God's] beginning, since, in itself, starting is always so beautiful?

Then Rilke poses this crucial question:

> If he is the most perfect one, must not what is less perfect *precede* him, so that he can choose himself out of fullness and superabundance? — Must not *he* be the last one, so that he can include everything in himself, and what meaning would we have if he whom we are longing for has already existed? As bees gather honey, so we collect what is sweetest out of all things and build Him.[47]

Rilke ends this remarkable passage with a call to vigilant attention and expectancy. Messianism at its best. The metaphor of the flowering, flourishing mustard seed is brought to a new poetic intensity. "Be patient," Rilke counsels the young poet, "and realize that the least we can do is to make coming into existence no more difficult for Him [God] than the earth does for spring when it wants to come."[48]

Here we return, as it were, to the "pregnant sense of the possible" noted in the quotation from Kierkegaard above — the interweaving of the divine and the human in patient prayer and longing. And this eschatological desire, as Rilke vividly reminds us, is not confined to human existence but involves, by extension, the entire expanse of the terrestrial universe as it awaits, yearns, and prepares itself for the coming *prima vera*.

My daughter, who brought this passage to my attention, told me this was a God she could believe in. Could I disagree?

Conclusion

So much depends, then, on what we mean by the *possible*. If one defines possibility according to established convention, as a category of modal logic or metaphysical calculus, then God is closer to the impossible than to the possible. But if one seeks, as I do, to reinterpret the possible as the eschatological *posse*, from a postmetaphysical poetical perspective, the stakes are very different. For now we are talking of a *second* possible (analogous to Ricoeur's "second naïveté") *beyond* the impossible, *otherwise* than impossible, *more* than impossible, at the *other side* of the old modal opposition between the possible and the impossible. And so we find ourselves close to Kierkegaard's "passion for the possible" as portal to faith.

I think it is crucial to recall here the telling distinction between two competing translations of the Greek term *dunamis*. On the one hand, we have the metaphysical rendering of the term as *potestas/potentia*, that is, as a potency understood in terms of an ecomomy of power, causality, substance—what Lévinas calls the economy of the Same (or Totality). On the other hand, we have an eschatological rendering of *dunamis* as *posse/possest*, that is, as a gracious and gratuitous giving that possibilizes love and justice in this world. It is this latter interpretation of *dunamis* that I have been seeking to promote in my three hermeneutic detours through the poetics of the possible (and, in more depth and detail, in *The God Who May Be*).

In triumphalist accounts of the Kingdom, the advent of the Messiah on the last day is often described in militaristic terms—as sublimely apocalyptic rather than lovingly vulnerable, as "almighty" rather than solicitous, as coercive rather than caring. By contrast, the divine *posse* I am sponsoring here is more healing than judgmental, more disposed to accept the "least of these" than to mete out punishment and pomp. If God can prevent evil from happening by re-creating the historical past, as the theologian Peter Damian once suggested, He is by implication a God of theodicy: namely, a God who has the power to decide whether history unfolds as good or evil. To me, this sounds like *potestas* rather than *posse*. A far cry from the divine power of the powerless that Etty Hillesum invokes when she summons us to help God to be God in the face of violence and war. A world away from the God of little things.

Sometimes I have been asked what would happen to the God of the Possible if we were to destroy the earth. How can God's promise of a kingdom on earth be fulfilled if there is no earth to come back to? What might be said of the existence of God in such a scenario? There are a few observations I would like to make here by way of conclusion, surmises that claim the poetic license of a "free imaginative variation."

First, I would say that as eternally perduring and constant (that is, as faithful and attentive to us in each *present moment*), God would live on as an endless *promise* of love and justice. This would be so even if we fail or frustrate this covenant by denying its potential for historical fulfillment *on earth*. In this case, God would be like a spouse abandoned by a spouse—to take up the bride/bridegroom analogy from the Song of Songs. A lover forsaken. Or, to borrow a metaphor from Hildegard of Bingen, the *posse* would be like a tree deprived of its greening (*viriditas*).[49] If denied its ultimate incarnation in the last days, the possible God would be like a flowering seed arrested before it could come to its full flourishing and fruition on the earth. It would still be *adventurus*, but no longer *futurus*. In other words, the divine advent would be deprived of a historical, human future but would remain, in each moment, enduringly faithful in spite of all. It would still be a "yes" in the face of our "no."

Second, as eternal *memory* (past), the divine *posse* would preserve all those eschatological "moments" from the past where the divine was incarnated in the flesh of the world every time (as Christ and Isaiah taught) someone gave a cup of cold water to someone else. In kairological as opposed to merely chronological time, these instants would be eternally "repeated" in divine remembrance. This would mark a rewriting of the old adage to read "The good that men do lives after them, the evil is interred with their bones" (to juggle with a line from Shakespeare's *Julius Caesar*). It would be in keeping with the repeated assurances of the biblical deity to remember the faithful who lived and died in history (e.g., Isaiah 49:15):

> Can a mother forget her infant, be without tenderness for the child of her womb? Even should she forget, I will never forget you.

And it would also be consonant with the contrary commitment to erase the memory of evil: "The Lord is close to the broken hearted/ The Lord confronts the evildoers/To destroy remembrance of them from the earth" (Psalm 34). There is, then, a deeply eschatological character to the biblical injunction to "remember" (*zakhor*). And this character is what translates God's mindfulness of creatures into a form of "anticipatory memory" (the term is Herbert Marcuse's)—a memory that preserves a future for the past. As Psalm 105 tells us, "He remembers forever his covenant which he made binding for a thousand generations—which he entered into with Abraham...." In other words, the promise made at the beginning of time is kept by the divine *posse* as an "eternal" remembrance of both the historical past and the present right up to *parousia*.

Third and finally, then, qua eternal *advent* (future), we might say that even though we would have deprived the divine *posse* of its future realization as a kingdom *come on earth*, we could not, by such an act of self-destruction, deprive God of the possibility of starting over again. Nothing *good* is impossible to God. And rebirth in the face of death is good. As in any nuptial promise or pledge, each partner can speak for himself or herself only: God can promise only for God, not for us. We are entirely free to break *our* part of the promise at any time. And if we do, if we engage in collective self-destruction (God forbid!), why should God not have a "second chance"? Is not *posse*, after all, the possibility of endless beginning?

Of course, the *posse* of the kingdom is not just a promise for humanity as a universal community (to be reassembled as the mystical body of Christ on the last day, according to the patristic notion of *anakephalaiosis*/recapitulation). *Posse* is also and equally a promise for each unique self whose singular good—but not evil—will be preserved eternally in the recollection of the *deus adventurus*: like each glistening speck of dust drawn in a comet's tail or each glint of plankton in the nocturnal wake of a ship. But if we destroy the earth, we also refuse the possibility of each of these virtually recollected and resurrected selves returning to a "new heaven as new earth" on the last day. They would return with *posse*—as eternal promise—but without the *esse* of the Second Coming. Unless, that is, God decided to start over again.

Several of the above remarks and conjectures find textual support, I believe, in the "Palestinian formula" of eschatological memory (*eis anamnesin*) prevalent in late Jewish and early Christian literature. The formula finds one of its earliest inscriptions in Psalm 111, "the righteous will be for eternal remembrance"; and again in Psalms 37 and 69, where the memory of God refers not just to creatures remembering their Creator in rituals and liturgies but also to the Creator recalling creatures, making the past present before God in a sort of eternal re-presentation that endures into the future and beyond. Likewise, in Ecclesiastes we find the repeated prayer that God might mercifully remember His children. As the biblical commentator Joachim Jeremias observes, such remembrance is an

> effecting and creating event which is constantly fulfilling the eschatological covenant promise.... When the sinner "is not to be remembered" at the resurrection, this means that he will have no part in it (*Ps. Sol.*, 3.11). And when God no longer remembers sin, he forgets it (Jeremiah 31:34; Hebrews 8:12, 10:17); this means that he forgives it. God's remembrance is always an action in mercy or judgment.[50]

The notion of eschatological memory is, as noted, also frequently witnessed in New Testament literature, where it takes the form of a double "repetition"—looking to past and future simultaneously. In the eucharistic formula "do this in remembrance of me" (*eis ten emen anamneisin*) (Luke 22:19; 1 Corinthians 11:24), the proper translation of the repetition injunction, in keeping with the Palestinian memorial formula, is this: "Do this so that God may remember me."[51] The appeal to divine memory during the eucharistic sharing of bread and wine may be seen, accordingly, as an echo of the third benediction of the grace after the Passover meal, which asks *God to remember the Messiah*—a benediction that is followed by a petition for "the remembrance of all thy people": "may their remembrance come before thee, for rescue, goodness. . . ."[52] The remembrance of past suffering is thus tied to the hope for the advent of the *parousia*—for Jews, the entry of the Messiah into Jerusalem; for Christians, the return of Christ on the last day. The petition for repetition—in the *kairological* rather than *chronological* sense—may be translated as "God remembers the Messiah in that he causes the kingdom to break in by the *parousia*."[53]

This allusion to a bilateral temporality whereby divine memory recalls the *past as future* is further evidenced in Paul's gloss on the eucharistic remembrance formula: "For as often as you eat this bread and drink this cup, you proclaim the Lord's death *until he comes*" (*achri ou elthei*; see 1 Corinthians 11:23–25). Indeed, the use of the subjunctive form *achri* often refers in the New Testament to the arrival of the *eschaton* (Romans 11:25; 1 Corinthians 15:25; Luke 21:24). The crucial phrase here—"until he comes"—may thus be read in light of the liturgical *maranatha* ("come, Lord!") invoked by the faithful in their prayers for the coming of God. So, rather than remembering the death of God as no more than a historical event of the past, the remembrance formula can be said to celebrate it as an eschatological advent—that is, as the inauguration of a New Covenant:

> This proclamation expresses the vicarious death of Jesus as the beginning of the salvation time and prays for the coming of the consummation. As often as the death of the Lord is proclaimed at the Lord's supper, and the *maranatha* rises upwards, God is reminded of the unfulfilled climax of the work of salvation "until [the goal is reached, that] he comes." Paul has therefore understood the *anamnesis* as the eschatological remembrance of God that is to be realized in the *parousia*.[54]

It is with this in mind that Luke speaks of the eschatological jubilation and "gladness" (*agalliasis*) that characterize the mealtimes of the earliest Christian communities (Acts 2:46).

In sum, the close rapport between the eucharistic request for repetition and the Passover ritual suggests that for both Judaism and Christianity the Kingdom's advent is construed as a *retrieval-forward of the past as future*. The remembrance formula might be interpreted, accordingly, as something like this: "Keep gathering together in remembrance of me so that I will remember you by keeping my promise to bring about the consummation of love, justice, and joy in the *parousia*. Help me to be God!" Or, as the Coptic version of the formula goes: "May the Lord come. . . . If any man is holy, let him come. *Marathana*. Amen."

The above conjectures operate, for the most part, in the realm of a hermeneutical poetics that enjoys a certain imaginative liberty vis-à-vis the strictures of theological dogmatics, speculative metaphysics, or empirical physics. However, I hasten to add, a fruitful dialogue remains open with all three disciplines.

Let me end with a final eschatological image from the poetics of the Kingdom—the invitation to the feast:

> I stand at the door and knock, says the Lord. If anyone hears my voice and opens the door, I will come in and sit down to supper with him, and he with me.

The great thing about this promise of an eschatological banquet is that no one is excluded. The Post-God of *posse* knocks not just twice but a thousand times—nay, infinitely, ceaselessly, until there is no door unopened, no creature, however small or inconsequential, left out in the cold, hungry, thirsty, uncared for, unloved, unredeemed. The Post-God keeps knocking and calling and delivering the word until we open ourselves to the message and the letter becomes spirit; the Word, flesh. And what is this message? It is an invitation to the Kingdom. And what is the Kingdom? The Kingdom is a cup of cold water given to the least of these, it is bread and fish and wine given to the famished and unhoused, a good meal and (we are promised) one hell of a good time lasting into the early hours of the morning. A morning that never ends.

13

Giving More
Jean-Luc Marion and Richard Kearney in Dialogue

This chapter is an edited transcript of a seminar held at the Mater Dei Institute, Dublin, January 2003.

RICHARD KEARNEY: This is a pretty open forum, there's nothing pre-prepared. I'm going to start by inviting Jean-Luc Marion to begin the seminar, and then we'll open it to the floor.

JEAN-LUC MARION: I take the opportunity of this seminar to answer a comment made by Richard Kearney which is very fruitful, and which is a very good example not only that we agree on most of the issues but also how far the concept of the saturated phenomenon can be applied. If we consider, as Richard did, Exodus 3:14, it's very fascinating, because there are three main possible interpretations. The first interpretation is the kataphatic: we take "I am who I am" as "I am, and I am an *ousia*, and more than that I am Being itself," and so on. Then you have the negative one (which is justified as well), the apophasis, saying, "I am who I am, and you will never know who I am"—which is a very old and traditional interpretation, too. And there is a third one, which is beyond affirmation and negation, which is the hyperbolical, where the two previous are both surpassed and assumed, which is "I am the one who shall be. Forever." Shall be what? He who can say "Here I am," because "Here I am" is the name under which the encounter between God and man is made,

243

throughout all revelation. So "I will be the one always able to answer or to call." And so, with the same words, the same intuition, to some extent, we have three possible significations, and we need at least those three. This is "mystical theology"; this is also a saturated phenomenon; this is also the possibility of an endless hermeneutic. This is a very good example, Exodus 3:14; the same thing may be repeated for other *logia*. So I think we deeply agree on that issue now.

RK: On that moment of consensus, let's open the discussion.

SANTIAGO SIA *(Loyola University, Marymount, Los Angeles, California):* This question, to both of you, is sparked off by two comments in Richard Kearney's paper. One is your suggestion of conceiving God as a God who may be, and then your reference to Eckhart, that we don't really have to abandon metaphysics. You have said that what Professor Marion is doing is phenomenology, and what you're doing is hermeneutics. What I'd like to suggest is that what we need, the third step, is the conceptualization of that suggestion, and that is that there is really a need to provide a new metaphysical vision (not "old" metaphysics). The reason is that it is important to be able to address many of the questions that arise when we try to conceive God in a systematic, in a consistent, and in an adequate way. The reason behind this observation is that that philosophical development, the concept of a God who may be, has already been done by people like Whitehead and Hartshorne, and I was wondering how much dialogue there has been between phenomenologists, hermeneutics, and process philosophers. . . .

JLM: Not very easy. I understand well the first two steps, but I question the legitimacy of the third one. Why do you call it metaphysics? Metaphysics is not a neutral word. It has a history—a very complicated and very long and very questionable history. And I think that even if, indeed, we need a more systematic frame to describe the new situation in which we hope to be now, I doubt that we should use the name of "metaphysics" again—because "metaphysics" is directly connected to the question of Being, to the question of Being according to the privilege of the *ousia*, and so on. So, even if you refer to process theology, and even if, in process theology, there is some use of metaphysics, perhaps it's quite a metaphorical use: it's quite different from the use of metaphysics by Armstrong and also the "new" analytical philosophers, because in that case they are right to use the word "metaphysics" because they are going back to the most strict acceptance of a set of categories by Aristotle. But, insofar as, I guess, you want to move far beyond that, perhaps it is not the word "metaphysics" that should be used. I think that to keep some distance with the word "metaphysics" is a positive gesture. We should, I think, keep in mind one of the final statements by Heidegger at the end of *Zeit und Sein:* that we should let metaphysics die itself. In other words, let metaphysics bury metaphysics, and don't use metaphysics as metaphor.

RK: Yes, we are in agreement here. But I would like to expand a little further. In *The God Who May Be* I tried to explore how Meister Eckhart revisits certain metaphysical terms—*sum, ego, qui est*, et cetera—and reinterprets them in a way that opens them up to a postmetaphysical, eschatological interpretation. And I think we could apply this move more generally to a variety of postmetaphysical movements in contemporary philosophy and theology. Maybe this is a slight difference of emphasis I have with Jean-Luc Marion, Heidegger, and Derrida. Rather than affirming "the metaphysics of presence," or ontotheology, which from Aristotle to Husserl is caught up in a metaphysics of "conceptual idolatry," what I try to advance with my notion of "diacritical hermeneutics" is the suggestion that in spite of the language of cause, substance, ground, *essentia, esse*, which easily lends itself to conceptual idolatry, there is also within metaphysics a metaphysical desire to understand, to conceptualize, to reason with, to reckon with, to make sense of, to debate with, questions of the ultimate. That metaphysical desire, it seems to me, is utterly respectable, and it can be recognized in most of the great metaphysicians. There are two ways of approaching Plato, for example. On the one hand, there is Plato as onto-theology and the metaphysics of presence. But on the other hand, there is Plato—as Lévinas revisits him—as the exponent of a metaphysics of eros, of desire. In that sense, when Lévinas speaks of metaphysical desire in *Totality and Infinity*, he is not saying we should return to Aristotelian or scholastic metaphysics qua speculative system. He's saying that there is some drive within all metaphysical attempts to name the unnameable, which is retrievable and which can be reread eschatologically. That's not true just of Plato: it's true of Augustine, where there is this restless desire for God; and it is true of Descartes, too. As Lévinas and Jean-Luc Marion have both pointed out, Descartes's "idea of the Infinite" is something that comes through metaphysics, but it can't be contained within metaphysics.

So, I would make that differentiation. Does this bring us close to something like process theology? As a metaphysical desire for God, yes. But not as a need to form a system, with grounds and causes and reasons and concepts that tend toward a "pantheism," where there's a beginning, middle, and end, and a Master Narrative which reduces God to an immanent, historical process. I don't have any quarrel with the description of God as an immanent, historical process, up to a point; but I think it is only half of the story. It's the story of us responding to the call of God and trying to work toward the kingdom. But there's another side to the story, which I don't really see recognized in Hartshorne or Whitehead, and that relates how historical becoming is a *response* to a call that comes from *beyond* history. So the question is: Is there a notion in process theology of God as radical transcendence, ulteriority, exteriority, alterity? Does process theology sufficiently acknowledge the *difference* between immanence and transcendence?

JOHN O'DONOHUE: Two points. First, in relation to desire, I think it's absolutely fascinating to mention Eckhart in this regard. Because when you bring the concept of desire into the Eckhartian system, it's very ambivalent: in a sense, all of our passion for God is imbued with desire, and yet the actual coming-into-the-presence has to happen through the exact opposite of what a saturated phenomenon is, namely, through total *Abgeschiedenheit* and detachment. There is in Eckhart this really subversive thing that *Gott wirt und Gott entwirt*, "God becomes and God un-becomes," and the suggestion is that God is only our name for it. And the closer we come to it, the more it ceases to be God.

The second thing, and perhaps this is a regressive point, given that we're talking about phenomenology and metaphysics . . . I wonder if there's any help to be gleaned from Hegel and his *Phenomenology of Spirit*, which undertakes an existential and epistemological journey through all the shapes of consciousness, from sense certainty to Absolute knowing, and has within it the desire of the dialectic and an implicit *memoria*, or memory, between the stages in the dialectic of consciousness, which constantly enriches each move; there is certainly enough inner critique within each shape that it's not allowed to become idolatrous and is pushed to the ultimate limits. Maybe here, in an earlier version of phenomenology, we might have a possible unity of Being and consciousness, where the deepest ground of consciousness is actually the awakening of Spirit, where the thing-in-itself becomes the thing-in-and-for-itself.

JLM: Your first point. Let us comment on *Gott wirt und Gott entwirt*. There is no contradiction between this and the saturated phenomenon. The very experience of the excess, for example, the intuition over signification makes clear that the excess may be felt and expressed as a disappointment. The experience of disappointment means that I have an experience which I cannot understand, because I have no concept for it. So the excess and the disappointment can come together. The saturated phenomenon doesn't mean that we are never in the experience of "being in the desert." The reverse is the case: the desertification is an excess, in some way. The experience of something that is unconditional is, for me, sometimes, made by the fact that I am disappointed: I am in the situation of making the encounter without having the possibility to understand it. And this is not nothing. This is a very important figure of phenomenality.

And so back to desire now, because there is a running question about desire. I would not be so optimistic about desire as some are. Indeed, in philosophy, from the beginning, there is something that is not purely conceptual working "behind," being the secret energy of the system, the desire of knowing things. Desire of knowing. Two remarks: first, either desire is quite different from knowledge itself— "All men desire to know," as Aristotle says. Only two possibilities: either the desire at the end is incorporated into the knowledge itself. To some extent this is done with, say, Hegel, where knowledge— rooted in the dialectic—includes in itself the desire to know. And so at that moment desire is kept, recalled within metaphysics. Or you may argue, and I think it was part of the argument of Lévinas about a very strange issue in Plato, that the desire is prior to the philosophical intention to know and has to be taken seriously as such. So you may try to focus your attention on desire "as such." This can explain a part of Neoplatonism, for instance, and psychoanalysis, if you want, considering desire "as such." But, in that case, the question is whether desire does not claim more than mere philosophy understood as a theory of knowledge. Perhaps the question of desire is too serious to be explained within the same horizons as the question of knowledge. Perhaps the question of desire cannot only not be answered but also cannot even be asked in the horizon of Being. So it's a reason why, I think, desire is the "backstage" of metaphysics, which was never enlightened by metaphysics (which is quite unable to do so). And so we have now perhaps to open a new horizon where the question of desire could be taken seriously. And it is not taken seriously, for instance, in psychoanalysis, because psychoanalysis can consider and describe desire, but it takes desire as simply a drive, an unconscious drive; it is nothing more than a drive, largely and perhaps forever. But there is perhaps a deep rationality and consciousness of desire which is other than and goes far beyond mere unconsciousness. To open this new horizon, we have to get rid of the horizon of Being, which is, at the end of metaphysics, quite unable, is not broad enough, to do justice to desire.

RK: Perhaps we could link the notions of "desert" and "desire." Take Eckhart's notion of *Abgeschiedenheit* as the abandonment of desire, the experience of release and dispossession. This is not incompatible with the experience of the saturated phenomenon but may actually be concomitant with it. I think there are two ways of approaching the divine saturated phenomenon. One is ecstasy—the traditional beatific vision of fusion with God, mystical *jouissance*. But there is also *Abgeschiedenheit*, the sense of being disinherited, disinvested—John of the Cross's dark night of the soul. Sometimes the saturated phenomenon seems closer to Augustine's or Dante's beatific vision; sometimes it approximates more to the experience of the desert, devastation, the void. At other times again, it can be both together.

In the transfiguration of Christ, for example, if we can take that as a divine saturated phenomenon, we witness an extraordinary fascination with the *whiteness* of the event, but also an experience of fear, such that the voice from the clouds has to say, "Do not be afraid." There is fascination but also recoil. Jesus cautions His disciples to keep a distance from the event, not to say anything to anyone about it, not to construct a monument or memorial. All these are ways, it seems to me, of acknowledging the importance of *Abgeschiedenheit*. One is very close to something that could burn us up. We need a distance, and to be faithful to it; we need to be cautious, discreet, and diffident. So I think it's a complex double move of ecstasy and *Abgeschiedenheit*, of attraction and disappropriation.

Relating this back to desire, I think it's important to distinguish between two different kinds—ontological and eschatological. Ontological desire comes from lack, which is, I think, the Hegelian and Lacanian definition of desire, but it also goes back, in fact, to Plato. One interpretation of Plato in the *Symposium* is that *eros* is the offspring of *poros* and *penia*, of fullness and lack, and therefore is a lack striving to be fulfilled. This *ontological* notion of desire strives for possession, fusion, atonement, and appropriation. I would oppose this to *eschatological* desire, which doesn't issue from lack, but from superabundance, excess, and surplus. This latter is also operative in Plato. But it's most emphatically evident, I think, in a biblical text like the Song of Songs, where there's a sort of theo-erotic drama between the divine and the human.

JLM: May I comment about that? You all know the formulation in the commentary on the Song of Songs by Gregory of Nyssa: What is eternity in paradise? It is the fulfillment of pleasure, where each fulfillment is a new *archē*, without end. That is exactly the reverse of our experience of biological desire, which cannot survive its fulfillment. And in that nonbiological, nonontical desire, which is not based on lack, the reverse is true: the more it is fulfilled, the more there is a rebirth of desire, without end. This kind of desire—which is nourished by excess, not destroyed by it—is quite different. When we feel that kind of desire, it's very clear that the original Platonic model, which is, I think, ruling all metaphysics until Lacan, is quite insufficient and cannot match the requirement of what is beyond even the way of knowledge. And also we are close, I think, on the concept of will, according to metaphysics. Because will, according to metaphysics, as will of will, will for knowledge, will for power, is quite different from the will involved in the question of meeting the other person, the question of love. So there is a real equivocity about concepts such as will, desire, and so on. And that equivocity is further evidence that there is really some limitation to metaphysics.

RK: Taking up Gregory of Nyssa's point, we might mention his notion of *perichoresis* to describe the love between the three persons of the Trinity. This is a telling analogy because what you've got here in the Three Persons is a love, a desire, a loving desire, that cedes the place (*cedere*), that gives room. But it is also a movement of attraction *toward* the other (*sedere*), a movement of immanence. Father to Son, Son to Spirit, and so on, in an endless circle. Hence the ambivalence of the double Latin translation as both *circum-in-Cessio* and *circum-in-Sessio*. But what is this movement that both yields and attracts? What does the *peri* or *circum* refer to? Around what? *Khora:* an empty space, a space of detachment, and distance, and disappropriation. The immanent movement in the free play of each person toward the other is accompanied by a movement of desire which is also a granting or ceding of a place to the other. And it's that double move of ecstasy-*Abgeschiedenheit* that you find within the very play of divine desire, which then translates into human-divine desire.

Just a comment on Hegel. Where I would have a difference with Hegel is on the question of the "Ruse of Reason." Whether Hegel's desire is an ontological drive or an eschatological one is open to interpretation. But certainly in the *Phenomenology* it seems to me that it's still caught in a kind of metaphysical totality. The movement is there, and the energy and dynamism is there, within the dialectic. But in the final analysis, there's a Cunning of Reason that has rigged the game. All the stakes are already set. Where I have a big problem with Hegel is not just with the definition of God as Absolute consciousness—a God who has really decided everything before the play has even begun—but also with his notion of evil. It's the question of theodicy, where everything is ultimately justified within the System. In contrast to Hegel, I propose a diacritical hermeneutics which approaches the problem of evil in a less extreme, more tolerant way, a way that allows for greater understanding. This is a very undogmatic claim, a hypothesis, a wager. It is a suggestion that this is a better way of doing things, as a description and as an interpretation. But the only way it can be shown to be better (or worse)—because I'm just part of a dialogue that others have begun long before me and will continue long after me—the only evidence is actually the intersubjective community of dialogue. In other words, it works if people are persuaded by this as an accurate description. As Merleau-Ponty says about the evidence of phenomenology, you read Husserl, you read Heidegger, and either you're persuaded by their descriptions or you're not. There are no extraphenomenological or extrahermeneutical criteria that you can appeal to as a metaphysical foundation, or ground, or cause, that prove you right and the others wrong. So in that sense it is always tentative. Indeed, it seems to me that the virtue of philosophy is this tentativeness—which doesn't mean being relativist or uncommitted. We all operate from beliefs, faiths, and commitments; all our philosophizing is preceded and followed by conviction. Before we enter the realm of philosophy we are already hermeneutically engaged. We come out the other end—no one being able to live by philosophy alone—we recommit to our convictions, our beliefs, and so on. But the important point is that one acknowledges when one goes into the philosophical debate that these are one's hermeneutical presuppositions, prejudices, and prejudgments—temporally and methodologically suspended for the sake of the conversation. Maybe, when you come back to your commitments again, you do so with a greater sensitivity to a plurality of interpretations. This is not relativism; it is a democracy of thought.

EILEEN BRENNAN *(Institut Catholique, Paris)*: In your paper, Richard, you recognized a great variety of interpretations of the saturated phenomenon, and you said there was no single interpretation that could be said to be the right one. In the same paper, you laid out your own hermeneutics, your onto-eschatological hermeneutics, which you carefully distinguished from the Romantic and the radical. My question is: Is there something in the act of working out a new hermeneutics that involves an implicit claim that this is better than the others, particularly as you distinguish yourself so carefully from them? And, if not, what's the motivation for producing such a hermeneutics?

RK: I don't think that the different hermeneutics have to be seen as conflicting or competitive or incompatible. If that were the case, then you'd have to say, "My hermeneutics is right, the saturated phenomenon is God, and Heideggerians are wrong to call it *Ereignis* and deconstructionists are wrong to call it *khora*." That's not what it's about. I would rather use the term *equiprimordial* here. For example, say you are depressed. You go to a Heideggerian philosopher, and she or he will tell you this is *Angst*, it's an existential experience of your being-toward-death. You go to a psychopharmaceutical therapist, and she or he will give you Prozac. The thing is, it's not a question of saying one is right and one is wrong. Here, I think, Julia Kristeva is correct. If you're to be more fully responsive to the pain of the sufferer, it is not a debate as to whether this is a biochemical crisis or an existential one. It can be both. And you can be helped at both levels. But it is not a matter of saying they're the same thing. They're operating at different levels. I think that's important: to recognize the different claims, interests, and levels of interpretation.

JLM: Yes. May I repeat that point in another way? There is no other argument to choose between different interpretations of the same data than the power of one interpretation in front of the other. This is a very fair battle, where the winner, posited at the end, is the one able to produce more rationality than the other, and you are convinced simply by the *idea vera index sui et falsi*. The hypothesis that produces more rationality than the other is the winner. And it is why it is a weakness in philosophy always to stick to a narrow interpretation of a situation, which is unable to make sense out of a large part of experience, and to say, "Well, you have no right to go beyond that limit." For me, this really is the defeat of reason, of philosophy, when a philosopher says, "You have no right to make sense of that part of experience; this is meaningless, and should remain meaningless." It is an improvement in philosophy when a new field, which was taken to be meaningless, suddenly makes sense.

EILEEN BRENNAN: Yes, I agree; but, if I may say, you both are demonstrating that you want to progress beyond existing interpretations and understandings, and yet at the same time you seem to want to pay great respect to those positions; you won't dismiss them. I understand there's a kind of generosity in your reading of other philosophers, but I feel that if there are people saying "You can't explore this," and you go ahead and explore it, clearly you are distancing yourselves from that. How can you both say "This is equally valid as a reading with mine," and yet at the same time you're. . . .

JLM: No, definitely no. You start in the situation where everyone has an even chance. Everyone can say "This sunset is a question of biology," or of aesthetics, or of religion. Everyone has their own possible interpretation, their constitution of the phenomenon. And everyone tries to go as far as they can. The result and the convictions which are gained, or not, are the result only of the power of that interpretation. Let us take the example of Lévinas. The question of the Other remained a puzzling issue until the move made by Lévinas, considering that, in the case of the phenomenon of the Other, we cannot understand it unless we reverse the intention. In that case, we no longer have an intention coming from me to the Other as the objective, the object; there is a reverse intentionality, and we have to reconstruct all of the phenomena that way. By saying that, suddenly a large range of phenomena were available, I would say for the first time in the history of philosophy. There is no other demonstration than the simple visibility of the phenomenon of the Other.

DAVID BLAKE *(Mary Immaculate College, Limerick):* I wanted to say that if we take the example of falling in love, and take that at its extreme situation, where somebody gets totally bowled over by somebody else, it seems to me that would be a good example of a saturated phenomenon: you are bedazzled, overcome, but you don't know the Other. The knowing will follow later. In this situation, you'd have an intuition, but what it is you know will only be revealed over time.

JLM: Indeed, the question of love is crucial. For instance, to fall in love implies a very special type of reduction, a self-reduction, but at the level of an erotic reduction; and it is very true that the experience of the Other, in love, is the experience of the saturated phenomenon par excellence. It's absolutely clear, you are right, that you will "see" the other before knowing him or her. It's a very special situation, you are right.

TIM MOONEY *(University College Dublin)*: "You've seen because you've believed; blessed are those who have not seen and believe." We've talked about a crisis in metaphysics and philosophy. Is the very idea of a saturated phenomenon not also a response to a crisis in belief—what Matthew Arnold called "we vague half-believers of our casual creeds"? And to that extent, just as phenomenology not only responds to crisis but also to the hidden nostalgia of modern philosophy, is this some sort of hidden nostalgia at the loss of faith, the long, melancholic withdrawal of the sea of faith?

JLM: A very good point. "Blessed are those who believe without seeing." What does that mean, exactly? It may be to some extent the distinction between philosophy and theology, simply that. Because in philosophy we have to "see," to believe. What does that mean, exactly, "to believe"? For us, because we start from a philosophical point of view, we spontaneously believe that to believe is to take for true, to assume something as if it were true, without any proof. This is our interpretation of belief. In that case, it is either belief or seeing. But is this the real meaning of belief? In fact, belief is also, perhaps, to commit yourself, and, in that case, it is also, perhaps, a theoretical attitude. Because by committing yourself to somebody else, you open a field of experience. And so it's not only a substitute for not knowing, it is an act which makes a new kind of experience possible. It is because I believe that I will see, and not as a compensation. It's the very fact you believe which makes you see new things, which would not be seen if you did not believe. It's the *credo ut intelligam*. So, all this makes clear that what's at stake with the end of metaphysics, and with phenomenology, is that the distinction between the theoretical attitude and the practical attitude should be questioned. At the end of metaphysics, both theory and practical situations are quite different. But I think there are practical or ethical requirements even in a theoretical point of view. There is no pure theoretical point of view. You assume a complete attitude toward the world. And this has to be questioned. It's why the questions of what's given, and what you believe, and of love, are perhaps the unavoidable issues now.

RK: On this question of seeing, I think it's important to recognize hermeneutically that there is a plurality of seeing. We can see in different ways. The empiricist sees the burning bush as a fact. John Locke would probably describe it in terms of impressions, and John Searle would probably start cooking sausages. That is a certain approach: a positivist, materialist, pragmatist approach. By contrast, Husserl or Heidegger, for example, might see it as a manifestation, a *Lichtung*, or disclosure of Being. For Husserl, it would be a kind of categorial seeing: we're not just looking at the fire as it burns, as it lights up, we're also looking at the *being* of the fire. Heidegger would deepen this ontological seeing. But then we could add a third mode of seeing, with a third reduction, which would be an eschatological seeing, where you hear the voice and you see the fire as a manifestation of the divine. Either you see it or you don't. And it doesn't mean, philosophically, that one is right and one is wrong. John Locke and the empiricists would come to Mount Horeb to describe the impression of a fire. Unlike Moses, who came with a burning question: How do I liberate my people from bondage in Egypt? Moses is lost, he is disoriented, his people are enslaved; he's looking for liberty, for hope. He comes with the desire for a promise, the desire for revelation. And so Moses sees something that the empiricist is not going to see. There are different modes of seeing. They're not incompatible: maybe Moses initially saw the fire empirically (you have to, to even approach it); but then he hears the voice. And that hearing and seeing *otherwise* is what trips the hermeneutic switch. Belief and desire are indispensable to interpretation.

As you know yourselves, when you're talking to someone about a difficult concept—love, beauty, the sublime, Being, God—you tend, even colloquially, to say "Do you see what I mean?" Now it's that "seeing as," that "Do you see it *as* I see it?" that signals a different mode of seeing. In all modes of seeing, there is a "seeing as," and therefore a belief, a presupposition, a reading (no matter how spontaneous or prereflective). In the case of Moses, there is what we might call a theological-eschatological "seeing as": he sees the burning bush *as* a manifestation of God. For Moses, and for subsequent believers, that is what it is, that is how it strikes them. But for someone who doesn't come with that faith, they're not going to see it that way.

JLM: Richard, is that "seeing as" simply the application of the same phenomenological "as structure" in Heidegger, in *Sein und Zeit*?

RK: Yes, although not at exactly the same level. It would be confessional rather than purely existential.

JLM: You suggest that the case of "seeing as" according to faith is a variation of *die Als-Struktur*? . . .

RK: Yes, but you will interpret the seeing eschatalogically, as a seeing of something that precedes you and overwhelms you and exceeds you . . .

JLM: What is very important to make clear against Barthian or Bultmannian ways of thinking is that there is some continuity between the general structure of hermeneutics and the case of faith, which is not irrational. This is my point. There is a deep rationality in the operations of faith, understanding, and interpretation, which cannot be reduced to the usual rules of hermeneutics and phenomenology. But there is a connection. I think we are no longer in a situation where you have "reason and faith." Reason is the construct. It is not optional, it is done. I would say that the difficulty for Christian theology now is perhaps that Christian theology assumes too much of the former figure of metaphysics and philosophy, which is already deconstructed. And this opens, I think, new fields for creative theology. But many theologians, if I may say so, have not taken quite seriously the end of metaphysics, as well as deconstruction, and so they miss open opportunities. It is perhaps surprising that philosophers are maybe more aware of new possibilities open to theology than theologians (or at least some of them).

RK: An afterthought on the question of the hermeneutic "as." I would say the everyday way of seeing the world is always inscribed by an "as." We see everything "as." Wittgenstein, of course, makes the same point. Seeing is always "seeing as." But when we go to practice philosophical hermeneutics, we bring the everyday "as" of prereflective lived experience (what Heidegger calls our pre-understanding, *Vor-verstandnis*) to a level of conscious clarification and critical reflection. I think we then switch the hermeneutic "as" into an "as if." There we enter into a position where we pretend we don't have our belief structures; we act "as if" we were free of convictions or presuppositions. It is a version of methodological bracketing or suspension. We put our everyday lived beliefs into parentheses. Not to renounce them, not to disown them, but to see them all the better. We go into a methodological laboratory of possibilities where our faith commitments and convictions—and it doesn't have to be religious faith, it can be political or cultural faith, et cetera—become certain ones among others. The so-called neutrality of philosophical hermeneutics is therefore strategic, artificial, contrived—but very helpful as a pull toward common understanding or consensus. I acknowledge the *seeing as* of my everyday pre-understanding, I put that on the table, and then I act *as if* I'm now open to empathizing with and listening to, with an open mind, these other perspectives. Then, finally, of course, one returns after the thought experiment of the hermeneutic "as if" to the former convictions of one's lived world. After the detour of methodological suspension, one returns to one's primordial *seeing as*—but hopefully with an enlarged, amplified, and more attentive attitude. An attitude more sensitive and open to other points of view.

FIACHRA LONG *(University College Cork):* My question is really one of clarification. I'm asking about the saturated phenomenon in time. As I understand it, Professor Marion would suggest that at a time $t1$ the encounter with the saturated phenomenon is fresh, original; then there's an attempt, if you like, to constitute the saturated phenomenon as an object in various ways and with various competing accounts, and so on. But at that stage certain cognitive habits begin to establish themselves, a sort of learning intervenes, so that at time $t2$ the encounter with the saturated phenomenon isn't quite the same, isn't as fresh or original as it was. So my question is: Is there any value in retaining the freshness of the saturated phenomenon? Should it be retained? Are tradition, learning, and such things obstacles or helps in the encounter with the saturated phenomenon?

JLM: Indeed, you are quite right to emphasize that there is a temporality of the experience of the saturated phenomenon, and you have exposed a dimension which is very important. We may be in quite different situations in front of the saturated phenomenon. Some saturated phenomena will, after a certain time, perhaps be reduced to average objects. Perhaps, after more information, other concepts, we shall be able to constitute them as objects. So there are some states—like admiration, according to Descartes—which change. Some admiration should disappear after time: no surprise anymore, complete understanding, no admiration left. We have that possibility. But there is the other possibility, with saturated phenomena, that the more we understand them, the more they keep appearing *as* saturated phenomena. For example, the saturated phenomenon of the ur-impression of time: it is always renewed. Or the experience of living and knowing the Other, when it is successful: the more you know the Other, the more it remains a saturated phenomenon. And you may perhaps assume the same about the historical event: the more you study the historical event, the more it appears again and again as a nonobjective phenomenon, a saturated phenomenon. So I think there are a lot of different epistemological situations. The saturated phenomenon does not stop epistemological inquiry, it makes it quite different.

And there is the other point you raise, and you are right: the question of tradition and education. Tradition and education are the way for us to face, in a more efficient and fruitful manner, some phenomena which otherwise we would not be able to face and stand in front of. So it is very important to emphasize this, as you did.

RK: It's come to the end of our time, here. It's been a great honor for me to be here with Jean-Luc, and I'd like to express thanks to Eoin Cassidy, Dermot Lane, and Ian Leask, and their colleagues, for hosting this symposium over two days. Above all, I'd like to thank Jean-Luc Marion, our guest, for gifting us with his presence . . .

The Absent Threshold: An Eckhartian Afterword

John O'Donohue

Jean-Luc Marion's philosophy of God has the excitement, clarity, and danger of something that has issued from the source. On the one hand, it has the imaginative warmth of a poetic sensibility that mines the silence in order to overhear the inner echoes of the transcendent and pierces the visual for tracings on the invisible. On the other, his thinking has the urgency of a blade that wants to cut the divine free from the metaphysical netting of conditional, reflexive thought. He wishes to make a clearance for undreamed dimensions of God to appear—free, unfiltered, and unframed by the constructive strategies of consciousness and intentionality. By invoking the majesty and autonomy of its true source, he wants to coax thought beyond its "native" matrix of reflexivity. In this way he hopes to free a space for the ineffable novelty of God to dawn. Marion pushes phenomenology beyond its own constructs; indeed, he challenges it to lay bare a horizon for the undreamed.

This is an ancient strain in philosophy and theology; it finds perhaps its classic exposition in the thought of Meister Eckhart. This chapter will explore Meister Eckhart's evocation of the divine and his "methodology" of clearance. Its purpose is not to contrast Marion and Eckhart but to see what light we might garner about Marion's

---

An earlier version of this article appeared in *The Eckhart Review* (2003). I thank the editors for their courtesy.

project through recalling this tradition in general and, in particular, the poetic and speculative brilliance of Eckhart's piercing thought.

Within the whole Western philosophical tradition there is no voice like the voice of Meister Eckhart. He constructed an utterly unique thought-world. He pushed thinking to its farthest boundaries, made it descend to the depths where the origin is opaque and ascend to the high summits where there is nothing but light. He put his eye to the earth at an amazing angle. What he glimpsed and managed to bring to word still fascinates us with its vitality, severity, and beautiful danger. His texts are real presences. To make their acquaintance is to begin a subversive and transforming thought adventure. After a time the texts cease to be mere objects of analysis or understanding. They begin to assume their own autonomy and, indeed, subjectivity. Often you feel that the texts are actually reading you or, at other times, that they have become wilderness guides luring you away from every domesticated domain of belief and thought. These are wilderness texts for any mind that has become in the least haunted by the Divine.

In the *Timaeus*, Plato claims that all thought begins in the recognition that something is out of place. The rupture between Being and consciousness arises in human subjectivity. Philosophical thought is the conceptual theater where this primal conversation between Being and consciousness unfolds and thematizes itself. Subjectivity is the place where Being becomes articulate. Subjectivity is eternally restless because it is the intimate threshold where duality awakens. Indeed, experience could be characterized as the arena where duality unfolds and engages itself. Subjectivity is that threshold between known and unknown, light and darkness, past and future, memory and possibility, language and silence, here and there, this and that, before and after, time and eternity, human and divine. The ongoing and creative tension between these oppositions is what animates experience and awakens the philosophical quest and question. Eckhart's thought is fascinating in the ways in which he thinks the threshold. He offers a dynamic of transfiguration where the threshold is subsumed in a more inclusive actuality.

The concept of threshold belongs to a family of concepts that name and order the outer edges of experience. The concept of *limit* indicates an end point. It may not be possible to go any farther; the limit suggests regions that remain out of reach. The *frontier* is a line that suggests limit but does contain the sense of an Outside that begins here; and while it may be out of reach, it does at least touch against the frontier. There is some sense, too, in which the notion of frontier almost invites the challenge to go beyond it. *Boundary* is a contour of given, appropriate, or chosen endings. The *threshold* is more than a boundary, frontier, or limit. It suggests an imminence of crossing. A threshold can be crossed from both sides; it is not merely the limit line of one domain; it is a more vital and fulsome line—a "line of betweenness." The domains that it divides often achieve their deepest intensification or refinement precisely on the threshold line. The domains are not simply adjacent in a way that the limit of one is the beginning of the other. "Threshold" suggests two sides deeply engaged and involved with one another. Forces coalesce at a threshold. At the threshold there is a concresence of experience. A threshold is a vital line of intense betweenness. In its deepest sense, to cross a threshold is more than an act of transition that would simply replace one idea, feeling, or situation with another. A threshold is a line of deeper change where the one who crosses is transformed. The concept of threshold carries the epistemological force of transformation.

A profound question inevitably opens a new threshold. The question is the place where the unknown becomes articulate in us. Beneath the surface of every culture and each individual consciousness there is the perennial presence of the primal questions. The "when" question refers to time. The "how" question addresses process. The "where" question points to space. The "what" question refers to the object. The "why" question explores meaning. The "who" question probes identity. At the heart of Meister Eckhart's thought, it seems, the subversive question is the "whence": the question of origin. Accompanying all his explorations, this question is like a subtle lantern that illuminates the different landscapes of his thought-world. God is the ultimate and intimate origin of all that is. For Eckhart, all these questions become more fully illuminated in the "whence" question. This recognition is also at the heart of his theory of Image. The question of our forgotten origin comes alive most intensely in Eckhart's portrayal of the soul.

The Soul as Threshold: Echkart's Methodology of Carefully Crafted Symmetries

For Eckhart the soul is the window into eternity. Were the soul to be subtracted from his work, the Divine would fall away into distance and anonymity. Subjectivity would be forever lost in the dispersal of multiplicity. Methodologically, the soul is the threshold along which Eckhart can outline and articulate the grounding conversation between the opaque depth of the Godhead and the gravity-laden fragmentation and dispersed multiplicity of finitude. In Sermon 72, he states:

> The soul is created as if at a point between time and eternity, which touches both. With the higher powers she touches eternity, but with the lower powers she touches time. She works in time not according to time but according to eternity.

Though Eckhart stakes everything on eternity, he does give worthy credence to the finite, on this side of the threshold. He constantly emphasizes the density and force of corporeality, multiplicity, and temporality in preventing us from hearing the eternal word (Sermon 57). The soul participates fully in the world in and through the body. While the soul is utterly central for Eckhart, he manages to avoid any soul-body dualism. The soul is in every member (Sermon 19). The soul animates the affective life: the essence of the soul lies chiefly in the heart (Sermon 62). The body is no empirical or mechanistic object in which the soul is a prisoner. Dualism arises when the intense but porous threshold at the center of duality is frozen and the fecundity of its inner conversation is deadened. Eckhart, however, reverses the traditional locationist theory: in Sermons 66 and 21 he states, "My body is more in my soul than my soul is in my body." This recognizes the body as an animated presence. He does not lose sight of the duality of body and soul, but he never permits this duality to become dualism. Existentially, this duality is apparent: as Sermon 72 has it, "[my] body and soul are united in one being, not in act."

The eternal and ineffable dimension of the soul, the soul's ground, is not stained or diminished by direct contact with finitude. The soul relates indirectly to the world through her powers. Eckhart describes the path of knowing in Sermon 19: the journey of knowing begins in the world of image and sense apprehension; then it rises from the senses into the questing intellect; then ascends farther into the intellect that does not seek.

When we consider the soul as the central threshold in Eckhart's thought, it becomes possible to discern a series of carefully crafted symmetries whose interactive dynamic constitutes the tension and creativity of Becoming in his thought. Technically defined, symmetry occurs when there are two things or forces that are mirror images of one another. Symmetry assumes some level of equality on each side of the threshold. This makes for both a sense of balance and an intensity of interaction. Rather than symmetry as repetitive mirror imaging, there is in Eckhart's thought more a series of carefully crafted symmetrical oppositions. There are also symmetries that are not oppositional, but inevitably they are already outside the tension of finite duality. The notion of the threshold is radically intensified when the two domains or forces are actually in dynamic, symmetrical opposition. Then the line of threshold is completely alive. When absolute engagement of each happens, the line of demarcation can no longer sustain its clarity. In that moment the threshold is subsumed in a deeper union and oneness.

Eckhart's philosophy is no description of a one-sided takeover of the finite by the eternal. There is a ground symmetry where the opposing forces within a duality can engage until the breakthrough to a deeper level occurs. In the conversation of Becoming, it is the force of oppositional symmetries that awakens transfiguration. Within the soul there is the symmetry of the temporal and the eternal. In the soul's engagement with existence, there is a symmetry between detachment and the lingering in the multiplicity. There is a symmetry between the reflexive knowing of objects and unreflexive knowing in the ground of the soul; a symmetry between the dispersal of particularity and singular simplicity of knowing the many in the one; a symmetry between the extensive patterns of sequence and the timeless knowing of the *nunc aeternitatis*, the eternal now; and a primal symmetry between the generation of the Logos and the Birth of God in the soul—this symmetry makes up the heart of the *creatio continua*, the eternal creating of creation. There is a symmetry of origin and existence, a symmetry between the opaque reticence of the Godhead and the coming forth of the persons in individual Trinitarian configuration.

These symmetries are not static. They live in dynamic and sustained tension with each other. The difficulty with the notion of symmetry is that it might suggest two dimensions engaging one another across a flat, horizontal plane. But Eckhart's thought-world is constructed along hierarchical planes, and one side of the symmetry, the eternal, always enjoys priority and greater force. The evolution of the transformation is realized when the lower side of the symmetry achieves uniformity with its higher opposite. To use colloquial parlance, Eckhart develops an "upwardly mobile" hierarchy where the thresholds that hold the symmetries gradually give way to uniformity and union.

Eckhart draws a fascinating portrait of the eternal dimension of the soul. This is the soul's ground, the essence of the soul. Here Eckhart's theory of the soul is subversive because he seems to suggest an ontological equivalence between the soul and God. He says, "When the soul is free of the obstructions of attachment and ignorance, then it glistens with beauty . . . only the uncreated God can equal its brilliance" (Sermon 5). Again he claims, "God loves my soul so much his being depends on it. If he were to stop, it would deprive him of his Godhead" (Sermon 5). And again, in relation to the ground of the soul: "There God is to the soul as if the reason for his being God were that he might be the soul's" (Sermon 78). The soul has a native longing for God. No thing, person, place, or event can reach the soul in this place. There it is fashioned for an absolute union with God. And, indeed, the dream of God seems to be this desire for utter intimacy with the soul. In this union there is no threshold, betweenness, or distance. God does not come to the soul through any means or modality. He comes totally as God Himself, the fullness of the divine. He does not withhold a hair's breath of His essence from the soul. It is a pure union, free of all forms. Eckhart states in Sermon 73, "Nowhere is God so really God as in the soul."

Beyond All Beyondness: The Secret of Detachment

The irony of this Divine fullness is that it happens precisely in the place where the soul dwells in Nothingness. This Nothingness liberates God: "God can afford no nature other than pure being . . . and the soul has no nature in her ground" (Sermon 61). In her ground, the soul is beyond time, space, and image. Because she is without image, the soul has no image of herself: "No image ever shone into the soul's ground" (Sermon 2). Eckhart says, "There is nothing so unknown to the soul as herself" (Sermon 1). It is crucial to Eckhart's notion of the union of soul and God that there is no reflection nor reflexivity in the ground of the soul. If there were reflexivity, the union could not be pure and total. God knows Himself without image. Therefore, the soul and He can be one in a clear union, in absolute stillness. This union would be misleadingly described as either a relationship or an encounter. It is devoid of all intention, identity, and otherness. There is nothing like it anywhere else in creation. It is without purpose or destination. It does not want to go anywhere. It simply is. This union is beyond time and context. It is whereless and timeless. Indeed, once it occurs, it evades language and concept.

No ripple flows from this union. Stillness, silence, nothingness, and nowness only remotely suggest its essence.

The severe clarity needed to enter this union emerges in Eckhart's treatise on *Abgeschiedenheit* (On Detachment). Detachment creates or, more correctly, *is* absolute clearance for nothing else but God. In Sermon 6, Eckhart states, "When the soul emerges into that unmixed light, she falls into her Nothingness." Yet it is difficult to describe Detachment. In his treatise Eckhart tells us, "Now Detachment comes so close to nothing that, between perfect Detachment and nothing, no thing can exist." There is no threshold here. Detachment does not share a boundary with any existential disposition or intention. Neither can it be understood as a reversal of our existential intentions or desires, nor has Detachment a boundary on the other side. There is no threshold between Detachment and God. Detachment is simplicity of being that does not place or posit itself over against anything else. It has no consciousness of itself, no engagement with what it is. In his treatise Eckhart states, "Nothing proceeds from Detachment, otherwise it would be a stain on it." Detachment is relieved of the future. It is also beyond the ethical and is "is free of compassion."

Detachment, Eckhart continues, is free of the dispersal of particularity: "The object of pure Detachment is neither this nor that. Detachment rests on absolutely nothing." A profound epistemological reversal occurs for the state of Detachment to come to preside. Detachment is absolute and direct. When the soul enters the state of Detachment, a logical necessity pertains that compels God to be one with the soul. This is not to be understood as the consequence of God's loving intention or as a divine reward for an achieved soul. Rather, God's nature is bound by necessity to become one with the detached soul. This is not an effect of anything else. It has to happen simply because it corresponds to the deepest nature of God: "God has stood in this unmoved Detachment from all eternity, and still so stands," in such a way that nothing transient can move him. Poetically, Eckhart suggests that "true Detachment is nothing else but a mind that stands unmoved by all accidents of joy or sorrow, honor, shame or disgrace, as a mountain of lead stands unmoved by a breath of wind." The oneness of God and soul is not a coming together. All thresholds vanish and, suddenly, they are uniform, not at one but one.

Detachment cannot be understood as the end product or arrival point of a committed dialectic of Becoming. Indeed, detachment seems to be beyond dialectic, namely, to be the opposite of the cumulative refinement and concresence of content that dialectic achieves. Neither could it be likened to a dialectic in reverse, namely, a dialectic that would unravel all content until pure Nothingness was reached. While pure Nothingness may be what Detachment is, it is still not a product or achievement of deliberate intentionality because such intentionality is always consciousness of an object. Such consciousness would only stain Detachment.

Given that Eckhart's concept of Detachment is a *unicum* in philosophy, it may be helpful to build a philosophical perspective in order to more positively suggest what Detachment might be. It has been a perennial dream of philosophy to outline a place outside thought and language, where the relentless pulse of identity and becoming gives way, yet a place that is not cold or dead; a place where it is possible to be fully present and yet beyond all entanglement, to be outside the chain of alternating oppositions that constitute continuity and becoming. In the Western philosophical tradition, the question of Being emerged first. Huge excavations occurred in classical and medieval philosophy. Then Descartes's scalpel cut away all that ontological webbing to delineate the naked and singular subjectivity stranded on the shore of a vast emptiness. Subsequent idealism endeavored to reintegrate the autonomy and constructive creativity of full-blown subjectivity into the substance of ontology. The emergence of idealism and especially of phenomenology underlines the relentless creativity of intentionality and consciousness. Fichte is especially interested in excavating the reflexive nature of consciousness and selfhood. Dialectic derives from and depends on the reflexive nature of consciousness. The intentionality of consciousness is curved; it simultaneously constructs the world outside and unfolds the self within. Language and thought also operate constantly within this circle of reflexivity. All attempts to dialectically break through this circle seem logically and epistemologically impossible—because the only tools to enable such a breakthrough—namely, language and thought—are themselves inherently reflexive. The best they can do is reveal the severity of the threshold that they are unable to cross. Language stutters here. Thought flickers and darkens.

Hundreds of years earlier than Fichte and idealism, Eckhart's theory of Detachment was finding a way out of the trap of reflexivity. Eckhart does not strive to dialectically transform the circle of reflexivity. The threshold is absent. Through a series of Not-sayings, of negations, he outlines this space of Detachment that is beyond all dialectic. Nothing stirs there, for there is only Nothing in its simple purity. Yet it is not a cold or vacuous Nothing. In Meister Eckhart's thought-world, Nothingness is neither vacant nor anonymous. It is not the acidic dissolution of each thing. Rather, it seems to be their ultimate realization as essence. It is a Nothing that has sprung free of reflexivity to become akin to the unrippled stillness of the primal Uncreated. It is the state in which the purest essence of the soul and the primeval stillness and silence of God are uniform. Detachment is beyond duality and dualism. It is also beyond unity as the autonomous and equal adjacency of two presences. Eckhart's Detachment would be a merely bland functional strategy of negation, coming at its object from outside, were it not underpinned by an ontology of passionate divine possibility, namely, the Birth of God in the soul. Through the severe clarity and Nothingness of Detachment, the glimmer of Divine Intimacy and Joy ultimately smiles through.

The Emergence of the Soul at the Heart of Divine Agency

In Sermon 8, Eckhart says:

> There is power in the soul which touches neither time nor flesh, flowing from spirit, remaining in the spirit, altogether spiritual. In this power, God is ever verdant and flowering in all the joy and all the glory that He is in Himself. . . .

And further on in the sermon, he says: "This power is void of all forms and free of all names . . . this same power wherein God ever blooms and is verdant in all His Godhead." While Detachment springs the soul into uniformity with God, this is not a temporary visitation or accidental likening of the soul and God. Eckhart sees it, rather, as the flowering of a primal ontological kinship. In Sermon 8 Eckhart does say that were I to have all images but have them without attachment, "I would be a virgin, untrammeled by any images, just as I was when I was not." It is a state of such pure clearance and clarity that it is akin to the purity of the uncreated. Again, in Sermon 51, he says, "Detachment of the understanding comprehends all things within itself without form or image—this comes from simplicity." Therefore Detachment is not withdrawal from the world. It is not spiritual catatonia.

Detachment is akin to the divine nature. God is absolutely in the world but untouched by all things. Detachment proclaims a new metaphysics of identity. True identity is not simply biography, the cumulative totality of experiences. True identity is not the linear unfolding of a life; it is, rather, this active, achieved, or returned intimacy of the divine and the human. God holds nothing back; consequently, the soul participates in the full agency of divine creativity. Having broken through to the source, the soul has now become the source. Now the source of divine creativity is to be sought nowhere else. In some swift curve of grace the soul has found the frequency of the divine; now God and soul create in seamless being. In Sermon 18, Eckhart says:

> Where time never entered, where no image ever shone in, in the inmost and highest part of the soul, God is creating the whole world. . . . All that is past, all that is present, and all that is to come, God creates in the inmost part of the soul.

The actual content of the intense dynamic of transfiguration in Eckhart is never portrayed. He describes the "before" and the "after," but the "during" seems to resist description. Perhaps this is because space and time, which normally frame the thresholds of our knowing and perception, are themselves transfigured here. The transition has already happened. The time here is the *nunc aeternitatis*, the "now of eternity" that admits of no sequence nor duration. Perhaps this is also the reason that, time and again, Eckhart insists that certain transitions happen without any means or mediation. In Sermon 74, he states, "Being flows without mediation from God, and life flows from being." In Sermon 14b, he says, "The Divine Image breaks forth from the fecundity of nature without mediation. . . . The simple divine image is impressed on the soul's inner nature without means." In Sermon 14a, he says:

> A master says, if all mediation were gone between me and this wall, I would be *on the* wall, but not *in* the wall. It is not thus in spiritual matters, for the one is always in the other: that which embraces is that which is embraced, for it embraces nothing but itself.

The clarity of Nothingness and Detachment seems to have absolved the need for mediator and mediation. This is also true of the relationship between the ground of the soul and her powers: "But in the soul's essence there is no activity, for the powers she works with emanate from the ground of being. Yet in that ground is the silent 'middle' . . . this part is by nature receptive to nothing save only the divine essence, without mediation" (Sermon 1). Underlying the absence of threshold here is a concept of absolute presence. One thing is not a vehicle for another nor is it its representative. Presence at the level of spirit is full presence. It is neither broken nor diminished by extension, separation, or distance. In his *Commentary on The Book of Wisdom*, Eckhart offers some interesting insights into the absence of threshold and medium:

> You should know that at the Son's coming into the mind it is necessary that every medium be still. The nature of a medium shrinks from the kind of union that the soul desires with and in God. The reason is, first, because existence of its nature is the First and the Last, the beginning and end, never the medium. Rather it is the Medium Itself by whose sole mediation all things are, are present within, and are loved or sought. But God himself is Existence Itself. . . . If anyone loves a medium or even beholds a medium, he does not love or see God.

The omnipresent Divine Actuality, the absolute Thereness of God, absolves the need for a medium. "Becoming and moving require a medium, but existing and possessing yield and are silent about any medium" (*Commentary on The Book of Wisdom*). Eckhart does not want to let a neutral, in-between world of mediation arise that would diminish or qualify presence. He makes this clear right through his writings. In Latin Sermon 9, he discusses the nature of image. And he is scrupulously careful to allow no distance to emerge between image and source: the image is in the source; the source is in the image. Eckhart's methodology does not need to employ a concept of mediation because he has a ready-made zone of pure eternity always at hand in the ground of the soul. Detachment is the door. And it is always open.

Eckhart places such singular emphasis on the soul as unique and exclusive Divine agency that it could at times seem as if the Incarnation might be relativized or unnecessary. But this is not the case, for the Divine agency of the soul is not to be restricted merely to the creation of creation. The soul's agency is absolutely within the primal depths of the Divine Interflow itself. The soul is active in the very Birth of God. In Sermon 79, Eckhart claims, "The soul brings forth in herself God out of God and into God: she bears him truly outside of herself: she does this by bearing God *there*, where she is Godlike: *there* she is an image of God."

The Birth of God in the Soul: Where Time and Eternity Are One

Eckhart says that neither God nor creature could ever sever this union. The uniformity is absolute. It would be ontologically impossible to sever this. In Sermon 71, he states, "God gives birth to Himself fully in me that I may never lose him." With the carefully crafted symmetry of forces in his ontology, Eckhart is able to evoke the confluence of time and eternity as simultaneity. In Sermon 61, he says, "The soul shoots out of this primal ground at the breaking forth of the Son from the Father." Eckhart does not practice a theology of sequence. His is a theology of simultaneity, articulated from within the circle of eternity. Therefore, the generation of the Son, the Incarnation, the Birth of God in the soul, and the *creatio continua* are distinct dimensions of what could be termed the one Divine Actuality. Simultaneity is the inclusive symmetry of time and eternity. Time as sequence and distance is transformed. In Sermon 79, Eckhart writes: "In the Eternal Now, God is bringing forth his Son all the time . . . .All things proceed from this." And in Sermon 65:

> The Father gives birth to His Son in the soul in the very same way as He gives birth to Him in eternity, and no differently . . . not only does He beget me as His Son, but He begets me as Himself and Himself as me, and me as His being and His nature.

Indeed, in terms of his theory of Image, a beautiful symmetry becomes evident here between the human person as *Imago Dei* and the Son as the Image of the Father. Eckhart says, "The soul differs in no way from our Lord Jesus Christ except in that the soul has a coarse essence . . . for his essence is in the eternal person." This coheres with Eckhart's intuition that in the Incarnation, God took on not just an individual person; rather, God assumed human nature. In Sermon 16, he says, "God became man that I might be born of God Himself." Then, more poetically, "There is a childbed in the Godhead." Ontologically, the intention of the Incarnation is that we may break through time and reenter the Divine Seamlessness. In Sermon 11, Eckhart writes, "To know the Father, we must be the Son." One could claim that for Eckhart, the Incarnation achieves full realization in the Birth of God in the soul. Furthermore, the Incarnation as the revelation of the Logos is in a sense also a revelation of the native intelligibility of the world. Intellect in its knowing is at the heart of reality: God is in all things as intelligence. Therefore, the intellect is the union of the mind and God, and of mind and world. As revealed intelligibility, the Incarnation demands its own metaphysics.

The theory of Detachment and the Birth of God in the ground of the soul are at the heart of Eckhart. They distinguish his thought and anchor his originality. A contrast with other styles of epistemology might serve to underline Eckhart's distinctiveness. His way contrasts starkly with the style of phenomenology. In Eckhart's thought-world, intentionality would be inadequate and untrustable. The Divine is not to be grasped. The heart of phenomenology is the explication of the structuring capacity of consciousness. In each moment consciousness co-constructs reality. This constructionist capacity would find no echo in Eckhart. The soul is about to enter the embrace of pure stillness in the Divine Birth. Here thought is no longer hungry with desire. Thought is no longer desperate to straddle the forked distance between the opaqueness of the object and the intimations of the subject. In Eckhart, created things are "occasions" inviting the possibility of detachment and transfiguration. In everything the soul wants to return home to the Divine Adjacency.

Yet here is where Jean-Luc Marion's phenomenology would find a great echo in Eckhart. In his transfiguration of the phenomenological strategy, Marion displaces the centrality of the subject in favor of the *pleroma* of the object. The excess of the object's givenness saturates the subject. The autonomy and majesty of the divine object are what set up and, indeed, structure the space for perception and relationship. Marion says that neither the place nor the language is ready for the visitation of God; indeed, to speak of preparing a place for God is idolatrous. The philosophy of Being covertly prescribes who God is to be. Marion's project is to create a conceptual space where the phenomenon might appear as it is, without becoming entangled in the finite grammar of identity and identification. God saturates and overflows all horizons of possibility.

Eckhart's thought-world can also be illuminated through contrast with the relational philosophy of dialogue. The whole plane of possibility for such encounter is utterly different in Eckhart. Through Detachment the subject enters into the freedom of Nothingness, wherein the union with the Divine eventuates itself. Rather than the confirmed autonomy and reciprocity of individuality, as in dialogical philosophy, in Eckhart the union of God and soul occurs in the ground where no other intention presides.

The Contemporaneous Origin

A contrast with dialectic, as in Hegel's *Phenomenology of Spirit*, might help to crystallize the difference of Eckhart. The arrival point in Hegel is determined negation. This is the epistemological harvest of the ever unfolding and cumulative determinations of the dialectic. The dialectic is the narrative of a continuity wherein experience unfolds and thematizes itself. Underpinning this continuity is a constant emergence of new possibility that, when realized in experience, becomes the ground of further emergent possibility and the invitation and entry into an ever deepening enrichment of experience. Ultimately, it is the refinement of consciousness toward the moment when Spirit/*Geist* emerges in the ground of consciousness. The secret and unfolding destination of consciousness is *Geist*. This is the *eschaton* of the dialectic. In Eckhart there is not so much a struggle toward a destination as the return home to the Origin. The Origin is not lost in the primeval past. The Origin is permanently adjacent to experience. Consequently, there is no necessity for the labor of a dialectic or the insistence on the emerging harvest of content through faithful and vulnerable continuity. In Eckhart the perspective is other; distance is not linear, it is unlikeness. Instead of an *eschaton*, there is a permanent and contemporaneous Divine Actuality. The realized union with God in the ground of the soul has the clarity, totality, and spontaneity of something epiphanic. The work of clearance and clarification springs the soul into the native actuality of its indwelling in God. Rather than successive and cumulative determination, the work of epistemology is anti-determining, the sundering of the soul from the gravity of attachment to particularity in order for the Divine Birthing to happen. This is not actuality as a merely theoretical construct. Eckhart's language is from within the event; it is a speculative poetry of Divine Presencing. Divine Actuality is an all-inclusive event. The soul leaves broken, sequential continuity to enter into the fluent continuum of the Divine. The whole metaphoric of birthing underlines this; this language suggests the new, the now, presence, recognition, realization, belonging, emergence, and arrival. It is a language charged with the excitement and danger of the Divine.

Eckhart seems to place little emphasis on experience of self or experience of the world as the doorway to a deeper eschatology of creation. Experience does not hold its contemporary attraction as an invitation to becoming. There is no sense of a passionate individuality thematizing and unfolding itself in and through experience. There is no sense of the matrix of experience as the arena for the discovery and realization of identity. It seems at every point that experience is herded toward the path of *askesis* in order to enter that secret door to God. This would be equivalent to annulling experience if Eckhart were working with a linear eschatology in which the soul eventually climbed out of sequence at the point of the Birth of God, to be wafted up a vertical channel into the opaque transcendent. The Birth of God would short-circuit the labor of creation. However, Eckhart's ontology is an ontology of Divine Actuality. Creation is neither annulled nor stopped. The deepest realization of experience is achieved when it awakens and enters its own essence. Time and again, Eckhart states that the Birth of God enables the soul to transfigure transience. And the soul in Eckhart is not a celestial prisoner in a temporary physical body. The soul is *the* threshold in Eckhart, the place where the full and vigorous experience of self and world can coalesce as transfigured. Therefore, in the Birth of God nothing is lost or forgotten. All is gathered inward from the dispersal and fragmentation of multiplicity. In this sense Eckhart's ontology opens a human life to the force and riches of its eternal birthright. Implicit in this ontology is the transfiguration of death as the wound where experience is severed into transience. In theological terms, Eckhart's Birth of God in the ground of the soul could be read as an ontology of resurrection. Death is subsumed in the eternity of creation. Memory is the place where our vanished days secretly gather. In this sense, eternal life is eternal memory. Ultimately, everything flows back into the intimate and ultimate origin. Echoing Augustine, Eckhart says in Sermon 50, "Memory, a secret, hidden art denotes the Father" and: "what is inborn in me remains."

In a sense, Eckhart's ontology is the poetic and speculative excavation of the contemporaneous origin. In order to delineate the richness of the origin in Eckhart, it may be helpful to outline a philosophical perspective against which the distinctiveness of the concept of origin might become clearer. Usually, we conceptualize experience in terms of "beginning" and "ending." Underpinning the notion of beginning and ending is the notion of a linear sequence. Eckhart's epistemology strives to think beyond the segmentation and distance of sequence, and endeavors to disclose a shape of unfolding more akin to a circle or perhaps a spiral. Endings and beginnings happen within the deeper circle of origin and completion. In this respect, Eckhart's thinking is deeply influenced by Neoplatonism's theory of the originary one and the inclusiveness and singularity of the outflow and inflow rhythms of emanation. Eckhart embraces and reshapes this rhythm of emergence, unfolding, and return to articulate his own Trinitarian ontology. It is no surprise that the figure of the Father plays such a huge role for Eckhart. In the Father the origin becomes evident. In Sermon 53, he says, "In the Father are the primal images of all creatures." Ideas are pre-things. This clearly attributes the origin of creation to a personal source, namely, the Father. The singularity and intimacy of the origin have imprinted its nature on all its descendant creatures and objects. Eckhart further states, "All creatures are striving to bring forth and to emulate the Father."

In his *Commentary on The Book of Wisdom*, Eckhart defines creation as the "conferring of existence after non-existence." But creation was not preceded by a vacuum. Everything that *is*, preexisted as idea in the mind of God. He continues, "The ideas of created things are not created, creatable as such. They are prior and posterior to things." The ideas are already in the Logos. "In him things are their ideas—In the beginning was the Word, or *Logos* which is the Idea." Later on, he underlines the artistic novelty of creation: "Creation is the production of things from nothing." He distinguishes the primal creativity that begot the Logos, that is termed "generation"; it is not of this world since it is not in time. Worldly creation is alteration, since it takes place in time and is of this world. The external existence of things confers autonomy on them, yet below the surface at a deeper level, alteration can never diminish their status as inhering in the Divine. They have proximate autonomy yet ultimate belonging.

The Divine Intellect as Primal Ontological Imagination

Informing and underpinning this whole ontology is the grounding recognition that God is Intellect. In the first of *The Parisian Questions*, Eckhart states that the intellect is more fundamental than Being in God:

> It is said in John 1, "In the Beginning was the Word, and the Word was with God, and the Word was God." The Evangelist did not say: "In the Beginning was Being, and God was Being." A word is completely related to intellect. . . .

Eckhart goes on to claim that intellect precedes Being. Being is not God but the creation of God. In other words, God exists because He knows. "Thus, I declare that it is not my present opinion that God understands because he exists, but rather that he exists because he understands." The affirmation of God as intellect confers a huge quality of intimacy on Being. Rather than appearing as a cold, fundamental category to ground the logic of identity and necessity, Being is already imbued with a quality of primal affinity. Ultimately, Being is belonging. Eckhart manages to ground here a single-source ontology that is intrinsically personal and ultimately creative. To express it in other terms of which Eckhart would not approve: Being is the ultimate creative act of the Divine Imagination. Beneath the most virulent oppositions and dualities, there reigns an ultimate affinity and belonging. At the heart of all opposition, duality is a threshold tensed for transfiguration.

In his *Commentary on John 14:8*—"Lord, show us the Father, and it is enough for us"—Eckhart deepens his portraiture of the Father as creator:

> According to the idea of existence and essence, God is, as it were, resting and concealed, hidden in himself, neither begetting nor begotten. . . . But according to the idea of Father or Paternity he first takes on and receives the property of fecundity, germination, and production.

In the *Commentary* Eckhart also stresses the originlessness of the Father, "the being that is not from another." All creation and creativity inhere ultimately in the Father. Eckhart says, "The Father is the source and principle of each and all emanation." The Father as ground of Being confers eternity and relationality on creation. Eckhart writes:

> Existence is the necessary goal of generation whose Principle is the Father. Existence is properly a repose; it is above time, and consequently nothing grows old there, nothing passes away, nothing changes.

And again:

> Because the essence is the source and cause of all the properties of a thing, it is what communicates everything. Therefore, the Father is shown when God is manifested through essence.

The fullness of what is, derives from the Father as First Source. Eckhart says, "And the First is rich in itself." In a beautiful recognition of the intimacy and belonging that the personal ontological origin exhibits, Eckhart writes in his *Commentary on John 14:8*:

The goal is God. He is the Principle and the goal. "The rivers return to the place from which they flowed."

Origin and completion constitute the all-embracing circle of presence.

At the human level there emerges a certain symmetry of primacy and priority in relation to intellect. In Sermon 54, Eckhart states, "The soul's intellect is the highest part of the soul." But the soul has not developed its intellect. It is a gift. In Sermon 73, he says, "The natural light of the intellect that God has poured into the soul is so splendid and so strong that all that God has created of bodily things seems mean and petty to it." He goes on to "locate" the Birth of the Logos in the soul through the intellect:

> In the night, when no creature shines or looks into the soul, and in the stillness when nothing speaks to the soul, then the Word is spoken to the intellect. This Word belongs to the intellect and means *Verbum* as it is and stands in the intellect.

This process is a mirror symmetry of the generation of the Logos in eternity. In Sermon 60, Eckhart says, "It is the light that lays hold of God, unveiled and bare, as He is in Himself, that is, it catches Him in the act of begetting." Intellect is the "place" where the ultimate creativity is stirred. Eckhart's ontology is rooted in the creativity of cognition. The passion of the soul is driven by the desire to know.

In Sermon 3, Eckhart describes the different levels of intellect and their role in the act of knowing:

> The active intellect abstracts images from outward things, stripping them of matter and accidents, and introduces them to the passive intellect and begets their mental image therein, and the passive intellect made pregnant by the active intellect in this way cherishes and knows these things with the aid of the active intellect. Even then, the passive intellect cannot keep on knowing these things unless the active intellect illumines them afresh . . . what the active intellect does for the natural man, that and far more God does for one with Detachment. He *takes away* the active intellect from him, and installing Himself in its stead, He Himself undertakes all that the active intellect ought to be doing. . . .

The entry of God to assume the work of the active intellect effects a radical transformation of the knowing act. The active intellect is caught among thresholds and boundaries. It is bound by the linear progress of sequence. Eckhart says, "The active intellect cannot entertain two images together, it has first one and then the other." The "author of nature," as Eckhart here terms God, enables the active intellect to enter the Divine Simultaneity of knowing. He says, "But God acts in the place of the active intellect, He engenders many images together in one point" (Sermon 3). This focus of simultaneous knowing is the majestic artistry of Divine Perception. In Sermon 2, Eckhart says:

> The blessed see God in a single image, and in that image, they discern all things. God sees Himself thus, perceiving all things in Himself. He need not turn from one thing to another as we do.

To use a coarse image, Divine Knowing is a telescoped knowing. Though Eckhart did not use the concept of totality, it can be used to unpack the inclusive cognition of the Divine. The singularity of the one image here is no ideologically compressed or syncopated multiplicity. Somehow, in the one image the totality of infinite presence is available. Without having its content injured, multiplicity can be coalesced in a profound and refined unity. Multiplicity has the potential to be one intimacy of presence. The condition of the possibility of this achieved unity lies in the secret and source of the intellect and idea. The idea is the ground of multiplicity, identity, affinity, and transfiguration. In Sermon 2, Eckhart says, "God is in all things as intelligence." And in Sermon 70, he claims, "For *there* is nothing but one, and where one is, there is all, and where all is, there is one." And in Sermon 69: "In God the soul knows total being." The ground of the soul inheres in the heart of divine actuality. The *seelen Funken*, the spark of soul, is already within Divine Presence and Divine Prevenience. In Sermon 53, Eckhart says, "This spark is so akin to God that it is a single impartible one, and it contains in itself the images of all creatures, imageless images and images above images."

At Home in the Source:
Beyond All Limits, Frontiers, and Thresholds

It is clear from the eternal quality of the soul's knowing that Eckhart is absolutely serious about the Birth of God in the soul. He draws ultimate conclusions from the depth of that union. In Sermon 4, he states:

> When you go out from your will and your knowledge, God with His knowledge surely and willingly goes in there and shines clearly . . . for you to know in God's way, your knowing must become a pure unknowing . . . a forgetting of yourself and all creatures.

At this point there is an epistemological equivalence between the Divine Intellect and the detached spirit. Sermon 66 says, "The same knowing in which God knows Himself is the knowing of every detached spirit, and no other." This epistemological equivalence finds wonderful and poetic expression in Eckhart's famous statement in Sermon 57: "The eye with which I see God is the same eye with which God sees me: my eye and God's eye are one eye, one seeing, one knowing and one love." This beautiful statement reveals more than any other the subversive Divine Reflexivity in which the detached soul now dwells. The image is built like a wonderful mirror: one eye confirms the other and is itself only through the presence of the other's seeing. The threshold between the Divine and the human has been utterly transfigured, clarified, and freed into a new identity in which God and soul emerge and sustain one another in a primeval *perichoresis* of seeing. One can glimpse in Eckhart's phrase the ontological resemblance between the way Father and Son gaze at one another in the Trinity and how God and soul dwell in the one act of seeing. This is identity as creative reciprocity. There is a profound epistemological simultaneity here. It invites us to understand Eckhart's theory of knowing in a completely different way from the usual image of a separated subject engaging an object over against a horizon.

To use the spatial image of the circle again. Finite knowing on its way toward this simultaneity of seeing could be imagined as a bright circle of illumination that is itself encircled by a deeper circle of Divine knowing. Normally this outer circle of Divine knowing is too bright for us, but when we become detached, perhaps what happens is that the ever present circle of outer Divine knowing is breaking in and through us. Indeed, in Sermon 24, Eckhart says of God, "He is the ground and encirclement of all creatures." This is an ultimate epistemological reversal: now it is God who knows in us. The one who was the object up to this point now *knows* in the subject. Ontology transfigures and suffuses epistemology.

The condition of the possibility of such seeing is the dynamic epistemological symmetry between the Divine Intellect and the intellect of the soul. The soul's intellect wants to go beyond God into the Godhead: "Delving deeper and ever seeking, she grasps God in his oneness and solitude, she seizes Him in His desert and in His proper ground" (Sermon 66). In Sermon 68, Eckhart describes how this knowing is beyond space and sequence; it knows in the eternal now, the *nunc aeternitatis*: "This power seizes God in his robing room." This is one of the most fascinating thresholds: the place where God arises from the Godhead. Current Western theology and spirituality have utterly neglected this opaque source of the Godhead. Without the Godhead, the Trinitarian persons become empty, functional ciphers. Jean-Luc Marion stands out as a unique thinker in contemporary philosophy and theology precisely because of his faithfulness to the exploration of the opaque source of the Godhead.

Echoes of Eckhart? Jean-Luc Marion's Philosophy of God

Though their thought-worlds differ profoundly, Jean-Luc Marion shares with Meister Eckhart a passionate concern with the Otherness and freedom of God. Marion's philosophy of God derives much of its urgency and edge from his attempt to rescue God from metaphysics. In a splendid display of counterinspiration, Marion develops his own thought through a critique of Heidegger. It is his contention that Heidegger's construct of *Sein-Dasein* ends up making God a prisoner of *Dasein*: ". . . the God of ontotheology is rigorously equivalent to an idol, that which is presented by the Being of beings thought metaphysically" (*IAD*, 18). Marion is at all times aware of the brilliance and far-reaching reflexivity of Heidegger's construct. While endeavoring to think beyond it, he is careful not to become unwittingly snared by its latent shape in any alternative thought field.

Marion develops an impressive methodological apparatus in order to think the autonomy of God. In framing his exploration, he wants to avoid becoming trapped in either Being or subjectivity. Consequently, he chooses to locate his thought source in the notion of "givenness." "Givenness" is both the source and the force at the heart of Marion's "ontology"; it is the originary impulse that projects, propels, and structures what is. It precedes identity; indeed, it confers identity. In a deft phenomenological maneuver, Marion is able to claim the "delay" in the initial self-activation of subjectivity as a key instance of the generosity and the prevenience of "givenness." It is before identity: only in and through its surge of generosity can the subject awaken to its selfhood. Similarly, it is the originary dynamic of "givenness" that actually bestows Being. This strategy enables Marion to sidestep the governing epistemological strain that comes with attributing foundational grounding to the ultimate category of Being. In this sense, Being is secondary to the originary and sourcing generosity of "givenness."

"Givenness" is not simple thereness nor the dead transfer of Being from an alien source. "Givenness" is more an activity, namely, the arrival and awakening of what is. Central, then, to "givenness" is the capacity for response that it awakens in the subject; the deeper this response, the more fully the "givenness" shows itself. Since Marion elucidates "givenness" in this way, he is easily able to render the desire within "givenness" to become explicit, that is, to show itself. In this elegant move, Marion satisfies the phenomenological necessity of presentation by a source that maintains its selfhood, autonomy, and otherness, a source beyond Being that evades the snares and reflexive netting of metaphysics. "Givenness" enjoys an enabling and transitive reflexivity that is beyond the confined symmetry of a metaphysics that would take its starting point from the dialectic of Being and *Dasein*. Marion's ingenious perspective confers full autonomy on the subject; however, this is a totally different concept of the subject from that delivered by the lonesome, self-constructing subject of the idealist tradition. Marion's subject enjoys full epistemological capacity, but it is an epistemological capacity awakened and conferred by the prevenient activity of "givenness": the more the subject is willing to receive, the more it comes to know.

There is a somewhat transcendental feel to Marion's thought. Yet, instead of a functional elucidation of the conditions of possibility, Marion is more concerned with exploring and articulating the conditions of impossibility. The figure of Denys and the aphophatic tradition glimmer like a rich shadow over his thought-world. With admiration, he quotes the principle of Denys: "It is necessary to understand the divine things divinely" (*ID*, 140). Through his poetic and speculative portraiture of the intensive geography of impossibility, Marion suggests the depths that reside in the Unknown and the Unthinkable; rather than being conundrums to logic and concept, he unveils them as their most profound source and abyss. At the heart of this radical epistemology Marion develops his fascinating notion of "distance." He is careful to clarify that "distance" is not to be confused with the ontological difference. In his essay on Denys, Marion says:

> Distance, precisely because it remains the Ab-solute, delivers the space where it becomes possible for us to receive ourselves. ... We discover ourselves, in distance, delivered to ourselves, or rather delivered for ourselves, given, not abandoned, to ourselves. ... In receiving himself from distance, man comprehends not only that distance comprehends him, but that it renders him possible ... anterior distance therefore governs positively that which it allows to be received in it. (*ID*, 153–54)

Through invoking the notion of "distance," Marion is able to protect and guarantee Otherness. The metaphor of "distance" also suggests a continuity with the Faraway that allows him to exploit a dynamic of separation that never becomes alienation and a dynamic of nearing that can never claim the Absolute. "Distance" becomes the root of possibility, the ground of longing, and the spur and invitation to participation; it is not merely a transcendental regulative principle that delivers a bare arithmetic of logical space. Ironically, it is precisely "distance" that creates the fecund space where the Absolute can become present. In this sense, "distance" is the poetics of divine space. Marion says, "In other words, radically prohibiting that one holds God as an object, or as a supreme being, distance escapes the ultimate avatar of a language of the object—the closure of discourse and the disappearance of the referent" (*ID*, 140). Marion sounds out the primal silence of the ur-language of the Absolute when he says, "The Unthinkable speaks even before we think we hear it, anterior distance holds out to us a language that precedes and inverts our predication" (*ID*, 143). This wonderfully poetic insight does not render our knowing redundant or unveil it as mere projection. Marion is after something else here. Like a poet, he is coming at our language and knowing in an oblique way in order to reveal something else. His goal is none other than that of making audible the primal music of the divine that dwells secretly within the poetry of language; in terms of knowing, it is "to know the Unknowing that our knowledges conceal" (see *ID*, 148). This Unknowing is not ignorance or the result of mere negation, but of utter fecundity and urgent invitation.

Marion's thought has journeyed far beyond the transcendental thresholds. Like Eckhart's, Marion's thought tastes of the divine flame. Somehow, here the attempt is being made to think God from within. This attempt subverts both the horizontal and the vertical leanings of concept and language. Despite the centuries of distance, both thinkers share the absolute concern with articulating the autonomy of God from Being. Eckhart says that intellect precedes Being and that Being is not God but the creation of God. In a striking similarity of language both argue for the primal clearance offered by the perspective of paternity. In his *Commentary on John 14.8*, Eckhart says, "According to the idea of . . . Paternity, [God] first takes on and receives the property of fecundity, germination and production." Marion says, "Paternal distance offers the sole space for filiation" (*ID*, 139). This primal perspective continues to maintain its clarity of severance over against any conceptual attempt to encroach on or claim it: "More, the paternal horizon of distance removes itself, by definition, from any inquiry that would claim to objectivate it" (*ID*, 204). While both thinkers endeavor to think God from within, their difficulty is to site a thought starting point that is already somehow the gift, the showing place, or the recognition point of the Absolute. For Eckhart this site is the Soul as threshold; for Marion it is the disclosure point and awakening place of "givenness."

The next methodological difficulty is to break or transfigure any false symmetry that might creep in, thus reducing the Divine to the limiting conditions of our epistemology. Marion achieves this through his careful elucidation of the "asymmetry of distance," which unveils the icon, precludes idolatory, and ultimately gives rise to the "saturated phenomen," the summit of the activity of "givenness." Eckhart's strategy is to outline the two regions of the soul, the one turned toward God and the other toward the world. For Eckhart, the soul is always a given, and through the interaction of intellect and soul the transfiguration of the existential dimension is realized. Whereas in Marion's thinking the impression of a journey prevails, in Eckhart's it is more a question of breaking into a simultaneity that always awaits us. The eternal quality of the soul's knowing enables an epistemology of simultaneity. Centuries before the birth of idealism and phenomenology, Eckhart's questions are not tempered by the hungers or straining of naked subjectivity. As we have seen, identity is more a question of returned intimacy than the journey of biography. Marion has a deep affinity with Eckhart here, in that identity for him seems to be the awakening and recognition of "givenness," and not a project of self-constitution, as in many other phenomenological thought-worlds.

Central to the dwelling in the eternal dimension is Marion's notion of Detachment. His "distance" maintains a phenomenological continuity with the Absolute. Eckhart's Detachment is more fierce and severely clear and bleak—a *unicum*. While Marion remains a unique and fascinating speculative poet of God beyond Being, the solitude and Otherness of Eckhart's God remains more tender and terrible — *fascinans et tremens*; his thought is rinsed with the severity, intimacy, and terror of the ultimate void. The tension in Eckhart also derives from the coupling of this severity with a tonality that is lyrical, evocative, and exhortative. His thinking is not descriptive or merely programmatic; it is, of course, a pinnacle of Western speculative thinking, but is flamed with an intimacy that has the immediacy of the ultimate poem of God.

Eckhart employs a whole family of concepts in order to elucidate this opaque frontier of Godhead, concepts such as Uncreated, Originlessness, the Unknowable, the Abyss of the Godhead, the Light That Darkens All Light, the Desert. What are the epistemological characteristics of these concepts? They suggest a delineated realm of Beyondness, a region unreachable through intellect, concept, or word. There is a suggestion of a richness too great to register on the limited radar of human consciousness and knowing. They are, furthermore, regions of absolute realization. The ordinary duality of knowing, the Sisyphean torment of desire, finds here the peace of ultimate Stillness. Though this realm lies beyond every frontier of Beginning, it is nevertheless suggested to be the preferred destination of the soul, the home of ultimate meaning and belonging. There is also a grounding sense or intuition that this realm (even the word "realm" is a misnomer), this No-Where, this No-Thingness, is not destructive. It is not a realm that unravels Being. It is not a realm of antithetical, dissembling Otherness. It is not a domain of anti-logic that dispirits essence. It is, rather, the place where essence finds its source, grounding, and ultimate destination. Logically, of course, because it is the utter unknown, one cannot convincingly claim anything for it. Even the claim that it exists is itself paradoxical. Nevertheless, one senses that Eckhart's confidence in this realm is grounded in the helpless kindness and love of God. Indeed, it seems that Eckhart can push thought beyond its own frontiers, toward the absolute unknowable, precisely because of his trust in the Incarnation as the Logos, the revealed principle of ultimate, trustable intelligibility.

Every limit, boundary, frontier, and threshold runs aground here. All the symmetries dissolve in the opaque and elegant swiftness of the originary asymmetry. Even the term "asymmetry" is inaccurate here because, after the realization of the Birth of God in the soul, the uniformity of God and soul is no longer over against any other force, opposition, or thing; there is nothing more outside. All the thresholds are transfigured. There is no distance or separation anymore. This is where this knowing comes up against that ultimate threshold where God recedes into Godhead. Eckhart says in Sermon 56, "God and Godhead are as different as heaven and earth." Then he coins one of the most radical phrases in the Christian theology of God: *Gott wirt und entwirt*, "God becomes and unbecomes." This is the diamond phrase of all aphophatic theology. It glistens like a strange half-prism that splits all our putative illuminations of the Divine. It is a phrase the returns us to the desert, to the bleak recognition that after all, God is only our name for it. The closer we come to it, the more it ceases to be God.

Notes

Introduction
Ian Leask and Eoin Cassidy

1. See Jean-Luc Marion, "The Voice Without Name: Homage to Lévinas," in his *The Face of the Other and the Trace of God*, ed. Jeffrey Bloechl (New York: Fordham University Press, 2000), pp. 224–42.

2. Derrida's most extended treatment of the theme of the gift can be found in his *Given Time*, vol. 1, *Counterfeit Money*, trans. Peggy Kamuf (Chicago: University of Chicago Press, 1992)/*Donner le temps*, vol. 1, *La fausse monnaie*, in the series La Philosophie en Effet (Paris: Éditions Galilée, 1991).

3. See Robyn Horner's comments in the introduction to her and Vincent Barraud's translation of *In Excess* (*IE*), p. xi.

Chapter 1. The Conceptual Idolatry of Descartes's Gray Ontology: An Epistemology "Without Being"
Derek J. Morrow

I would like to thank Philipp W. Rosemann for his valuable comments on an earlier draft of this paper.

1. Dominique Janicaud, *Le tournant théologique de la phénoménologie française* (Paris: L'Eclat, 1991), English translation in *Phenomenology and the Theological Turn: The French Debate* (New York: Fordham University Press, 2000), pt. I: Dominique Janicaud, "The Theological Turn of French Phenomenology," trans. Bernard Prusak, pp. 16–103; for criticism leveled against Marion, see esp. pp. 50–66. For Marion's response to Janicaud, see, inter alia, *BG*, 38–39 and 336, n. 80 (*ED*, 59–60 and 60, n. 1); *BG*, 71–74

and 342–43, nn. 1–6 (*ED*, 103–8: 104, nn. 1–2; 105, n. 1; 106, nn. 1–2; 107, n. 1); *BG*, 328, n. 8 (*ED*, 8, n. 4); *BG*, 340, n. 112 (*ED*, 91, n. 1). Janicaud in turn takes up the argument of *Being Given* in his *La phénoménologie éclatée* (Combas: Éditions de l'Éclat, 1998). For discussion of the debate in the literature, see John D. Caputo, "Derrida and Marion: Two Husserlian Revolutions," in *Religious Experience and the End of Metaphysics*, ed. Jeffrey Bloechl (Bloomington: Indiana University Press, 2003), pp. 119–34; Thomas A. Carlson, "The Naming of God and the Possibility of Impossibility: Marion and Derrida between the Theology and Phenomenology of the Gift," in chap. 6 of Carlson, *Indiscretion: Finitude and the Naming of God* (Chicago: University of Chicago Press, 1999), pp. 190–236; Jean Grondin, "La tension de la donation ultime et de la pensée herméneutique de l'application chez Jean-Luc Marion," *Dialogue* 38 (1999): 547–59; Robyn Horner, *Rethinking God as Gift: Marion, Derrida, and the Limits of Phenomenology* (New York: Fordham University Press, 2001), and the review of this work by Derek J. Morrow in *American Catholic Philosophical Quarterly* 75, no. 4 (Fall 2001): 633–39; Marie-Andrée Ricard, "La question de la donation chez Jean-Luc Marion," *Laval théologique et philosophique* 57, no. 1 (2001): 83–94; James K. A. Smith: "Respect and Donation: A Critique of Marion's Critique of Husserl," *American Catholic Philosophical Quarterly* 71, no. 4 (Autumn 1997): 523–38; "Liberating Religion from Theology: Marion and Heidegger on the Possibility of a Phenomenology of Religion," *International Journal for Philosophy and Religion* 46 (1999): 17–33; and *Speech and Theology: Language and the Logic of Incarnation* (London: Routledge, 2003), esp. chap. 2; Marlène Zarader, "Phenomenology and Transcendence," trans. Ralph Hancock et al., in *Transcendence in Philosophy and Religion*, ed. James E. Faulconer (Bloomington: Indiana University Press, 2003), pp. 106–19. For a more general treatment of the topic in which the analysis is guided by the later writings of Derrida, see Hent de Vries, *Philosophy and the Turn to Religion* (Baltimore: Johns Hopkins University Press, 1999).

2. John Milbank: "Can a Gift Be Given? Prolegomena to a Future Trinitarian Metaphysic," *Modern Theology* 11, no. 1 (Jan. 1995): 119–61, repr. in *Rethinking Metaphysics*, ed. L. Gregory Jones and Stephen E. Fowl (Oxford: Blackwell, 1995), pp. 119–61; "Only Theology Overcomes Metaphysics," *New Blackfriars* 76 (July–Aug. 1995): 325–43, repr. in Milbank's *The Word Made Strange: Theology, Language, Culture* (Oxford: Blackwell, 1997), pp. 36–52; "The Soul of Reciprocity, Part One: Reciprocity Refused," *Modern Theology* 17, no. 3 (July 2001): 335–91; "The Soul of Reciprocity, Part Two: Reciprocity Granted," *Modern Theology* 17, no. 4 (Oct. 2001): 485–507; "Postmodernité," in *Dictionnaire critique de théologie*, ed. J.-Y. Lacoste (Paris: Presses Universitaires de France, 1998; Quadrige, 2002), pp. 924–25. Most recently, Milbank has repeated this criticism in his *Being Reconciled: Ontology and Pardon* (London: Routledge, 2003), pp. 138–61, esp.

pp. 152–57. For an interesting assessment and critique of Milbank's position, see Gavin Hyman, *The Predicament of Postmodern Theology: Radical Orthodoxy or Textual Nihilism?* (Louisville, Ky.: Westminster John Knox Press, 2001).

3. "Les *Regulae* ne permettent pas une lecture obvie. Mieux, nombre de leurs caractéristiques tendent finalement à les soustraire à une entreprise de calme lecture, pour les maintenir dans une étrange indécision, où elles flottent, comme un texte sans texte, "sans titre, sans généalogie ni postérité—en un mot, sans lieu, utopique" (The *Regulae* do not admit of a precautionary reading. Better: many of their characteristics tend finally to shield them from the enterprise of a calm reading, in order to maintain them in a strange indecision, where they float, like a text without a text, without a title, without either genealogy or posterity—in a word, without a place, utopic"; *OG*, 13; my translation). "Without a text," because the autographs of the *Regulae* are no longer extant; "without a title," because the manuscripts we do possess contain conflicting variants for the title; and "without either genealogy or posterity," because the subject matter of the (incomplete and unpublished) *Regulae* is discontinuous with that of Descartes's earlier unpublished writings and nevertheless fails to merit an express or implicit mention in any of the later, published works (*OG*, 13–16).

4. All translations from *OG* provided in the text and in the notes are my own.

5. For Marion's articulation of the proposals and their deficiencies, see *OG*, 17–18.

6. Generalizing a claim that Marion makes specifically only for *Rule VI*: "The situation of schizocosmenia becomes clear only if *Rule VI* is read and deciphered as a strangely constant and precise dialogue with Aristotle" (*OG*, 78–79).

7. Generalizing what Marion affirms of the conclusions reached by his exegesis of *Rule II*, "[c]onclusions que seul le décryptage aristotélicien de la *Règle II* rend formulables" ("[c]onclusions that only the Aristotelian deciphering of *Rule II* makes it possible to formulate; *OG*, 43). Cf. the similar claim made for *Rules V, VI*, and *VII*: "Ces textes [*Rules V, VI*, and *VII*], souvent dangereusement sous-estimés et méconnus, exigent, en effet, une rigoureuse lecture comparative, où le rapport constant à la thématique aristotélicienne procure *seul* quelque sûreté dans le décryptage de la pensée cartésienne" ("These texts [*Rules V, VI*, and *VII*], often dangerously underestimated and misunderstood, indeed demand a rigorous comparative reading, one in which the constant link to the Aristotelian thematic could *alone* procure some confidence in the deciphering of Cartesian thought; *OG*, 71; emphasis added).

8. *OG*, 20, citing Henri Gouhier, *Les premières pensées de Descartes: Contribution à l'histoire de l'Anti-Renaissance* (Paris: Vrin, 1964), p. 143.

9. Thus, for example, Desmond Clarke, who subordinates the *Regulae* to the *Discourse* in a manner similar to Gilson, believes that "[t]he justifica-

tion for a direct confrontation of Descartes and Aristotle is somewhat strained in the introductory chapter" of *OG* (Desmond Clarke, review of *Sur l'ontologie grise de Descartes*, by J.-L. Marion, *Studia Leibnitiana* 9, no.1 [1977]: 120–22, at 120). Despite this criticism—or rather, in direct contradiction to it—Clarke nevertheless concedes that Marion's approach to the Cartesian text is "evidently a fruitful one" (ibid.), and that his "exposition of the *Regulae* throws much light on the many vague and elusive concepts which govern the interpretation of the text" (ibid., 121). Clarke does not appear to consider the possibility that, within the field of hermeneutics at least, explanatory "fruitfulness" is itself a pertinent—and therefore valid— criterion of justification. For another evaluation of Marion's thesis that exhibits weaknesses similar to those of Clarke, see Zeljko Loparic, "À propos du cartésianisme gris de Marion," *Manuscrito* (Campinas, Brazil) 11, no. 2 (1988): 129–33.

10. On this point, cf. the judgment of Gregor Sebba: "It is not the least of Marion's achievements to have recognized the true significance of this inconspicuous passage." "Retroversion and the History of Ideas: J.-L. Marion's Translation of the *Regulae* of Descartes," in *Studia Cartesiana*, 2 vols. (Amsterdam: Quadratures, 1979–81), vol. 1, pp. 145–65, at 155.

11. René Descartes, *Regulae ad directionem ingenii* (Rule III, AT, X, 369.1–10), in *The Philosophical Writings of Descartes*, vol. 1, trans. John Cottingham, Robert Stoothoff, and Dugald Murdoch (Cambridge: Cambridge University Press, 1985), p. 14. (Hereafter cited parenthetically as "*PWD*, I," followed by the page number.)

12. Marion understands *AT*, X, 369.1–10, to be stating "'generally' [*generaliter; AT*, X, 369.3] a principle that is valid for the whole of the *Regulae*" (*OG*, 22).

13. With Marion, Gregor Sebba finds in this passage from *Rule III* "Descartes' Declaration of Independence from the School and . . . from Aristotle, with explicit reference to the term 'intuitus' on which his [Descartes's] disagreement with Aristotle is fundamental" ("Retroversion and the History of Ideas," 155; ellipsis in the original; cf. ibid., 155, n. 28, which cites the relevant texts from *RUC* and *OG*).

14. *RUC*: René Descartes, *Règles utiles et claires pour la direction de l'esprit en la recherche de la vérité. Traduction selon le lexique cartésien, et annotation conceptuelle par Jean-Luc Marion, avec des notes mathématiques de P. Costabel* (The Hague: Martinus Nijhoff, 1977).

15. In his exposition of Marion's *principe de métaphorisation*, Sebba notes that "[t]he gap between word and meaning in this analysis thus occurs throughout the *Regulae* wherever Descartes finds himself basically at variance with Aristotle. This disagreement is, however, not expressed by contradicting Aristotle—[because, ironically,] mere contradiction would still be a mark of dependence" ("Retroversion and the History of Ideas," 155). Thus Descartes's reticence to contradict Aristotle directly can be traced to

the former's desire to achieve a *greater* conceptual autonomy from the latter than would be possible by engaging him in direct contradiction.

16. For the fragment (which Marion translates in extenso at *OG*, 22), see *AT*, X, 204.6–13. Cf. *RUC*, 127, "Annotations," n. 12, in which this fragment is cited again to support the claim that Descartes employs a "principle of metaphorization" in the *Regulae*.

17. Marion regards the *transferre* of *AT*, X, 369.9, as an allusion to the Aristotelian definition of metaphor given in *Poetics* 1457b6f (*RUC*, 127, "Annotations," n. 12).

18. Cf. *OG*, 71, which states regarding "the epistemic operations" deployed in the *Regulae* that "the condition of their epistemic possibility imposes the destruction of certain ontological concepts, a destruction that is not justified nor, perhaps, brought about, but is only sketched by a simple setting to one side."

19. On this precise point, see the comments of Pierre Adler, who explains that for Marion, "Cartesian ontology . . . conceals itself under an epistemological discourse" in such a way that "the Cartesian ontology of the *Rules* is a half-tone substitute for [Aristotelian] ousiology, which stands alongside ousiology and as such does not deny that the *pragmata* really exist" (Pierre Adler, in Jean-Luc Marion, "On Descartes' Constitution of Metaphysics," paper delivered at Columbia University, Oct. 1, 1985; published in *Graduate Faculty Philosophy Journal* [New York] 11, no. 1 [1986]: 21–33, at 31, n. 12, editor's note).

20. Ibid. Adler's note here seeks to explain what Marion means by the phrase "gray ontology." Cf. *OG*, 186: For Marion, Descartes subscribes to a "[g]ray ontology, because this ontology does not at all declare itself, and because *it is concealed within an epistemological discourse* [my emphasis], but especially because it has to do with the thing, inasmuch as the thing departs from its irreducible οὐσία in order to take on the visage of an object, being submitted entirely to the demands of knowledge." Adler does not specifically reference this passage in his note, but as the italicized portion indicates, he does appear to have it in mind when he speaks of Descartes's gray ontology as "conceal[ing] itself under an epistemological discourse."

21. Invoking the language of Husserl, Marion will describe this methodological *mise entre parenthèses*, enacted by Descartes throughout the *Regulae*, as "the ἐποχή of the nature of the thing as such" (*OG*, 79).

22. The title of *OG*'s second chapter expresses this idea succinctly as "The Constitution of Order as the Dismissal [*destitution*] of the Categories of Being" (*OG*, 71).

23. J.-L. Marion, "Le paradigme cartésien de la métaphysique," *Laval théologique et philosophique* 53, no. 3 (Oct. 1997): 785–91, at 788.

24. Marion's first systematic discussion of the *Regulae*'s distinctly *metaphysical* ambivalence occurs in "L'ambivalence de la métaphysique cartésienne," *Les études philosophiques* 4 (1976): 443–60 (repr. in *OG*, 191–208).

Published just one year after the appearance of the first edition of *OG*, "L'ambivalence" argues that the *Regulae* and the *Meditationes* display a parallel vacillation in their respective understandings of the meaning and content of "first philosophy"; taken together, these two vacillations articulate the ambivalence and the ambiguity of Cartesian ontology as such (see *OG*, 197, n. 18). The argument of "L'ambivalence" has as one of its intentions to clarify and to elaborate the presentation first given in *OG*, §11, regarding how the *Regulae*'s *mathesis universalis* "transcribe[s] into an epistemological register" (*OG*, 192) Aristotle's first philosophy. As such, *mathesis universalis* effects the Cartesian "transcription of ontology into epistemology" (ibid.) in such a way that "in the *Regulae* the primacy of epistemology does not conceal the necessity of a *metaphysica generalis* (for the science of the object plays, by means of this primacy, the role of an ontology of the thing, in gray)" (*OG*, 197).

25. Marion, "L'ambivalence de la métaphysique cartésienne," in *OG*, 191–208, at 192.

26. As opposed to its form, since "[f]ormally, Cartesian philosophy is deployed as an explicit and avowed non-ontology" (*PMD*, 80).

27. Already in Merleau-Ponty, one finds the locution "ontology of the object" being used to designate Descartes's equivocal (hence "gray") transcription of the language of traditional metaphysics into an epistemological register: "In Descartes, for example, the two meanings of the word 'nature' (nature in the sense of 'natural light' and in the sense of 'natural inclination') adumbrate two ontologies (an ontology of the object and an ontology of the existent" (Maurice Merleau-Ponty, *Annuaire du Collège de France* [1958], repr. in *Le visible et l'invisible* [Paris: Gallimard, 1964], pp. 219–20, as cited in Marion, *DMP*, 126, n. 72/*PMD*, 134, n. 72).

28. For the syntagma *de omni re inquantum scibili*, see Jean-François Courtine (*Suarez et le système de la métaphysique*, in the series Épiméthée [Paris: Presses Universitaires de France, 1990], p. 489), who follows Marion on this point: "[T]he *Regulae* constitute very precisely an enterprise of general ontology: *de omni re scibili*; or better: *de omni re inquantum scibili*," and 489, n. 7: "Let us add that, for Descartes, there is no other possibility for considering [*envisager*] the reality of any thing whatsoever, except to consider it, precisely, *inquantum scibili* [insofar as it is knowable]." Courtine has in mind expressly (ibid., 489) *Rule VI, AT* X, 381.9–13, which asserts that "*res omnes* per quasdam series posse disponi, *non* quidem *in quantum* ad aliquod genus entis referentur, sicut illas Philosophi in categorias suas diviserunt, *sed in quantum* unae ex alijs *cognosci possunt*" ("*all things* can be arranged serially in various groups, *not in so far as* they can be referred to some ontological genus [such as the categories into which philosophers divide things], but *in so far as* some things *can be known* on the basis of others"); *PWD*, I, 21; emphasis added). For Marion's treatment of *Rule VI*, see the following texts: *OG*, 71–99 (§§12–15); *DMP*, 73–78/*PMD*, 80–85.

29. Subsequently, Marion will explicate Descartes's deconstruction and construction of Aristotelian οὐσία as (respectively) an elimination and a reduction of the categorial *ens*. Elimination, because "[e]ach time the *Regulae* evoke the *genus entis*, they eliminate it as radically as possible" (*DMP*, 75/ *PMD*, 82). Reduction, because in the *Regulae*, "the elimination of the *ens philosophicum* [of Aristotle] is reached only on a tangent and always admits a residue" in which "*ens* indicates purely and simply the lowest-level object [*l'objet minimum*] offered to the imaginative gaze of the mind, and it is enjoined to it [*il s'ordonne à lui*] all the more perfectly as it results from it" (*DMP*, 76/*PMD*, 83). Thus the *Regulae*'s "reduction of the *ens* to the lowest level of objectness" (*DMP*, 78/*PMD*, 85; "la réduction de l'*ens* à l'objectité minimale") reveals how Descartes's selective reworking of Aristotelian οὐσία in fact presupposes (ironically) the irreducibility of οὐσία, such that any attempt to eliminate it completely—even methodologically, as here—nonetheless fails because it "always admits a residue" (*l'objet minimum*) that cannot be completely subsumed by "the imaginative gaze of the mind."

30. So Graham Ward, "Introducing Jean-Luc Marion," *New Blackfriars* 76, no. 895 (July/Aug. 1995): 317–24, at 319. Ward explicitly links Marion's elaboration of this particular feature of Descartes's gray ontology with Derrida's playful pun on the word *déconstruction*: "Derrida always insists that *déconstruction* is also *de construction*" (ibid.).

31. Marion's claim that *mathesis universalis* is a "universal science" characterized by a "nonmathematical mathematicity" that as such "is universal only insofar as it is no longer purely mathematical" stands in direct contradiction to the venerable (and influential) interpretation of Gilson, for whom "the idea of the unity of science" in Descartes consists precisely in "the universalization of the mathematical method" (Étienne Gilson, *René Descartes, Discours de la méthode. Texte et commentaire* [Paris: Vrin, 1925; 4th ed., 1966], p. 152). Emmanuel Martineau, in light of "the demonstration by Marion of the 'meta-mathematicity' of *mathesis*" (alluding to *OG*, 64, which speaks of "a universal *mathesis*, a nonmathematical meta-mathematicity"), finds "the expression 'the universalization of the mathematical method'" in this passage from Gilson to be "extremely equivocal," since "Descartes, far from universal*izing* anything whatsoever, in establishing being in its Being as order [*en fixant l'étant dans son être comme ordre*] accedes on the contrary to universal*ity*, which is quite different, and signals the epagogic leap (in other words, the ontological leap)" (E. Martineau, "L'ontologie de l'ordre," *Les études philosophiques* 4 [1976]: 475–94, at 482–83; emphasis in the original). See also *OG*, 61, a text that seems to have Gilson's interpretation specifically in view: "By bringing out [*dégager*] the mathematicity of mathematics, Descartes—far from claiming to 'mathematize' all knowledge—undertakes the task of unearthing the secret that certainty and the organization of the sciences share in common. This secret, because it is prior to mathematics, is able to be extended beyond the region of mathematics."

32. Cf. Martineau, who asks whether there is at work in the *Regulae*, "if not a new concept of metaphysics, at least an actual ontological meditation." In response to his own question, he notes that "one massive fact, first of all, gives one good hope, a fact that Marion is the first one in France to highlight: 'universality' is the very ether in which the *Regulae* move" (Martineau, "L'ontologie de l'ordre," 476).

33. See *Rule VIII*, AT, X, 396.3–4: "veritatem propriè vel falsitatem non nisi *in solo intellectu* esse posse" ("there can be no truth or falsity in the strict sense except *in the intellect alone*"; PWD, I, 30; emphasis added).

34. On Marion's use of this metaphor in *OG*, see the comments of Desmond Clarke (*Studia Leibnitiana* 9, no. 1 [1977]: 121), who complains rather laconically that "there are some central theses in the book which might have been more perspicuous with a less metaphorical exposition. For example, the center of gravity along the subject–object relation (Ch. 1) . . . would . . . be considerably improved by more direct language." Yet given that Marion employs the "center of gravity" metaphor precisely to emphasize the profound *inversion* of the Aristotelian *ens inquantum ens* by the Cartesian *mathesis universalis*, with the result that *ens* is now dependent upon thought rather than the reverse, one is hard pressed to see what in the metaphor is objectionable or unclear—such that a nonmetaphorical substitute would convey a "more perspicuous" reading of Marion's argument. What could be "more perspicuous"—and therefore more faithful to Marion's central claim—than the image of radical *bouleversement* that is conjured by this metaphor?

35. J.-L. Marion, "Descartes et l'onto-théologie," *Bulletin de la Société Française de Philosophie* 76, no. 4 (1982): 117–71, at 155, n. 12.

36. Cf. DMP, 58–59 (mod.)/PMD, 64: "The Cartesian *prima philosophia* lays claim to metaphysical dignity, not by virtue of privileged beings, but, beyond them, by virtue of the arrangement in order [*la mise en ordre*], as the single correct determination of before and after, of the principle and the derivative. It claims that putting in order by and for the sake of making evident [*la mise en ordre par et pour la mise en évidence*] is enough to constitute a metaphysics; no recourse to an *ens in quantum ens* is needed. In Cartesian terms, this amounts to a *mathesis universalis*, in which being as known mimics, without ever being summed up in, being as being."

37. Marion depicts the purely epistemological primacy of *mathesis universalis* even more forcefully in DMP, 63/PMD, 68–69.

38. "Un néant d'ontologie" is the heading given to PMD, §6.

39. *Rule XII*, AT, X, 418.1–3: "Dicimus igitur primò, aliter spectandas esse res singulas in ordine ad cognitionem nostram, quam si de ijsdem loquamur prout revera existunt" ("First, when we consider things in the order that corresponds to our knowledge of them, our view must be different from what it would be if we were speaking of them in accordance with how they exist in reality"; PWD, I, 44). Cf. Marion's translation of this passage: "Nous disons donc premièrement, qu'il faut considérer chacune des

choses *quand elles sont ordonnées à notre connaissance* autrement, que si nous parlions des mêmes pour autant qu'elles existent réellement" ("We say, therefore, firstly, that one must consider otherwise each of the things *when they are ordered to our knowledge*, that if we were speaking of the same things insofar as they really exist"; *RUC*, 45; emphasis added). As the italicized passage indicates, Marion's rendering of *in ordine ad cognitionem nostram* construes the "ordering" of things by the mind, effected by the method, in a much more active sense than do the translators of *PWD*.

40. *RUC*, 238, n. 21. That "the required order is constituted first *in ordine ad cognitionem nostram*" (in the order that corresponds to our knowledge) states the "first precept of *Mathesis Universalis*" (ibid.).

41. At *RUC*, 238, n. 21, Marion identifies the *in ordine ad cognitionem nostram* (in the order that corresponds to our knowledge) of *Rule XII* (*AT*, X, 418.2) with the *aliquis ordo vel mensura examinatur, ad Mathesim referri* (a certain order or measure is examined, to be referred to as *Mathesis* of *Rule IV*; *AT*, X, 378.1–2). When one reads this last text, Marion tells us, "it is crucial to see that here it is a question of an order that could be other than it is, precisely because it results from an act of institution [*un établissement*"] (*RUC*, 159, n. 32).

42. "Fiction of thought": to illustrate "the alternative [that between the tacitly rejected natural order and the actively instituted methodic order], in which the *Regulae* undoubtedly allows to come to the surface the final thought that gives rise to them" (*OG*, 77), Marion goes on to cite a passage from *Rule X* (*AT*, X, 404.22–27), where Descartes states that we must "read into" nature an orderliness that is not inherently present in it. In commenting on this text, Marion concludes that for Descartes, "order must appear here, when indeed even the existing thing would not suffice to present it; in such a case, observation is committed to mastering a unique order [*un ordre seul*], one obtained by dint of the *cogitatio*, by a fiction of thought—a manufactured fiction of an order where none appeared, but one that is never understood as a falsifying order" (ibid.).

43. Cf. *DMP*, 145/*PMD*, 155, where Marion identifies this transition as "the principle presupposed by *all* [his emphasis] the metaphysics of modernity."

44. A controversy made famous, for example, by the views of Gilson on the one hand, and of Brunschvicg on the other. For a brief summary of the specifics of the debate, along with representative texts, see Martineau, "L'ontologie de l'ordre," 484–85.

45. Cf. *DMP*, 82/*PMD*, 88, where Marion asks: "Shouldn't it therefore be admitted, once and for all, that the Cartesian enterprise decidedly does *not* [his emphasis] belong to metaphysics?" Although he admits that such a conclusion "would join up with the opinions of certain celebrated commentators who insist on emphasizing in Descartes the end of all 'realism' and the commencement of a pure reign of 'consciousness' [L. Liard; see ibid., n.

22], or who deplore in him a 'degradation' [J. Maritain; see ibid., n. 22] of ancient philosophy" (*DMP*, 82/*PMD*, 88), nevertheless Marion contends that "it is not acceptable to give in to this all too simple conclusion" (*DMP*, 82/ *PMD*, 89).

46. Martineau discerns in this text a "remarkable formula, but one that does not fully satisfy me" ("L'ontologie de l'ordre," 485) because, in describing the duplication of orders thus instituted as a *problem* (namely, "the problem of a gap between two orders"; *OG*, 78, n. 17), Marion's text can be read as implying that this duplication constitutes a (for Martineau, nonexistent) difficulty in Descartes's thought that awaits a solution in his more mature work: "Marion seems to maintain that the duplication of orders in fact poses a difficulty, and that the latter awaits a solution; it being insinuated (the reader may well think) that the *Méditations* and the *Responses* will end up by solving this difficulty. Now, it is the necessity of just such a presupposition that I wish to revoke in doubt" (ibid.). For his part, Martineau claims that "it is nothing but natural that the author of the *Regulae* should profess a deliberate—not to say provocative—dualism," for the simple reason that "there is not a *problem of order* [in the *Regulae*], but *a question of the way* that leads up to Being" (ibid., 490; emphasis in the original).

47. J.-L. Marion, "What Is the Method in the Metaphysics? The Role of the Simple Natures in the *Meditations*," in *CQ*, 43–66, at 47/*QC*, 75–109, at 81 (hereafter cited parenthetically by page number).

48. The hermeneutic importance Marion attaches to "the very schizocosmenia that presides over the bifurcation of order" (*OG*, 78) can be glimpsed by comparing the title of *OG*, §14 ("La subversion de l'ordre: 'οὐσία' relativisée") with that of its earlier recension ("Le dés/ordre comme le *totius artis secretum*"), in J.-L. Marion, "Ordre et relation: Sur la situation aristotélicienne de la théorie cartésienne de l'ordre selon les *Regulae* V et VI," *Archives de philosophie* 37 (1974): 243–74, at 258 (title for §3). Given that Marion regards the principle *Rule VI* sets forth of a consciously *imposed* epistemological order—Descartes's *artis secretum* (*AT*, X, 381.8)—as so central for understanding the project of the *Regulae* that in a later work he can say of the *artis secretum* that it "sums up the entire *Regulae*" (*DMP*, 62/*PMD*, 68), the two formulations of *OG*, §14, and "Ordre et relation," §3, if equivalent, suggest what is truly at stake for Marion in thematizing Cartesian *schizocosmie* ("Le dés/ordre"): namely, the wholesale sidelining of οὐσία ("'οὐσία' relativisée") that is tacitly presupposed by the *totius artis secretum*.

49. Jean-Robert Armogathe, "Sémanthèse d'IDÉE/IDEA chez Descartes," in *IDEA: VI Colloquio internazionale del Lessico intellettuale europeo, January 5–7, 1989*, in the series Lessico Intellettuale Europeo, ed. M. Fattori and M. L. Bianchi (Rome: Edizioni dell'Ateneo, Centro di Studio del CNR, 1990), pp. 187–205, cited by Marion in *CQ*, 171, n. 2/*QC*, 76, n. 2.

50. That is, in the *Meditationes*, "The idea determines thought through the action of thinking, rather than [as with Aristotle] determining the thing

directly according to its essence" (*CQ*, 45 [mod.]/*QC*, 78). Marion sees in this development "an irreversible shift of the center of gravity [*Ainsi le centre de gravité s'est-il déplacé irréversiblement*]: the idea informs the raw material [*le matériau*] — that is, thought — rather than the matter [*la matière*] of the thing itself" (*CQ*, 45 [mod.]/*QC*, 79). By the metaphorization of schizocosmenia, Descartes "displaces" enmattered being by transferring its "form" to the "matter" of thought; with this *déplacement*, form (*idea*, εἶδος) no longer informs Aristotelian ὕλη (*la matière*), but Cartesian *pensée* (*le matériau*).

51. Respectively, *CQ*, 44 (mod.), 45 (mod.), 46/*QC*, 76, 78, 80.

52. The *natura simplicissima* (*Rule VIII*, AT, X, 399.17) is distinguished from the *natura simplex* (*Rule XII*, AT, X, 418–28, passim) only verbally; Descartes uses the former expression to stress the self-evident character of the noncomposite *natura simplex* (see *Rule VIII*, AT, X, 399.5–21). Cf. *OG*, 135–36: "In the phrase *natura simplicissima*, therefore, simplicity signifies the sizing up [*le calibrage*] of the thing by and for evidence, a calibration that enables only the intelligible nature (according to the new meaning of that term) to subsist as a result of it. . . . [T]he simple natures do not constitute the elements of the objective world; they constitute, rather, the most simple (=intelligible) terms for the construction of an intelligible model — a model that is in no way 'real' — of the phenomenal world."

53. For Marion's extremely detailed exposition of this reworking, see *OG*, 113–48 (§§18–24), "chap. 3: The Deconstruction of the [εἶδος and the Construction of the Object."

54. *CQ*, 47 (mod.)/*QC*, 82: "Cette nature résulte donc de la connaissance, loin de la normer: en tant qu'objet connaissable, objet précisément en tant que connaissable, elle se substitue donc à l'οὐσία, qu'elle [la nature simple] exclut définitivement de la métaphysique moderne. . . ." *Caveat lector*: The English translation provided in *CQ* is seriously misleading at this point in the text; I have emended it considerably in order to convey Marion's meaning with the requisite precision.

55. See also *DMP*, 79/*PMD*, 86: "the simple natures, which, *by definition*, are completely and perfectly knowable" (emphasis added).

56. See *RUC*, 238, n. 21.

57. For the copious references to Descartes's texts adduced in support of this point, see ibid., n. 46.

58. Cf. *DMP*, 92/*PMD*, 99: "[F]or Descartes the *ens* is not defined in its relationship with φύσις, but uniquely and sufficiently according to objectivity [*l'objectivité*]."

59. Cf. *DMP*, 75 (mod.)/*PMD*, 81: "the simple natures, which are simple, or better, which are quite simply, only inasmuch as they are diverted [*détournées*] from what they are *revera*; they are, in a word, only "respectu intellectus nostri" ([AT, X] 418.9; 419.6–7 = [*PWD*, I] 44; [*PWD*, I] 44).

60. Cf. *DMP*, 75/*PMD*, 82: For Descartes, "Knowledge begins when there disappear, as determining authorities, the matter and therefore the

form that, each time, "specialize" it [the extramental *res*], specify it, give it *forma* and *essentia*, εἶδος and therefore οὐσία. Knowledge begins when the *res* loses all its own essence, therefore when the order imposed by the *ens* and its different meanings is effaced."

61. Cf. *OG*, 189: From the moment it is subjected to the *Regulae*'s schizocosmenia, "the thing loses its rights over itself in the following way: each of its 'causes' is mortgaged in order to benefit the *Ego* [*au profit de l'Ego*]; the thing, losing its self-referential sufficiency, loses all immediacy to Being, in a relation that the imposed *Ego* mediates (being—*Ego*—only known οὐσία/ Being)."

62. That is, the simple natures are "perfectly" constructed in the twofold sense of being (1) "wholly constructed" and (2) "constructed without defect." The second sense is consequent upon the first, in that the flawless character of the simple nature—its transparent intelligibility—is due to its having been entirely produced by the intuitive mind and its methodic gaze.

63. J.-L. Marion, "Descartes à l'encontre d'Aristote," in *Aristote aujourd'hui*, ed. M. A. Sinaceur (Toulouse: Érès, and Paris: UNESCO, 1988), pp. 326–30, at p. 327. For the French text and the fuller context of this citation, see note 65.

64. Ibid., p. 328. Cf. *DMP*, 90–91/*PMD*, 98.

65. "*Grâce* à la permanence du site aristotélicien, comme métaphysique (et non pas seulement *malgré* elle), la nouveauté cartésienne devient précisément mesurable. C'est donc la constitution aristotélicienne de la métaphysique qui peut et doit introduire dans la nouveauté selon laquelle Descartes reprend les lieux aristotéliciens, les déplace, et donc les (re)pense. A l'encontre d'Aristote, donc à sa rencontre" (Marion, "Descartes à l'encontre d'Aristote," p. 327; emphasis in the original). ("*Thanks* to the permanence of the Aristotelian site, as metaphysics (and not only *in spite of* it), the Cartesian novelty becomes clearly measurable. Hence it is the Aristotelian constitution of metaphysics that can and must usher in the novelty according to which Descartes takes up the Aristotelian topoi, displaces them, and therefore (re)thinks them: against Aristotle, thereby encountering him.")

66. Following the lead of Jeffrey Kosky, I translate Marion's *la reconduction* somewhat woodenly in this context as "reconduction" in order to make clear Marion's intention to highlight its literal, etymological sense of "leading back." See, for example, *PMD*, 98: "Voici le point décisif où tout se retourne: la réduction cartésienne du monde advenant à son statut réduit et conditionnel d'objet ne déserte pas totalement la reconduction du monde à son statut d'étant, mais la répète à un déplacement près" (*DMP*, 90: "Here is the decisive point about which everything else revolves: the Cartesian reduction of the world to its reduced and conditional status as object does not totally abandon reconducting the world to the status of being; it repeats it, with a slight displacement").

67. This particular feature of the *Regulae*'s gray ontology, in which the Being of beings is re(con)duc(t)ed to the status of an object, Marion names

the *objectité* ("objectness" or "objectity") of the object. See, for example, *DMP*, 92–93/*PMD*, 100.

68. *OG*, 151: "Whence the surprising face of the semantics for the term ὑποκείμενον. . . . The ὑποκείμενον can only be relieved [*se destituer*] of possessing any self-sufficient substrate (-κείμενον), since knowledge only proceeds by making a complete abstraction from it; there remains, besides this impossible subsistence [*demeurance*], only submission (ὑπο-), but one in which the direction is inverted: no longer a presence, or a substrate, of a certain irreducible (and perhaps irreducibly unknowable) thing, but a being-put-at-the-disposal [*mise à la disposition*] of a higher authority; *subject* [Marion's emphasis], originally from substrate, comes to designate *a subjection* of the substrate" (my emphasis).

69. Already in *L'idole et la distance*, Marion will associate "the human gaze" (*le regard humain*) with the production of "a conceptual idol" (*IAD*, 13/ *ID*, 31).

70. In this text, Marion understands the *objectum purae Matheseos* of the *Meditationes* (*AT*, VII, 71.8 and 15; 74.2; 80.9–10) to refer "to what *Regula IV* names a *Mathesis valde diversa a vulgari*" (*AT*, X, 376.4), namely, the *Mathesis universalis* that has as *objectum* (378.3) ". . . illa omnia tantum in quibus aliquis ordo vel mensura examinatur" (*AT*, X, 377.23–378.1) (*DMP*, 91, n. 34/ *PMD*, 98, n. 34). Subsequently, however, in a more recently published essay, he appears to qualify this judgment: "There is an unavoidable connection here with the *mathesis universalis* of *Rule IV*, but it does not follow that the two notions are identical. The *mathesis* of the 1641 meditations (which is *not* [Marion's emphasis] characterized as "universal") is explicitly restricted to the material (and common) simple natures, and involves the use of imagination, whereas the *mathesis* of the 1627 *Regulae*, explicitly described as *universalis*, extended in principle (if not de facto) to all the simple natures, including the intellectual ones. The restricted scope of this science or *mathesis* in the *Meditations* nevertheless goes hand in hand with an enlarging of the effective use made of the simple natures" (*CQ*, 174, n. 22; cf. the earlier, slightly different version of this footnote in *QC*, 95–96, n. 20).

71. Marion follows Heidegger in regarding the "subjectity" of modern subjectivity as less a psychological phenomenon (in which human consciousness suddenly becomes more aware of itself) than a metaphysical phenomenon (in which one particular "subject"—understood in the older sense of *hypokeimenon*—decides to privilege itself as the organizing polestar for all knowledge, and ultimately for all being). See, for example, *OG*, 188.

72. Marion's playfulness here is difficult to convey in translation; the French text of this passage reads: "Descartes, et par lui la pensée moderne, n'aborde la chose qu'en y 'regardant précisément la chose qui lui est obje(c)t(ée), *rem sibi objectam*' (*Rule XII* [*AT*, X], 423.2–3), la chose en tant qu'objet. L'objet se résume en ce que le regard de l'esprit admet dans le domaine de son évidence; et donc il ne recouvre de la chose initiale que ce que le jeu composé des natures simples en saisit, et en propose au regard."

73. In his French translation of Descartes's *Regulae* (*RUC*, "Annexe I," pp. 295–302), Marion insists that "despite the authority of almost all the translators since Victor Cousin" (ibid., 302), *intuitus* must be rendered as *le regard* if Descartes's meaning is to be preserved and accurately conveyed.

74. Once again, in this passage, the reader encounters yet another instance in which the playfulness of Marion's French is nearly untranslatable: *intuitus* refers to "un regard qui garde à vue l'objet" (a gaze that keeps its object in view), that is, "[un regard qui] garde sous sa vue la chose qu'il met en évidence" ([a gaze that] keeps within its sight the thing that it places in evidence; *RUC*, "Annexe I," p. 302). Marion's phrasing, which plays with the polysemy of the verb *garder* (= "to keep," but also "to guard; to look after"), and with the relation of *garder* to its cognate noun, *le regard* ("gaze; look; stare; regard"), suggests a certain vigilance and resoluteness that is consistent with the willfulness required of the idolatrous: *intuitus*, one might say, is "the regard that stands guard" over its arraigned object.

75. *OG*, 181 ("la déréalisation de la chose en un objet"); by this intriguing turn of phrase, Marion means to indicate the removal of the *res* from the thing that is carried out by the gaze when it constricts the being of the *ens* by regarding it solely as a representable *objectum*. The intuitive gaze brings about "the transformation (or, rather, the a-formation'; that is, the disappearance of the form) of the given, individual thing. By means of an abstraction, the thing is reduced to that which thought can accept from it, as the object of thought" (*OG*, 62, n. 70: "la transformation (ou plutôt la disparition de la forme, l'a-formation) de la chose donnée et individuelle qui, par abstraction, se réduit à ce que la pensée peut admettre en elle pour son objet").

76. As indeed even a cursory reading of *Sur la théologie blanche de Descartes* will confirm, a crucial element of Marion's interpretation of Descartes gains its very point of departure by reflecting on the *irreducible* distinction Descartes insists on making between philosophy and theology. Moreover, according to Marion, Descartes's insistence on the irreducibility of this distinction condemns to failure—even while, paradoxically, it constitutes—his attempt to rescue the Christian theological tradition from its own idolatrous embrace of univocity. Thus if we see in the *Regulae* a Descartes who is veering toward idolatry, in the letters to Mersenne of 1630 we find another Descartes: namely, one who seeks to overcome idolatry (at least in part), but lacks the conceptual tools to do so—and thereby furthers the very idolatry he seeks to overcome (see *TB*, 27–159, "Livre I: L'analogie perdue de Suarez à Galilée," sec. 1, "L'achèvement théologique de l'analogie et la critique cartésienne de l'univocité de l'*ens*").

77. *BG*, "Preface to the American Translation," p. x.

78. *IAD*, xxxvii/*ID*, 13. The full text reads: "I mobilize here a precise conceptual pair, idol/icon, without giving it a sufficient phenomenological and cultural description: I freely admit this. And not without a certain vio-

lence, I transpose this pair from the properly cultural domain into the conceptual domain" (*IAD*, xxxvi–xxxvii/*ID*, 13). In applying this text to the argument presented in *God Without Being*, I assume that the latter may be said to have supplied the requisite "phenomenological and cultural description" of the idol/icon omitted from *L'idole et la distance*, even while it has carried over the "violence" originally enacted there by the transposition of the idol/icon "from the properly cultural domain into the conceptual domain."

79. Cf. *GWB*, 7/*DSE*, 15: "The idol does not indicate, any more than the icon, a particular being or even class of beings. Icon and idol indicate a manner of being for beings, or at least for some of them."

80. Marion follows Heidegger in construing "the theo-logy of metaphysics" as a "the*io*-logy" (a neologism derived from the Greek term for the divine, Tὸ Θεῖον) that, as such, provides the constitutive ground (*Verfassung*) of all beings without restricting the actual content of this ground to a specific ontic instance in which this constitution is exhibited (cf. *TB*, 447: "Following Heidegger, I admit that metaphysics, according to its essential constitution, deploys the ambivalence of an ontology and a the[i]ology"; *TB*, 448: "[T]he theology of an onto-theology consists as much in a the*io*logy — that is, in a search for the divine (Tὸ Θεῖον) — as it does in theology, which, strictly speaking, is a search for the god(s), or even God. What is meant by 'the divine'? Precisely those privileged beings that are able to secure the role of serving as a principle for other beings: the*io*logy inquires after first principles, to the extent that these principles exist as beings." Thus in *DMP*, 95–103/*PMD*, 103–11, for example, Marion sets forth his reasoning as to why the Cartesian *ego* of the *Meditationes* is legitimately interpreted as an instance of this constitution (see esp. *DMP*, 98/*PMD*, 106). Marion sees this the*io*-logic constitution at work already in the *Regulae* (albeit still only in an implicit manner) insofar as the *Regulae*'s gray ontology reconducts all beings in their Being to the status of "object" for the *mens humana* as its *cogitata* (*DMP*, 96/*PMD*, 104). On the implicit the*io*logy of gray ontology, which as yet lacks a rigorously identified ontic foundation in the *Regulae*, see *TB*, 449 (citing *OG*, 67 and 69, at 449, n. 4). On why such the*io*-logy is more accurately termed a "constitution" rather than a "structure," see *OG*, 194, n. 12.

81. *GWB*, 12 (emphasis added)/*DSE*, 21.

82. *ITN*, 34 (mod.)/*DS*, 181/*IE*, 150 (mod.).

83. *Rule XII*, *AT*, X, 423.3; *PWD*, I, 47.

84. "Now, conceiving the world also implies producing it: producing a world, instead of articulating [*dire*] *this* world [Marion's emphasis], splitting the world into a real but unknown or ill-known world and a world that is radically knowable precisely because produced insofar as it is known — this is the function of ideology" (*PC*, 33 [mod.]/*PAC*, 47).

85. "Why do we appeal to technology? Because it constitutes, par excellence, the form of rationality that, at the terminal point of metaphysics, submits beings in their totality to man as their master and possessor. How?

By substituting another world for the world such as it is. This substitution clearly assumes no falsification, for it goes back to the conditions for the possibility of modern science itself. Ever since Galileo, and metaphysically with Descartes, the human mind postulates that "when we consider things in the order that corresponds to our knowledge of them, our view of them must be different from what it would be if we were speaking of them in accordance with how they exist in reality [*Rule XII, AT,* X, 418.1–3; *PWD,* I, 44]. The conditions for certain and evident knowledge refer things to the *mens humana,* to the point of distinguishing them from the essence, as it were, that constitutes them in themselves. . . . Henceforward, the essence of technology appears to precede the empirical practice of the technologies. In other words, the various technologies would not produce any (technological) object if, first of all, the essence of technology—science as method, and not as contemplation of *ousia*—did not constitute the parameters of clear and distinct knowledge as sole reality. In short, technology, considered in its essence, deploys a rationality that depends entirely on the *ego cogitans*" (*PC,* 35–36/*PAC,* 49–50). In this quotation, the influence of Heidegger's "Die Frage nach der Technik" is evident enough.

86. For the meaning of "a-formation," see note 75, above.

87. Thus, in following out the phenomenological analysis of the idol and the icon presented in *God Without Being,* one may conclude that it is not the gaze per se that renders gray ontology idolatrous, but rather its restricted scope that desires to see only itself. On this point, see the recent essay, "What Love Knows," in *PC,* 153–69 (at 164–65): "How do we distinguish the other from an object, supposing that we go about this conscientiously? By noting that the object regards us not, while the other does. The object certainly 'regards' us, in the sense that it 'concerns' us, and eventually becomes of interest to us, which is to say, is able even to arouse our desire. But regarding us in that sense only signifies that we feel the weight of our own interest weighing upon us, reflected back by the object upon which it exerts itself. We certainly take an interest in this object, but always through our desire with respect to it, so that we experience our desire reflected by it, more than we experience it itself; or rather, this object is worthy of its name (that which opposes itself to us) only insofar as it reflects and sends back to us our desire. The object regards itself, but sends back to us only our own 'regard,' our own gaze, like a mirror (or, let us say, an idol). *The other, in contrast, modifies from top to bottom the rules for the exercise of the gaze*: he, and he alone, opposes a gaze to my gaze; he no longer passively reflects my gaze, like an eventually unfaithful object of my desire, but is always its faithful mirror; he responds to my gaze not with a reflection of my own, but with another gaze. *The other, or the uncontrollable gaze*" (emphasis added). See also *IAD,* 66/*ID,* 91: "The danger of the person consists in the fact that the person is never possessed, never fixed, never represented."

88. In its original context, the question inquires after the idolatrous implications of the Nietzschean will to power: "*Dasein,* as will to power, must,

in all its forms (above all in the capacity of an organism), receive a perspective from a gaze" (*IAD*, 39/*ID*, 63). As part of his response to this question, Marion shows that the conceptual idolater need not aspire to divinity in order to covet its prerogatives: "Would one have to become a god in order that, at the heart of nihilism, things should again become a 'world'? . . . To evaluate the world is the very act of a god; or better—to evaluate is the act in which man and world assume a finally divine face. It is not necessary to be, or to replace, the idolatrous 'God' in order to play this game—on the contrary. For this game renders divine only those who play it with uncovered face—not idolatrously" (*IAD*, 39–40/*ID*, 64).

Chapter 2. I Am, I Exist
Lilian Alweiss

I should like to thank the Irish Reseach Council for the Humanities and Social Sciences for awarding me a fellowship for the academic year 2003/4, which made this research possible. I should also like to thank Ian Leask for his advice and support throughout.

1. Descartes, Letter to Mersenne, May 25, 1637, *AT*, I, 376. Not included in the English translation; cited in *MP*, 131.

2. Ibid.

3. Cf. J. Hintikka "*Cogito, Ergo Sum*: Inference or Performance?" in *Descartes: A Collection of Critical Essays*, ed. Willis Doney (Garden City, N.Y.: Anchor Books, 1967), pp.108–39. It is surprising not to find a single reference to this article in Marion's work, considering that his reading is virtually identical to that of Hintikka.

4. Cf. Hobbes's "Objections to *Second Meditation*," *AT*, VII, 172; and Gassendi's, *AT*, VII, 259.

5. *AT*, VII, 259; also cited by Hintikka, "*Cogito, Ergo Sum*," p. 112.

6. *Nouveaux essais* [1704], trans. A. G. Langley (La Salle, Ill.: Open Court, 1949), IV, 7, sec. 7; cited by Hintikka, "*Cogito, Ergo Sum*," p. 113.

7. It is worth noting Descartes's response to this: "When someone says 'I am thinking, therefore I am, or I exist,' he does not deduce existence from thought by means of a syllogism, but recognizes it as something self-evident by a simple intuition of the mind. This is clear from the fact that if he were deducing it by means of a syllogism, he would have to have had previous knowledge of the major premise: 'Everything which thinks is, or exists'; yet in fact he learns it from experiencing in his own case that it is impossible that he should think without existing. It is in the nature of our mind to construct general propositions on the basis of our knowledge of particular ones" (*AT*, VII, 140/1). He thus does not argue that the 'ergo' here should be understood syllogistically. Yet as Bernard Williams observes in his *Descartes: The Project of Pure Enquiry* (Harmondsworth, U.K.: Penguin/Hassocks, U.K.: Harvester Press, 1978), p. 89, "since not all inferences are syllogistic, the possibility remains open that the cogito is some other sort of inference." Indeed, it could be understood as an explication.

8. Heidegger, *Being and Time*, trans. John Macquarrie and Edward Robinson (Oxford: Basil Blackwell, 1962), §10, pp. 45–46.

9. Hintikka, "*Cogito, Ergo Sum*," p. 122.

10. Cf. ibid., p. 118.

11. Ibid., p. 121. Emphasis added.

12. Ibid., p. 128. Bernard Williams (*Descartes*, p.74) refers to a pragmatically self-defeating or self-falsifying contradiction that should not be confused with a logical contradiction.

13. Hintikka, "*Cogito, Ergo Sum*," p. 139.

14. Ludwig Wittgenstein, *Tractatus Logico-Philosophicus*, trans. D. F. Pears and B. F. McGuinness (London: Routledge, 1958), pp. 116–17, 5.633.

15. Ibid., 5.641.

16. Marion is indebted to the thought of Michel Henry, who equally sought to show that the reflectivity of thought is not crucial for Descartes. Cf. Marion's "Générosité et phénoménologie: Remarques sur l'intérpretation du *Cogito* cartésienne par M. Henry," *Les études philosophiques* 1 (1988): 51–72/CQ, 96–117.

17. Marion here believes that intentional thought is necessarily representative or reflexive. Indeed, this is a view that Edmund Husserl tried to establish, even though he was not able to uphold it. Yet, as I argue below, intentionality can also be nonreflexive. See also Lilian Alweiss, *The World Unclaimed: A Challenge to Heidegger's Critique of Husserl* (Athens: Ohio University Press, 2003), chap. 2, §§42–43, 90–97.

18. Jean-Paul Sartre, *Being and Nothingness: An Essay on Phenomenological Ontology*, trans. Hazel Barnes (London: Routledge, 1969), p. xxix; emphasis added.

19. Jean-Paul Sartre, *Transcendence of the Ego: An Existentialist Theory of Consciousness*, trans. Forrest Williams and Robert Kirkpatrick (New York: Octagon Books, 1957), p. 49. This position is close to Hume's notion of personal identity, according to which there is no permanent self that accompanies all my perceptions. See Hume's *Treatise of Human Nature*, sec. VI, "Of Personal Identity."

20. Sartre, *Transcendence of the Ego*, p. xxx.

21. Ibid.

22. "*I am thinking, therefore I exist*" (AT, VI, 32–33).

23. Hintikka, "*Cogito, Ergo Sum*," p. 120.

24. It is curious to see that this insight has influenced both Nietzscheans and positivists. For Nietzsche, the view that there is thinking in the same way as there is a lighting was crucial, since he wished to break causal reasoning by postulating that there is a deed without a doer or becoming without being. For positivists such as Mach or Schlick, it was of importance because it pointed to the neutrality of experience.

Chapter 3. Hubris and Humility: Husserl's Reduction and Givenness
Timothy Mooney

1. These remarks show my deep indebtedness to Merleau-Ponty's "The Philosopher and His Shadow," in *Signs*, trans. Richard C. McCleary (Evanston, Ill.: Northwestern University Press, 1964), p. 160/"Le philosophe et son ombre," in *Signes* (Paris: Gallimard, 1960), p. 202. I am similarly indebted to Derrida's early studies cited below.

2. *Reduction and Givenness*, trans. Thomas A. Carlson (Evanston, Ill.: Northwestern University Press, 1998), pp. 4, 11–13/*Réduction et donation* (Paris: Presses Universitaires de France, 1989), pp. 11–12, 22–24. Hereafter abbreviated as *RG* and *RD*, respectively.

3. *Logical Investigations*, trans. J. N. Findlay and ed. Dermot Moran, 2 vols. (London: Routledge, 2001), vol. 1, pp.168, 178. Hereafter abbreviated as *LI*, followed by the volume number/*Husserliana* XIX/1, *Logische Untersuchungen*, vol. II/I, ed. Ursula Panzer (The Hague: Martinus Nijhoff, 1984), pp. 10, 27. Hereafter abbreviated as *Hua* XIX/1.

4. *LI* 2, 278–79/*Husserliana* XIX/2, *Logische Untersuchungen*, vol. II/2, ed. Ursula Panzer (The Hague: Martinus Nijhoff, 1984), pp. 668–69. Hereafter abbreviated as *Hua* XIX/2.

5. *LI* 2, 273, 312/*Hua* XIX/2, 660, 721.

6. *LI* 1, 194/*Hua* XIX/1, 47; *RG*, 23/*RD*, 39.

7. *RG*, 25, 34–35/*RD*, 42–43, 56.

8. *RG*, 15, 30/*RD*, 28, 50–51.

9. *LI* 2, 83/*Hua* XIX/1, 359–60.

10. *RG*, 33–34/*RD*, 54–55.

11. *LI* 2, 206–7/*Hua* XIX/2, 566–67.

12. *RG*, 32–33/*RD*, 53.

13. Ibid. See also *RG*, 53/*RD*, 85–86.

14. *Being Given: Toward a Phenomenology of Givenness*, trans. Jeffrey L. Kosky (Stanford, Calif.: Stanford University Press, 2002), p. 20/*Étant donné: Essai d'une phénoménologie de la donation* (Paris: Presses Universitaires de France, 1997), pp. 32–33. Hereafter abbreviated as *BG* and *ED*, respectively.

15. *The Idea of Phenomenology*, trans. William Alston and George Nakhnikian (The Hague: Martinus Nijhoff, 1964), p. 49/*Husserliana* II, *Die Idee der Phänomenologie*, 2nd ed., ed. Walter Biemel (The Hague: Martinus Nijhoff, 1958), p. 61. Hereafter abbreviated as *IOP* and *Hua* II, respectively. Quoted in *RG*, 53/*RD*, 85–86.

16. *IOP*, 59/*Hua* II, 74.

17. *The Crisis of European Sciences and Transcendental Phenomenology*, trans. David Carr (Evanston, Ill.: Northwestern University Press, 1970), p. 234/*Husserliana* VI, *Die Krisis der europäischen Wissenschaften und die transzendentale Phänomenologie*, 2nd ed., ed. Walter Biemel (The Hague: Martinus Nijhoff, 1962), p. 237. Hereafter abbreviated as *CES* and *Hua* VI, respectively.

18. Translation slightly emended.
19. *CES*, 217, n. 31/*Hua* VI, 81, n. 31.
20. *Ideas Pertaining to a Pure Phenomenology and to a Phenomenological Philosophy, First Book*, trans. Fred Kersten (The Hague: Martinus Nijhoff, 1982), p. 44/*Husserliana* III.1, *Ideen zu einer reinen Phänomenologie und phänomenologischen Philosophie: Erstes Buch*, rev. ed., ed. Karl Schuhmann (The Hague: Martinus Nijhoff, 1976), p. 51. Hereafter abbreviated as *IDS* I and *Hua* III.1, respectively.
21. *LI* 2, 338 (translation emended)/*Hua* XIX/2, 756–57.
22. *BG*, 12–13/*ED*, 21–22.
23. *RG*, 50–51, 53/*RD*, 81–82, 86; *BG*, 13–14/*ED*, 22–23.
24. *IOP*, 3, 7, 8/*Hua* II, 5, 9, 11; *IDS* I, 96–97/*Hua* III.1, 93.
25. *RG*, 53/*RD*, 85–86; *BG*, 23–26/*ED*, 37–40.
26. *IDS* I, 101, 110–11/*Hua* III.1, 97, 104–5.
27. *RG*, 23/*RD*, 40; *LI* 1, 194/*Hua* XIX/1, 47.
28. *BG*, 194–95, 222/*ED*, 273–74, 310–11.
29. *IDS* I, 153–56/*Hua* III.1, 141–44.
30. *IOP*, 59 (translation slightly emended)/*Hua* II, 74.
31. *BG*, 32–33/*ED*, 49–50.
32. *IDS* I, 93/*Hua* III.1, 90.
33. *RG*, 56, 62/*RD*, 90, 97.
34. *Cartesian Meditations*, trans. Dorion Cairns (The Hague: Martinus Nijhoff, 1960), pp. 40, 44–45/*Husserliana* I, *Cartesianische Meditationen und Pariser Vorträge*, 2nd ed., ed. Stephen Strasser (The Hague: Martinus Nijhoff, 1963), pp. 78, 82–83. Hereafter abbreviated as *CM* and *Hua* I, respectively.
35. One interpretation of the panopticon "broadened to the dimensions of the world" is that it refers to the reduction of all possible experiences of individual beings to spatiotemporal form. The possibility of intellectual or mystical intuitions would be closed off in advance. But it seems to me that Marion does not pursue these last routes in the works under consideration, and cannot do so without abandoning phenomenology altogether. His remark that the horizon assigns the nonvisible to this or that focal point suggests that the panopticon is invoked in a literal sense, as a worldview from everywhere in sensuous intuition and imagination. Drawing on Husserl, Maurice Merleau-Ponty criticizes the "view from everywhere" hypothesis, arguing that it is in effect a view from nowhere. See *Phenomenology of Perception*, trans. Colin Smith (London: Routledge and Kegan Paul, 1962), pp. 67–72/*Phénoménologie de la perception* (Paris: Gallimard, 1945), pp. 81–86.
36. *Phenomenological Psychology*, trans. John Scanlon (The Hague: Martinus Nijhoff, 1977), p. 66 (translation emended)/*Husserliana* IX, *Phänomenologische Psychologie*, ed. Walter Biemel (The Hague: Martinus Nijhoff, 1968), p. 88. Hereafter abbreviated as *PP* and *Hua* IX, respectively.
37. *RG*, 16–17/*RD*, 29–30.

38. *RG*, 201/*RD*, 301; *BG*, 249–51/*ED*, 344–47.

39. *BG*, 267, 370, n. 31/*ED*, 368, 368, n. 2. See also *Experience and Judgment*, ed. Ludwig Landgrebe, trans. James S. Churchill and Karl Ameriks (Evanston, Ill.: Northwestern University Press, 1973), p. 77/*Erfahrung und Urteil*, ed. Ludwig Landgrebe (Hamburg: Meiner, 1999), p. 81.

40. *RG*, 204–5/*RD*, 305.

41. "The Saturated Phenomenon," trans. Thomas A. Carlson, *Philosophy Today*, 40 (1996): 103–24/"Le phénomène saturé," in *Phénoménologie et théologie*, ed. Jean-François Courtine (Paris: Criterion, 1992), pp. 79–128.

42. *BG*, 218/*ED*, 303–4.

43. *BG*, 213–14, 215–16/*ED*, 298–99, 301.

44. *BG*, 209–11, 217, 226/*ED*, 293–96, 302, 315.

45. *BG*, 220–21/*ED*, 307–9.

46. *On the Phenomenology of the Consciousness of Internal Time (1893–1917)*, trans. John Barnett Brough (Dordrecht: Kluwer, 1991), pp. 48–49/*Husserliana X, Zur Phänomenologie des inneren Zeitbewusstseins (1893–1917)*, ed. Rudolf Boehm (The Hague: Martinus Nijhoff, 1966), p. 47. Hereafter abbreviated as *PCIT* and *Hua* X, respectively.

47. *PCIT*, 42, 84–85, 88/*Hua* X, 40, 80–81, 83.

48. *PCIT*, 30–31/*Hua* X, 28–29.

49. *BG*, 32–33/*ED*, 50.

50. *BG*, 9–10, 16, 26–27/*ED*, 15–17, 26–27, 41–42.

51. "Foundational Investigations of the Phenomenological Origin of the Spatiality of Nature," trans. Fred Kersten, in *Husserl: Shorter Works*, ed. Peter McCormick and Frederick A. Elliston (Notre Dame, Ind.: University of Notre Dame Press, 1981), pp. 230–31/"Grundlegende Untersuchungen zum phänomenologischen Ursprung der Räumlichkeit der Natur," in *Philosophical Essays in Memory of Edmund Husserl*, ed. Marvin Farber (Cambridge Mass.: Harvard University Press, 1940), p. 324. Hereafter abbreviated as *FI* and *GU*, respectively. See also *CM*, 83–84/*Hua* I, 116–17.

52. *Formal and Transcendental Logic*, trans. Dorion Cairns (The Hague: Martinus Nijhoff, 1969), p. 237/*Husserliana* XVII, *Formale und transzendentale Logik*, ed. Paul Janssen (The Hague: Martinus Nijhoff, 1974), pp. 243–44. See also 244/251. Hereafter abbreviated as *FTL* and *Hua* XVII, respectively.

53. *FTL*, 250–51/*Hua* XVII, 221–22.

54. *FTL*, 251/*Hua* XVII, 222.

55. *Writing and Difference*, trans. Alan Bass (Chicago: University of Chicago Press, 1978), pp. 131–32/*L'écriture et la différence* (Paris: Seuil, 1967), pp. 192–94. Hereafter abbreviated as *WD* and *EDF*, respectively.

56. *IDS* I, 58–59, 61/*Hua* III.1, 63, 65.

57. *CM*, 151/*Hua* I, 177.

58. *History of the Concept of Time: Prolegomena*, trans. Theodore Kisiel (Bloomington: Indiana University Press, 1992), p. 113/*Gesamtausgabe 20.*

Prolegomena zur Geschichte des Zeitbegriffs, ed. Petra Jaeger (Frankfurt: Klostermann, 1979), pp. 155–56.

59. *RG*, 155–56/*RD*, 231–33; *IDS* I, 21/*Hua* III.1, 26–27; *FTL*, 148/*Hua* XVII, 153–54.

60. *IDS* I, 87/*Hua* III.1, 85; *CES*, 159–60/*Hua* VI, 162–63.

61. *IDS* I, 166/*Hua* III.I, 155. In using the term "anexact," which has no connotations of deficiency, I am again borrowing from Derrida. See Derrida's *Edmund Husserl's Origin of Geometry: An Introduction*, rev. ed., trans. John P. Leavey, Jr. (Lincoln: University of Nebraska Press, 1989), p. 123/ *Introduction à "L'origine de la géométrie" par Edmund Husserl*, rev. ed. (Paris: Presses Universitaires de France, 1974), pp. 131–32.

62. *IDS* I, 187/Hua III.I, 176.

63. *IDS* I, 94–95/*Hua* III.I, 91–92.

64. *IDS* I, 94–95/*Hua* III.1, 92.

65. James K. A. Smith, "Respect and Donation: A Critique of Marion's Critique of Husserl," *American Catholic Philosophical Quarterly* 71, no. 4 (1998): 531–34. In reading Jamie Smith's excellent article I have discovered that he already refers to Husserl's remark, cited by Derrida and above, that conscious production hardly signifies that I invent and make the divine transcendency. See p. 535, n. 44.

66. *IDS* I, 92/*Hua* III.I, 89.

67. Ibid.

68. *CM*, 109/*Hua* I, 139; *WD*, 124/*EDF*, 182.

69. *Analyses Concerning Passive and Active Synthesis: Lectures on Transcendental Logic*, trans. Anthony J. Steinbeck (Dordrecht: Kluwer, 2001), p. 48/ *Husserliana* XI, *Analysen zur passiven Synthesis: Aus Vorlesungs- und Forschungsmanuskripten (1918–1926)*, ed. Margot Fleischer (The Hague: Martinus Nijhoff, 1966), p. 11. Hereafter abbreviated as *APS* and *Hua* XI, respectively.

70. *CM*, 53–54/*Hua* I, 89–90.

71. *APS*, 58/*Hua* XI, 20–21.

72. *IDS* I, 102, 364/*Hua* III.I, 97–98, 353. See also *APS*, 59/*Hua* XI, 22.

73. *APS*, 77/*Hua* XI, 38.

74. *APS*, 264(translation slightly emended)/*Hua* XI, 212.

75. *IDS* I, 9/*Hua* III.I, 14.

76. *APS*, 43/*Hua* XI, 7.

77. *Ideas Pertaining to a Pure Phenomenology and to a Phenomenological Philosophy, Second Book*, trans. Richard Rojcewicz and André Schuwer (Dordrecht: Kluwer, 1989), pp.199, 231/*Husserliana* IV, *Ideen zu einer reinen Phänomenologie und phänomenologischen Philosophie: Zweites Buch*, ed. Marly Biemel (The Hague: Martinus Nijhoff, 1952), pp.189, 219–20. Hereafter abbreviated as *IDS* II and *Hua* IV, respectively.

78. *PCIT*, 57/*Hua* X, 55. See also *IDS* I, 106–7/*Hua* III.I, 101–2.

79. *IDS* I, 51–52/*Hua* III.I, 57.

80. *APS*, 197, 210–11/*Hua* XI, 150, 162–63.

81. *APS*, 196–97, 213, 523/*Hua* XI, 148–49, 164–65, 419.

82. *APS*, 48–49/*Hua* XI, 11–12. So far as I am aware, Marion himself rejects the possibility of an unthematic outer horizon serving as or even approaching a saturated phenomenon. The saturated phenomenon does not have a halo of the not yet known behind it or around it. That is to say, it is not at all articulated into the intended and co-intended and given and co-given. See *BG*, 209–10/*ED*, 293–94. But if certain phenomena can exceed their horizon, "[t]his does not mean dispensing with a horizon altogether, since this would no doubt forbid any and all manifestation; it means using the horizon in another way so as to be free of its delimiting anteriority." *BG*, 209/*ED*, 293.

83. *PCIT*, 57/*Hua* X, 55.

84. If signification is restituted after the astonishment phase (assuming that astonishment is temporally finite), Marion would turn out to be remarkably close to Husserl. Interestingly, Marion admits something very like this, in a passage already referred to in brief above: "Couldn't one fear that the very hypothesis of a phenomenon saturating a horizon is a danger—one that should not be underestimated since it is born from the most real experience: that of a totality without door or window, excluding every possible, every other, every Other? But this danger, while no doubt undeniable, results less from the saturated phenomenon itself than from the misapprehension of it. When this type of phenomenon arises, it is most often treated like a common-law phenomenon, indeed a poor phenomenon, one that is therefore forced to be included in a phenomenological situation that by definition it refuses, and is finally misapprehended. If, by contrast, its specificity is recognized, the bedazzlement it provokes would become phenomenologically acceptable, indeed desirable, and the passage from one horizon to another would become a rational task for the hermeneutic. The saturated phenomenon safeguards its absoluteness and at the same time dissolves its danger when it is recognized as such, without confusing it with other phenomena." *BG*, 211/*ED*, 295–96.

85. See *Of Grammatology*, trans. Gayatri Spivak (Baltimore: Johns Hopkins University Press, 1976), 266/*De la grammatologie* (Paris: Minuit, 1967), 376. See also *WD*, 280/*EDF*, 411.

86. *IDS* I, 53, 57/*Hua* III.I, 58, 61.

87. John Scanlon, "Husserl's *Ideas* and the Natural Concept of the World," in *Edmund Husserl and the Phenomenological Tradition: Essays in Phenomenology*, ed. Robert Sokolowski (Washington, D.C.: Catholic University of America Press, 1988), pp. 225–28. See also *IDS* I, 81–82/*Hua* III.1, 80. Scanlon gives a very useful summary of Avenarius's ideas as set out in *Der menschliche Weltbegriff*, 3rd ed. (Leipzig: Reisland, 1912). For Avenarius, our natural conception of the world, once it has been liberated from superstition and the subsequent philosophical overlays of skeptical empiricism and idealism, is of a material environment whose component parts stand in various

relations of dependence. All the "mere things" and their relations are mechanical. The thoughts of the human being can be translated into the operations of the central nervous system, and the claim that the sounds and movements we make have more than mechanical significance is nothing but a hypothesis. This account absolutizes the world, and is the foil for Husserl's alternative.

 88. Scanlon, "Husserl's *Ideas*," pp. 228ff.
 89. *IDS* II, 189, 193/*Hua* IV, 179, 183–84.
 90. *IDS* II, 192–93, 199/*Hua* IV, 183, 189–90.
 91. *IDS* II, 10–11, 191, 196–99/*Hua* IV, 8–9, 182, 186–89.
 92. *IDS* II, 191, 193/*Hua* IV, 182, 183.
 93. *IDS* II, 185–86, 200/*Hua* IV, 176, 190.
 94. *IDS* II, 200–3, 239–41, 286–90/*Hua* IV, 190–93, 228–29, 273–77.
 95. *IDS* II, 201/*Hua* IV, 191.
 96. *PP*, 46/*Hua* IX, 62.
 97. *PP*, 66/*Hua* IX, 89.
 98. *FI*, 224–25/*GU*, 312–13.
 99. *IDS* II, 165–67/*Hua* IV, 158–59.
 100. *FI*, 226–27/*GU*, 314–16.
 101. *FI*, 227–29/*GU*, 318–21.
 102. *IDS* II, 384–85/*Hua* IV, 374–76.
 103. *CES*, 144, 381/*Hua* VI, 147, 460–61.
 104. *CES*, 142–43 (translation slightly emended)/*Hua* VI, 145–46.
 105. *CES*, 186–87/*Hua* VI, 190–91.
 106. *CES*, 367/*Hua* VI, 376.
 107. *CES*, 51–53/*Hua* VI, 51–53.
 108. *RG*, 203–4/*RD*, 303–4; *BG*, 13–16/*ED*, 22–27.
 109. *CM*, 35, 152–53/*Hua* I, 73, 179; *CES*, 145, 150/*Hua* VI, 148, 153. Near the start of *Being Given*, Marion claims that the phenomenological method should produce the indubitability of the apparition of things without producing the certainty of objects. The way in which the reduction operates par excellence is in dissolving the false realities of the natural attitude. As noted above, however, the addendum is that it must be done in order to undo it, in order to show that what appears through it is finally without it. It seems fairly clear that Marion is speaking of Husserl's reduction insofar as it is to be supplemented by his own reduction. He appears to retain the view that the former's reduction, when practiced by itself, leads back to a negative characterization of mundane things as poor in intuition and lacking variety. *BG*, 9–10/*ED*, 15–16.
 110. *BG*, 26/*ED*, 41.
 111. *BG*, 27/*ED*, 42.
 112. The uncovering of the givens of the entirely natural attitude is not Husserl's sole motivation. Some of his last comments on the reduction center around the claim that it had to be reworked because it passed too quickly

over the "uniqueness and personal indeclinability" of the ego of the epochē or primal "I" into the sphere of transcendental intersubjectivity. *CES,* 154–55, 247, 264/*Hua* VI, 157–58, 250–51, 267–68. The uniqueness as such of the subjective a priori is incapable of objectification or eidetic subsumption, and here we may recall the statement from Husserl's 1911 *Logos* article that, for phenomenology, "the singular is eternally the *apeiron.*" "Philosophy as a Rigorous Science," in *Phenomenology and the Crisis of Philosophy,* trans. Quentin Lauer (New York: Harper & Row, 1965), p. 116/*Philosophie als strenge Wissenschaft* (Frankfurt: Klostermann, 1981), p. 43.

113. *Signs,* p. 161/*Signes,* p. 204.

Chapter 4. Glory, Idolatry, *Kairos*: Revelation and the Ontological Difference in Marion
Felix Ó Murchadha

1. It was not, however, *totally* without philosophical importance in the classical period: it is a concept which is to be found in Aristotle, for example. On *kairos* in Aristotle, see Pierre Aubenque, *La prudence chez Aristote* (Paris: Presses Universitaire de France, 1986), pp. 95–105.

2. Martin Heidegger, *Phänomenologie des religiösen Lebens, Gesamtausgabe* 60 (Frankfurt: Klostermann, 1995), p. 102/*The Phenomenology of Religious Life,* trans. Matthias Fritsch and Jennifer Anna Gosetti-Ferencei (Bloomington: Indiana University Press, 2004), p. 71 (translation modified).

3. There are, in the context of the present discussion, clear connections between *paradoxa* and *doxa* in its meaning of "glory." The meaning of *doxa* as glory will be discussed below. On the connections between glory and paradox, see *ID,* p. 25.

4. See Dominique Janicaud, *Le tournant théologique de la phénoménologie français* (Paris: Éclat, 1991)/Dominique Janicaud et al., *Phenomenology and the "Theological Turn": The French Debate* (New York: Fordham University Press, 2000).

5. See, on authority, *ED,* 327f./*BG,* 235. On phenomenality, see Marion, *SP,* p. 103: "[the] religious phenomenon poses the question of the general possibility of the phenomenon."

6. For the following, see Gerhard Kittel, ed., *Theologisches Wörterbuch zum Neuen Testament* (Stuttgart: Kohlhammer, 1935), vol. 2, pp. 235–55.

7. K. Rahner, "The Hiddenness of God," in his *Theological Investigations,* trans. Cornelius Ernst, vol. 16 (London: Darton, Longmann and Todd, 1979), p. 243.

8. Marion talks in this context of bedazzlement. See his "Evidence and Bedazzlement," in *PC,* pp. 66f. Bedazzlement arises when the gaze cannot bear what appears to it. This appearance must be perceived in order to bedazzle. It bedazzles, however, only if seen as a gift of love, and this is possible only through love "which bears all" (1 Corinthians 13:7). See also *SP,* 114: "the glory of the visible weighs and it weighs too much."

9. See 1 Corinthians 1:22–24.

10. See Marion: "the speech offered to God sings, that is, it praises" (*ID*, 133).

11. See K. Rahner, "Theses on Prayer 'in the Name of the Church,'" in his *Theological Investigations*, vol. 5 (London: Darton, Longmann and Todd, 1966), p. 166.

12. See John 1:10, 1 Corinthians 1:21. See also the discussion of this theme in Heidegger, "Von Wesen des Grundes," in his *Wegmarken* (Frankfurt: Klostermann, 1978), pp. 141–43; "On the Essence of Grounds," in *Pathmarks*, ed. and trans. William McNeil (Cambridge: Cambridge University Press, 1998), pp. 111–12.

13. Heidegger, *Einführung in die Metaphysik* (Tübingen: Niemeyer, 1987), p. 79/ *Introduction to Metaphysics*, trans. Ralph Manheim (New Haven, Conn.: Yale University Press, 1987), p. 104.

14. *Einführung*, p. 78/*Introduction*, p. 103.

15. Heidegger, "Zeit und Sein," in his *Zur Sache des Denkens* (Tübingen: Niemeyer, 1988), p. 12/*On Time and Being*, trans. Joan Stambaugh (Chicago: University of Chicago Press, 2002), p. 12.

16. See "Nachwort zu 'Das Ding,'" in his *Vorträge und Aufsätze* (Pfullingen: Neske, 1990), p. 176/"The Thing," in his *Poetry, Language, Thought*, trans. Albert Hofstadter (New York: Harper & Row, 1971), p. 183.

17. See Heidegger, *Beiträge zur Philosophie: Von Ereignis, Gesamtausgabe* 65, ed. Friedrich-Wilhelm von Hermann (Frankfurt: Klostermann, 1989), p. 396/*Contributions to Philosophy (from Enowning)*, trans. Pavis Emad and Kenneth May (Bloomington: Indiana University Press, 1999), p. 277.

18. "Zeit und Sein," p. 9/*On Time and Being*, p. 9.

19. See *RD*, 284–302/*RG*, 189–202.

20. See *GWB*, 8/*DSE*, 16: "The idol and the icon determine two manners of being for beings, not two classes of being."

21. "Von Wesen der Sprache," in his *Unterwegs zur Sprache* (Pfullingen: Neske, 1971), p. 211/"The Nature of Language," in his *On the Way to Language*, trans. Peter D. Hertz (San Francisco: Harper & Row, 1982), p. 104. For a cogent discussion of the alterity of things in Heidegger, see S. Benso, "The Face of Things: Heidegger and the Alterity of the Fourfold," *Symposium* 1, no. 1 (1997): pp. 5–15.

22. *Sein und Zeit* (Tübingen: Niemeyer, 1986), p. 85/*Being and Time*, trans. Joan Stambaugh (Albany: State University of New York Press, 1996), p. 79.

23. See Heidegger, "Von Wesen der Wahrheit," in his *Wegmarken*, p. 185/"On the Essence of Truth," in his *Pathmarks*, p. 144.

24. See Heidegger, *Die Kunst und die Raum/L'art et l'espace* (Zurich: Erker, 1983), p. 9.

25. Heidegger, "Nachwort zu 'Das Ding,'" p. 173/"The Thing," p. 181.

26. See *SP*, 119: "The saturated phenomenon refuses to let itself be looked upon as an object, precisely because it appears with a multiple and indescribable excess that suspends any effort at constitution."

27. I am grateful to Prof. James Mensch for bringing home to me the importance of emplacement in relation to the sacred.

28. See, on the difference between respect and reverence, W. Desmond, "On the Betrayals of Reverence," *Irish Theological Quarterly* 65 (2000): p. 216.

29. In "The Origin of the Work of Art," Heidegger sees the splendor or the glory (*Glanz*) of the god being in the work. *Holzwege* (Frankfurt: Klostermann, 1980), p. 29/*Off the Beaten Track*, trans. Julian Young and Kenneth Haynes (Cambridge: Cambridge University Press, 2002), p. 22.

30. See "Der Satz der Identität," in his *Identität und Differenz* (Pfullingen: Neske, 1957), pp. 18f./"The Principle of Identity," in his *Identity and Difference*, trans. Joan Stambaugh (London: Harper & Row, 1969), pp. 30f.

31. See Heidegger, "Phänomenologie und Theologie," in his *Wegmarken*, pp. 47–77/ "Phenomenology and Theology," in his *Pathmarks*, pp. 39–61.

32. "The Final Appeal of the Subject," in *Deconstructive Subjectivities*, ed. Simon Critchley and Peter Dews (Albany: State University of New York Press, 1996), p. 98.

33. See Marion's discussion of "incident," *ED*, 213–18/*BG*, 151–54.

34. For a detailed account of the importance of kairos in Heidegger's thought, see Felix Ó Murchadha, *Zeit des Handelns und Möglichkeit der Verwandlung: Kairologie und Chronologie bei Heidegger im Jahrzehnt nach "Sein und Zeit"* (Würzburg: Königshausen & Neumann, 1999).

35. Heidegger, *Phänomenologie des religiösen Lebens*, p.104.

36. Ibid., pp. 102ff.

37. Rémi Brague, *La sagesse du monde* (Paris: Fayard, 1999), pp. 74–78.

38. See "Von Wesen und Begriff der Φύσις," in his *Wegmarken*, pp. 238f./"On the Essence and the Concept of Φύσις," in his *Pathmarks*, pp. 184 f.

Chapter 5. Reduced Phenomena and Unreserved Debts in Marion's Reading of Heidegger
Brian Elliott

1. Unless otherwise indicated, all translations of the Latin and German texts are my own.

2. Here I understand the notion of *gratia* in its orthodox Christian sense of a free gift of God that can in no way be effected by human acts. Close attention to Heidegger's lectures from the early Freiburg period between 1919 and 1923 reveals that at that time he granted this doctrine of grace signal importance within his interpretation of Christian theology. Among the few explicit indications of this is the following, taken from a report of his current research on Aristotle written by Heidegger in the au-

tumn of 1922, in order that Paul Natorp might endorse his move to the University of Marburg. Here Heidegger is referring to the role of a "destruction" of Christian theology for the purpose of arriving at a historically rigorous philosophical anthropology: "The center of such an [anthropological] interpretation of Augustine, in relation to the ontologically and logically basic constructions of his doctrine of life, is to be found in the writings on the Pelagian dispute and his ecclesiastical doctrine" ("Phänomenologische Interpretationen zu Aristoteles: Anzeige der hermeneutischen Situation" ["Natorp Report"], *Dilthey-Jahrbuch* [1989]: 228–74, at 251). For a detailed analysis of Heidegger's 1920/21 lectures on the phenomenology of religion, see Brian Elliott, "Existential Scepticism and Christian Life in the Early Heidegger," *The Heythrop Journal* 45 (July 2004): 273–89. Beyond the initial working out of his *Ereignisdenken* in the latter half of the 1930s, Heidegger's interpretations of poetic thinkers such as Hölderlin, Rilke, and Trakl evince the continued presence of a notion akin to Christian grace. A notable example of this is offered by the text of the 1950 lecture on Trakl, "Die Sprache" (in *Unterwegs zur Sprache*, 10th ed. [Stuttgart: Günther Neske, 1993], pp. 11–33). Marion's failure to advert to the presence of such an idea throughout the development of Heidegger's thought allows him, I believe, to insist on what is a merely specious sense of distance between his own idea of givenness and Heidegger's thinking.

3. Thus despite such comments as the following: ". . . the Heideggerian transgression does not distinguish itself from the Husserlian reduction by a retrogressive return toward the naïve position of the world; it distinguishes itself by passing beyond, toward the meaning of the Being of being" (*RG*, 66). Breaking out of the sphere of objecthood toward the meaning of Being is for Marion ultimately a Pyrrhic victory, since Heidegger's transformation of phenomenology must face up to one necessary question: "The path toward Being in general that is presented by *Dasein*—and therefore also by the (restricted) 'ontological difference' that it sets into play—is this path *a* path, is it even the sole and *unique* path?" (*RG*, 137). This question relating to "the priority of *Dasein*" (*RG*, 139) is motivated by an interpretation of *BT* that Marion shares with many other commentators: namely, that the project of fundamental ontology came to grief through an emergent sense of systemic unsustainability. That this was *not* the case can be shown not only with recourse to Heidegger's subsequent self-interpretation in the *Letter on "Humanism."* It is also now evident from the early Freiburg lecture manuscripts that Heidegger's pursuit of the "meaning of Being" by means of an initial focus on that being that for him alone understands Being represented a methodological, and not a constitutive, privileging of human existence. Thus, already in his second Freiburg lecture course from the winter semester 1919/20, Heidegger speaks of a methodological focusing on the "self-world" (*Selbstwelt*) that would eventually have to be rescinded (see *GA* 58, *Grundprobleme der Phänomenologie* [Frankfurt: Klostermann, 1992], passim).

GA refers to Heidegger's *Gesamtausgabe*, ed. Friedrich-Wilhelm von Herrmann (Frankfurt: Klostermann, 1975ff).

4. *GA* 24, *Grundprobleme der Phänomenologie* (Frankfurt: Klostermann, 1975).

5. This omission can be situated within Marion's more general disinclination to thematize the whole *temporal dimension* of Heidegger's thought. When it is recalled that in *BT* the idea of thrownness stands in the immediate vicinity of facticity and that the latter, with its essential dynamic of "falling" (*Verfallen*), is grasped there as basic existential "motility" (*Bewegtheit*), it may be said that Marion signally fails to appreciate the fundamental dynamic-temporal sense of *Dasein*'s understanding of Being, and hence of the ontological difference itself. Once again, the early lectures on religion amply demonstrate how the figure of grace or givenness at work in Heidegger's early thought is grasped in terms of a sense of eschatological temporality (see *GA* 60, *Phänomenologie des religiösen Lebens* [Frankfurt: Klostermann, 1995], pp. 98ff., 141, 144, 151ff.).

6. *GA* 9, *Wegmarken* (Frankfurt: Klostermann, 1976).

7. *SZ* refers to *Sein und Zeit*, 16th ed. (Tübingen: Niemeyer, 1993).

8. Where Marion does explicitly deal with the connection between situatedness and being-given-over-to, in his discussion of flesh in the work *In Excess* (*IE*), pp. 82–103, it is again noteworthy that Husserl's notion of *Leib* from *Ideas II* takes center stage rather than Heidegger's account of *Befindlichkeit*. Marion's treatment of flesh also exhibits signal internal tensions. Accordingly, Marion initially follows Husserl in asserting that "the *ego* casts itself in flesh in order to fix, if not to freeze, itself, and in this way take its first *self*" (*IE*, 91), only to contradict this explication of flesh as *actively assumed selfhood* by subsequently holding "I do not give myself flesh; it gives me to myself in giving itself to me—I am given over [*adonné*] to it" (*IE*, 99). The broader context of Marion's discussion involves a rather counterintuitive defense of Descartes's acknowledgment of the necessity of incarnation, whereby Husserl's Cartesianism is by implication defended against Heidegger's radical critique. In his lectures on Leibniz from 1928, Heidegger remarks, "*Dasein* as such contains the inner possibility for the factical dispersal (*faktische Zerstreuung*) into embodiment (*Leiblichkeit*) and thereby into sexuality. . . . *Dasein* as factical is in each case among other things individuated into a body and at once among other things in each case two-sidedly [individuated] into a particular gender" (*GA* 26, *Metaphysische Anfangsgründe der Logik* [1928; 2nd ed., Frankfurt: Klostermann, 1992], p. 173). According to Heidegger, the phenomena of embodiment and sexuality are aspects of the more general existential structure of thrownness, which itself denotes the sense of *Dasein*'s historical situatedness (see *GA* 26, 174). Thus, Marion's failure even to mention Heidegger's notion of *Befindlichkeit* in his treatment of the theme of flesh strengthens my contention that Marion conspicuously fails to acknowledge a debt to Heidegger on the issue of

grasping phenomenality as givenness. In this way Marion follows a key move in Lévinas's interpretation of Heidegger whereby aspects of Heidegger's account of existence are implicitly appropriated and yet explicitly held to be fundamentally absent from the Heideggerian position. Such an obfuscating strategy is common to many commentators who view their task as some defense of Husserlian phenomenology in the face of the Heideggerian "distortion."

9. Marion is here presumably following Heidegger's own initial note from the first edition of the *Letter on "Humanism"* (Frankfurt: Klostermann, 1949), which states that what is said in the letter relates back to a path of thinking embarked upon in 1936. Between 1936 and 1938 Heidegger attempted to set out his *Ereignisdenken* (see *GA* 65, *Beiträge zur Philosophie: Vom Ereignis* (Frankfurt: Klostermann, 1989).

10. See *BG*, 69–70. In his gloss on Heidegger's concept of the phenomenon in its phenomenological sense given in *BT* and other texts from the same period, Marion places exclusive emphasis on the self-showing aspect of the Heideggerian formulation: "Das, was sich zeigt, so wie es sich von ihm selbst het zeigt, von ihm selbst her sehen lassen" (to let that which shows itself be seen from itself in the very way in which it shows itself from itself; *SZ*, 34). Yet, Heidegger at this time repeatedly alluded to the danger of understanding phenomenology as a kind of idle speculation directed to what is in some sense "simply there." To stave off such a sense of radical passivity with respect to phenomenological investigation, Heidegger had to insist on the aspect of *facilitating or letting* something show itself as itself from itself. As awkward as this formula is, its sense as a middle voice that eschews both subjective distortion and objective self-sufficiency with respect to the phenomena is made sufficiently clear in *BT* and elsewhere. It is also clear that Marion's figure of pure givenness aims at humbling the achievement of *Dasein* in its letting things show themselves in the name of a Lévinasian notion of radical passivity never subjected to critical scrutiny in Marion's key texts.

11. See *BG*, 199ff.

12. "Senseless" in at least two senses. First, because every showing must literally "take place," that is, be situated concretely. It is one of the merits of Heidegger's thought, I believe, to have insisted that both phenomena and what were traditionally called noumena equally require or entail location. Second, the situatedness of the phenomenon implies not only that that which shows itself has concrete location, but also that what witnesses such showing equally "takes place." In other words, "letting" things show themselves entails embodiment and thus sentience. Inheriting the philosophical tradition of Bergson and Merleau-Ponty, Marion's thinking exhibits a peculiar aversion to acknowledging the necessity of embodiment. In turning to Kant's organization of the categories in order to articulate the basic characteristics of the saturated phenomenon and in alluding to the figure of the Kantian sublime via Turner's paintings, Marion offers an unre-

mittingly intellectualist reading of Kant's notion of experience. Where, one must ask, are such key Kantian ideas as temporality, schematism, sensibility, and "orientation in thinking" in Marion's exposition? The truth of the matter is that concrete location and embodiment have long since been buried by Marion's concept of phenomenality. Thus, already in *God Without Being* the rejection of concrete embodiment is evident in Marion's understanding of the Eucharist: "A spiritual body, in other words a body infinitely more united, more coherent, more consistent—in a word, more real—than any physical body" (*GWB*, 179/*DSE*, 253).

13. Heidegger had already glossed *ich bin* (I am) as *ich wohne* (I dwell) in *BT*. After the turn away from fundamental ontology and its central guiding thesis that time constitutes the basic horizon of ontological understanding, from the mid-1930s onward the centrality of the place of dwelling becomes increasingly evident in Heidegger's thought. From the beginning, Heidegger articulates place as event of appearance and attempts to bring into reciprocal relation a sense of the historical-destinal and that of an interface of the human and superhuman or divine. An early instantiation of this idea of place is given by Heidegger in his description of the Greek temple in his essay "The Origin of the Work of Art" (see *GA 5, Holzwege*, 2nd ed. [Frankfurt: Klostermann, 2003]/*Basic Writings*, ed. David F. Krell, 2nd ed. [London: Routledge, 1993]).

14. An example of this parallel development of the motifs of place and language is offered by Heidegger's lecture "Hölderlin and the Essence of Language," delivered in Rome in the same year as the artwork lectures (1936). Here the linkage of language and place with a sense of the divine is equally in play: "Since language properly happens as dialogue, the gods are expressed and a world appears. But again it is necessary to see that the presence of the gods and the appearance of the world are not at first a consequence of the happening of language; rather, they are simultaneous with it" (*Seitdem die Sprache eigentlich als Gespräch geschieht, kommen die Götter zu Wort und erscheint eine Welt. Aber wiederum gilt es zu sehen: die Gegenwart der Götter und das Erscheinen der Welt sind nicht erst eine Folge des Geschehnisses der Sprache, sondern sie sind damit gleichzeitig*; GA 4, Erläuterungen zu Hölderlins Dichtung, 2nd ed. [Frankfurt: Klostermann, 1996], p. 40). Given the historical context of this lecture, the political resonance of Heidegger's insistence on man's historical "belonging to the earth" (*Zugehörigkeit zur Erde*; p. 36) could hardly have been missed by his audience.

Chapter 6. The Reason of the Gift
Jean-Luc Marion

1. "To give everything [*tout donner*]" is perhaps an odd expression, because on the occasions when I say that I give "everything," most of the time I in fact give nothing (nothing real, no thing—first paradox), and this very fact allows me to give all that I can, namely, to give myself (almost) without

reserve or restraint (second paradox). But what is the significance of this gift where I give nothing in order to give myself—precisely not as a thing, but as an "unreal" gift, completely given and yet repeatable? From the very outset, we find ourselves in an aporia.

2. The normal English translation of *donataire* is "recipient." However, in *Being Given*, Kosky introduces "givee," which preserves the common root of *donateur, donataire, don*, and *donner*. Because of the parallels between *Being Given* and this chapter, we have followed Kosky's choice. (Trans.)

3. On the question of the gift, its possible contradiction, and the critique of my treatment of it in *RG*, see, in succession: Jacques Derrida's remarks in *Given Time. 1: Counterfeit Money*, trans. Peggy Kamuf (Chicago: University of Chicago Press, 1992), esp. pp. 12ff. and 50ff.; translation of *Given Time, Donner le temps. 1: La fausse monnaie*, in the series La Philosophie en Effet (Paris: Éditions Galilée, 1991), pp. 24ff. and 72ff.; my response in *BG*, 74ff./*ED*, 108ff; and our debate, *OTG*.

4. It is appropriate here to acknowledge the analyses of Camille Tarot, *De Durkheim à Mauss, l'invention du symbolique: Sociologie des sciences de la religion* (Paris: La Découverte, 1999); and Alain Caillé, *Anthropologie du don: Le tiers paradigme* (Paris: Desclée de Brouwer, 2000).

5. Anne Robert Jacques Turgot, *Reflections on the Formation and Distribution of Wealth* (written in 1766, published in 1768–70), in *The Economics of A. R. J. Turgot*, ed. and trans. P. D. Groenewegen (The Hague: Martinus Nijhoff, 1977), §31, p. 57.

6. Antoine-Augustin Cournot, *Researches into the Mathematical Principles of the Theory of Wealth*, trans. Nathaniel T. Bacon, in the series Reprints of Economic Classics (New York: Macmillan, 1927; repr. New York: Kelley, 1971), §2, p.10, and §6, pp.16–17.

7. Ibid., §2, p. 8; Cournot's emphasis.

8. Though one could easily refer to Descartes (e.g., *Discourse on Method*, *AT*, VI, 61–62), Cournot refers more to Leibniz: "We have already sketched elsewhere [*Traité de l'enchaînement des idées fondamentales*, II, chap. 7] the principles of this *superior dynamic* for which Leibniz had the idea, and which shows us, in the laws that govern the work of machines, a proper example for conceiving the much more general laws under whose empire the perpetual conversion of natural forces into one another is brought about; in the same way, one can establish a comparison between the phenomenon of economic production and the work of machines, so as to adjust [*rendre sensible*] the analogies they present" (*Principes de la théorie de richesses* [1860], ed. Gerard Jorland, in Cournot's *Oeuvres complètes*, vol. 9 [Paris: Vrin, 1981], p. 39; Cournot's emphasis). In his own way, Diderot fully recognized and stated that the "economy" is inscribed in the deployment of a *mathesis universalis* in its strictly Cartesian meaning, on which it depends from beginning to end for the radicality of objectification: "One holds forth, one investigates, one feels little and reasons much; one *measures everything to the scrupulous level of*

method, of logic and even of truth.... Economic science is a fine thing, but it stupefies us." *Salon de 1769*, in Diderot's *Oeuvres complètes*, vol. 16, *Beaux-arts III*, ed. Herbert Dieckmann and Jean Varloot (Paris: Hermann, 1990), 657; emphasis added.

9. *Rendre raison* means to give a rational explanation or reason, thereby making something appear reasonable. However, because both "render" and "reason" are important terms in this chapter, *rendre raison* is translated throughout by the somewhat clumsy "render reason." (Trans.)

10. Jean-Baptiste Say, *A Treatise on Political Economy or The Production, Distribution and Consumption of Wealth* (New York: Claxton, Remsen & Haffelinger, 1880), translation of *Traité d'économie politique ou Simple exposition de la manière dont se forment, se distribuent et se consomment les richesses*, 6th ed., ed. Horace Say (Paris: Guillaumin, 1841; 1st ed., 1803), vol. 1, p. 455, and vol. 1, p. 117.

11. Karl Marx, *Capital: A Critique of Political Economy. Book One: The Process of Production of Capital*, trans. from the 3rd German ed. by Samuel Moore and Edward Aveling, ed. Frederick Engels (London: Lawrence and Wishart, 1954), chap. 19, p. 506; chap. 18, p. 500; chap. 6, p. 172; chap. 1, sec. 4, pp. 84f. (emphasis added). The excess of surplus value, which does not appear in the exchange's formulation, destroys its equality. This fact contradicts not only social justice, and Ricardo's or Smith's theory of value, but also invalidates the very notion of a political economy (henceforth dubbed "bourgeois"). Excess—even the invisible excess of surplus value— destroys the terms of exchange, and thus the economy. Certainly, Bataille envisages an economy based on excess: "The solar radiance ... finally finds nature and the meaning of the sun: it is necessary for it to give, *to lose itself without calculation*. A living system grows, or lavishes itself *without reason*," such that "in practical terms, from the perspective of riches, the radiance of the sun is distinguished by its unilateral character: it loses itself *without counting, without consideration. The solar economy* is founded on this principle" ("The Economy to the Proportion of the Universe," trans. Michael Richardson, in *Georges Bataille: Essential Writings*, ed. Michael Richardson [London: Sage, 1998], pp. 75 and 74; translation of "L'économie à la mesure de l'univers," first published in *La France libre* no. 65 [July 1946], repr. in Bataille's *Oeuvres complètes* [Paris: Gallimard, 1976], vol. 7, p. 10; Bataille's emphasis). But one can question the legitimacy of thinking (and naming) this excess (without reason or measure) of expenditure starting from an economy, unless one assumes an economy deprived of exchange, price, and calculation; that is, the contrary of what economists understand by this term.

12. Marx relies here on Aristotle's arguments. On the one hand, equality defines justice, and therefore exchange: "Since the unjust man is unequal and the unjust act unequal, it is clear that there is also an intermediate for the unequal. And this is the equal." On the other hand, injustice consists in upsetting equality by appropriating "more" (value): "The man who acts

unjustly has too much, and the man who is unjustly treated too little, of what is good." *Nicomachean Ethics*, trans. W. D. Ross, rev. J. O. Urmson, in *The Complete Works of Aristotle: The Revised Oxford Translation*, ed. Jonathan Barnes, Bollingen Series 71:2, vol. 2 (Princeton, N.J.: Princeton University Press, 1984), V.3.1131a10–11; V.3.1131b19–20.

13. Leibniz strongly emphasizes that this universality of the principle of sufficient reason extends to the contingency of the event. "*No fact* can be real or actual, and no proposition true, without there being a sufficient reason for its being so and not otherwise" (*G. W. Leibniz's Monadology: An Edition for Students*, trans. Nicholas Rescher [Pittsburgh, Pa.: University of Pittsburgh Press, 1991], §32, p.116; emphasis added); or "The principle in question is the principle of the want of a sufficient reason *for a thing to exist, for an event to happen*" ("Fifth Letter to Clarke," in *G. W. Leibniz: Philosophical Essays*, ed. and trans. Roger Ariew and Daniel Garber [Indianapolis, Ind.: Hackett, 1989], §125, p. 346; emphasis added). Or again: "Constat ergo omnes veritates *etiam maxime contingentes* probationem a priori seu rationem aliquam cur sint potius quam non sint habere. Atque hoc ipsum est quod vulgo dicunt, nihil fieri sine causa, seu nihil esse sine ratione (It is therefore established that all truths, *even the most contingent*, have an a priori proof or some reason why they are rather than are not. And this is what the vulgar say: Nothing comes to be without cause; or: Nothing is without reason)"; untitled text described on the contents page by the editor [Gerhardt] as "Ohne Überschrift, in Betreff [Untitled, in] der Mittel der philosophischen Beweisführung [Reference to the Means of Philosophical Demonstration]," in *Die philosophischen Schriften von Gottfried Wilhelm Leibniz*, ed. C. I. Gerhardt, 7 vols. (Berlin: Weidmann, 1875–90), vol. 7, p. 301; emphasis added.

14. Without repeating the Cartesian *causa sui*, which submits even God to causality (*de ipso Deo quaeri potest* [which can be asked even about God himself], *IIae Responsiones*, AT VII, 164, l. 29)—or, in His case alone, to reason—Leibniz nevertheless thinks God as being a reason (His own sufficient reason) for Himself: "Vides quid ex illo theoremate sequatur, *nihil est sine ratione* . . . omnia, quae sibi ipsi ratio cur sint, non sunt . . . ea tamdiu in rationem, et rationem rationis, reducenda esse, donec reducantur in id quod sibi ipsi ratio est, id est Ens a se, seu Deum (You see what follows from the thesis: *nothing is without a reason* . . . everything that is not a reason for its own existence . . . is to be reduced to its reason, and its reason's reason, until it is reduced to what is its own reason, namely, the Being of itself, that is, God)"; *Confessio philosophi*, in Leibniz's *Sämtliche Schriften und Briefe*, ser. 6, vol. 3, *Philosophische Schriften: 1672–1676*, ed. Leibniz-Forschungsstelle der Universität Münster (Berlin: Akademie-Verlag, 1980), p. 120; Leibniz's italics.

15. Pierre Corneille: "Cinna, let us be friends! An end to strife!/You were my enemy; I spared your life;/Despite your base designs—that plot

insane—/I'll spare my would-be killer's life again!/Let's now compete and time its view deliver/On who fares best—recipient or giver./My bounties you've betrayed; I'll shower more:/You shall be overwhelmed, as ne'er before!" (*Cinna or The Clemency of Augustus*, in *Le Cid; Cinna; Polyeuct: Three Plays*, trans. Noel Clark [Bath: Absolute Classics, 1993], V, 3, vv. 1701–8). Admittedly, Cinna receives the gift as it is given—but we are here in Corneille's world and not in ours.

16. See my analysis in *IE/DS*, chap. 5.

17. The French *conscience* can mean either "conscience" or "consciousness." (Trans.)

18. Fatherhood gives *itself* only to the extent that it gives. Thus it inverts and bears out the definition of "the gifted [*l'adonné*]," who receives *himself* from what he receives. See *BG*, § 26, esp. pp. 266ff./*ED*, 366ff.

19. On the phenomenon's determinations as given, see *BG*, bk. 3, pp. 119ff./*ED*, 169ff. I mention only some of them here, but fatherhood also validates the others (anamorphosis, facticity, fait accompli, incident, etc.).

20. "Givenness" is the obvious English translation for both *donnéité* and the German *Gegebenheit*. "Givenness" is, however, already well established as the English translation for Marion's *donation*. To avoid any confusion, "givenence" has been introduced as an alternative. (Trans.)

21. See Roland Barthes: "Historically, the discourse of absence is carried on by the woman: Woman is sedentary, Man hunts, journeys; Woman is faithful (she waits), man is fickle (he sails away, he cruises). . . . It follows that, in every man who speaks of the absence of the other, *the feminine* declares itself: this man who waits and who suffers from it, is miraculously feminised." Roland Barthes, *A Lover's Discourse: Fragments*, trans. Richard Howard (London: Jonathan Cape, 1979), pp.13–14; translation of *Fragments d'un discours amoureux* (Paris: Seuil, 1977), p. 20; Barthes' emphasis.

22. Michel Henry does this with an exemplary rigor, by opposing reciprocity—"The phenomenon that is at the economy's origin is exchange, the concept of which cannot be formed independently of that of reciprocity"—to that which goes beyond it—"the nonreciprocity of the interior relation that connects us to God signifies the intervention of another relation than that which is established among men," that [relation] precisely where "each person is son of God and of him alone . . . no living being having the power to bring itself into life." *Paroles du Christ* (Paris: Seuil, 2002), pp. 37, 46, 47.

23. Leibniz, *Monadology*, §31, p. 21.

24. Leibniz, *Monadology*, §32, p. 21.

25. See *BG*, §§17–18 (and bk. 3, passim).

26. This gift, which imposes itself to be given and received of itself, could be described, with Barthes, as *adorable*, for "*Adorable* means: this is my desire, insofar as it is unique: 'That's it! That's it exactly (which I love)!' Yet the more I experience the specialty of my desire, the less I can give it a

name; to the precision of the target corresponds a wavering [*tremblement*] of the name; what is characteristic of desire, proper to desire, can produce only an impropriety of the utterance. Of this failure of language, there remains only one trace: the word 'adorable' (the right translation of 'adorable' would be the Latin *ipse*: it is the self, himself, herself, in person)" (Barthes, *A Lover's Discourse*, p. 20/*Fragments d'un discours amoureux*, p. 27). In fact, the ipseity and the pure self of this phenomenon—that which it is a question of loving, hence of receiving, hence of giving—come to it perhaps from precisely what they liberate from my desire and from its language, which, in this adorable, see only fire, only a manifest object of an obscure desire.

27. On the transition from "show itself" to "give itself," see *BG*, §6, pp. 68ff.

28. Thus this remark, which Barthes makes in passing, would take on all its weight: "The gift then reveals the test of strength of which it is the instrument" (*A Lover's Discourse*, p. 76/*Fragments d'un discours amoureux*, p. 91).

29. Thomas Aquinas, *Summa theologiae*, IIa IIae, q. 58, a. 11 (emphasis added), referring to Aristotle (*Nicomachean Ethics*, V), who does not, however, use this exact formula.

30. Leibniz, *Elementa verae pietatis* (1677–78), in Gaston Grua, *Textes inédits*, 2 vols. (Paris: Presses Universitaires de France, 1948), vol. 1, p. 13; emphasis added. See also vol. 1, p. 25; and "Specimen inventorum de admirandis naturae generalis arcanis," in Leibniz's *Die philosophischen Schriften*, vol. 7, p. 309.

31. See Oscar Bloch and Walther von Wartburg, *Dictionnaire étymologique de la langue française*, 8th ed. (Paris: Presses Universitaires de France, 1989; 1st ed., 1932), p. 546; Alfred Ernout, *Morphologie historique du latin*, 3rd ed., Nouvelle Collection à l'Usage des Classes, no. 32 (Paris: Klincksieck, 1953; 1st ed., 1914), §207, p.136; and Antonio Maria Martin Rodriguez, *Los verbos de "dar" en latín arcaico y clásico* (Grand Canary: Universidad de Las Palmas, 1999), *ad loc*. This is confirmed by Vincent Carraud, who emphasizes this "fundamental meaning" (*donner la raison* [to give reason], *ratio reddenda/ratio reddita*, etc.) even in the formulas of the history of metaphysics (*Causa sive ratio: La raison de la cause, de Suarez à Leibniz* [Paris: Presses Universitaires de France, 2002], pp. 27ff., 436, 462 and n. 1, 492, etc.).

32. On the determinations of the phenomenon as pure given, see *BG*, bk. 3.

33. On the analysis of saturated phenomena, see *BG*, bk. 4, §§21–23, and *IE*, passim.

Chapter 7. The Gift: A Trojan Horse in the Citadel of Phenomenology?
Joseph S. O'Leary

1. Heidegger, *Wegmarken*, *Gesamtausgabe* 9, ed. Friedrich-Wilhelm Herrmann (Frankfurt: Klostermann, 1976), p. 334.

2. See Theodore Kisiel, *The Genesis of Heidegger's Being and Time* (Berkeley: University of California Press, 1995), p. 246.

3. Aristotle, *Metaphysics*, 1004b20.

4. As suggested by Jocelyn Benoist, "L'écart plutôt que l'excédent," *Philosophie* 78 (2003): 77–93, at 83.

5. Jacques T. Godbout, with Alain Caillé, *L'esprit du don* (Paris: La Découverte, 2000), p. 287.

6. See Marcel Hénaff, *Le prix de la vérité: Le don, l'argent, la philosophie* (Paris: Éditions du Seuil, 2002), pp. 156, 188.

7. Godbout, *L'esprit du don*, p. 182.

8. Ibid., p. 173.

9. Hénaff, *Prix de la vérité*, p. 277, referring to Jane Cobbi, "L'obligation du cadeau au Japon," in *Lien de vie, noeud mortel*, ed. Charles Malamoud (Paris: EHESS, 1988).

10. Godbout, *L'esprit du don*, pp. 188–89.

11. Hénaff, *Prix de la vérité*, pp. 179, 181.

12. Ibid., p. 266.

13. Godbout, *L'esprit du don*, p. 231.

14. Hénaff, *Prix de la vérité*, p. 216.

15. See ibid., p. 237.

16. See Godbout, *L'esprit du don*.

17. See John D. Caputo, "Apôtres de l'impossible: Sur Dieu et le don chez Derrida et Marion," *Philosophie* 78 (2003): 33–51, at 38.

18. Godbout, *L'esprit du don*, p. 275.

19. Ibid., p. 295.

20. Guy Bugault, *Nāgārjuna: Stances du milieu par excellence* (Paris: Gallimard, 2002), p. 64.

21. Godbout, *L'esprit du don*, pp. 324–25.

22. Gérard Granel, *Le sens du temps et de la perception chez E. Husserl* (Paris: Gallimard, 1968), pp. 34–35.

23. Ibid., p. 47.

24. The literal reading of the Gospel here carries over from Marion's first, and freshest, presentation of the triple reduction: "Esquisse d'un concept phénoménologique du don," *Archivio di filosofia* 62 (1994): 75–94.

25. See Marion, *Le phénomène érotique* (Paris: Éditions Bernard Grasset, 2003), chap. 1.

26. *The Perfection of Wisdom in Eight Thousand Lines*, trans. Edward Conze (Bolinas, Calif.: Four Seasons Foundation, 1975), p. 70.

27. See Nāgārjuna, *Le traité de la grande vertu de sagesse*, trans. Étienne Lamotte (Louvain: Institut Orientaliste, 1970), pp. 570–781.

28. Ibid., p. 708.

29. Ibid., p. 709.

30. Ibid., p. 707.

31. Ibid., p. 650 (quoting the Perfection of Wisdom sutra).

33. See Benoist, "L'écart plutôt que l'excédent."
34. Bugault, *Nāgārjuna*, p. 50.
35. Ibid., p. 19.

Chapter 8. Phenomenality in the Middle: Marion, Romano, and the Hermeneutics of the Event
Shane Mackinlay

1. Jean-Luc Marion, "The Reason of the Gift," chap. 6 in this volume.

2. Romano's major work is published in two complementary volumes: *L'événement et le monde*, Épiméthée: Essais Philosophiques (Paris: Presses Universitaires de France, 1998), and *L'événement et le temps*, Épiméthée: Essais Philosophiques (Paris: Presses Universitaires de France, 1999). Some of the key features of these volumes are sketched in an earlier essay, in the context of an analysis of aspects of Heidegger's thought: "Le possible et l'événement," *Philosophie* 40 (Dec. 1993): 68–95, and 41 (Mar. 1994): 60–86. A revised version of this essay appears in a collection of Romano's essays: *Il y a*, Épiméthée: Essais Philosophiques (Paris: Presses Universitaires de France, 2003), pp. 55–111. The text of Romano's that I will draw on most often is *L'événement et le monde* (hereafter, *EM*).

3. Martin Heidegger, *Being and Time*, trans. John Macquarrie and Edward Robinson (New York: Harper, 1962), translation of *Sein und Zeit*, 18th ed. (Tübingen: Max Niemeyer, 2001) (hereafter, *BT*).

4. Romano, *Il y a*, p. 10.

5. In *Being Given*, Marion proposes the event as the "ultimate determination" of the given phenomenon (*BG/ED*, §§17–18), and as the paradigm of phenomena that are saturated according to quantity (§23.3). *In Excess* (*IE*) is a collection of occasional lectures that Marion framed as a series of studies of the types of saturated phenomena he had set out in *BG*. Chapter 2 of *IE* ("The Event or the Happening Phenomenon") deals with the event.

6. I have chosen to follow Horner in leaving *adonné* untranslated. Kosky proposes "gifted," which is succinct and retains a clear connection with the root of *adonné* in the French *donner* (to give). However, the primary meaning of "gifted" in English is "talented," which is quite misleading.

7. "The fact, precisely insofar as it wells up in fact [*en fait*], annuls the legitimacy of asking it about its cause. First of all, because its cause or causes are unimportant, seeing as it is already found there well and truly, in fact [*de fait*]. Next, because if the inquiry into its cause or causes ever becomes possible, this will only happen after the fact [*après coup*], by relying on the fact that it already arrived in fact [*le fait qu'il arriva déjà de fait*]" (*BG*, 140/*ED*, 199; translation modified).

8. An asterisk following a page reference indicates that the translation has been modified.

9. Emphasis used within quotes is that of the original author unless "emphasis added" follows the quotation.

10. For example: "That which shows *itself*, first *gives itself* [*Ce qui se montre, d'abord se donne*] —this is my one and only theme" (*BG*, 5*/*ED*, 10).

11. "I do not make it [the phenomenon] by my fact, ahead of the fait accompli; I let (myself) be made, I let it make me [*je ne le fais pas de mon fait, devant le fait accompli, je (me) laisse faire, je le laisse me faire*]" (*BG*, 146*/*ED*, 207).

12. As Marion develops the idea of givenness, he places far more emphasis on its being an active giving rather than a middle-voiced happening. This privileging of the active/passive structure may contribute to his insistence that *donation* be translated in English as "givenness" (cf. Horner, translator's introduction to *In Excess* [*IE*, xi]), despite the connotations this has of something that is given in a fixed way, and that must simply be received. Other options, such as "givingness," may have more successfully evoked the actual occurring of giving (and appearing), on which he wants to focus. See, for instance, Marion's clarification of the title *Being Given*, in which he emphasizes that "being" should be read as a verb (i.e., the present participle of "to be") rather than as a noun (i.e., "*a* being"): "The given verbally unfolds its givenness in it [*le donné déplie verbalement en lui sa donation*]" (*BG*, 2/*ED*, 6).

13. Heidegger contends that human existence is hermeneutic *in its very happening*, and not just in the epistemic acts of interpretation with which we recount it. This *"primary* sense" of hermeneutics as the "interpretation of Dasein's Being [*Auslegung des Seins des Daseins*]" (*BT*, §7, 62/*SZ*, §7, 38) can be seen in Heidegger's analysis of the "as-structure" of understanding and interpretation (*BT*, §§32–33). An assertion that interprets an entity by describing it *as* something does not add signification to the entity; rather, it discloses that entity *as* already embedded in a network of relations and significations.

14. More recently, Marion makes a similar response to Richard Kearney. See "A Dialogue with Jean-Luc Marion," *Philosophy Today* 48 (2004): 12.

15. Jean Greisch suggests that Romano's evental-evential distinction should itself be regarded as "ontological." Greisch, "'L'herméneutique événementiale': De la mondification à la temporalisation du temps," *Critique* 57, no. 648 (2001): 404.

16. "The event has reconfigured my intrinsic possibilities, articulated among themselves—my world; it has opened a new world in and by its welling up [*surgissement*]" (*EM*, 55).

17. Romano's description of an innerworldy fact as a "fait accompli" should not be confused with Marion's description of the event as a "fait accompli" (*BG*/*ED*, §15). Marion carefully distinguishes the fait accompli of an event from the actuality of an effect, while Romano's innerworldly fact is precisely such an actuality.

18. "Selfhood, in its evential sense, always signifies, as we will see, the capacity of the *advenant* to appropriate the possible possibles [*possibles évent-*

uels] articulated in a world and arising from the event, and to understand oneself on the basis of them" (*EM*, 118).

19. "The *advenant* is the title for describing the event constantly in course of my own coming [*advenue*] to myself from the events which happen to me [*m'adviennent*] and which, in being destined to me, give me a destiny: adventure [*aventure*] without return. It designates neither a privileged being, nor an ontological instance, but rather the very opening to the event in general" (*EM*, 72).

20. Romano believes that his focus on birth is the decisive factor that frees his analysis from the Cartesian elements of *Dasein*. He argues that Heidegger's restriction of possibility to *Dasein*'s own self-projection depends on his ignoring the significance of birth. In turn, this allows Heidegger to present death as one of my actual and appropriable possibilities, thus avoiding the need to grapple with death as something radically other that happens *to me* (Romano, *Il y a*, pp. 57–88).

21. "To be born is to be a self originally [*originairement*], but not originarily [*originellement*]; it is to be free originally, but not originarily; it is to understand the meaning of one's adventure originally, but not originarily; it is to make possible [*possibiliser*] the possible (by projecting it) originally, but not originarily, etc." (*EM*, 96).

Chapter 9. The Dative Subject (and the "Principle of Principles")
Ian Leask

1. Husserl, *Ideas Pertaining to a Pure Phenomenology and to a Phenomenological Philosophy*, bk. 1, trans. Fred Kersten (Dordrecht: Kluwer, 1983), sec. 24, p. 44/*Ideen zu einer reinen Phänomenologie*, Halbband 1, text of first three editions, ed. K. Schuhmann (Dordrecht: Kluwer, 1977), *Husserliana* III/1, pp. 52–53.

2. Kant, *Kritik der Urteilskraft*, sec. 57, n. 1.

3. Heidegger, *On Time and Being*, trans. Joan Stambaugh (New York: Harper & Row, 1972), pp. 62–63/*Zur Sache des Denkens* (Tübingen: Niemeyer, 1969), pp. 69–70.

4. As Marion demonstrates, Heidegger's critique of Husserlian "Cartesianism" masks a particular (if reconstituted) egology of its own: Heidegger's *sum* may be temporal ipseity, but it is characterized, nevertheless, in terms of a nonsubstitutable Self-Constancy, an anticipatory resoluteness that brings about the true "mineness" of the Self's Selfhood. Even in the *Destruktion* of the cogito there lurks a creeping autarchy. See "L'ego et le *Dasein*: Heidegger et la 'destruction' de Descartes dans *Sein und Zeit*," *Revue de métaphysique et de morale* 92 (Jan. 1987): 25–53, trans. in *RG*, pp 77–107; and "Le sujet en dernier appel," *Revue de métaphysique et de morale* 96 (1991): 77–95. See also "Interloqué," in *Who Comes After the Subject?*, ed. Eduardo Cadava, Peter Connor, and Jean-Luc Nancy (New York and London: Routledge, 1991), pp. 236–45.

5. A prime example here is the treatment of boredom. Where Heidegger's stunning analysis of *Langeweile* (in the *Fundamental Concepts of Metaphys-*

ics) has an ulterior motive (achieving a Dionysian awakening "at dreaming's end," a self-transformation in the face of our fully revealed worldhood), Marion, by contrast, is prepared to treat "boredom itself" as a "counterexistential," irreducible to any (evaluative) nihilism, to anxiety, to negation, or to any "suffering awareness of Nothing." (True boredom, Marion shows, has no function, no interest [*GWB*, 115, 117]; it suspends the *Anspruch* and means "the dissolution of worldhood" [*RG*, 191/*RD*, 290].)

6. For fuller descriptions, see SPCG, especially 137–40.

7. After all, "the 'I' finds itself, instead of the constituting 'I' that it remained in the face of common law phenomena, constituted by a saturated phenomenon" (SP, 119/PS, 121).

8. Husserl, *Ideas*. See note 1.

9. Cf. SPCG, 137: "If the recipient preceded the gift and remained independent of its occurrence, it could condition, provoke, or even offer it."

10. In the original: "La charge d'ouvrir ou fermer le flux entier de la phénoménalité."

11. Emmanuel Lévinas, *Otherwise Than Being; or, Beyond Essence* [*OB*], trans. Alphonso Lingis (The Hague: Nijhoff, 1981), p. 87/*Autrement qu'être; ou, Au delà de l'essence* [*AE*] (The Hague: Nijhoff, 1974), p. 111.

12. *OB*, 192, n. 20/*AE*, 109, n. 20. Cf. *OB*, 101/*AE*, 127; and *OB*, 194, n. 5/*AE*, 130, n. 5.

Chapter 10. Marion's Ambition of Transcendence
Mark Dooley

1. See especially John D. Caputo, "Apostles of the Impossible: On God and the Gift in Derrida and Marion," in *God, the Gift, and Postmodernism*, ed. John D. Caputo and Michael J. Scanlon (Bloomington: Indiana University Press, 1999), pp. 185–222; and Dominique Janicaud, "The Theological Turn of French Phenomenology," in *Phenomenology and the "Theological Turn": The French Debate* (New York: Fordham University Press, 2000), pp. 3–106. See also the excellent book-length study of the Derrida-Marion debate by Robyn Horner, *Rethinking God as Gift: Marion, Derrida, and the Limits of Phenomenology* (New York: Fordham University Press, 2001).

2. Friedrich Nietzsche, *The Will to Power*, trans. Walter Kaufmann and R. J. Hollingdale, ed. Walter Kaufmann (New York: Vintage Books, 1967), p. 301.

3. Ibid., p. 11.

4. This chapter is an attempt to examine and appraise the notion of the saturated phenomenon from the point of view of a Rortian (after Richard Rorty) perspective. For some time now I have been moving in the direction of Rorty's postfoundational pragmatics in an effort to underscore the benefits of anti-essentialism. For more on why I believe Rorty has the edge over his fellow anti-essentialists, see Mark Dooley: "Private Irony vs. Social Hope: Derrida, Rorty, and the Political," *Cultural Values* 3 (July 1999):

263–90; "A Civic Religion of Social Hope: A Reply to Simon Critchley," *Philosophy and Social Criticism* 27, no. 5 (2001): 35–58; "On Circumventing the Quasi-Transcendental: Caputo on Rorty," in *A Passion for the Impossible: John D. Caputo in Focus*, ed. Mark Dooley (Albany: State University of New York Press, 2003), pp. 201–235 (includes Caputo's response, "Achieving the Impossible").

5. See SP, 180–85.

6. Immanuel Kant, *Critique of Judgment*, trans. Werner S. Pluhar (Indianapolis, Ind.: Hackett, 1987), p. 182. Cited in SP, 196.

7. Richard Rorty, *Philosophy and Social Hope* (Harmondsworth, U.K.: Penguin, 1999), p. 48.

8. Ibid, p. 54.

9. Hilary Putnam, *Realism with a Human Face*, ed. James Conant (Cambridge, Mass.: Harvard University Press, 1990), p. 28. Cited in Rorty, *Philosophy and Social Hope*, p. xxvii.

10. Robert Brandom, "Heidegger's Categories in *Being and Time*," *The Monist* 66 (1983): 387–409, at 389.

11. Cited by Rorty in his *Essays on Heidegger and Others* (Cambridge: Cambridge University Press, 1991), p. 64.

12. Richard Rorty, *Consequences of Pragmatism: Essays, 1972–1980* (Brighton, U.K.: Harvester Press, 1982), p. xx.

13. Ibid.

14. This citation appears at several junctures throughout Rorty's most comprehensive treatment available of the consequences for religion of his particular brand of neopragmatism, "Cultural Politics and the Question of the Existence of God," in *Radical Interpretation in Religion*, ed. Nancy Frankenberry (Cambridge: Cambridge University Press, 2002), pp. 53–77.

15. Rorty, *Consequences of Pragmatism*, p. xix.

Chapter 11. *Le phénomène érotique:* Augustinian Resonances in Marion's Phenomenology of Love
Eoin Cassidy

1. *Le phénomène érotique* (PE) (Paris: Grasset, 2003). All English translations of PE are my own.

2. See PE, 22–23. Marion draws attention to his *Prolégomènes à la charité* (PC).

3. See *Confessions*, 2.ii.2 and 3.i.1. Both passages situate the desire for love within the context of the compelling attraction of erotic love—a love that, for Augustine, can all too easily blur the lines between love and lust.

4. "La philosophie se définit comme 'l'amour de la sagesse,' parce qu'elle doit en effet commencer par aimer avant de prétendre savoir. Pour parvenir à comprendre, il faut d'abord le désirer" (PE, 10). See also PE, 11: "La philosophie ne comprend qu'à la mesure où elle aime—j'aime comprendre, donc j'aime pour comprendre" (Philosophy understands only to the ex-

tent that it loves—I love to understand, therefore I love in order to understand).

5. See Marion's comment, made in the course of an appreciation of his friend Cardinal Hans Urs von Balthasar: "The Christian outlook facilitates the resurgence and appearance in the world of phenomena that have up until then remained invisible, on the basis of which a new interpretation of already visible phenomena becomes thenceforth legitimate. What is this new given and this new interpretation? The answer is charity, which gives itself and allows itself to be seen only by those who love it." See Marion's "Christian Philosophy and Charity," *Communio* 19 (Fall 1992): 469.

6. As Marion puts it in chapter 13 of this volume: "Perhaps the question of desire cannot only not be answered but also cannot even be asked in the horizon of Being. So it's a reason why, I think, desire is the 'backstage' of metaphysics, which was never enlightened by metaphysics (which is quite unable to do so)."

7. "Je peux bien reconnaître 'je pense, donc je suis' très certainement—pour aussitôt annuler cette certitude en me demandant 'à quoi bon?' La certitude de mon existence ne suffit jamais à la rendre juste, ni bonne, ni belle, ni desirable—bref, ne suffit jamais à l'assurer" (*PE*, 42).

8. Ecclesiastes, 1:2–3: "Vanity of vanities, says the Preacher, vanity of vanities! All is vanity. What does man gain by all the toil at which he toils under the sun?" (RSV, 1966).

9. As Marion has put it in "Christian Philosophy and Charity," p. 471: "If the words *Crede ut intelligas*, which stem from an Augustinian order, at first seem valuable for theology, the Christian outlook that trains itself on the created world in general pursues another variant of this phrase, namely—*Ama, ut intelligas*. And, as a result, the more love grows, the more it sees phenomena that stem from a third order; the more, indeed, it loves."

10. *Confessions*, trans. R. S. Pine-Coffin (Harmondsworth, U.K.: Penguin, 1961), 3.iv.7, p. 59.

11. See *Confessions*, 5.xiv.24 and 6.i.1. See also 6.iv.5: "Anxiety about what I could believe as certain gnawed at my heart all the more sharply as I grew more and more ashamed that I had been misled and deluded by promises of certainty for so long and had talked wildly, like an ignorant child, about so many unconfirmed theories as though they were beyond question." Pine-Coffin trans., 6.iv.5, p. 115.

12. "Nisi credideritis, non intellegetis" (Unless you believe, you will not understand). See *De magistro*, 2.37; *De libero arbitrio*, 1.ii.4; *In Joannis evangelium*, tract. 29.6.

13. One of the most interesting paths to trace is Augustine's commentaries on the phrase from the beatitudes "Blessed are the pure in heart." In his earlier writings he speaks of faith that purifies the heart; but as his life progresses, he increasingly speaks of love as that which purifies the heart. See *In Johannis epistulam*, tract. 9.10. Note also Augustine's many references

to Paul's Letter to the Galatians, 5:6 ("Faith works through Love") to emphasize the essential link between faith and love. Neither can be understood in isolation from the other.

14. The most sustained treatment of this theme is in Augustine's fourth homily on the first Letter of St. John. In particular, see *In Johannis epistulam*, tract. 4.6: "The whole life of the good Christian is a holy longing. What you long for, as yet you do not see; but longing makes in you the room that shall be filled, when that which you are to see shall come."

15. For a detailed treatment of this and related themes, see Eoin Cassidy, "Augustine's Homilies on John's Gospel," in *Studies in Patristic Christology*, ed. Thomas Finan and Vincent Twomey (Dublin: Four Courts Press, 1998), pp. 122–43.

16. *In Johannis evangelium*, tract. 25.3.

17. Ibid., tracts. 18.6, 38.2, 53.8.

18. See ibid., tract. 18.7: "Rise, seek, sigh, gasp with longing, and knock at the closed doors. But if we do not yet long, do not yet eagerly desire, do not yet sigh, we shall cast down our pearls to all sorts of persons, or we ourselves shall find pearls of no value. Can I therefore, my dear friends, encourage desire in your hearts." See also ibid., tract. 34.7.

19. Ibid., tract. 18.11.

20. Ibid., tract. 26.1.

21. Note the manner in which Augustine reflects on his failure to "knock at the door." See *Confessions*, 6.iv.5 and 6.vii.11.

22. Ibid., 1.i.1.

23. Ibid., trans. Pine-Coffin, 8.vii.16, p.169.

24. See *PE*, 64–69. As Marion writes, "La réduction érotique destitue toute identité de soi à soi, qui se fonderait sur la pensée de soi" (The erotic reduction dismisses all notion of self-identity that would seek to base itself on the thought of itself; p. 64).

25. *PE*, 43–47.

26. The motif of the call is, of course, an established concern in Marion's writings; see, for example, *ED/BG*, sec. 28. More recently, Marion has related the notion of "call" to his earlier concern with the "icon," making the point that "what imposes its call must be defined not only as the other person of ethics (Lévinas) but more radically as the icon. The icon gives itself to be seen in that it makes me hear (understand) its call" (*IE*, 118–19).

27. The "Me voici" is a central motif in Lévinas's writings. For Lévinas, "Me voici" is not a statement of self-assertion (something that can be implied by the English translation); rather, "Me voici," formulated in the accusative, suggests something like an acknowledgment of my passivity in the face of the other: it is an acknowledgment that "the other is in me and in the midst of my very identification otherwise *than Being* (Beyond Essence, trans. Alphonso Lingis [The Hague: Martinus Nijhoff, 1981], p. 125). This corresponds closely to Marion, who, in his use of this phrase, is concerned

to highlight the manner in which I receive my identity in responding to the call from the other.

28. "Autrui ne doit donc pas seulement me dire 'Me voici' dans l'instant, il doit aussi me le promettre pour tout instant encore à venir. Il ne doit pas me dire la signification, il doit me la promettre. La signification, qui permet seule à mon intuition de faire apparaître le phénomène d'autrui pour moi, surgit comme un serment—ou elle manque toujours" (The other must therefore not only say 'here I am' in the moment, he or she must also promise it for every moment to come. He or she must not only utter the significance of the words but must also promise them. This symbol of meaning which alone permits my intuition to reveal the phenomenon of another for me, surges forth as a pledge—or it will be lacking forever; *PE*, 165).

29. Ibid., pp. 170–71. Note the following: "Lui et moi naissons, rennaissons même (la réduction érotique abolit un monde et crée une intrigue) comme amant et aimé—et réciproquement, car lui aussi endure la même conversion" (The other and myself born, and even reborn (the erotic reduction abolishes a world and creates a love [affair] as lover and loved—and reciprocally, because the other also undergoes the same conversion; *PE*, 170).

30. Unquestionably, this is one of the most profound insights to be gleaned from the "réduction érotique." As Marion puts it: "J'ai donc dû admettre qu'aucune question ne m'atteignait plus radicalement que celle qui me demandait non pas 'suis-je en pensant?,' mais 'm'aime-t-on d'ailleurs?' Bref, 'être ou ne pas être,' telle n'est plus la question, mais uniquement 'm'aime-t-on d'ailleurs?'" (I must therefore acknowledge that no question touches me more radically than that which asks me not 'do I obtain selfhood in thinking?' but rather 'does anyone love me?' To put it succinctly, 'to be or not to be,' this is no longer the question, but uniquely 'does anyone love me?'"; *PE*, 68). Again, the spirit of Lévinas looms large.

31. See *PE*, 161–63

32. In *PE*, sec. 41 (pp. 327–31), titled "Même soi," Marion places considerable emphasis on this notion that I am able to love myself only because I am first loved by another. It is a theme that runs through the whole book. See, for example, p. 71: ". . . elle m'assigne donc, sans retour à dépendre de ce que je ne peux ni maîtriser, ni provoquer, ni même envisager—un autre que moi, éventuellement un autrui pour moi, en tout cas une instance étrangère—venant de je ne sais où—en tout cas pas de moi" (. . . it [am I loved?] assigns me therefore, irredeemably, to be answerable to that which I can neither control, nor challenge, nor even contemplate—an other than myself, eventually an other to me, in any case an outside presence—coming from I do not know where—in any case not from me).

33. "L'assurance m'arrive toujours, non plus d'un ailleurs ontique qui me conserverait dans mon étantité, mais d'un ailleurs plus intime à moi que moi-même" (*PE*, 133). (See also *PE*, 72.) Marion has frequently reflected on this Augustinian theme; see, for example, *PC*, 153–55, and *IE*, 23–24.

34. "Je deviens moi-même et me reconnais dans ma singularité, lorsque je découvre et admets enfin celui que je désire; celui-là seul me manifeste mon centre le plus secret—ce qui me manquait et me manque encore" (*PE*, 172).

35. "Mon désir me dit à moi-même en me montrant ce qui m'excite" (*PE*, 172).

36. For a detailed treatment of this theme in Augustine's anthropology—including a discussion of the celebrated phrase "love and do what you will" (*dilige et quod vis fac*)—see Eoin G.Cassidy, "Augustine's Exegesis of the First Epistle of John," in *Scriptural Interpretation in the Fathers: Letter and Spirit*, ed. Thomas Finan and Vincent Twomey (Dublin: Four Courts Press, 1995), pp. 201–20.

37. *Confessions*, 13.ix.10. The full passage reads: "Pondus meum amor meus; eo feror, quocumque feror" (In my case, love is the weight by which I act. To whatever place I go, I am drawn to it by love).

38. In particular see *Confessions*, 2.iv.9–2.x.18.

39. Ibid., 8.viii.19.

40. Ibid., 3.iv.7.

41. Ibid., trans. Pine-Coffin, 3.vi.10, pp. 60–61. For a sustained treatment on the relation between the desire for truth and the search for happiness, see ibid., 10.xxiii.33–34.

42. Richard Kearney, in his "Desire for God," in *God, the Gift, and Postmodernism*, ed. John D. Caputo and Michael J. Scanlon (Bloomington: Indiana University Press, 1999), p. 113, describes Augustine's portrayal of *curiositas* or *concupiscentia oculorum* as "the ocular-erotic drive to appropriate the ephemera of the visible universe." He observes: "At its most sophisticated, this lust of the eyes took the form of an obsessive epistemological *curiositas* with regard to absolute knowledge." For an extended treatment of *curiositas*, see Augustine's *De vera religione* [*On the True Religion*], XXXVIII, 69–71.

43. See *Confessions*, 2.ii.2 and 3.i.1.

44. Ibid., 7.xvi.22.

45. Luke 15:11–32.

46. *Confessions*, trans. Pine-Coffin, 10.xxvii.38, pp. 231–32.

47. This is well expressed in *Confessions*, 3.vi.11: "Tu autem eras interior intimo meo et superior summo meo" (Yet you were deeper than my inmost understanding and higher that the topmost height that I could reach; ibid., 3.vi.11, p. 62).

48. See *In Iohannis epistulam*, 7:4–10, where Augustine comments on the passage from 1 John 4:10, which reads: "In this is love, not that we loved God but that he loved us. . . ."

49. For Augustine, desire is always linked to delight. A key Augustinian theme is that God prompts us to take delight in praising Him: it is only in and through the gift of delight that desire is awakened. See the celebrated

passage from *Confessions*, 1.i.1: "You prompt us to take delight in praising you, because you have made us for yourself, and our heart is restless until it finds rest in you."

50. "Au moment d'aimer, l'amant ne peut croire ce qu'il dit et ce qu'il fait, que sous un certain aspect d'éternité" (*PE*, 173).

51. For an extended treatment of this theme, see *PE*, 286–302, 318–31.

52. See *PE*, 286–302. For a slightly different approach to this theme, see *IE*, 123–27.

53. "Le phénomène érotique, que demande l'amant, exige la longue et profonde fidélité. Mais la fidélité requiert rien de moins que l'éternité" (The erotic phenomenon, which the lover demands, requires a long and profound fidelity. But fidelity requires nothing less than eternity; *PE*, 286). See also *PE*, 287: "Ainsi aimer demande non seulement la fidélité, mais la fidélité pour l'éternité. La fidélité temporalise donc le phénomène de l'amour, en lui assurant son seul avenir possible" (Therefore love requires not only faithfulness but faithfulness for eternity. Thus faithfulness grounds the phenomenon of love, thus ensuring its only possible future).

54. See *PE*, 302–3, 320.

55. "Je m'accomplis comme amant, parce que je peux (et cela ne dépend que de moi) aimer à chaque instant comme pour l'éternité" (*PE*, 322).

56. See *PE*, 322: "Car l'éternité ne vient pas comme de l'extérieur . . . ; elle surgit du serment lui-même comme sa requête intime et intransigeante, . . ." (Because eternity does not come as if from the outside . . . it surges up from the covenant itself as its intimate and uncompromising requirement, . . .)

57. "Les amants accomplissent leur serment dans l'adieu—dans le passage à Dieu, qu'ils convoquent comme leur dernier témoin, leur premier témoin, celui qui ne part et ne ment jamais. Alors, pour la première fois, ils se disent 'adieu': l'année prochaine à Jérusalem—la prochaine fois à Dieu. Penser à Dieu peut se faire, érotiquement, dans cet 'adieu'" (PE, 326).

58. *Confessions*, 4.iv.7–4.ix.14.

59. Ibid., trans. Pine-Coffin, 4.vi.11, pp. 77–78.

60. See *In Johannis epistulam*, tract. 4.1–3. In this passage, Augustine identifies the path to interiority with that of justice, thus graphically illustrating the social character of human nature. For a more detailed treatment of this and related themes, see Eoin Cassidy, "Le rôle de l'amitié dans la quête du bonheur chez S. Augustin," in *Actualité de la pensée médiévale: Recueil d'articles*, ed. J. Follon and J. McEvoy (Louvain: Éditions Peeters, 1994), pp. 171–201; and Eoin Cassidy, "Friendship and Beauty in Augustine," in *At the Heart of the Real*, ed. F. O'Rourke (Dublin: Irish Academic Press, 1992), pp. 51–66.

61. *Confessions*, 4.vii.12.

62. Ibid.

63. "L'amant, dès le début de son avance, anticipe sur l'éternité. Il ne la désire pas, il la présuppose" (*PE*, 299).

64. *Confessions*, trans. Pine-Coffin, 4.ix.14, pp. 79–80.

65. To underpin the importance of the inclusive nature of ordered love, Augustine always emphasizes the triadic—or more precisely, in the context of his faith, the Trinitarian—character of true love. One of the most celebrated of his many meditations on the nature of God draws on the imagery of love—the lover, the beloved, and love itself. (For Augustine, love as the Holy Spirit includes all and draws them into the mystery of God's love.) See *De Trinitate*, 8.x.14: "What does the soul love in a friend except the soul? And, therefore, even here there are three: the lover, the beloved, and the love."

66. See *In Johannis epistulam*, tracts. 1.9, 7.10, 8.10. In the course of these commentaries, Augustine seeks to ensure that the Johannine emphasis on fraternal love is interpreted in a manner that respects the importance of the love of enemies.

67. Augustine's monastic spirituality is based on the centrality of fraternal love, as reflected in the phrase "one soul and one heart in God" (*anima una et cor unum in Deum*)—adapted from Acts 4:32. The words *in Deum* are added by Augustine and are thus a reminder of the importance he attaches to them. In his earlier life he interprets these words as "in God," whereas in his later life, conscious of the eschatological perspective, he interprets them as "toward God." See Eoin Cassidy, "Le rôle de l'amitié dans la quête du bonheur chez S. Augustin."

68. In *Confessions*, 7.x.16, there is an evocative reflection on God that links the motifs of Truth, Love, and Eternity: "All who know the truth know this light, and all who know this light know eternity. It is the light that charity knows. Eternal Truth, true Love, beloved Eternity—all this my God, you are, and it is to you that I sigh by night and day."

69. Marion introduces this viewpoint in *PE*, 14–15, but the theme receives its most detailed treatment in the final section of the book (*PE*, 331–42). As Marion puts it: "L'amour ne se dit et ne se donne qu'en un sens unique, strictement univoque.... L'amour se définit comme il se déploie—à partir de la réduction érotique et uniquement d'elle; il n'admet donc nulle autre variation que celle des moments de cette unique réduction" (Love is said or given in only one way ... love defines itself as it is expressed—from the "réduction érotique" and uniquely from it: it therefore admits of no other interpretation than that which is charted by this unique reduction; *PE*, 334).

70. Ibid., 277–83.

71. Ibid., 336–39.

72. Ibid., 340.

73. The following passage from PE, 341, is an extract from an extended phenomenological reflection on God perceived as love: "Il [Dieu] fait l'amant, comme nous—passant par la vanité (des idoles), la demande qu'on l'aime et l'avance d'aimer le premier, le serment et le visage (l'icône), la chair

et la jouissance de la communion, la douleur de notre suspension et la revendication jalouse, la naissance du tiers en transit et l'annonce du tiers eschatologique, qui finissent par s'identifier dans le Fils incarné, jusqu' à la promulagation unilatérale par lui de notre fidélité, à nous" (He [God] is a lover like us—traversing the vanity (of idols), the desire to be loved and to be a lover, the pledge and the face (the icon), the flesh and the joy of communion, the sadness of our silence and jealous resentment, the birth of a third person on his way and the announcement of an eschatological trinity, who will eventually identify himself with the incarnate Son, until he is in a position to proclaim our fidelity to each other.).

74. "Dieu nous précède et nous transcende, mais en ceci d'abord et surtout qu'il nous aime infiniment mieux que nous n'aimons et ne l'aimons. Dieu nous surpasse au titre de meilleur amant" (*PE*, 342).

75. 1 John.4:8–10. See Augustine's commentary on these verses, *In Johannis epistulam*, tract. 7.5–9. As he states in verse 9, "Here is love, not that we loved him, but that he loved us. We did not first love him. He loved us, to the end that we might love him."

76. It must be noted, however, that at times Augustine seems to interchange the words *amor*, *dilectio*, and *caritas* without too much concern for the classical distinctions.

77. See Aristotle, *Eudemian Ethics*, 1244b1–1245b19. See also *Nicomachean Ethics*, 1170a14–1170b19. For a detailed treatment of this theme, see Eoin G. Cassidy, "The Significance of Friendship: Reconciling the Classical Ideals of Friendship and Self-sufficiency," in *Amor Amicitiae: On the Love That Is Friendship. Essays in Medieval Thought and Beyond in Honor of the Rev. Professor James Mc Evoy*, ed. Thomas A. F. Kelly and Philipp W. Rosemann, Recherches de Théologie et Philosophie Médiévales, Bibliotheca 6 (Louvain/Paris/Dudley, Mass.: Peeters, 2004), pp. 39–62.

78. This theme is treated in some detail in Eoin G. Cassidy, "The Recovery of the Classical Ideal of Friendship in Augustine's Portrayal of Caritas," in *The Relationship Between Neoplatonism and Christianity*, ed. Thomas Finan and Vincent Twomey (Dublin: Four Courts Press, 1992), pp. 127–41.

79. *In Johannis epistulam*, 8.5, trans. John Burnaby, in *Augustine: Later Works* (Philadelphia: Westminster Press, 1955), p. 321.

80. *Confessions*, trans. Pine-Coffin, 6.xvi.26, p. 132. Cf. *De diversis quaestionibus*, 83, q. 31, 3: "Friendship consists in wishing well to someone because he is the person that one loves, with, on his part, a similar disposition" (*Eighty-three Different Questions*, trans. D. L. Mosher, Fathers of the Church series, 70 (Washington, D.C.: Catholic University of America Press, 1977), pp. 60–61.

81. 1 John 4:8–10.

82. See *Confessions*, 1.i.1.

83. See *Sermo*, 105.2, in *Patrologiae cursus completus, series Latina (PL)*, vol. 38, ed. J. P. Migne (Paris, 1841), p. 619.

84. *De civitate Dei*, 10.3, trans. D. Knowles (Harmondsworth, U.K.: Penguin, 1972), p. 376. See also *Confessions*, 6.vii.12: "You used me to set him [Alypius] on the right path"; ibid., 7.vi.8: "So to cure my obstinacy you found me a friend." Cf. *De sermone Domini in monte*, 1.38; and *Sermo*, 81.7, in *PL*, vol. 38, p. 504..

85. *Epistle*, 130, trans. W. Parsons, Fathers of the Church series, 18 (Washington, D.C.: Catholic University of America Press, 1955), pp. 376–401. It is the same perspective that marks Augustine's understanding of *caritas* that is extended to enemies. See, for example, *Confessions*, 4.xii.18: "If your delight is in souls, love them in God. . . . Love them, then, in him and draw as many with you to him as you can" (trans. Pine-Coffin, p. 82).

86. This theme is dealt with at some length in *In Johannis epistulam*, tract. 7.4–8, and in particular ibid., tract. 9.0, where one finds the phrase "love is God."

Chapter 12. Hermeneutics of the Possible God
Richard Kearney

1. Husserl, *Husserliana*, VII, 274, 350. The *Husserliana* series will henceforth be referenced in the abbreviated form *Hua*. For exact translation and publication details of each of these volumes, see Jean Greisch's bibliography in *Le buisson ardent et les lumières de la raison: L'invention de la philosophie de la religion*, vol. 2 (Paris: Le Cerf, 2003), pp. 67–69. I am indebted to my longtime friend and colleague Jean Greisch for his wide-ranging scholarship and research on Husserl. Most of the quotes and remarks on Husserl that follow were brought to my attention by Greisch.

2. Husserl, *Hua*, VI, 140, 156; *Hua* XXVII, 125–26.
3. Husserl, *Hua*, XXVII, 101.
4. Cited by Greisch in his *Buisson ardent*, p. 38.
5. Husserl, *Hua*, XXVII, 102.
6. Ibid.
7. See Marion's *BG*, para. 24, pp. 234ff.
8. Husserl, *Hua*, XXVII, 102.
9. Husserl, letter to Gerda Walther, cited by Greisch in his *Buisson ardent*, p. 50.
10. Husserl, *Hua*, III/1, 126.
11. Husserl, *Hua*, XVII, 335, 221.
12. Cited in Greisch, *Buisson ardent*, p. 50.
13. Husserl, *Hua*, XXVII, 235.
14. Greisch, *Buisson ardent*, p. 51.
15. Husserl, *Hua*, XV, 378–86; and manuscript B II, 2, 53.
16. Husserl, *Ideas: General Introduction to Pure Phenomenology* (New York: Collier, 1962), pp. 200–1.
17. Husserl, manuscript B II, 2, 53.
18. As cited by Greisch in his *Buisson ardent*, p. 56.

19. Husserl, *Hua*, XXVII, 234.
20. Husserl, manuscript F I, 24, 70.
21. Greisch, *Buisson ardent*, p. 57.
22. Søren Kierkegaard, *The Sickness unto Death: A Christian Psychological Exposition for Upbuilding and Awakening*, ed. and trans. Howard Hong and Edna Hong (Princeton, N.J.: Princeton University Press, 1980), p. 40. I am grateful to my Boston College colleague Vanessa Rumble for bringing this passage to my attention.
23. Martin Heidegger, *Die Metaphysik des deutschen Idealismus (Schelling)*, ed. Günter Seubold (Frankfurt: Klostermann, 1991), p. 49. Cited by Greisch in his *Buisson ardent*, p. 371.
24. In his introduction to *Being and Time*, trans. John Macquarrie and Edward Robinson (Oxford: Blackwell, 1962), Heidegger states that, for phenomenology, "possibility stands higher than actuality" (p. 63). Later in this text, he refers to *Dasein*'s pre-awareness of its own death in *Angst* as a specific mood in which it "finds itself face-to-face with the 'nothing' of the possible impossibility of its existence" (p. 310). This existential-human experience of "possible impossibility" may be usefully contrasted with the deconstructive notion of "impossible possibility" in Derrida's "Comme si c'était possible . . . ," *Revue internationale de philosophie* 3, no. 205 (1998); and in John D. Caputo's "The Poetics of the Impossible and the Kingdom of God," in *The Blackwell Companion to Postmodern Theology*, ed. Graham Ward (Oxford: Blackwell, 2001), pp. 469ff., and "The Experience of God and the Axiology of the Impossible," Villanova University Conference Paper, Nov. 8–10, 2001. For a critical discussion of the differences between (a) the deconstructive reading of the impossible advanced by Derrida and Caputo and (b) my hermeneutic reading of the possible as *posse*, see Richard Kearney, "The Kingdom: Possible and Impossible," in *A Postmodern Phenomenology of the Cross*, ed. David Goicoechea (New York: Fordham University Press, forthcoming). For a detailed critical discussion of Heidegger's various concepts of possibility in *Being and Time* and subsequent texts, see Richard Kearney, "Heidegger's Poetics of the Possible," in his *Poetics of Modernity: Toward a Hermeneutic Imagination* (Atlantic Highlands, N.J.: Humanities Press, 1995), pp. 35–48, and *Poétique du possible* (Paris: Beauchesne, 1984). See also the rapport between Heidegger's notion of the possible and that of Husserl, Ernst Bloch, and Jacques Derrida in Richard Kearney, *The God Who May Be: A Hermeneutics of Religion* (Bloomington: Indiana University Press, 2002), ch. 5, "Possibilizing God," pp. 80ff.
25. See Kearney, *Poetics of Modernity*, p. 219, n. 34, on Edgar Lohner's contentious translation of *Vermögen* in his version of the "Letter on Humanism," in Richard Zaner and Don Ihde, *Phenomenology and Existentialism* (New York: Capricorn Books, 1973), pp. 147–81.
26. On the significance of this "Turn," see William J. Richardson, *Heidegger: Through Phenomenology to Thought* (The Hague: Nijhoff, 1963; rev. ed., New York: Fordham University Press, 2003).

27. For a more elaborate commentary on this key passage, see Kearney, "Heidegger's Poetics of the Possible," pp. 44–48 and p. 220, n. 36, and "Heidegger, le possible et Dieu," in *Heidegger et la question de Dieu*, ed. Richard Kearney and Joseph O'Leary (Paris: Grasset, 1980), pp. 125–67. On the various theological interpretations of Husserl's and Heidegger's phenomenology, especially by figures such as Marion, Lévinas, and Henry, see Dominique Janicaud, *Le tournant théologique de la phénoménologie française* (Paris: L'Éclat, 1991). See also Richard Kearney, "Heidegger's Gods," in his *Poetics of Modernity*, pp. 50–64; Jean-François Courtine, ed., *Phénoménologie et théologie* (Paris: Criterion, 1992); and George Kovacs, *The Question of God in Heidegger's Phenomenology* (Evanston, Ill.: Northwestern University Press, 1990).

28. Kearney, "Heidegger's Poetics of the Possible," p. 220, n. 37.

29. Ibid., p. 45. My translation.

30. See Nicholas of Cusa, *Trialogus de possest*, ed. R. Steiger (Hamburg: Felix Meiner Verlag, 1973); and P. J. Casarella, "Nicholas of Cusa and the Power of the Possible," *American Catholic Philosophical Quarterly* 64, no. 1 (1990): 7–35. Casarella makes some interesting comparisons between Nicholas's divine *possest* and Heidegger's power of the "loving possible." Another contemporary commentator to note the intriguing links between Heidegger and Nicholas on the notion of the possible—though from an ontological rather than an eschatological perspective—is Giorgio Agamben, *Potentialities: Collected Essays in Philosophy* (Stanford, Calif.: Stanford University Press, 1999), esp. pp. 192–204.

31. Heidegger, "Letter on Humanism," pp. 172–73.

32. Martin Heidegger, interview, "Nur noch ein Gott kann uns retten," *Der Spiegel*, May 31, 1976, pp. 193–219; and *Beiträge zur Philosophie (Vom Ereignis)*, *Gesammelte Arbeiten*, 65 (Frankfurt: Vittoria Klostermann, 1994); on this Heidegger-Schelling connection, see George Seidel, "Heidegger's Last God and the Schelling Connection," *Laval théologique et philosophique* 55, no. 1: 91ff.

33. Martin Heidegger, *An Introduction to Metaphysics*, trans. Ralph Manheim (New York: Doubleday, 1961), pp. 6ff. See also the analysis of this analogy of proper proportionality between ontology and theology in Kearney, *Poétique du possible*, pt. 4, "Le chiasme herméneutique," pp. 211–56.

34. Martin Heidegger, ". . . Poetically Man Dwells . . . ," in his *Poetry, Language, Thought*, trans. Albert Hofstadter (New York: Harper & Row, 1971), p. 215.

35. This essay is published as a supplemtary text in Heidegger's *On Time and Being*, trans. Joan Staumbaugh (New York: Harper & Row, 1972), p. 54.

36. Ibid, pp. 59–60.

37. Ibid., p. 8. See also Kearney, *Poetics of Modernity*, pp. 220–21, n. 41, on the crucial link between "possibility" and "Being understood as time

which absences as it presences." See also the fascinating study by Hent de Vries, "Heidegger's Possibilism," in his *Philosophy and the Turn to Religion* (Baltimore: Johns Hopkins University Press, 1999), pp. 279–96.

38. See Heidegger's hermeneutical retrieval of Kant's critical project in *Kant and the Problem of Metaphysics* (Bloomington: Indiana University Press, 1962) as it pertains to his understanding of possibility (p. 252): "Kant must have had an intimation of this collapse of the primacy of logic in metaphysics when, speaking of the fundamental characteristics of Being, 'possibility' (what-being) and 'reality' (which Kant termed 'existence'), he said: 'So long as the definition of possibility, existence and necessity is sought solely in pure understanding, they cannot be explained save through an obvious tautology.'" But Heidegger does not ignore Kant's subsequent retreat to the logicist model: "And yet, in the second edition of the *Critique* did not Kant re-establish the supremacy of the understanding? And as a result did not metaphysics, with Hegel, come to be identified with 'logic' more radically than ever before?"

39. Walter Benjamin, "Theologico-Political Fragment" (1921), in his *One Way Street*, trans. Edmund Jephcott and Kingsley Shorter (London: NLB, 1979), pp. 155ff.

40. Rashi, *The Torah: With Rashi's Commentary*, trans. Yisrael Isser Zvi Herczeg (Brooklyn, N.Y.: Mesorah Publications, 1997). It would be interesting to relate Rashi's rabbinical interpretation to Isaac Luria's kabbalist reading of God in terms of a generous withholding or "withdrawal" (*zimzum*) that invites human creatures to subsequently retrieve and reanimate the fragments of the "broken vessels" of divine love that lie scattered like tiny seeds throughout the created universe. This reading, which exerted a deep influence on Hasidic thinkers as well as on philosophers such as Simone Weil, seems to confirm my own account of God's refusal to impose Himself on creation—as some kind of omnipotent fulfilled being (*Ipsum Esse subsistens*), Sufficient Reason, or Supreme Cause (*ens causa sui*)—preferring instead to relate to humans in the realm of the "possible" rather than of the purely "actual" or "necessary." I am grateful to my Boston College colleague Marty Cohen for bringing the insights of the Lurianic kabbala to my attention. See in particular his article "Sarach's Harp," *Parabola* 22, no. 3 (Fall 1997).

41. Etty Hillesum, *An Interrupted Life*, trans. Arnold Pomerans (New York: Owl Books, 1996), p. 176.

42. Nicholas of Cusa, *Trialogus de Possest*, in Jasper Hopkins, *A Concise Introduction to the Philosophy of Nicholas of Cusa* (Minneapolis: University of Minnesota Press, 1980), p. 69. The original Latin reads: "Deus est omne id quod esse potest."

43. Pseudo-Dionysius the Areopagite, *The Divine Names and Mystical Theology*, trans. John D. Jones (Milwaukee, Wis.: Marquette University Press, 1980), p. 182.

44. Ibid., p. 188. For a further exploration of the link between negative theology and microeschatology, see Stanislas Breton, *The Word and the Cross* (New York: Fordham University Press, 2002), pp. 8–11, 49–50, 60–70, 80–91, 112–14. See in particular Breton's radical claim that we must give to God the being He has not, qua thirsting, kenotic, crucified stranger (pp.121–22). The *dunamis* of God is here identified with the *germen nihili* or "power of nothing" that reveals itself as a "double nothingness" and powerlessness that liberates those oppressed by the power of *ta onta*, sowing the seed of nonbeing epitomized by the Beautitudes so that the eschatological tree of love and justice may flower and flourish (pp. 80–84 and xxiv–xxvi). For it is in and as a "seed of nonbeing" that, in Eckhart's resonant phrase, "God becomes verdant in all the honor of his being" (quoted p. 80).

45. See the illiminating reading of Hopkins in Mark Patrick Hederman, *Anchoring the Altar: Christianity and the Work of Art* (Dublin: Veritas, 2002), pp. 131ff. It is important to note that this microtheological emphasis on God as less rather than more is not confined to the Judeo-Christian tradition. It is also found in much of the Buddhist and Hindu wisdom literature. See, for instance, the following passage from Krishnamurti: "The silence which is not the silence of the ending of noise is only a small beginning. It is like going through a small hole to an enormous, wide, expansive ocean, to an immeasurable, timeless state." See Jiddu Krishnamurti, *Freedom from the Known* (San Francisco: Harper, 1969), p. 109.

46. Robert Musil, *The Man Without Qualities*, cited in Kearney, *Poétique du possible*, p. 3.

47. Rainer Maria Rilke, *Letters to a Young Poet*, trans. Stephen Mitchell (New York: Vintage Books, 1986), pp. 61–63.

48. Ibid., p. 63. The emphasis here on the earth as correspondent for divine eros highlights, once again, the incarnational tendency of theo-eroticism. The earth is full of the seeds of the divine (what Augustine, borrowing from the Stoics, called *logoi spermaticoi*), incubating within the finite historical world like latent potencies waiting to be animated and actualized by the infinitely incoming grace of God as transcendent *posse*. If one removes transcendent *posse* from this equation, one relapses into a purely immanentist dialectic (evolutionary materialism or, at best, process theology). On the other hand, if one ignores the immanence of terrestrial and human potencies, one is left with an inordinately inaccessible and abstract deity—a sort of acosmic alterity without face or voice (e.g., deism or deconstruction). A hermeneutical poetics of divine *posse* tries to preserve a delicate balance between these opposite extremes.

49. I am grateful to my wise friend and teacher, Peggy McLoughlin, for this reference. Here is one verse in which the term *viriditas* appears: "O most noble greening power (*O nobilissima viriditas*)/Rooted in the sun,/Who shine in dazzling serenity/In a sphere/That no earthly excellence/Can comprehend./You are enclosed/In the embrace of divine mysteries,/You blush like

the dawn/And burn like a flame of the sun." See Selina O'Grady and John Wilkins, eds., *Great Spirits 1000–2000: The Fifty-two Christians Who Most Influenced Their Millennium* (New York: Paulist Press, 2002).

50. Joachim Jeremias, *The Eucharistic Words of Jesus* (Philadelphia: Fortress Press, 1977), p. 249. I am indebted to two of my colleagues at Boston College, Gary Gurtler and John Manoussakis, for bringing these comments and references by Dionysius and Jeremias to my attention.

51. Ibid., p. 252.

52. *The Passover Haggadah* (New York: Schocken Books, 1953), p. 63.

53. See Jeremias, *Eucharistic Words*, p. 252. One might detect an echo of this eschatological pattern of forgetting and remembering from the finite human perspective in Dante's *Divine Comedy* ("Purgatory," canto 28), where the Pilgrim encounters two inexhaustible streams of the garden, Lethe and Eunoe; the former washes away all memory of sin, while the latter retrieves the memory of the good deeds and life-giving moments.

54. Jeremias, *Eucharistic Words*, p. 253.

Chapter 14. The Absent Threshold: An Eckhartian Afterword
John O'Donohue

The following translations were used.

Meister Eckhart, *Sermons and Treatises*, ed. and trans. Maurice O'C. Walshe (London: Watkins, 1979).

Meister Eckhart, *The Essential Sermons, Commentaries, Treatises and Defense*, trans. Edmund Colledge and Bernard McGinn, Classics of Western Spirituality (New York: Paulist Press, 1981).

Meister Eckhart: Teacher and Preacher, ed. Bernard McGinn, Classics of Western Spirituality (New York: Paulist Press, 1986).

Master Eckhart: Parisian Questions and Prologues, trans. Armand A. Maurer (Toronto: Pontifical Institute of Mediaeval Studies, 1974).

Contributors

Lilian Alweiss: Lecturer in the Philosophy Department at Trinity College Dublin. A graduate of the University of Durham, she obtained her M.A. at the University of Essex, a Diplome d'Études Approfondies at the University of Strasbourg, and her Ph.D. at the University of Essex. Her publications include *The World Unclaimed: A Challenge to Heidegger's Critique of Husserl* (Ohio University Press, 2002) and she edited a special edition of *Journal of the British Society of Phenomenology* on John McDowell.

Eoin Cassidy: Lecturer in philosophy, Mater Dei Institute, Dublin. Educated at University College Dublin; the Pontifical University of St. Thomas, Rome; the Pontifical University of Maynooth; and the Institut Supérieur de Philosophie, Université Catholique de Louvain. He has published widely on Augustine, early medieval philosophy, early Christian theology, and applied philosophy. He has recently edited *Measuring Ireland: Discerning Values and Beliefs* (Dublin, 2002), and, with Andrew McGrady, *Media and the Marketplace: Ethical Perspectives* (Dublin, 2001).

Mark Dooley: Formerly visiting research fellow at the Department of Philosophy, University College Dublin. His many publications in the area of contemporary European philosophy include *The Politics of Exodus: Kierkegaard's Ethics of Responsibility* (Fordham University

Press, 2001); *Questioning God*, with John D. Caputo and Michael J. Scanlon (Indiana University Press, 2001); *Questioning Ethics*, with Richard Kearney (Routledge, 1999); *A Passion for the Impossible: John D. Caputo in Focus* (State University of New York Press, 2003); and *The Catastrophe of Memory* (Acumen, 2004).

Brian Elliott: Lecturer in the Philosophy Department, University College Dublin. He received his M.A. from Edinburgh University and his Ph.D. from Freiburg University. His publications include *Anfang und End in der Philosophie* (Duncker & Humblot, 2002) and *Phenomenology and Imagination in Husserl and Heidegger: Images of Thought* (Routledge, 2004).

Richard Kearney: Charles Seelig Professor in Philosophy at Boston College and visiting professor of philosophy at University College Dublin. Internationally renowned for his work in Continental philosophy, aesthetics, and ethics, he has recently added to his extensive list of publications by completing a trilogy titled Philosophy at the Limit: *On Stories* (Routledge, 2001), *The God Who May Be* (Indiana University Press, 2001), and *Strangers, God and Monsters* (Routledge, 2002).

Ian Leask: Lecturer in philosophy at the Mater Dei Institute, Dublin. Educated in Scholastic Philosophy at Queen's University Belfast, he has published *Questions of Platonism* (2000), and numerous articles on Continental philosophy, ancient philosophy, and the philosophy of religion.

Shane Mackinlay: Currently studying the role of hermeneutics in the phenomenology of Jean-Luc Marion for a doctorate in philosophy at Katholieke Universiteit Leuven (Belgium). He lectures in philosophy at Catholic Theological College (Melbourne) and has lectured in philosophy and ethics at Australian Catholic University. He has an M.A. in philosophy from K.U. Leuven, and undergraduate degrees in theology and physics.

Jean-Luc Marion: Professor of philosophy at the Université de Paris I–Sorbonne. As well as publishing widely on Descartes, Professor Marion has written groundbreaking religious works (most notably *God Without Being*) and equally radical phenomenological studies, such as *Reduction and Givenness* (awarded the 1992 religious works (most notably *God Without Being*) and equally radical phenomenological studies, such as *Reduction and Givenness* (awarded the 1992 Grand Prix du Philosophie de l'Académie Française), and *Being Given*.

Timothy Mooney: Received his B.A. from the National University of Ireland and his Ph.D. from the University of Essex. He is currently College Lecturer in Philosophy at University College Dublin. He has co-edited *The Routledge Phenomenology Reader* with Dermot Moran (Routledge, 2002) and is the author of several studies on phenomenology, deconstruction, and process philosophy.

Derek Morrow: Currently a doctoral student at the University of Dallas and assistant editor of the *American Catholic Philosophical Quarterly*. His dissertation, "De-nominating God as *Ipsum Esse:* The Postmodern Thomism of Jean-Luc Marion," aims to situate the disparate treatments of Aquinas in Marion's corpus within the larger context of Marion's extensive scholarship on Descartes and his more recent work in contemporary phenomenology and Continental philosophy of religion.

John O'Donohue: Philosopher and poet. He has published two collections of poetry, *Echoes of Memory* (1994) and *Conamara Blues* (2001). He is also the author of two books in which he has attempted to develop a lyrical, philosophical spirituality: *Anam Cara* (1997) and *Eternal Echoes* (1999). He published a book on Hegel, *Person als Vermittlung: Die Dialektik von Individualität und Allgemeinheit in Hegels "Phänomenologie des Geistes." Eine philosophisch-theologische Interpretation* (Matthias-Grünewald-Verlag, 1993), and is currently working on a *Habilitationsschrift* on Meister Eckhart at the University of Tübingen.

Joseph S. O'Leary: Philosopher and theologian. He studied theology in Maynooth College, Ireland, and at the Gregorian University, Rome. During his stay in Paris, from 1977 to 1979, he brought the thought of Heidegger and Derrida to bear on patristic texts, drawing inspiration from Marion's *L'idole et la distance*. He organized, with Richard Kearney, a celebrated colloquium, published as *Heidegger et la question de Dieu* (Grasset, 1980), to which Marion contributed the central essay of *God Without Being*. He pursued these reflections further in *Questioning Back: The Overcoming of Metaphysics in Christian Tra-*

dition (Winston-Seabury, 1985). A resident of Japan since 1983, he collaborates with the Nanzan Institute for Religion and Culture and teaches literature at Sophia University. In *Religious Pluralism and Christian Truth* (Edinburgh University Press, 1996), he engaged the thought of Derrida and Marion alongside that of Nāgārjuna.

Felix Ó Murchadha: Lecturer in philosophy at the National University of Ireland, Galway. Educated at University College Galway and University College Dublin, Ireland; McMaster University, Canada; and Bergische Universität Wuppertal, Germany. His publications include a monograph titled *Zeit des Handelns und Möglichkeit der Verwandlung. Kairologie und Chronologie bein Heidegger im Jahrzehnt nach "Sein und Zeit"* (Königshausen und Neumann, 1999) and numerous articles and book chapters focusing on hermeneutics, phenomenology, time, and the philosophy of religion. His research interests include phenomenology, philosophy of religion, hermeneutics, philosophy of time, philosophy of art, and Heidegger, Lévinas, Ricoeur, and Merleau-Ponty.

Index

Adonné, 169–73, 180, 188
Angelus Silesius, 227, 231–32
Aquinas, 20, 87, 137
Aristotle, 13, 14, 15, 16, 17, 18, 19, 20, 21, 24, 25, 26, 27, 28, 35, 36, 83, 216, 232, 245, 247
Augustine, 87, 94, 140, 164, 201–202, 203–206, 208–10, 212–14, 216–19, 245, 248, 272

Being, 2, 3, 28–32, 76, 80, 85–86, 88–95, 136–39, 185–86, 225–28, 244, 278–79, 312n3, 313n5
Boredom, 77, 324n5
Brandom, Robert, 194, 196, 198

Cicero, 203, 209
Cogito, see 'Ego'.
Cusanus, Nicholas, 227, 233

Dasein, 3, 88–92, 94, 167–69, 173–74, 177, 180, 181, 197, 225–26, 278–79, 312n3, 313n5, 313n8, 314n10, 324n19
Denys the Areopagite, 150, 233–34
Derrida, Jacques, 1, 5–7, 47, 56, 58, 92, 136, 137, 144, 148, 149, 154, 162, 164, 191, 245
Descartes, René, 2, 4, 12–36, 37–46, 256, 265

Eckhart, Meister, 227, 244, 245, 246, 248
Ego, 37–46, 154, 167–68, 184–85, 186, 188, 191–92, 202–203, 206–207
Event, 169–73, 177–78

Face, 79–80
Fatherhood, 6–7, 117–23, 125, 157–59, 161–63

Gift, 5–6, 102, 103, 104–34, 140, 141, 142–66, 168
Glory, 71–75
God, 2, 3, 55–56, 58, 70–75, 80–81, 84–86, 93, 135–136, 139–42, 186, 195, 203, 204, 205, 209, 210, 212, 213–14, 215, 217–19, 220–42, 245–50, 258–64, 266–83, 299n80, 318n14
Gregory of Nyssa, 249
Greisch, Jean, 223, 224

Hartshorne, Charles, 244, 246
Hegel, G. W. F., 147, 148, 149, 233, 246, 247, 250, 271
Heidegger, Martin, 2, 3, 38–39, 41, 50, 57, 69–70, 74–77, 78–82, 84–86, 88–96, 130, 132, 135, 136, 138, 148, 152, 163, 166, 167–69, 172, 173–74, 176, 177, 180, 181, 182, 185, 194, 197, 198, 220, 224–28, 245, 250, 254, 255, 278
Hillesum, Etty, 232, 233, 238
Hintikka, J., 37–38, 39–40, 42, 45
Hopkins, Gerard Manley, 234–35
Husserl, Edmund, 47–68, 88, 92, 95, 152, 155, 156, 167–69, 182, 184, 185, 188, 197, 220, 221–24, 225, 245, 250, 254

Icon, 3–4, 78, 328n26
Idol, 3, 33–36, 78–79
Infinite, 2
Intuition, 48–51, 54

Janicaud, Dominique, 11, 69, 136, 137
John of the Cross, 248

Kant, Immanuel, 37, 38, 40–42, 43, 95, 184, 221, 232
Kierkegaard, Søren, 193, 225, 237, 238

Lacan, Jacques, 158, 249
Leibniz, G., 38, 132, 232, 233
Levinas, Emmanuel, 2, 3, 4, 5, 84, 136, 149, 188, 189, 194, 207, 231, 238, 245, 247, 252
Love, 78–79, 81–83, 149–50, 201–19, 252–53

Mahayana Buddhism, 159–61
Mathesis universalis, 17, 19–21, 27–28
Mauss, M., 92, 142
Merleau-Ponty, Maurice, 47, 50, 68, 149, 250, 290n27
Milbank, John, 11, 286n2
Musil, Robert, 235–36

Nagel, Thomas, 191, 193, 194
Nietzsche, Friedrich, 30, 31–33, 45, 143, 191, 192
Nygren, Anders, 149–50

Paul, Saint, 33, 71–74, 83, 84, 227
Philo of Alexandria, 139–40
Plato, 245, 247, 248–49, 259

Reduction, 48–54
Ricoeur, Paul, 142, 149, 224, 237
Rilke, Rainer Maria, 235–37
Romano, Claude, 167, 169, 173–81
Rorty, Richard, 191, 193, 194, 195, 197

Sartre, J.-P., 43–46, 149
Saturated Phenomenon, 4–5, 93–94, 183–84, 192–93, 194, 307n82

Thing, 79–80

Vanier, Jean, 232

Whitehead, A. N., 244, 246
Wittgenstein, Ludwig, 40, 191, 193, 255

Perspectives in
Continental Philosophy Series
John D. Caputo, series editor

1. John D. Caputo, ed., *Deconstruction in a Nutshell: A Conversation with Jacques Derrida*
2. Michael Strawser, *Both/And: Reading Kierkegaard: From Irony to Edification*
3. Michael D. Barber, *Ethical Hermeneutics: Rationality in Enrique Dussel's Philosophy of Liberation*
4. James H. Olthuis, ed., *Knowing Other-wise: Philosophy at the Threshold of Spirituality*
5. James Swindal, *Reflection Revisited: Jürgen Habermas's Discursive Theory of Truth*
6. Richard Kearney, *Poetics of Imagining: Modern to Post-modern*. Second edition
7. Thomas W. Busch, *Circulating Being: From Embodiment to Incorporation. Essays on Late Existentialism*
8. Edith Wyschogrod, *Emmanuel Lévinas: The Problem of Ethical Metaphysics*. Second edition
9. Francis J. Ambrosio, ed., *The Question of Christian Philosophy Today*
10. Jeffrey Bloechl, ed., *The Face of the Other and the Trace of God: Essays on the Philosophy of Emmanuel Lévinas*
11. Ilse N. Bulhof and Laurens ten Kate, eds., *Flight of the Gods: Philosophical Perspectives on Negative Theology*
12. Trish Glazebrook, *Heidegger's Philosophy of Science*
13. Kevin Hart, *The Trespass of the Sign: Deconstruction, Theology, and Philosophy*

14. Mark C. Taylor, *Journeys to Selfhood: Hegel and Kierkegaard*. Second edition

15. Dominique Janicaud, Jean-François Courtine, Jean-Louis Chrétien, Michel Henry, Jean-Luc Marion, and Paul Ricœur, *Phenomenology and the "Theological Turn": The French Debate*

16. Karl Jaspers, *The Question of German Guilt*. Translated by E. B. Ashton. Introduction by Joseph W. Koterski, S.J.

17. Jean-Luc Marion, *The Idol and Distance: Five Studies*. Translated with an introduction by Thomas A. Carlson

18. Jeffrey Dudiak, *The Intrigue of Ethics: A Reading of the Idea of Discourse in the Thought of Emmanuel Lévinas*

19. Robyn Horner, *Rethinking God as Gift: Marion, Derrida, and the Limits of Phenomenology*

20. Mark Dooley, *The Politics of Exodus: Søren Kierkegaard's Ethics of Responsibility*

21. Merold Westphal, *Toward a Postmodern Christian Faith: Overcoming Onto-Theology*

22. Edith Wyschogrod, Jean-Joseph Goux, and Eric Boynton, eds., *The Enigma of Gift and Sacrifice*

23. Stanislas Breton, *The Word and the Cross*. Translated with an introduction by Jacquelyn Porter

24. Jean-Luc Marion, *Prolegomena to Charity*. Translated by Stephen E. Lewis

25. Peter H. Spader, *Scheler's Ethical Personalism: Its Logic, Development, and Promise*

26. Jean-Louis Chrétien, *The Unforgettable and the Unhoped For*. Translated by Jeffrey Bloechl

27. Don Cupitt, *Is Nothing Sacred? The Non-Realist Philosophy of Religion: Selected Essays*

28. Jean-Luc Marion, *In Excess: Studies of Saturated Phenomena*. Translated by Robyn Horner and Vincent Berraud

29. Philip Goodchild, ed., *Rethinking Philosophy of Religion: Approaches from Continental Philosophy*

30. William J. Richardson, S.J., *Heidegger: Through Phenomenology to Thought*

31. Jeffrey Andrew Barash, *Martin Heidegger and the Problem of Historical Meaning*

32. Jean-Louis Chrétien, *Hand to Hand: Listening to the Work of Art*. Translated by Stephen E. Lewis

33. Jean-Louis Chrétien, *The Call and the Response*. Translated with an introduction by Anne Davenport

34. D. C. Schindler, *Hans Urs von Balthasar and the Dramatic Structure of Truth: A Philosophical Investigation*

35. Julian Wolfreys, ed., *Thinking Difference: Critics in Conversation*

36. Allen Scult, *Being Jewish/Reading Heidegger: An Ontological Encounter*

37. Richard Kearney, *Debates in Continental Philosophy: Conversations with Contemporary Thinkers*

38. Jennifer Anna Gosetti-Ferencei, *Heidegger, Hölderlin, and the Subject of Poetic Language: Toward a New Poetics of Dasein*

39. Jolita Pons, *Stealing a Gift: Kierkegaard's Pseudonyms and the Bible*

40. Jean-Yves Lacoste, *Experience and the Absolute: Disputed Questions on the Humanity of Man*. Translated by Mark Raftery-Skehan

41. Charles P. Bigger, *Between* Chora *and the Good: Metaphor's Metaphysical Neighborhood*

42. Dominique Janicaud, *Phenomenology "Wide Open": After the French Debate*. Translated by Charles N. Cabral